Catholics' Lost Cause

Catholics' Lost Cause

*South Carolina Catholics
and the American South, 1820–1861*

Adam L. Tate

University of Notre Dame Press

Notre Dame, Indiana

Library of Congress Cataloging-in-Publication Data

Names: Tate, Adam L., 1972– author.
Title: Catholics' lost cause : South Carolina Catholics and the American
    South, 1820–1861 / Adam L. Tate.
Description: Notre Dame, Indiana : University of Notre Dame Press, 2018. |
    Includes bibliographical references and index. |
Identifiers: LCCN 2018036125 (print) | LCCN 2018042823 (ebook) | ISBN
    9780268104191 (pdf) | ISBN 9780268104207 (epub) | ISBN 9780268104177
    (hardback : alk. paper) | ISBN 0268104174 (hardback : alk. paper)
Subjects: LCSH: Catholic Church—South Carolina—History—19th century. |
    South Carolina—Church history—19th century.
Classification: LCC BX1415.S6 (ebook) | LCC BX1415.S6 T38 2018 (print) | DDC
    282/.75709034--dc23
LC record available at https://lccn.loc.gov/2018036125

For Eugenie

CONTENTS

ACKNOWLEDGMENTS

One often works under the illusion that writing and research are solitary and lonely tasks. But such thoughts soon fade after considering the numerous people who contribute to one's labors. I have incurred many debts while working on this project and wish to acknowledge a few of the many people who have assisted me.

Three fellow scholars often listened to me and offered their advice. Kevin Schmiesing, my old friend, encouraged me frequently during the project and read the manuscript. His probing questions and careful eye for detail made me think through many of my assumptions. Nathan Coleman took time from his own work to read chapters of the manuscript as I was working on them. He assisted me greatly in honing my argument and rewriting awkward spots. He demonstrated his friendship by encouraging me throughout the process. I am greatly in debt to him. Finally, my good friend and colleague David Gilbert read the manuscript, asked pointed questions, offered critiques, and pushed me to write clearly. I could not have completed the project without his steady support. All mistakes in the book, of course, are mine.

Others too have supported the project. The librarians at Clayton State University, particularly Barbara Dantzler and Rhonda Boozer, fielded my many requests for materials. Archivists at Emory University, the University of South Carolina, and the Archives of the Diocese of Charleston, especially Melissa B. Mabry, provided critical assistance. My colleague R. B. Rosenburg helped me in the research process through his mastery of navigating numerous databases. My editor at the University of Notre

Dame Press, Eli Bortz, patiently led me through the peer review process and offered great advice and support. Sheila Berg assisted me in producing a polished product. Peer review, as usual, improved the manuscript greatly, and I owe thanks to the anonymous reviewers.

Finally, I wish to acknowledge the support of teachers, friends, and family. Obviously, I could not have written this book without the early guidance of many professors who took their valuable time to teach me how to write and argue as a historian. My graduate school mentor Forrest McDonald died as I was completing the manuscript. I thought of his example and advice often during the process, and I hope his lessons about writing have paid off here. My good friend Charles Rumore encouraged me to write when I thought I would never be able to begin. He also listened to various ideas and insights. Finally, my wife and children endured much as I researched and wrote. I dedicate this book to my wife, Eugenie, who has supported me so much through our years together. I could not have done this without her. Thank you.

Introduction

In the Confederate Museum in New Orleans, Louisiana, there is a hand-made crown of thorns supposedly given to Jefferson Davis after the Civil War by Pope Pius IX. The display suggests a deep sympathy between the pope and the Confederacy, alludes to a link between the Catholic Church and the American South, and could imply that southern Catholics, per-haps unlike their northern coreligionists, had accommodated well and comparatively easily to a region in which their numbers were small. While Pius did send Davis a personal letter, the crown of thorns story is false. Scholars have demonstrated that the Confederate president's wife, Varina, actually made the item.[1]

The story of the crown of thorns hints—at least in the minds of some people—that there was a natural affinity between Catholicism and the South. The claim has had some durability, appearing in both contempo-rary accounts and in modern scholarship. Before 1840 most of the Catho-lic dioceses in the United States were southern.[2] During the antebellum period, some northern evangelicals, who despised both southerners and Catholics, connected the two and labeled each as regressive and un-American. Abolitionists made those claims frequently.[3] After the Civil War, northern nativists often labeled Confederates and Catholics equally

as destroyers of the nation.[4] W. Jason Wallace has shown how those attitudes influenced antebellum American politics, and the literary scholar
Jenny Franchot has illuminated the same theme in the literature of the
early nineteenth century.[5] Eugene Genovese maintained that southern
conservatism and Catholicism overlapped in several areas. Catholics, he
noted, "found a much warmer reception among the slaveholders of the
South than among the propertied classes of the North."[6] Andrew Stern's
recent work on Catholic-Protestant relations in the South adopts and
expands Genovese's arguments. Stern studied the experiences of Catholics in Charleston, Mobile, and Louisville. He concluded that Catholics
and Protestants collaborated in a friendly manner more often than they
fought with one another.[7] David Gleeson, the foremost authority on the
Irish in the antebellum South, also perceives a region friendly to Irish
Catholic immigrants in the nineteenth century. He writes, "Native tolerance was crucial to Irish integration into society. Poor foreign immigrants from Ireland could not have become southerners without the help
of what one of them called the 'chivalrous people.'"[8] While the nineteenth-
century South remained largely Protestant, both contemporaries and
scholars have recognized a certain compatibility between the region and
Catholicism.

Literary scholars also have examined the theme of Catholic-southern
affinity, noting the influence of postbellum writers, particularly twentieth-
century southern Catholic writers, on the subject. Allen Tate, one of the
Vanderbilt Agrarians, converted to Catholicism, as did his wife, Caroline Gordon. Flannery O'Conner and Walker Percy, two of the most
famous southern writers of the mid- to late twentieth century, wrote as
Catholics. Thomas Haddox and Bryan Giemza, adding to the insights
of Franchot, have examined in detail the literature of Catholic southerners. These scholars argue that the affinity between Catholicism and
the South was not essential but a conscious creation of writers to serve
polemical purposes. One scholar, John Thompson, has underlined the
irony in this posited affinity. Of prominent southern converts to Catholicism, Thompson remarked, "These conversions stand out for their
very unusualness—not because the converts were famous writers, but
because so few Southerners of any kind have turned to Rome in the
twentieth century. Intensely anti-Catholic, militantly fundamentalist,
the South has not been receptive to the Church's message. Those who

have responded to it have trod a lonely path that has directed their footsteps away from solidarity with their region and their people."[9] If conversion brought alienation, did an affinity really exist?

Some scholars have suggested that southern Catholics abandoned their religious principles in order to accommodate to the culture around them. Thus their affinity to the South came at the cost of the purity of their faith. "The [Catholic] Church," Randall Miller suggests, "like the Protestant churches, yielded to social and political pressures and adopted a Southern stance on social issues. Almost in spite of itself, the Southern Church adapted to local conditions, with little appreciation of the consequences." According to this interpretation, Catholics in the South "won social and political acceptance" by "sanctifying the secular order of slavery and states' rights."[10] Other scholars have portrayed the Irish as being "confined" by southern culture or as willing participants in institutions of oppression in order to serve their own economic interests.[11] In these interpretations, accommodation hardly respected the integrity of the Catholic faith.

Both arguments—that of a natural affinity and that of an unthinking accommodation that endangered the faith—are plausible and marshal important evidence. But a third possibility remains, one pursued in part by the literary scholars mentioned above. Southern Catholic clerical leadership deliberately cultivated an affinity with non-Catholic southerners as a means to resolve the pesky problem of cultural accommodation. Catholic leaders sought a way to engage, rather than capitulate to, southern culture. As the religious scholar Philip Jenkins wrote of Christianity's relationship to non-Christian regimes during another era, "Too little adaptation means irrelevance; too much leads to assimilation and, often, disappearance."[12] South Carolina Catholic clergy wished to avoid both extremes. The posited affinity between Catholicism and the South, then, existed as a strategy of engagement based on the specific cultural environment of the nineteenth-century South.

The question of affinity relates to broader historiographical questions of nineteenth-century nationalism and the ways minority groups related to a broader culture. For the past forty years, scholars of the American South have spent a great deal of energy uncovering the roots of southern and Confederate nationalism. Southerners, like other Americans as well as Europeans during the nineteenth century, participated eagerly in nationalist movements. As Paul Quigley has detailed in his book *Shifting Grounds*, southern nationalism resembled broader efforts to define one people under one government but also had unique features thanks in particular to American federalism.[13] Nationalist movements in the United States in both the North and the South conceptualized a homogeneous, unified people, often defined in ethnic, religious, and historical terms.[14] Given that Catholics in the South were a small minority and were largely foreign immigrants, their incorporation into the southern "people" was not a given. Catholics becoming southerners and, later, Confederates thus illuminates important characteristics of southern nationalism.

Whereas many nineteenth-century nationalists demanded one homogeneous people forming the national community, there was an older, alternative form of nationalism in the South that could apply to southern Catholics. As scholars have recognized, American nationalism focused on the role of the American Revolution in creating the nation.[15] One of the important effects of the Revolution was to bind together through common sentiments those who had experienced the conflict. The historian Kevin Gutzman has pointed to the importance of this idea in early national Virginia. Patrick Henry, as well as devoted Virginia republicans, Gutzman writes, "viewed the American union not as a mere legal fiction, but as a hard fact." "It was based," he continues, "on ties of consanguinity, of experience, and of language."[16] In other words, although blood relations and ethnicity played a role, the Union—the "imagined community," to use Benedict Anderson's phrase—was also one of sentiment and shared experiences. In addition, as Peter Kastor has ably pointed out, this brand of nationalism demanded loyalty to republican government.[17] Positing ties based on feeling, history, and loyalty to republicanism rather than strict cultural homogeneity allowed a union of sentiment to include minority groups who thus identified. A union of sentiment could include a variety of groups, even Catholics.

Both Thomas Jefferson and John C. Calhoun articulated this alternative nationalism at various times. In 1804 Jefferson wrote to Joseph Priestley about the recent Louisiana Purchase. Discussing the possibility of future separation between East and West due to the immense size of the United States, Jefferson insisted, "Whether we remain in one confederacy, or form into Atlantic and Mississippi confederacies, I believe not very important to the happiness of either part. Those of the western confederacy will be as much our children & descendants as those of the eastern, and I feel myself as much identified with that country, in future time, as with this."[18] Jefferson thus trusted in common sentiment, history, and blood over any legal ties of union.

Calhoun expressed a similar conception of nationalism in his 1842 speech in the Senate concerning the presidential veto power. He asserted, "Instead of a nation, we are in reality an assemblage of nations, or peoples (if the plural noun may be used where the language affords none), united in their sovereign character immediately and directly by their own act, but without losing their separate and independent existence."[19] Calhoun's contention that the United States was an "assemblage of peoples" offers an important insight into this version of nationalism. Heterogeneous peoples could unite for a common purpose under such a conception of the Union. This perhaps explains in part Calhoun's religious toleration. As Genovese writes, "Calhoun hated religious bigotry and condemned, in particular, the rabid anti-Catholicism expressed most notably in the convent-burning that disgraced the Northeast but not the South."[20] Catholics could, following Calhoun's conception of the Union, become southerners and Americans by becoming part of the "assemblage of peoples." Presumably, they could preserve their separate religious identity at the same time.

The Diocese of Charleston makes a good test case for the question of affinity because of the prominence of its Catholic leadership in the American church and the importance of Charleston as a cultural and political center. The diocese, founded in 1820, originally included the states of North Carolina, South Carolina, and Georgia. Two of the bishops during the antebellum period, John England and Patrick Lynch, played significant roles in the church nationally during the nineteenth century. The Diocese of Charleston also left an important source for scholars, the *United States Catholic Miscellany*, the first national Catholic newspaper in the United States. The paper operated almost continuously from 1822 to 1861. Since other primary sources on Catholicism in South Carolina are quite limited, the newspaper is an important window into Catholic engagement of the South and the United States generally. The newspaper, along with the rich record of primary sources on Charleston and nineteenth-century South Carolina, provides the data for this study's contextual approach.

Like the nineteenth-century nationalists Benedict Anderson has studied, the bishops and clergy who promoted and edited the *Miscellany* used it to create an "imagined community" of Catholics, a people seeking inclusion in the broader "assemblage of peoples." The newspaper played an essential role by projecting the clerical leaders' visions for the diocese and served as a primary avenue of engagement with non-Catholic South Carolinians. By selecting stories to print, events to promote, and voices to be amplified, its editors marked the rhetorical boundaries of the state's Catholic community. But, to use Anderson's memorable phrase, this was a "community in anonymity."[21] Dispersed throughout the state, Catholics could hardly constitute a real community of neighbors any more than the people of South Carolina could be called a community. The *Miscellany*'s clerical editors, however, claimed to speak on behalf of their people—Catholics in the southern Atlantic states—and posited an affinity with their non-Catholic neighbors.

The affinity between Catholicism and southerners relied on two factors that operated simultaneously. First, Catholics and southerners shared a conscious identity as minorities. Second, the Catholic clerical leadership of South Carolina developed cultural, religious, and political strategies to build an affinity between Catholic and non-Catholic southerners. Their efforts sometimes succeeded because they could draw on the conception of the Union as an assemblage of peoples. This allowed Catholics to claim ownership in the South while safeguarding their religious commitments. Ideally, it allowed them to be southerners and Catholics with little cognitive dissonance. Catholic attempts, however, sometimes failed and raised the ire of their non-Catholic neighbors. When that occurred, the tensions that arose between Catholics and southerners revealed weaknesses in Catholic assertions of affinity between their faith and their adopted region of the United States.

The common feeling of minority status created important similarities between Catholic and southern strategies of cultural and political engagement. Scholars as far back as Jesse Carpenter in his 1930 study, *The South as a Conscious Minority*, have recognized the importance of minority status for the politics and culture of the Old South. Carpenter highlighted two primary effects. First, minority status strengthened the bonds between members of the group and solidified identity. Second, it gave rise to a narrative of oppression and called for legal protections for the minority group. While southerners such as Calhoun worried about declining southern political power in the federal government and growing attacks on slavery, Catholics in the South faced an energized, aggressive, and often anti-Catholic nativist movement.

The combination of minority status and hostile opposition accentuated feelings of difference in both Catholics and southerners. Both groups were extremely sensitive to outside criticism and responded aggressively to perceived slights and outright attacks. In the face of opposition, both groups stressed their unique identities and their ability to fit into the larger group under certain conditions. Narratives of oppression had a role as well. For example, the fact that many Catholics in South Carolina were Irish exacerbated feelings of victimization. At the same time, Catholics pointed out to their neighbors the oppression suffered by Catholics in northern Europe after the Reformation to counter nativist claims of Catholic tyranny. As Quigley has noted, southern nationalists likewise thrived on a sense of victimhood.[22]

Finally, Catholics and southerners insisted on legal protections. The bishops of Charleston included on the masthead of the *Miscellany* the first amendment to the Constitution, a reminder to nativists of legal protections for religion. Calhoun's theory of nullification attempted to impart a legal process in order to protect the southern political minority. His successors tried the same thing in 1860, demanding a federal slave code for the territories. Minority status strengthened the affinity between Catholics and southerners and allowed them to collaborate more closely during the 1850s when they were attacked by common enemies: northern reformers and evangelical nativists.

Catholic leadership in South Carolina urged an affinity between the South and Catholicism in part for pragmatic reasons. As Randall Miller has argued, "Building the institutions of the Church became the principal concern of Church leaders in the Old South, for they understood that without an institutional framework Catholicism could not exist."[23] The bishops' determination to build a lasting presence forced them to engage their cultural and political environment. Thus any appreciation of Catholic actions in antebellum South Carolina must consider the broader context of the state and region in order to comprehend Catholic actions and ideas.

In their engagement efforts, the Catholic leadership developed a moderate approach to the issue of cultural accommodation. Catholics wished to be good citizens and true to their faith but also recognized that faith and culture could come into conflict. Catholic leaders thus positioned themselves intellectually in a place where they did not seem to be compromising their principles to accommodate the culture but instead interacted with their neighbors on Catholic terms. Sometimes they succeeded. As the sectional crisis of the 1850s wore on, Catholics faced intense pressure to accommodate fully to the secular culture. Catholic leaders in the diocese also recognized that they shared common enemies with their southern neighbors, a situation that brought them closer together.

The Catholic strategy in South Carolina could only work within a Jeffersonian conception of the Union as a bond of sentiment among peoples who shared a history. It is not surprising that South Carolina Catholic leadership implicitly understood this. The *Miscellany* frequently printed stories about colonial Maryland and Catholic participation in the Revolution. Catholics claimed a common history with their neighbors, implying that the bonds of sentiment qualified them to be part of the nation.[24] The demands of sentiment also help to explain Catholic sensitivity to prejudice in South Carolina and their appeals to both honor and toleration. If non-Catholics despised their Catholic neighbors and believed vile propaganda about the Catholic religion, then the bonds of sentiment would be lacking. Catholics would be left outside of the community.

The Catholic strategy of appealing to both religious and regional identities resembled other antebellum southern negotiations of contested identities. For example, Calhoun's conception of nullification stressed a moderate position between consolidation and secession. Just as South Carolina Catholics wished to be seen as southern Americans and Catholics, Calhoun claimed identity as both an American and a Carolinian. Nullification, by eschewing complete separation, allowed him to claim both simultaneously. The prominent South Carolina writer William Gilmore Simms posited a middle way in literature. He noted that his novels of the South were a way to demonstrate both his southern and American identities. "To be *national* in literature," he wrote, "one must needs be *sectional*."[25] In positing dual identities, the strategies of Calhoun, Simms, and the Catholic leadership of the Diocese of Charleston resembled one another in their logic.

This book argues that antebellum affinity between Catholicism and the South was not essential, but it became real. The desire for this affinity shaped the public actions of South Carolina's Catholic leaders, from promoting Catholicism to publishing a newspaper, engaging in religious disputes, selecting church architecture, celebrating Irish ethnicity, choosing effective political strategies, and thinking about slavery. I examine through various episodes how clerical leaders developed this affinity, how it was challenged, and how it grew as the Civil War approached. This study seeks to root Catholic actions deeply in the southern context. Strategies of accommodation necessarily were grounded in specific context and events. Abstract ideas met concrete realities, causing both conflict and adjustment. Without understanding the context of the time, the meanings of actions are obscured. Far from being merely anachronistic, attention to context reveals the contingent nature of the past and the contested realms of human action. Rather than a chronological narrative of antebellum Catholicism in South Carolina, this book explores important or particularly revealing episodes in which Catholic leaders engaged the culture of the state. It focuses on the perspectives of the clergy, because it was the clergy who devised the public stance of the church and because of the limitations of the primary source record.[26] Priests of Irish descent predominated in the Diocese of Charleston. "Between 1820 and 1880," Gleeson writes, "71 of the 101 priests who served there were Irish or of Irish heritage."[27] Anderson has noted that Irish clergy played significant roles in Ireland by "mediating" nationalism to the common people.[28] They performed the same role in South Carolina for their flocks, so their actions warrant deeper exploration.

This book begins by introducing the broad context of the state and the church during the antebellum era and provides the biographical background of Charleston's bishops, the men most responsible for building the idea of affinity. Chapter 2 describes Catholic efforts at institution building, which rooted them in the community and required cultural strategies of accommodation. The Deep South presented four great challenges to the bishops of Charleston: a dearth of clergy and resources, intellectual hostility, cultural prejudice against Catholics, and the geographic extent of the region. To meet these challenges the bishops supported education, publishing, and charitable works. In addition, they traveled throughout the diocese, meeting and engaging both Catholics and non-Catholics. The chapter also compares Catholic and evangelical religious strategies, demonstrating their similarities. As will be shown,

Catholicism was part of the southern religious experience, not an exception to it. Chapter 3 examines Catholics' uses of apologetics in their vigorous public debates with their non-Catholic neighbors. Catholics rooted themselves in their community but faced many who doubted their commitment to republicanism. Catholics publicly fought these charges and appealed to the honor culture of the South for vindication. The *Miscellany* carried a seemingly endless series of debates with a plethora of non-Catholic opponents. The chapter examines two debates with John Bachman, the leading Lutheran minister in South Carolina. Both clergy and laymen of the diocese joined the second public debate with Bachman, attempting to defend both their specific religious points of view and their status in the state as citizens. Chapter 4 looks at Catholic efforts at self-representation by examining three St. Patrick's Day celebrations in Charleston as well as the construction of a cathedral in the city. As the clergy portrayed these events in the *Miscellany*, Catholics regardless of sex, race, ethnicity, or class supported Catholic engagement with the wider culture. They raised money for the new cathedral and paraded through the streets on St. Patrick's Day to demonstrate their loyalty to both church and state. Rather than a liability, Catholics used their ethnic and religious differences as proof of their fitness for republican citizenship. In this, they celebrated the Jeffersonian conception of the Union.

The last two chapters investigate Catholic engagement with southern politics and the institution of slavery, familiar ground in the historiography of the American South. Chapter 5 traces Catholic strategies of political engagement during the nullification crisis and the 1850s. The clergy, attuned to both international and national events, crafted political responses that reflected their vision of a global church as well as their local situation. During the nullification debates, the rise of the Know Nothing Party in the early 1850s, and the secession crisis, Catholic leaders built political alliances with their neighbors to demonstrate their worth as fellow citizens and southerners. Chapter 6 considers Catholic engagement on the issue of slavery. Like the Protestant churches in South Carolina, the Catholic Church included African Americans and struggled to balance black religious participation with the odious and oppressive institution of slavery. The chapter revises many scholarly treatments by placing the writings of Bishops England and Lynch in the context of discussions of slavery in the state. As with other issues, Catholics tried to maintain their religious principles and southern affinities when discussing slavery. But this attempt at balance ultimately failed.

South Carolina afforded Catholics a place to live that differed from the northeastern cities where many antebellum Catholic immigrants made their homes. Catholic leaders recognized and took their opportunities to plant their faith, appreciating that religious freedom and a Jeffersonian understanding of the union provided them opportunities to be southerners, Americans, and Catholics simultaneously. By 1861 Catholics had succeeded in establishing Catholicism as part of the state's cultural geography. Layered identities do not, however, always integrate smoothly. Loyalty has to be renegotiated constantly as situations change. Loyalty also comes with a price. For South Carolina Catholics, the destruction of the Civil War was a price they paid, costing all Catholics in the state the hard-won progress their antebellum predecessors had sacrificed so much to achieve. The war, then, gave South Carolina Catholics their own version of the Lost Cause.[29]

CHAPTER ONE

The Context of Catholicism in Antebellum South Carolina

The dominant scholarly narratives of nineteenth-century American Catholicism, with a few notable exceptions, have proceeded along national rather than regional lines. They have focused on the Americanization of Catholic life, ideas, and practice, as well as the challenges presented by a large immigrant church,[1] and have devoted less attention either to Catholicism in the American South or to how the regional context of the United States influenced cultural accommodation. Thus to set the stage for an argument that hinges on a regional rather than a national narrative, it is necessary to describe broadly the context of antebellum South Carolina and to provide brief biographical sketches of Catholic leaders in the Diocese of Charleston.

South Carolina presented specific challenges to Catholics during the antebellum period. Not only did the state have the reputation as the most radical southern state, but the economic, social, and political indicators revealed a state in serious flux.[2] The cotton trade dominated the economy of antebellum South Carolina. While rice cultivation along the coast had shaped the colonial economy during the eighteenth century and helped slavery take root in the colony, the Lowcountry's economic dominance peaked by 1820.[3] The expansion of short staple cotton to the Upcountry reshaped the state's economy and spread slavery throughout South Carolina. So the state continued its export economy based squarely on slave labor. Cotton proved profitable for South Carolina whites, but the prosperity, as Lacy Ford noted, was "fragile."[4] The antebellum economy experienced booms and busts that affected the state's politics significantly. For example, the Panic of 1819 made for tough economic times during the 1820s, contributing to the nullification movement.[5] The economy recovered during the 1830s only to fall prey to the Panic of 1837. The 1840s also proved difficult economically, but the decade of the 1850s, as Ford wrote, "was the most profitable decade in history for growing cotton." Like other southern states, South Carolina built railroads and preached economic diversification.[6] South Carolina in 1860 remained overwhelmingly dependent on cotton agriculture and exports to fuel its economy.

South Carolina's social order resembled that of the other cotton states—with a few differences. The population during the antebellum period grew but at a slower rate than other southern states. The state's population stood at 502,741 in 1820 and 703,708 in 1860.[7] During economic downturns, thousands of South Carolinians migrated west seeking better, more productive cotton lands. The reliance on cotton also meant that the population was largely rural. Of the state's few cities, Charleston was the largest and most significant, having a population of about 40,000 in 1860. Columbia followed, with an 1860 population of around 8,000.[8] Both cities had white majority populations in 1860. Charleston possessed a vibrant and well-documented intellectual life, as well as a range of benevolent institutions to address various social needs.[9]

During the nineteenth century South Carolina exhibited some religious diversity among its white population. The Second Great Awakening made evangelical Protestantism a major but not dominant force. After 1820 South Carolina evangelicals built numerous institutions to consolidate their gains in church membership, firmly establishing their presence in the state.[10] Yet the Protestant Episcopal Church as well as the Presbyterian churches remained strong and produced important public figures.

Regardless of denomination, the social ideal accepted and preached by the white population of the state was personal independence, a concept that had important political repercussions. South Carolina possessed a strong republican political tradition whose values and tenets were widely shared by the white population.[11] Republicans in South Carolina depicted politics as a "moral struggle" in which independent, honorable men of virtue and public devotion battled vicious, self-interested individuals who, purely for self-gain, conspired against the liberties of the community.[12]

The icon of antebellum South Carolina republicanism was John C. Calhoun. Calhoun solidified his power in the state during the tumultuous 1820s and, as vice president during Andrew Jackson's first term, led the divisive nullification movement. During the 1830s and 1840s he cultivated political unity in the state and stressed the antiparty aspects of the republican tradition in an attempt to keep the two-party system at bay. After Calhoun's death, however, this unity dissolved. The Know Nothing Party made a brief appearance in the state, and Democrats were divided between those who wished for a stronger presence in the national Democratic Party and radicals who preferred an independent course. South Carolina contained a strong contingent of southern nationalists, but for the most part they stressed the same republican values of personal independence, virtue, and honor shared by the white population. South Carolina politicians accepted the existence of slavery as a given and viewed northern abolitionists as a serious threat to the peace of the state. The strident defense of slavery in the state, the presence of a significant radical faction that embraced secession, and devotion to republican principles of independence definitely shaded Carolina's politics and created a political culture for which the Catholic minority would have to account.

Catholicism had a troubled history in South Carolina. During the colonial period few Catholics lived there, and Catholicism was publicly reviled. In addition, the Stono Rebellion of 1739, the largest slave rebellion in South Carolina's history, possessed a Catholic element. Some of the rebels were Catholics and attempted to march to Spanish Florida to gain their freedom. Catholicism thus became linked to slave rebellions, certainly not a way to win accolades from the ruling class of the colony.[13] It is not surprising, then, that South Carolina lacked religious freedom until 1790, when the laws against Catholic officeholding were removed from the state constitution. Around the same time, a small group of Catholics in Charleston began forming a congregation and, in 1789, bought a building for a church, St. Mary's. Randall Miller notes that Catholicism in South Carolina before 1820 was marred by "ethnic rivalry."[14] Irish and French factions were the most prominent. The Irish priest Simon Felix Gallagher became pastor of St. Mary's in 1793. But Gallagher had troubles with Archbishop John Carroll of Baltimore, who possessed ecclesiastical jurisdiction of the area, and was removed as pastor. A French priest, Father Cloriviere, a dedicated monarchist, arrived at St. Mary's but alienated many of the French-speaking parishioners who had settled in the city after fleeing the slave revolt on Santo Domingo. Some members of the Irish congregation disliked Cloriviere because of his poor command of the English language. The lay trustees of St. Mary's asserted their authority to select a priest for their congregation, but this brought them into conflict with the archbishops of Baltimore, resulting in a brief schism. In 1820 the pope created the Diocese of Charleston and named Fr. John England of Cork, Ireland, as bishop, hoping thereby to end the contentious behavior of the lay trustees.[15]

Originally, the Diocese of Charleston encompassed the states of North Carolina, South Carolina, and Georgia. According to the 1820 census, the population of these states was 1,482,559. Thirty years later, the census recorded 2,228,938 people in the diocese, a significant increase but well below the national and northern averages for growth. The population of the country, due to natural increase and immigration, more than doubled during the same thirty-year span. New England, which received numerous immigrants during the period, doubled its population as well.[16] Still, the pope created the Diocese of Savannah in 1850, separating the state of Georgia from the Diocese of Charleston. In 1860 the latter contained 1,696,330 individuals (Catholic and non-Catholic).[17] Despite the seemingly large population numbers, Georgia, South Carolina, and North Carolina, like the rest of the nation, were overwhelmingly rural, and since the War of 1812 the population of these states had spread into the vast interior of the coastal South.

Catholics in the Diocese of Charleston made up a small percentage of the total population. Jay Dolan captured contemporary opinion about Catholicism in the South: "Catholicism was in a sorry state, and the complaint most frequently heard in these parts was the scarcity of priests and the neglect of religion."[18] Since no church census exists for the period, the historian James Woods, using U.S. Census data from 1850, presented the number of church buildings as a better way to estimate the size of the Catholic population. In 1850 the southern states possessed 21.2 percent of all the Catholic churches in the United States. But two-thirds of those churches were located in three states: Maryland, Kentucky, and Louisiana. The census recorded 14,996 churches in the South in 1850. Just 1.7 percent of these were Catholic churches.[19] The *Metropolitan Catholic Almanac and Laity's Directory* for 1851 listed the churches and Catholic institutions in the Diocese of Charleston, which by this time covered only North and South Carolina. The almanac counted eighteen churches and forty "stations," which were stops for missionary priests to offer mass and preach, sixteen clergymen, five seminarians, and an estimated five thousand Catholics.[20] This was in a population of 1,141,570. In South Carolina, Catholic churches made up 1.1 percent of the state's church buildings.

Catholics in the Diocese of Charleston lived near the few cities in the region and varied in regard to ethnicity and economic status. The historian Michael McNally noted, "Catholicism in the South was and is concentrated in the urban centers and made little headway in rural areas." "Practicing Catholics," he continued, "most of them immigrants," resided near cities, "where churches and clerical ministry were more conveniently available."[21] In particular, the Irish played a significant role in the Diocese of Charleston, constituting a majority of clergy during the antebellum period. The U.S. Census of 1850 recorded that 1.6 percent of the white population in the South was foreign-born Irish. Over a third of all foreign-born inhabitants of the region in 1850 were Irish.[22] Charleston, an important port city, attracted Irish Catholic immigrants, many of whom fled the depressed economic conditions in Ireland that had resulted after the Napoleonic Wars. As David Gleeson has shown, many Irish immigrants to the Deep South chose to settle in urban rather than rural areas because they perceived greater economic opportunity there. Ethnic Irish newspapers in northern cities often advertised favorable economic conditions in southern towns.[23] Charleston also claimed French Catholics and, after 1850, German Catholics. A number of Maryland Catholic families migrated to the diocese, creating a settlement in Locust Grove, Georgia, near Augusta. In addition, there were

African Americans among the Catholics of the diocese. A segment of the Catholic population was poor, but others arrived with some means. For example, the parents of Fr. James Corcoran, editor of the *United States Catholic Miscellany* during the 1850s, migrated to Charleston from Ireland after the War of 1812 and owned a small store and eventually three slaves.[24] Some of the French-speaking immigrants from Santo Domingo brought slaves with them.[25] Others, like Julia Datty, who had been educated in Paris before having to flee Santo Domingo in the 1790s, opened a school in Charleston and later joined and led Bishop England's Sisters of Charity of Our Lady of Mercy.[26]

Counting the Catholic population without definitive data is impossible, but a few anecdotes can provide a sense of the Catholic population and its growth. On August 1, 1829, the *Miscellany* published a short notice about the number of communicants in the city of Charleston. Under the heading "Statistics," the editor wrote, "From a note in the handwriting of the Rev. Mr. Cloriviere it appears that at Easter 1818, the number of communicants in this city was *whites*, men 26; women 79; *coloured* persons 17. Total 122. In 1820, the number was, we believe, 173: at last Easter it was considerably over 400."[27] Counting communicants is not the same as counting participants in services or those who considered themselves Catholic, but the numbers showed growth over time. In 1851, in its information about weekly services at the Cathedral of St. Finbar in Charleston, the *Metropolitan Catholic Almanac* noted, "Catechism at 9 ½ on Sunday. About 150 attend. The catechism for colored persons takes place after Vespers. About 175 attend." The almanac also mentioned the efforts of the Sisters of Our Lady of Mercy in Charleston, noting that they "give religious instruction to colored persons four evenings during the week." Both accounts noted racial diversity in the Catholic population of Charleston and relatively small numbers. The historian Andrew Stern, accepting the difficulty of counting the population of the diocese, estimates there were ten thousand Catholics in North and South Carolina in 1860.[28]

Outside of Charleston, there were a few Catholics dispersed widely over the rural landscape. In the first history of the diocese (1879), Rev. Jeremiah O'Connell, a missionary priest for over thirty years, told the history of Catholicism primarily by describing the Catholic families dispersed throughout Georgia and the Carolinas who had kept the faith alive and passed on the traditions they had received. For example, reflecting on his labors in middle Georgia during the 1840s, O'Connell commented, "In Monroe, Covington, Monticello, and over the entire country, I found but three families permanently settled who were Catholics." Of Georgia's state capital at the time, Milledgeville, O'Connell remarked that the city had a population of three thousand, "a dozen of whom were Catholics." He continued, "Among these were the brothers Michael and James O'Brien. Louisa, the wife of the latter, became a Catholic. This was a kind and hospitable family."[29] The O'Briens allowed O'Connell to offer mass in their home for the few local Catholics. The story contained a trope familiar to O'Connell's narrative. A family, usually of Irish origin, kept the faith in the home, frequented the sacraments whenever a priest was available, and married Protestants, who often converted to Catholicism.

These isolated Catholic families sometimes played important roles in the history of the Diocese of Charleston. The third bishop of Charleston, Patrick Lynch, came from such a family. His parents, Conlaw and Eleanor, migrated to the United States from Ireland in 1818. They eventually made it to Georgetown, South Carolina, where they were recruited to settle in Cheraw in the Upcountry. Cheap land certainly enticed Conlaw Lynch, who plied his trade as a carpenter and eventually built a Catholic church in the town. The Lynches were devout and relied on visiting priests for the sacraments. Their second son, Patrick, showed great intellectual promise, and they sent him to study with Bishop England in Charleston in 1829. On the other hand, Michael O'Connor, an immigrant from Limerick, Ireland, settled in Beaufort, South Carolina, in the Lowcountry. He married a local Baptist woman who eventually converted to Catholicism. O'Connor built a Catholic church in Beaufort. One of his sons, Michael P. Connor, studied at St. John's College (later Fordham University) in New York City before establishing a distinguished political and legal career in Charleston.[30]

Father O'Connell also identified Irish laborers as Catholics in the diocese, although many of them did not remain in the region for long. O'Connell mentions that in Marietta, Georgia, there lived "Molony, a carpenter, who plied his art all over the country for a period of fifty years." Molony, he continued, "travelled a long distance to receive the sacraments." O'Connell also mentions his experiences in the Upcountry town of Greenville, South Carolina, in the early 1850s where he found "only two families who were Catholic, and very poor." But in 1854 a large number of Irish laborers and their families arrived in the area to lay railroad tracks. O'Connell ministered to the families, organized a temperance society, and created a "priest's bank" to teach the workers how to save their wages.[31] But once the railroad work ended, most left the area. Christopher Silver, who studied the demographics of Charleston during the 1850s, noted the same phenomenon of Irish labor there. Many of the Irish workers came to the city from New York and stayed only as long as they could find work.[32] A transitory, poor population presented difficulties to the priests who ministered to their needs, but they boosted the numbers of Catholics in the diocese.

Catholics in the Charleston diocese faced some of the same conditions as their coreligionists in the North but differed in other respects. Like Catholics in the North, those in South Carolina were ethnically diverse and concentrated in urban areas.[33] Charleston, Augusta, Savannah, Wilmington, and Columbia contained Catholic populations large enough to sustain parishes and support schools, nuns, and clergy. These cities stood out as economic and cultural outposts in a swath of seemingly endless farmland. Catholics in the Diocese of Charleston shared with northern Catholics the challenge of geography—the sheer size of the country—and the need to build Catholic institutions, particularly parishes and schools, in order to nourish the faith. Of course, Catholics in both regions faced anti-Catholic outbursts, which often produced an acute awareness of their minority status.

At the same time, Catholics in South Carolina confronted additional challenges. Because of their small numbers, Catholics remained impotent as an independent political force. The only case in which they exercised influence was in Charleston city politics in the late 1850s, as Irish laborers constituted a small but growing percentage of the population. Catholics' minority status required that they join existing political factions and adapt to the dominant political culture if they wished to have any influence. The other notable difference between the North and the South for Catholics was the institution of slavery. Absent in the North, slavery remained integral to South Carolina's economy. Southern Catholics would have to address the issue in a context very different from their northern coreligionists.

The Diocese of Charleston had three energetic leaders during the antebellum period, each of whom shaped significantly Catholic engagement with southern culture. John England, the inaugural bishop of the diocese was, as James Woods indicates, "the most significant prelate in the South, and perhaps the whole United States, during the antebellum era."[34] England shaped many of the strategies of engagement that his successors attempted to follow. Ignatius Reynolds, Bishop England's successor, traveled the diocese extensively and strove to fund and administer the institutional framework his predecessor had created. In addition, Reynolds constructed a Gothic Revival–style cathedral in Charleston, a significant architectural feature in the city. Patrick Lynch, the third bishop, had been recruited into the seminary by Bishop England. Possessing a powerful intellect, Lynch found himself tapped for service in many areas. As bishop during the Civil War, Lynch served the people of Charleston as well as the Confederate States of America as a diplomat to Rome. After the war, Lynch labored for two decades to rebuild the diocese's institutional apparatus. Though the Catholic population of the diocese was small, the three antebellum bishops enjoyed powerful reputations in the South and were respected within the American church. Their stature and ambition made them hard to ignore.

John England exemplified the Irish influence on American and southern Catholicism. Born in Cork, Ireland, on September 23, 1786, England was a precocious youngster. He grew up under the British penal system, suffering discrimination on account of his Catholicism. He attended a Protestant school as a boy and then studied for the priesthood at the Theological College of Carlow. Ordained in 1808, the young Father England quickly joined political activists, including Daniel O'Connell, in protesting the penal laws. The British Parliament proposed in 1808 to emancipate Irish Catholics and pay Catholic clergy with state funds in return for a parliamentary veto of candidates for Catholic bishoprics in Ireland. In 1811, Cork hosted several protest movements against the so-called Veto Bill. In 1813 England gained control of a newspaper, the *Cork Mercantile Chronicle*, and used it to attack the Veto Bill and defend the church. He suffered for his outspoken views, and his newspaper fell victim to legal harassment. England was not solely interested in politics, however. He also led efforts to educate the Irish laity, particularly the urban poor, and served as a prison chaplain, where he ministered to many who were unjustly imprisoned under the penal laws. England's biographer Patrick Carey explains, "The experience of the penal system . . . encouraged Irish Catholics to perceive the union of church and state as inimical to their own interests." England, Carey added, learned from his bitter experiences as a young man and young priest that "the state did not grant favors without expecting reciprocation."[35] Father England took these lessons to South Carolina, building a style of Catholicism that meshed well with American republicanism.[36] On September 21, 1820, in St. Finbar's Cathedral in Cork, England was consecrated bishop of the new Diocese of Charleston.

Bishop England inherited numerous problems when he reached South Carolina in December 1820. To deal with his new situation, he drew on his experiences in Ireland and sought a pastoral approach that would spread and preserve Catholicism in the Deep South. In a revealing document written to the cardinal prefect of the Propaganda in Rome, Bishop England described his goals and the obstacles that stood in the way.[37] The letter, written halfway through his tenure as bishop, identified both internal and external problems that made his tasks particularly laborious.

In his letter, Bishop England expressed to Rome his desire to develop a style of leadership and Catholic life that would be suited to the cultural environment of the American South. He believed it to be his "principal duty" on arriving in the United States to study the American legal environment so as to settle the troubling lay trustee problem that plagued the three Catholic churches in the city.[38] In 1820 laymen had owned the parish churches, leading to bitter conflicts between clergy and their lay congregations. Bishop England wrote to the cardinal prefect that he solved the trouble by promulgating a diocesan constitution in which "the laity are empowered to cooperate but not to dominate" church governance. His nod to American republicanism, he reported, had established "peace and mutual confidence and a pleasant concord between the clergy and the laity."[39] England also lamented the poverty and size of the diocese. Because Catholics lived at great distances from one another, the bishop found it difficult to reach his flock, a problem aggravated by a shortage of priests. He bemoaned in particular the absence of "native youths who would present themselves for Holy Orders."[40] The lack of priests and the lack of social prestige were mutually reinforcing. Bishop England wrote that the "previous dissentions" among Catholics in Charleston, that is, before 1820, "had so lowered them in public estimation that those who wished to maintain a certain dignified position in society abandoned the Church through shame."[41] Clearly, then, the bishop's second area of focus would have to be the secular culture in which he lived.

From the beginning, Bishop England intended to improve the image of Catholicism among his southern neighbors by founding strong institutions. Catholics in the Diocese of Charleston were poor, divided, few in number, and generally lacked social status, providing a public relations nightmare for Bishop England. He founded a "good school of belles-lettres" in Charleston, but Protestant opposition made the project difficult to maintain, and it eventually closed.[42] He also attempted to promote female education. He sought, he told the cardinal prefect, Ursuline nuns to educate young ladies. He indicated his intentions regarding the non-Catholic population:

Though for the most part Protestants, they hold in great esteem the qualifications of these nuns, and I am sure that they will confide their children to them; and thus their prejudices will be removed and many conversions will follow; or at least the way will be opened through the good ladies educated by the nuns to exercise a very powerful influence on the whole mass of society.[43]

In order to reach the Protestant and secular publics and improve the reputation of Catholicism, he founded a weekly newspaper, the *United States Catholic Miscellany*. He noted that Americans read many newspapers, and often these newspapers repeated "the vilest and most shameful calumnies against Catholics." To "counteract this evil," he started the paper, which has "dissipated many prejudices and has silenced many enemies."[44] By speaking to non-Catholics in forms they were accustomed to, Bishop England demonstrated facility with American institutions and culture.

While the bishop also mentioned his work among the poor and enslaved in his diocese, he clearly indicated that the major challenge for Catholicism in the South was its lack of social status. Catholics could not hope to increase their presence and influence until they gained institutions that garnered respect from the non-Catholic majority. Lacking the means to status, Catholics depended on the secular culture to credential them. They had to participate in the institutions created by their non-Catholic neighbors in order to build respectability. In this sense, the Catholic experience in the Deep South resembled the situation of early southern evangelicals. Scholars have shown that in order for evangelicalism to grow in the South, it had to achieve respectability. Evangelicals achieved this in part by building institutions such as colleges that could serve as entry points for members of evangelical denominations into the ranks of the elite.[45] Catholics, however, did not have such luxury; they had no significant institutions. Part of Bishop England's plan was to build Catholic institutions that could provide Catholics with places free from anti-Catholic prejudice and could, over time, convey social respectability to Catholics as they interacted in secular society. Respectability would then build cultural capital that could be drawn on by future generations of Catholics.[46]

Bishop England labored hard to achieve his goals. He began a religious community of women, the Sisters of Our Lady of Mercy, and invited a group of Ursuline nuns from Cork to open a convent in Charleston. He opened a seminary in Charleston to increase the number of clergy in the diocese. On the national scene, England advocated for provincial councils of American bishops to coordinate their efforts in the United States. He traveled to Europe seeking funds for his new diocese and even served as the papal representative to Haiti. Exhausted by his efforts, he died on April 11, 1842. He had acted according to his vision but in the process saddled his successors with large financial obligations and tremendous expectations.

Ignatius Reynolds succeeded Bishop England in 1844, putting his own stamp on the Diocese of Charleston in his decade-long episcopate. Born on August 22, 1798, in Nelson County, Kentucky, Reynolds came from a Catholic family who had migrated from Maryland. He spent his youth on the family farm and then entered the Theological Seminary at Bardstown, Kentucky. In 1821 he moved to Baltimore to attend St. Mary's Seminary. Ordained a priest in 1823, Reynolds returned to Kentucky where he taught at and then administered St. Joseph's College in Bardstown. In 1833 he won acclaim for ministering to the people of Bardstown during a cholera outbreak. Later he became vicar general to Bishop Benedict Flaget and moved to Louisville, Kentucky, where he lived and worked from 1841 to 1844. It was the Fifth Provincial Council of Baltimore that recommended him to replace Bishop England, a task

no one apparently wanted. On March 19, 1844, Reynolds was consecrated bishop in Cincinnati and made his way to Charleston.[47]

Bishop Reynolds recognized and embraced the tremendous financial
commitment required to maintain the infrastructure of the diocese. He
sometimes complained about the poor financial health of the diocese and
even privately chided some of his clergy about spending too much
money.[48] But he continued to publish the *United States Catholic Miscellany*
and incurred the costs to publish a five-volume edition of Bishop England's works, both important intellectual contributions to the church in
the South. Reynolds also undertook a major financial campaign to construct a new cathedral. He hired Patrick Keely of New York, a practitioner of the Gothic Revival style, to build the Cathedral of St. John and
St. Finbar. The building, dedicated on April 6, 1854, demonstrated Catholic commitment to the region and the city of Charleston. Reynolds also
won a reputation for visiting far-flung reaches of his diocese, and the *Miscellany* captured some of the great labors this entailed. Reynolds died on
March 9, 1855, lamented by his clergy and flock. He had continued both
Bishop England's task of building infrastructure and England's devotion
to the people of the South, rooting the church more deeply in the region.

The life of the third bishop of Charleston, Patrick Lynch, proved the
success of Bishop England's strategies. Born on March 10, 1817, in
Clones, County Monaghan, Ireland, Lynch spent little time in his an-
cestral homeland. His parents migrated to the United States when Patrick was a baby. After arriving in Philadelphia, the family moved to
Georgetown, South Carolina, and in 1819 settled in Cheraw, a village in
the northeast part of the state. Conlaw Lynch worked as a carpenter and
eventually built up enough capital to acquire slaves.

Young Patrick demonstrated both religious devotion and great intelligence. He spent some time in school at Cheraw Academy before enroll-
ing in 1829 in Bishop England's Seminary of St. John the Baptist in
Charleston. In 1834 England sent Lynch along with a Charleston or-
phan of Irish parents, James Corcoran, to Rome to attend the seminary
of the Sacred Congregation for the Propagation of the Faith. The Propaganda, as it was called, oversaw missionary activity in the church, and
the United States was mission territory at the time. Both Lynch and
Corcoran excelled at the seminary. Lynch acquired fluency in seven languages and showed remarkable interest in science and mathematics.

Ordained in Rome in 1840, the young Father Lynch returned to South Carolina, where Bishop England appointed him to teach in the Seminary of St. John the Baptist. Between 1842 and 1844, he assisted at the cathedral. Under Bishop Reynolds he ran the seminary until the bishop closed it in 1851, and he also served as vicar general of the diocese.

During the 1840s Lynch periodically edited the *Miscellany* and engaged in an acrimonious public debate with a Presbyterian minister and South Carolina College professor, James Henley Thornwell.[49] David Heisser, Lynch's biographer, detailed Lynch's intellectual pursuits. Lynch participated in several intellectual clubs in Charleston and wrote at least once for the *Southern Quarterly Review* when South Carolinian William Gilmore Simms served as editor. He also offered advice on public works projects to acquire fresh drinking water for the city of Charleston, indulging his interest in geology. His major task under Bishop Reynolds was to oversee the construction of the new cathedral, which experienced many delays and cost overages. Lynch demonstrated consistently the talent and aptitude of his mentor, Bishop England.[50]

Patrick Lynch served the Diocese of Charleston as bishop for close to a quarter century. He became the administrator of the diocese in 1855 on Reynolds's death and on March 14, 1858, was consecrated bishop. Lynch served in trying times. During the 1850s, his old friend and classmate Rev. James Corcoran edited the *Miscellany*, fighting battles against nativists and European-style liberals whom he perceived as great dangers to the church worldwide. Like Bishop England, Lynch attempted to skirt direct commentary on pressing political matters. But once South Carolina seceded, Lynch and Corcoran celebrated the Confederate States of America and encouraged loyalty to the new regime. In 1861 Lynch exchanged letters, eventually published in newspapers, on secession with his old friend Archbishop John Hughes of New York. Lynch defended secession and blamed the North for embracing the radicalism that destroyed the Union.[51]

In December 1861, Catholic infrastructure in the city suffered a blow when a great fire swept through Charleston. The new cathedral and other church buildings were destroyed. As the Civil War progressed, Union gunboats blockaded Charleston and shelled the city, causing numerous hardships for civilians. Lynch spent most of his time ministering to the sick and wounded. He also had new administrative tasks related to slavery. Heisser detailed Lynch's struggles as a slave owner, having acquired slaves for the diocese through a bequest in the will of a wealthy Irish Catholic, William McKenna. In 1864 Lynch agreed to go to Rome to represent the Confederate States of America at the Vatican. He met Pope Pius IX, but the pope did not receive him as an official representative of a foreign government, and Vatican recognition for the Confederacy did not materialize. Lynch then tried his hand at propaganda, penning a defense of southern slavery for European newspapers in an attempt to stir sympathy for the Confederacy.[52]

The end of the Civil War brought tremendous challenges for Bishop Patrick Lynch. In Europe when the war ended, Lynch, because of his mission to Rome for the Confederacy, had to obtain a presidential pardon to return to the United States. The diocese was in shambles, and many clergy believed that Lynch had abandoned it during the toughest times at the end of the war. He faced seemingly insurmountable odds to rebuild his diocese, which was in worse condition than when Bishop England had arrived in 1820. Ironically, Lynch spent a lot of time in the North, soliciting funds to pay off the diocese's debt and rebuild infrastructure. He and James Corcoran, who had moved to St. Charles Borromeo Seminary in Philadelphia after the war, attended the Vatican Council in Rome during the 1870s. Lynch continued to publish articles in Catholic journals but could not revive the *Miscellany*. He died on February 26, 1882, having raised most of the money needed to retire the diocese's debt. Despite a life of vigorous activity and intellectual labor, Lynch's episcopacy was a lost quarter century. He spent himself trying to rebuild what the war had destroyed.[53]

Catholics in South Carolina worked to establish their churches and build a presence in the state during the most tumultuous years of the nineteenth century. Although a small minority and sometimes facing determined opposition, South Carolina Catholics sought to express their faith in ways their neighbors could understand. One continuous effort during the antebellum period involved building Catholic institutions that would allow South Carolina Catholics to increase their presence in the region.

CHAPTER TWO

Spreading the Word

In November 1839 Bishop England used the occasion of the annual convention of the Diocese of Charleston to reflect on the obstacles to establishing a dynamic Catholic presence in the South. First, the bishop addressed
the issue of clergy and resources. He noted that when he arrived in the diocese in 1820, he had only "five priests." By 1839, however, there were
"eighteen in the several stations of the diocese." Furthermore, he mentioned that he had built a seminary to educate clergy for the diocese and
pointed out that the laity had "to exert themselves more strenuously to
support their clergy in a becoming manner." In addition to donations by
the laity of the diocese, the bishop reported, he had repeatedly raised
money in Europe, particularly in France, Ireland, Italy, and from "the Leopoldine Society in Austria." He also identified the many misrepresentations of Catholicism by the press, particularly the Protestant press, as a
serious problem. Thus he remarked that he had "always considered it to be
essential to our well-being to have a periodical paper," the *United States
Catholic Miscellany*, to defend the church and counter intellectual hostility.
He hoped the laity would continue to fund the paper.[1]

Along with these appeals, Bishop England reflected on cultural prejudices against Catholicism and the geographic expanse of the diocese as

further challenges. Cultural prejudice, he suggested, could be overcome by selfless acts of charity. He commented on the recent outbreak of yellow fever in Augusta, Georgia, as an opportunity for service. Not only did two priests in Augusta help the victims, but three members of the Sisters of Our Lady of Mercy, an order founded by Bishop England, cared for sick patients. The sisters, he insisted, had "also the consolation of knowing that even here below, their charity and devotion have been duly prized by men, though intended by them only as an offering to that God to whom they are so deeply indebted." Catholics in Savannah and Locust Grove, Georgia, had also provided relief to the victims. Bishop England, referring to his visitation of the diocese in 1839, noted that the number of Catholics was growing but that "the districts are . . . much too extensive," making travel difficult. The geographic expanse meant that the diocese needed more clergy to service the Catholic population adequately. The need for clergy would become greater "as the internal improvement of the states advance[d]" and the population began "to spread towards the interior."[2] Southern Catholicism's four main difficulties—a dearth of clergy and resources, intellectual hostility, cultural prejudice, and the geographic expanse of the South—overlapped. To address them the bishop needed strong Catholic institutions and, most of all, more resources.

Bishop England's diagnosis was not unique. Even though Catholics were a small minority in the Diocese of Charleston, their experiences resembled those of other Christians in the South, particularly Protestant evangelicals. Ironically, common experiences and approaches to rooting and spreading the Christian faith in the South united Catholics and Protestants in a common endeavor despite their mistrust of one another. Southern Catholics, like their evangelical neighbors, faced a similar material environment and thus common challenges. In fact, scholarship on southern Christianity has stressed that evangelical Protestantism was not native to the region. Like Catholics, then, evangelicals had to fight to plant their churches in southern soil. Both groups also grappled with southern culture. In regard to spreading their faith, Catholics differed little from their Protestant neighbors and devised similar approaches to overcome comparable difficulties. Catholics were simply thirty years behind. Catholics in the South faced some unique challenges, however, especially due to their ethnic composition, their immigrant status, and their particular intellectual concerns. But the Catholic experience in the

South reveals an unexpected affinity with southern evangelicals that placed Catholics within the southern religious experience, not as outliers or exceptions to general trends.[3] The common experiences of southern Christians helped cement Catholic perceptions of belonging to the common "peoples" of the region.

The sacraments—such as baptism, the eucharist, confirmation, and matrimony—are central to Catholic life, and for most of them an ordained minister is required or preferred. Thus, the church needed a large number of clergy to operate and grow. Bishop England remarked to the diocesan convention in South Carolina in 1827, "The great want under which we at present labour in this state is that which affects the whole diocess [sic]; the want of a sufficient and efficient clergy." The bishop reminded the diocese that it was "our duty to provide as far as in our power, for the wants of those scattered members of our flocks."[4] This meant that the diocese had to find ways to attract and keep clergy. England repeatedly addressed the problem of Catholics leaving the faith because of the lack of Catholic institutions and clergy to support them. In 1835, for example, he told the convention of the diocese that the number of those who had left the church in the past half century had "been incalculably greater than those who have reunited themselves thereto." The vast majority, he believed, left because of "the want of missionary attention." He noted that some individuals were to blame for moving to areas without Catholic institutions. But he also recognized the cultural pressure to conform to community norms. Many avoided "singularity by frequenting strange [Protestant] meetings for the purposes of religion."[5] Often, it seems, churchgoing served as a means of cultural assimilation for immigrants. Therefore, Bishop England charged his flock with finding ways to expand its institutional footprint to recapture lost Catholics. To do this required clergy.

Protestant denominations faced similar challenges in navigating the geography of the South to reach their members and potential converts with a limited supply of clergy. Anne Loveland writes, "The chief problem evangelicals encountered in the country was that posed by the dispersal of the population." For example, Methodists used circuit-riding preachers to reach rural congregations. But the system was taxing on ministers, who generally preferred urban assignments. Some ministers had responsibility for as many as ten congregations and were expected to preach during the week as well as on weekends. Baptists in the South used itinerant preachers too but in many locales implemented the "once-a-month system of preaching." Rural Baptist churches might have a minister who came to preach one or two times a month and rotated among different congregations. Baptists disliked this system and tried during the late antebellum period to create more stable assignments.[6] Presbyterians also suffered from clergy shortages and, like Catholics, required seminary instruction for their ministers. Some scholars have argued that these educational requirements placed Presbyterians at a competitive disadvantage with Baptists and Methodists.[7]

Despite these challenges, evangelical Protestants had achieved success in the South, a situation Bishop England recognized and wished to emulate. He told South Carolina Catholics in 1830 that "owing to similar causes" Protestants labored "under a like necessity" in the South. "How many are the establishments which have been created, and are abundantly maintained" by the Protestants, he exclaimed. They had built their infrastructure "by means of subscriptions, of collections, of donations, and of bequests." This way the Protestants "have largely placed the means of maintaining professors, erecting buildings, creating libraries, supporting candidates, and aiding missionaries, besides also erecting their churches, and providing for their pastors."[8] In 1835 England again shamed the diocesan convention in Georgia by pointing to Protestant successes in building institutions in the state. He hoped Georgia Catholics would "do the same."[9] The bishop and his diocese, however, faced tremendous obstacles in attracting clergy.

Europe could, and did, provide clergy to Charleston and the United States. Priests born in France, in Ireland, and in German-speaking lands were common throughout the clergy-starved American church during the nineteenth century. But Bishop England hesitated to rely on foreign clergy for several reasons. For example, he doubted the fitness of many volunteer European clergy for service. He told a gathering of Catholic laity in 1836 that while the diocese had benefited from "many a meritorious and useful clergyman" from Europe, it had also received some unworthy candidates. Foreign bishops were "more ready to part with those who would be more detrimental than useful to our infant missions."[10] Bishop England realized that he too felt pressure to send out clergy as quickly as possible to fill the needs of the laity. "Under other circumstances," he told Georgia Catholics in 1827, some clergy "would have been at least subjected to a more lengthened probation." Failure to enforce this produced "consequences" that "have been extremely unpleasant in more instances than one." Having learned his lesson, Bishop England promised "to leave churches vacant" rather "than to make any similar appointment in future."[11] He calculated in an 1829 letter to Petit De Villers, Esq., of Savannah that he had lost fourteen clergy to various causes, three of whom he sent away "for misconduct."[12]

Bishop England also believed that many foreign clergy struggled to understand American culture and only reinforced nativist stereotypes that Catholicism was a religion foreign to the United States. He particularly worried about French clergy, in part a demonstration of his ethnic bias.[13] In 1835 England told a correspondent, "Still I am daily more and more convinced that the genius of the nation and the administration of the French are not easily reconciled." The French, he commented, "never can become American," and relying on French clergy reinforced "prejudice against our religion." Many Americans believed Catholicism "is not American, that it is the Religion of strangers, of aliens, & c." The Irish, however, were "easily amalgamated with the Americans," he asserted. "Their principles, their dispositions, their politics, their notions of government, their language and their appearance become American very quickly, and they praise and prefer America to their oppressors at home."[14] During an 1829 address to South Carolina Catholics, Bishop England demanded clergy who shared American culture. They should possess "knowledge of American laws, intimacy with American people, the attachment to American institutions, the habit of American discipline, the zeal for American improvement, and devotion to American rights." Effective clergy had to be able to adapt "the great principles of faith, of morality, and of science to American circumstances."[15] Not surprisingly, foreign clergy struggled to fulfill Bishop England's criteria.

Bishop England's final reason for eschewing a reliance on foreign clergy was more pragmatic: foreigners had to undergo a period of "seasoning" to survive the climate of the Deep South. The geography of Lowcountry South Carolina and the Georgia coast encouraged malarial mosquitoes. In 1824 Bishop England listed as one of the challenges facing clergy of the diocese "the peculiarity of our climate," which "requires an adaptation of the bodily system."[16] The bishop understood all too well the challenge, having suffered numerous bouts of illness during his first two years in the country. In February 1822 he wrote to his friend William Gaston, a Catholic lawyer and state judge in North Carolina, "I have had two other serious attacks since I received your letter from Raleigh . . . but I trust I now am sufficiently reduced to bear this climate."[17] England's addresses to the diocesan conventions as well as remembrances of diocesan priests detailed the numerous clergy who did not survive. Fr. Jeremiah O'Connell, who served as a missionary priest in the diocese for more than thirty years, remarked that half of the priests who had lived in the diocese had either died or left to escape the harsh conditions of the Deep South.[18] England often lamented the fevers and other illnesses that frequently prevented clergy from performing their duties.[19] The climate made it unlikely that the diocese would attract enough foreign priests to serve. Bishop England wished to rely, therefore, on southern Catholics to fill the clerical ranks.

England's desire for native clergy led him to found in 1825 the Seminary of St. John the Baptist in Charleston, a financially demanding project. The commitment to the seminary led to two courses of action. First, he articulated a philosophy of church funding under the system of religious freedom in the United States. Second, he devised practical means to cover his expenses. But his practical decisions did not always work and contributed to several problems for the diocese.

Throughout his career in Ireland and the United States, England strongly supported a voluntary system of church support.[20] In Ireland he had written against efforts by the British Parliament to pay the salaries of Irish bishops, fearing the state control that would likely follow. In 1839, in the context of a discussion of finances, he told the diocesan convention, "In this life, we cannot look for absolute perfection in human institutions; we must only endeavor to follow in practice that system which, in our actual position, gives us the greatest good, with the least evil."[21] Bishop England was no utopian. Nor did he try to impose on others the system that worked best in his context. For example, in an undated manuscript, England wrote that he would neither "strip the Church of her possessions" gained through state support nor "advise the clergy of a nation, which upon a long regulated system was dependent upon the government, to fling away its bounty and to throw itself upon the people." But he also advised those who supported a religious estab-

lishment not to universalize their preference. Pointing to the Irish example, he noted that "during three centuries the Irish clergy have had no
such [government] pay, and their Church has not perished." Religious
establishments made the church dependent "upon the caprice or the policy, upon the vices or virtues, of statesmen." He believed that "it would
be a great blessing to the Church, if she was free from this control of either good or bad men." While he preferred "a state of perfect ecclesiastical freedom," he understood that it too had its weaknesses.[22]

The voluntary system of church funding depended on "the zeal of the
people," wrote Bishop England, and therein lay its strength. Like the
school of American republican ideology that relied on popular virtue for
vigor, England's ecclesiastical system rested on the virtue of the laity.[23]
Ideally, the people would feel pressed to support their clergy and church
because they would be responsible financially. The voluntary system
would help the clergy to behave, for it would be in their "interest" to
"secure [the laity's] affection." At the same time, the priest would not be
"the slave of any individual nor of any faction" for funding. As England
insisted, the clergyman "must endeavor to conciliate all." The priest
should recognize "that the affections of his people and the esteem of his
superior are secured only by the correct and zealous discharge of his
duty."[24] Clerical leaders would have to find ways to inspire the people to
virtue. As he wrote to his friend Simon Bruté, then a seminary professor
in Maryland, in 1827, "The more I study the people the more am I convinced of this principle. 'They must be led by their habits.' You cannot
drive them."[25] For Bishop England the voluntary system was not intended to democratize the structure of the church but to make the clergy
and the laity feel it was in their interest to perform their religious duties.

He realized, however, that individuals suffered temptations to shirk
their duties, making a system that relied on the zeal of individuals sometimes fragile. Again, this concern mirrored American republican fears of
declension.[26] In an 1827 address to South Carolina Catholics, Bishop
England reminded them that they should be concerned with others: "As
in the natural, so in the mystical body, the affliction or suffering of one
member affects the whole, and the others should be active in their aid."
Bishop England then described what economists have called the free
rider problem. When individuals provide public goods, there is a tendency for the individual to withhold his small efforts because he will still

enjoy the benefits of everyone else's contributions. "Individuals even who are well disposed," he said,

> find that much is not required from them, and each persuades himself that his omission of that little will not be any serious injury, whereas it is plain that all our exertion is but the combination of the acts of individuals, and all our means the sum of their small and separate contributions; and if each yields to this too generally prevailing delusion, we shall be left without efficient officers, or any funds.[27]

Recognizing that many people are willing to let someone else carry their load, England had to become a tireless exhorter and fund-raiser. On the one hand, he sought native clergy in order to better engage in missionary endeavors; on the other, the atmosphere of religious voluntaryism transformed him into, at least in part, a fund-raising bureaucrat. It was a role that was necessary for his quest to meet his goals and a role his successors would have to play as well.

Bishop England tried various approaches to acquire funding for his efforts to educate and train native clergy. Initially, he attempted to raise money from the broader community by operating a school. The June 12, 1822, edition of the *Miscellany* announced the opening of the Philosophical and Classical Seminary of Charleston. Students could take courses in English, belles-lettres, classics, mathematics, and philosophy, for which they paid tuition quarterly.[28] Although courses in Catholicism were conspicuously absent from the curriculum, local Protestants attacked the school during the summer of 1822 as a plan to convert Protestant children to Catholicism. The bishop responded to these charges in the pages of the *Miscellany*. He wrote that "several respectable gentlemen" asked for the school and that he had publicly pledged "that the religion of the children placed under my care, should not be interfered with." He resented that his "reputation" had been questioned. He noted that because the school received no public money, he owed explanations only to the parents of his students. Thus he would make no further public statements in defense of the school. He assured the public that he did not teach Catholicism to students or hold Catholic liturgies at the school. He also noted that students pledged not to discuss religious differences among themselves at school. Bishop England insisted that he had prom-

ised not to proselytize students and had kept his word. To suggest otherwise was an insult to his honor.[29]

While it was true that Bishop England did not use the school to make
converts, he did tie the school to his plans to facilitate the education of a
native clergy. In September 1822 he apologized to William Gaston for
his delinquency in corresponding, pointing to his clerical duties as well
as his role as superintendent of his new school. He admitted to Gaston
his intentions for the school. First, he hoped "by its profits to aid in pur-
chasing the ground for the church, & of having a school in which candidates for orders [the priesthood] should I be so fortunate as to meet any,
might be properly educated." Second, he believed that the school "has
made itself a character which if it can support will throw all the respectable portion of Carolinian education into our hands." He mentioned that
the "Presbyterians have been furious in their attacks upon it" but that the
school had grown to "twelve Catholic children & fifty-one of other persuasions & of the most respectable families of this state."[30] But the bishop's optimism proved short-lived. In 1824 he admitted to Gaston that
some Protestants had not been happy about funding the bishop's plan for
clergy. "Our good friends here," he wrote, "have discovered our intention
to be frugal & to spare what we can to aid candidates for holy orders." As
a result, many Protestant parents pulled their children out of the Philosophical and Classical Seminary and rebuilt a decrepit Protestant school
for their children. The bishop grumbled, "We were thus by their good &
liberal conduct, involved in debt." In order to salvage his school, he had
to teach many of the classes himself, draining valuable time and energy
from his other duties.[31] In 1824 he told the diocesan convention in
Charleston that the school "has been far from being a source of emolu-
ment." "Henceforth," he said, "we shall expect from it the only benefits
of education for such of our candidates as may be improved in its
classes."[32] The bishop's plan to fund the education of native Catholic
clergy from the tuition of wealthy Protestant students had failed.

The school survived until the mid-1830s, but Bishop England became
increasingly bitter about the controversy. He mentioned it often in his
writings and addresses to explain in part the general poverty of his diocese despite his best efforts. Privately, he commented on the incident to
point to Protestant hostility to Catholics. He wrote Francis Lieber in
1835 that he had been "the victim of conspiracy of the clergy of several

other denominations" who had prompted Protestants to pull their children from the school, thus leaving him in debt. He commented, "[The incident] has taught me that I made a most disastrous mistake in imagining that what I deemed liberality was to be found in the land to which my predilections were given because I thought that those men left each other free in their intercourse with heaven."[33] It is not surprising that Protestants would have objected to the bishop's use of profits from the school to educate clergy of a religion to which they objected. After all, the bishop had recognized Protestant concerns about Catholicism by prohibiting the teaching of religion or the discussion of religious differences at the school. In 1837, soon after the Philosophical and Classical Seminary closed, the bishop remarked that he had not tried "to enrich myself" but had hoped to fund a seminary for candidates to the priesthood.[34] He would have to find another source of funding.

By necessity, Bishop England, like most of his fellow American bishops, turned to Europe for assistance. The bishop's turn to Europe in the 1830s coincided with the intensification of Protestant nativism and, in the phrase of James Bratt, the "reorientation of American Protestantism." The growth of Catholicism in the United States, mostly as a result of immigration, began to change American Christianity by establishing, as Bratt indicated, "Protestant versus Catholic" instead of "popular versus elite or pro- versus antirevivalist postures" as the basic religious divide in the country.[35] This context ensured hostility to Bishop England's plans.

During the 1830s Bishop England acknowledged publicly the importance of foreign donations to sustaining his seminary.[36] In this period two European organizations in particular provided funds to the Diocese of Charleston, the Association for the Propagation of the Faith in Lyons, France, and the Leopoldine Association in Austria. Both had been founded to assist foreign missions, particularly those in the United States.[37] In 1833 Bishop England remarked to a convention of South Carolina Catholics that "our poverty was aided by the charity and munificence of many of our brethren in France and in Austria." He noted that on his recent travels in Europe he had met with representatives of the charitable societies to give specific information about the needs of southern Catholics. In Vienna, he said, the Austrian leaders were "altogether uninformed of the actual state of our churches."[38] He obtained a meeting with the emperor to thank him for his support. In his convention address the next year, he told the delegates that his cultivation of both societies had paid off with more donations. In 1835 he again reported European donations, noting that they were "intended to sustain our seminary and to support those [the diocese's] missions."[39]

By 1835, however, these foreign contributions to Catholics had provoked vocal opposition from the Protestant press, which Bishop England tried to answer. Most notably, Samuel F. B. Morse, inventor of the telegraph and a notorious anti-Catholic, published pamphlets in 1834 and 1835 attacking Catholic immigration as the preeminent danger to the Republic. In his 1835 *Imminent Danger to the Free Institutions of the United States through Foreign Immigration, and the Present State of the Naturalization Laws,* Morse identified an Austrian plot to spread absolute monarchy to the United States by funding American Catholicism through the Leopoldine Society, by sponsoring Jesuit priests to undermine republicanism, and by sending "ship-loads of Roman Catholic emigrants" to convert the United States "to the *religion* of Popery." Morse refused to believe Catholic rebuttals to his charges. For example, Catholics pointed out that most Catholic immigrants, particularly the Irish, supported the Democratic Party, not monarchy. But Morse countered, "Yes; to be sure they are on the side of Democracy. They are just where I should look for them. Judas Iscariot joined with the true disciples." Catholics professed to be loyal Democrats but did so only *"to cover their designs"* to overthrow republicanism.[40]

Bishop England responded to such charges in his 1835 address to the convention of South Carolina Catholics. He denied that European missionaries sought to overthrow republicanism, quoting an anonymous French missionary funded by the Propaganda in Lyons who claimed that while he was in the United States "it was [his] duty to be a republican." England exclaimed, "Yet this is the society which has furnished us in two years with one thousand dollars to destroy the republicanism of the two Carolinas and of Georgia!!!" He wondered when the non-Catholic people of the region would "exhibit in respect to our religion and its institutions the same good sense and discernment that they manifest upon every other question."[41] Although the bishop continued to rely on foreign donations, he realized that this dependence reinforced anti-Catholic prejudices. He would have to raise funds domestically to support his clergy.

In February 1836 the bishop addressed the Society of St. John the Baptist, his domestic solution to raising funds for clergy support, on its first anniversary. He admitted that "after upwards of fourteen years of labour and suffering, it was found that it would be unwise to place our chief reliance upon foreign aid."[42] Surely, nativist attacks played a role. The *Miscellany* in 1835 was filled with reports of nativism, particularly the notorious burning of the Ursuline Convent in Charlestown, Massachusetts, in 1834. On January 24, 1835, the bishop placed in the paper a copy of a constitution for a "Roman Catholic Missionary Society of the Diocess of Charleston" that would be organized to collect donations from members by subscription. The editorial introduction to the constitution indicated that southern Catholics needed to imitate the successes of their "brethren of other communions." Protestants had been able to fill "up the vacancies of their ministry" and to extend "their ministrations to places that were unprovided," the paper noted. In addition, Protestants "have even undertaken to enlighten their fellow citizens who are sunk in the darkness and degradation of what they are pleased to call *Popery*," the bishop jibed. While American Protestants sent missionaries throughout the world, southern Catholics "have been comparatively negligent in sustaining our own ministry," despite having "been aided by the charitable contributions of our brethren in Europe." The bishop charged that Catholics must "begin with something like the energy of those by whom we are surrounded."[43] On February 15, 1835, "at the church of St. Mary, Hassell Street," a group of Catholics "ratified" the constitution and called themselves the Roman Catholic Society of St. John the Baptist.[44]

Bishop England believed that a stated interest in native clergy would bring success to the society. The laity would recognize the importance of supporting a seminary and missions throughout the diocese. He told the society that there was no other way to fund these efforts "but by the voluntary contributions of those whose sense of duty, whose zeal for religion, whose patriotism and whose provident love for their own offspring will induce their cooperation." Protestants had succeeded by soliciting rather "small subscriptions, regularly paid."[45] The society would do the same. Bishop England told Georgia Catholics in 1835 that the society was "a voluntary association, founded upon the same principles, and for the same objects, as the association for propagating the faith which exists in France, and the Leopoldine Association in Germany."[46] He hoped the society could contribute to the diocese without arousing the nativism associated with foreign donations. It did successfully raise money for the seminary, but contributions from the laity depended on the health of the economy. So when the Panic of 1837 devastated the country's economy, donations declined. Such was the cost of the bishop's plan. His successors continued the society, but Bishop Reynolds closed the Seminary of St. John the Baptist in 1851.

The search for adequate clergy consumed much of Bishop England's time and energy. Like evangelical Protestants, the bishop recognized the importance of numerous and competent clergy to spread religion and build lasting institutions. The voluntary nature of American religion demanded much of the bishop, but despite his great efforts the numbers of native clergy remained small.

Alexis de Tocqueville noticed the ubiquity of newspapers during his 1831 travels in the United States and attributed their great number to the new individualism emerging in the country. Individuals unattached to traditional institutions would act in common only if they were convinced the proposed actions served their interests. Newspapers facilitated this realization; they were "the only way of being able to place the same thought at the same moment into a thousand minds," Tocqueville commented. Americans were "spread over a wide area" and had limited ability to travel widely. Thus, he insisted, "a means of daily communication has to be found which does not require contact." The newspaper served to bind a community of readers, "sweeping them along all the more readily as they are individually powerless."[47] For Tocqueville, America, in a sense, substituted the newspaper for the face-to-face interactions of traditional life and produced powerful senses of community that could lead to common action.

As Tocqueville recognized, newspapers played a central role in American culture during the early republic by disseminating information and ideas. American colonists had launched their Revolution from the printing press, creating a vibrant print culture of protest that announced to the world their justifications for seeking independence from Great Britain. Americans' consumption of newspapers increased dramatically after the Constitution was ratified in 1789. In 1790, 92 weekly and biweekly papers were published in the United States. According to Joyce Appleby, 371 papers, "many of them dailies," were printed in the country in 1810.

That year Americans purchased 24 million newspapers, roughly 3.4 newspapers per person. By 1820 the ratio had increased to 5.1 newspapers per person. In 1820 the U.S. population was 8 million. As Appleby pointed out, half of the population in 1820 was under the age of sixteen, and around 20 percent were enslaved. This means that literate adult white Americans, a minority, consumed a great deal of news. Appleby noted that the United States had "the largest aggregate [newspaper] circulation of any country of the world, regardless of size."[48] R. Laurence Moore has pointed out that "getting into print became the primary way to prescribe and contest values during the nineteenth century." "To matter," he continued, "what was said had to find a publisher."[49]

The explosion of print culture was due in part to laws that encouraged its proliferation. In 1792 Congress passed the Post Office Act. It set extremely low rates for sending newspapers through the mail and also empowered Congress with establishing "new post routes."[50] The immediate result was an explosion in the number of post offices and newspapers carried through the mail. In 1790 the United States had 75 post offices handling 300,000 letters and 500,000 newspapers. Fifty years later there were 13,468 post offices handling 40.9 million letters and at least 39 million newspapers. Richard John calculated that in this period "newspapers made up as much as 95 percent of the weight of the mail, while accounting for no more than about 15 percent of the revenue." The government also allowed newspaper editors to receive, "free of charge, one copy of every other newspaper in the country."[51] This led to the common practice of editors clipping stories from other newspapers and reprinting them in their own papers. It was thus not uncommon for a reader to encounter news from numerous locales. By the 1840s railroads and telegraph lines spread the news and the mail more quickly, facilitating wider dissemination of information.[52] As steam presses came into use by 1850, information could be produced and spread rapidly and relatively cheaply.[53]

Naturally, the Protestant press also grew in size and importance during the nineteenth century. Nathan Hatch, echoing Tocqueville, wrote that "the absence of strong ecclesiastical institutions in the American republic exalted the role of the religious press." Editors, Hatch added, "could impart a sense of coherence and direction to widely scattered congregations."[54] Evangelicals since George Whitefield in the 1730s used the press to build a cohesive religious movement. Evangelical efforts to

create a religious culture in the United States through reading Christian works, particularly the Bible and short religious tracts, resulted in
strong institutions dedicated to using the media for Christian purposes.[55]
Founded in 1825, the American Tract Society (ATS) became "the leading publisher and distributer of cheap religious books and tracts in the
antebellum era." By 1841 the ATS had created a nationwide network of
salesmen, colporteurs, to distribute its literature. As David Paul Nord
has noted, the goal of the ATS "was to employ modern technologies of
printing, modern principles of business organization, and modern methods of distribution to place into the hands of readers a timeless message
contained in two-hundred-year-old books."[56] But the ATS also issued
tracts hostile to Catholicism and targeted immigrant Catholics for conversion. One ATS pamphlet from 1836 expressed the hope that through
converting Catholics to Protestantism there would be "another reformation more pure and spiritual than the first."[57] Other Protestant groups
distributed literature and printed journals and periodicals.[58] By creating
a reading public and supplying the public with various forms of literature
cheaply, evangelical Protestants built cultural influence.

Bishop England planned to found a newspaper in the Diocese of
Charleston almost immediately on his arrival, having recognized the
power that newspapers possessed in modern culture. While a priest in
Ireland, England had edited the *Cork Mercantile Chronicle*, using it in ecclesiastical and political battles. Carey noted that during England's editor-
ship of the Cork newspaper and his participation in public meetings of
political protest, he "learned to value democratic methods."[59] On February
16, 1822, Bishop England wrote in his diary that he "issued a prospectus
for the publication of a weekly Catholic newspaper to be called the United
States Catholic Miscellany."[60] Two days later he wrote to William Gaston
that the greatest need of Catholics in the diocese was "some common
organ of communication," a newspaper. The "common organ" could bind
together the small number of Catholics otherwise dispersed throughout
the diocese. He summarized his plan to Gaston, focusing on the need to
defend Catholicism from Protestant attacks and to educate readers on
Catholic doctrine.[61] When Bishop England published the *United States
Catholic Miscellany* in June 1822 it became the "first strictly religious journal established in this county in defense of Catholic doctrine."[62] The *Miscellany* was England's greatest intellectual labor. Reflecting back on the

founding of the *Miscellany* in the 1830s, he wrote to the cardinal prefect of the Propaganda Fide, "On my arrival in America I soon found that the Press was one of the greatest instruments for good or evil; for there everybody reads the daily or weekly papers, while the reading of books is not so common." He estimated that "more than fifty" religious journals and papers viciously attacked "our holy Religion" regularly.[63]

Bishop England envisioned the *Miscellany* as primarily concerned with countering intellectual hostility to Catholicism. In the first issue, he noted that he would not introduce the project with a flowery essay because, as he had been told, "America was a republic in which people liked plain transaction of business, and preferred work to promises." He followed with an allegory, explaining that the paper sought to present the truth about Catholicism to counter the "fiction" and "misrepresentation" found in hostile papers.[64] In the newspaper's prospectus, he listed as his principles "candour, moderation, fidelity, charity, and diligence." He then listed six "topics" that the paper would "embrace." First, it would explain Catholic doctrine clearly in order to dispel misunderstandings. Second, it would examine "history for the purpose of investigating the truth of many assertions which have been, perhaps, too lightly hazarded." Third, it would print news of Catholicism in other parts of the world, particularly in Europe and the Americas. The final three goals aimed to support Catholics in America. The *Miscellany* would include "memoirs and anecdotes" of famous Catholics and enemies of the church, summarize "political events and domestic occurrences," and provide "occasional reviews of religious publications." Overall, the paper sought "vindication" for Catholicism.[65] Reflecting in 1835 on the first decade of the paper's existence, Bishop England expressed gratification: "At the time of its establishment and for some years after, no other paper in the Union undertook to correct the many misrepresentations which issued from not only what is called the religious, but even from the secular press."[66]

The *Miscellany* not only defended Catholicism from attacks, but served other purposes in the diocese. As Tocqueville had suggested about newspapers in general, the *Miscellany* tried to strengthen southern Catholics. This resulted in part from Bishop England's intention to provide broad treatment of Catholicism: doctrine, history, and current events. In the first issue of the paper, Bishop England noted that bringing together the news into a coherent whole was extremely difficult.

"Persons are inclined to think," he wrote, "that every body knows as well as they do, the public facts which take place before their eyes, or they think them so little interesting, that they decline communicating them to the public." Those "mistakes" meant that "we are frequently left without much interesting news."[67] As a result, the bishop had to solicit stories from those he knew and then select and present that information in the paper. He hoped that the paper would build a network of individuals to provide news from the United States and throughout the world. Although the *Miscellany* had correspondents, its foreign news consisted primarily of reprints of articles in British papers. But by selecting the news to print, the editors could present a common vision of Catholicism that would inform the Catholics who read it. By reprinting stories and letters from around the diocese, the paper could forge bonds among the people. Rev. Jeremiah O'Connell told of one priest in the diocese who "never read any newspaper except the *Miscellany*."[68] Thanks to Bishop England's efforts, Catholics in the South read the addresses of their bishops and priests and saw vigorous debates with prominent southern Protestant ministers and editors—men such as James Henley Thornwell, Robert Breckinridge, Benjamin Gildersleeve, John Bachman, and Frederick Dalcho. The combativeness of the paper provided a sense that southern Catholics stood united against their opponents and could hold their own with the most learned Protestants.

While serving its purposes ably, the *Miscellany* suffered from a number of problems, particularly financial ones. In his addresses to the conventions of his diocese, Bishop England usually stressed the need to continue funding the paper despite its continuous debt. In his 1831 address to Georgia Catholics, for example, he lamented that "though extensively circulated" the *Miscellany* had "such poor returns as to have never met fully the expenses of its publication." "I do strenuously and emphatically press upon you the important duty of its support," he said.[69] Bishop England told the cardinal prefect of the Propaganda that the paper "has dissipated many prejudices and has silenced many enemies," but it was only one of a small number of Catholic papers combatting a deluge of Protestant publications.[70] The bishop also realized that financial difficulties contributed to the poorer quality of the paper and drained his time. In a July 22, 1826, editorial, he explained the recent six-month suspension of publication. In addition to the obvious financial reasons, he cited

"the slovenly manner in which our paper had been latterly published."
He planned to accept more advertisements, tighten the process of collecting subscription payments, and provide more "variety in the detail"
of the paper.[71] But to provide more variety, he needed more contributors.
Thus in his letters to Gaston he asked for contributions of information.
He also solicited his clerical friends. For example, he told Simon Bruté in
1825, "You must pay for your Miscellany by sending information."[72] The
lack of contributions meant that England himself had to take on more of
the writing. Having to reprint articles from other papers decreased the
amount of diocesan news, potentially weakening the ability to draw together local Catholics. But the paper continued to be published until
December 1861, becoming an important institution in the diocese and a
major source of Catholic news in the South.

England's successor, Bishop Ignatius Reynolds, recognized the importance of the *Miscellany* in reducing hostility to southern Catholics,
but he believed that the diocese needed to publish a lasting and substantial intellectual defense, a collection of Bishop England's writings.
Newspapers, as Tocqueville recognized, were ubiquitous and ephemeral.
A multivolume collection of England's writings would elevate his stature
as a serious intellectual contributor not only to American Catholicism
but also to the South.[73] So Reynolds obtained a complete run of the *Miscellany* and then established a committee of priests who had known England to establish what had come from his pen. Some of the Ursuline
nuns in Charleston assisted the committee. At the same time, Reynolds
recognized that the publication of Bishop England's works would be
costly and expressed his "anxiety" over his financial commitment to the
project. Nevertheless, he wrote that his "chief motive has been, to preserve for this and future ages the labors of a writer, well acquainted with
the important subjects which he treated, and singularly gifted with the
powers of close and exact logic, and with the happy talent of communicating his thoughts, in a style remarkable for perspicuity and strength . . .
and sometimes elevating us by its sublimity." He recognized that Bishop
England had the ability "of accommodating himself to the circumstances, and spirit of the age, in which we live" and of "making every
thing available for the great and holy cause, to which he had consecrated
his life." Not only did Reynolds believe England's writings would inspire
others and decrease hostility to the faith, but he also noted their histori-

cal value as "among the first *in time*,—as in merit,—of the contributions of the Catholic Church in these States, to Literature, Science and
Theology." The writings were proof "of the learning and zeal of our
clergy in this, as well as in every other age and country."[74] *The Works of
the Rt. Rev. John England* would stand as an intellectual monument to
southern Catholicism, legitimizing its reputation and perpetuating
Bishop England's vision for Catholics in the American South.

Although sales of *The Works of the Rt. Rev. John England* were slight,
the initial reviews confirmed Reynolds's expectations. Newspaper and
journal reviews acknowledged Bishop England's importance in both
Catholic and southern letters. Southern papers praised England's writings
on slavery, which had tried to demonstrate that the church did not share
the cause of northern abolitionists. In October 1849 the *Charleston Courier*
announced the publication of the *Works*, noting, "In Charleston, the scene
of his labors,—the city where a daily intercourse with men of the most
distinguished abilities developed the resources of his gigantic mind, his
works will doubtless be eagerly sought for."[75] On January 5, 1850, the *Miscellany* reprinted a review from the *New Orleans Bulletin*. It too recognized
the "attachment of Bishop England to his adopted country, and his devotion to the South in particular." Bishop England's "profound learning and
elegant scholarship" should attract readers "throughout the Southern
States," noted the review. It also praised the bishop's letters on slavery,
recommending them to southern "divines" as "an armory of weapons to
use against those at the North who would excommunicate them."[76] In
1851 *De Bow's Review* published a brief mention of the *Works*, acknowledging "the courtesy of Bishop Reynolds in the presentation of these volumes." After a brief listing of the contents of the volumes, the reviewer
opined that Bishop England's letters on slavery "are among the ablest papers ever written upon the subject" and noted that the influence of the
letters elevated "the Bishop very high throughout the Southern States."[77]
The *Boston Pilot*, a Catholic paper, did not comment on the letters regarding slavery but praised Bishop Reynolds for publishing "a valuable addition to the Catholic literature of this Continent."[78] Finally, *Brownson's
Quarterly Review* devoted numerous pages to reviewing the *Works* in 1850.
The anonymous reviewer praised Bishop England's writings but warned
readers of England's "Gallicanism," a product of his education in Ireland.
In addition to Bishop England's weak treatments of the papacy, the

reviewer warned that he exaggerated when he called the church's structure "republican."[79] Despite these criticisms, the review praised the *Works*
as intellectually important. The reviewers in both secular and Catholic
papers agreed that the *Works* served as a significant monument to American and southern Catholicism, thus fulfilling Reynolds's intention.

Like the *Miscellany* itself, however, the *Works* caused financial strain.
Rev. Jeremiah O'Connell later remarked, "This publication cost a very
large sum, and was a heavy drain on the diocesan fund; the subscription
did not meet the full expense of publication."[80] But in 1855 Bishop
Reynolds noted in the *Miscellany* that the print run of two thousand copies had been sold, allowing the diocese to meet the "heavy expenses attending the enterprise."[81] The *Works* and the *Miscellany* demonstrated the
commitment of southern Catholics to defending Catholicism through
intellectual means and the modern print industry to establish themselves
as fixtures on the southern cultural landscape for both their contemporaries and future Catholics. In this path they followed their Protestant
neighbors.

American reform movements exploded nationwide after the War of
1812. Although not completely religious in inspiration, the movements
drew inspiration, energy, and leadership from evangelical Protestantism.
Evangelical beliefs in progress and postmillennialism directed many to
attack social evils like intemperance, crime, and poverty.[82] Although the
locus of reform movements lay in the North, Charleston shared in the
push for benevolent reform and undertook a number of projects designed
to better the lives of urban dwellers. Catholics, like other groups, participated in the benevolent empire even if they did not share the same ratio-
nale or degree of participation as their evangelical neighbors. The historian Barbara Bellows stresses the interfaith character of the city's reform:
"Religious benevolence in Charleston reflected the presence of multiple
traditions: the social ethic of the Anglicans; the drive for proselytizing
voluntary associations among Evangelicals; Jewish benevolent practices;
the search for acceptance by Catholics."[83] In addition to theological justifications for charitable labors, Catholic leaders in Charleston understood that social work could reduce cultural prejudices against Catholicism by demonstrating Catholic willingness to sacrifice for the broader
community and work alongside their neighbors to improve social conditions. Charity could build affinity among neighbors.

In 1829 Bishop England brought four women from Baltimore to form the nucleus of the Sisters of Our Lady of Mercy, a community that would carry out charitable activities in the diocese.[84] In November 1839 he told the diocesan convention that he had founded the community "for the purpose of educating female children, of having care of orphans, and of assuaging the sufferings of the sick and aiding towards their recovery." The bishop's decision was risky, for Catholic religious women were stock characters in anti-Catholic literature. In 1835, for example, the *Miscellany* devoted considerable space to exposing the Maria Monk hoax, in which a woman published an exposé of a convent in Canada where she allegedly suffered sexual assaults. The book sold thousands of copies before being exposed as a fraud by the press. Given this atmosphere, it was important that the Sisters of Our Lady of Mercy were seen to be working hard among the poor in the diocese. The bishop remarked, "Already have the sisters earned for themselves the lasting gratitude of numbers upon whom they conferred great benefits."[85] The Sisters particularly fulfilled the bishop's purpose for them during the 1839 yellow fever outbreak in Augusta, an important city in the diocese.

Yellow fever epidemics in the nineteenth-century South made the service of the Sisters of Our Lady of Mercy especially memorable. Scientists did not discover the cause of yellow fever, the *Aedes aegypti* mosquito, until the turn of the twentieth century. The historian Margaret Humphreys has written that the "death and disorder yellow fever brought to the South made it the preeminent concern of southern boards of health." She noted that "yellow fever had an impact out of proportion to its mortality because of its concentration of deaths within the span of a few weeks and the horror and rapidity of its course."[86] People understood that the fever disappeared after a heavy frost and thus they had to wait for nature during the long fever season stretching from July to November. John R. Pierce and Jim Writer noted that often boards of health "were too slow to attack an emerging epidemic" because they had to consider both public health and the effect of fever rumors on the commerce of their towns.[87] By 1840 physicians doubted that yellow fever was contagious like smallpox was, but in the face of outbreaks citizens usually ignored the doctors and fled the infected cities. Those who were too poor or sick to leave stayed behind to grapple with the hated Yellow Jack. Many southerners realized, as Humphreys indicated, that "yellow fever was greatly damaging their region's interests."[88]

Yellow fever hit Augusta hard in August 1839. The city lay at the fall line on the Savannah River. Founded in 1735 by James Oglethorpe, the city became, in the words of Milton Heath, "the principal inland trade center of Georgia."[89] The August 29 edition of Augusta's *Georgia Constitutionalist* reprinted an August 23 notice from the city's board of health, which had just met. The board asked that doctors of Augusta meet "at the Rail Road Bank" to give "their opinion of the prevailing fever."[90] A few days earlier, the *Charleston Courier* had published a notice that Augusta suffered from a fever, citing as its source a passenger on the railroad connecting the two cities. In the August 30 edition of the *Courier*, the editor noted that "there is no diminution of cases, and that the panic still continues." "Crowds of the inhabitants," the editor remarked, "are leaving daily, and business of all kinds is almost entirely suspended," an ominous sign for an important commercial depot during the cotton harvest season. The editor hoped that some Charleston physicians would travel to Augusta to help their medical colleagues since "four of the principal Physicians of that place have been taken sick."[91] Not surprisingly, the September 5 edition of the *Constitutionalist* counseled calm. The paper blamed for the panic "the erroneous statements of numerous letter writers from our city" published in Charleston papers. "*Fright*," the editor declared, "has caused more deaths in the city within the last few weeks than any prevailing epidemic." He admitted that Augusta citizens "have been panic stricken" and that "every one that could remove himself or family has done so." The paper tried to bring calm by printing Mayor Alfred Cumming's rejection of assistance from Charleston physicians, which had been offered by Mayor Pinckney of Charleston. Cumming assured the public that Augusta's doctors were sufficient to handle the crisis and that the fever was not contagious. The paper then printed the opinion of a Dr. Antony, one of the founders of Augusta's Medical College of Georgia, that the outbreak was not yellow fever and that reports of the fever's virulence had been exaggerated. Unfortunately, Dr. Antony died later that fall from the fever.[92]

As the fever persisted, conditions in Augusta worsened. Even the city's newspapers suspended publication of their daily editions. The editor of the *Constitutionalist* wrote on September 5, "We are still short handed in our office, and it will be a week or more before we are able to resume our usual publication of a tri-weekly paper."[93] The *Augusta Chronicle & Sentinel* suspended publication of its daily paper for two months, resuming on

November 11.[94] So many people fled the city that business suffered. In the October 24 edition of the *Constitutionalist* the editors advised readers "to keep away until we have a frost" but then implored "our country friends" to "bring in their produce" during the day. The merchants were waiting, and there was no "fear of danger."[95] Nearby papers complained that news of the yellow fever was hard to obtain since Augusta papers had suspended their daily editions and did not offer much commentary on the fever in their weekly editions. The Athens, Georgia, *Southern Banner* mentioned on September 27 that it was "without regular reports of the fever in Augusta for the past week." The *Charleston Courier* published a letter from an Augusta correspondent on September 10 noting that despite protests from the Augusta Board of Health, the reports in the *Courier* on the fever were good, but "the facts are really worse than I have seen in any extract." He continued, "The suffering among the poorer classes is unprecedented. Nurses and attendants for the sick cannot in all cases be had." The city struggled to bury the dead. He doubted "whether much if any over 1000 whites sleep in the city."[96] Augusta's population at the time was around 6,500. The *Chronicle & Sentinel* estimated that there were between 1,500 and 2,000 cases of yellow fever; 240 people died.[97] Yellow Jack persisted through November 8. The *Constitutionalist* reported on November 12 that Augusta had three "black frosts" that week, thus ending the fever threat.[98]

Southerners shared an understanding of the devastation wrought by yellow fever outbreaks, and nearby communities offered aid to Augusta. On September 23, Robert Charlton, mayor of Savannah, wrote a letter to Mayor Cumming offering $1,000 on behalf of the city council to help care for the city's suffering.[99] The Augusta Board of Health on October 3 thanked the Presbyterian Church of Athens for sending $233.50 "for the relief of our sick poor."[100] Mayor Cumming worked diligently to care for those stricken by the fever. Refusing to abandon the city, even though the fever killed three city councilmen and he himself fell ill, Cumming continued to work hard. His labors won him widespread acclaim. On November 19 Augusta citizens gathered at the Masonic Hall to honor him as one of the "few who remained" to care for the sick.[101] The Augusta papers did not mention Catholic aid, but the *Miscellany* on November 16 printed letters of appreciation from Mayor Cumming and the board of health and detailed Catholic assistance.

Like other groups, Catholics contributed both time and money to relief efforts for Augusta. The *Miscellany* reported that in August, as the fever hit, Fr. John Barry, priest at Holy Trinity Church in Augusta, offered "the residence which he occupied" to "the disposal of the Board of Health, as a temporary hospital." Mayor Cumming asked Father Barry to request from Bishop England some Sisters of Our Lady of Mercy to nurse the sick. The bishop sent three sisters and Rev. T.J. Cronin via railroad to Augusta to help. Mayor Cumming welcomed them, and they quickly got to work in the makeshift hospital at Holy Trinity Church. The *Miscellany* noted that they cared for seventy patients, twenty of whom died. The sisters returned to Charleston on November 2. Augusta's city council had offered to defray the costs of their fares and stay in the city. But Father Barry, on behalf of Bishop England, refused "as the Catholics of Charleston felt that in the affliction of their sister city, they ought at least not make any charge for charitable aid, and the more especially as a great portion of the patients were Roman Catholic." The *Miscellany* mentioned too that the Catholic parish in Locust Grove sent a donation to relieve "the sick of Augusta." Catholics had supported the city well.[102]

The responses of Mayor Cumming and the Augusta Board of Health demonstrated that the labors of the sisters and priests helped remove some cultural prejudices. After all, Mayor Cumming had thanked Bishop England "for the signal kindness manifested by you in directing the efforts of the Sisters of Charity to the relief of the afflicted of our city." He also wrote to Father Barry, "May God long preserve you for the exercise of that unbounded charity and benevolence which has so much endeared you to this community." The board of health also expressed its gratitude to both men. It commended the bishop "for his promptness and liberality in furnishing aid to our sick poor" and thanked Father Barry "for the use of his parsonage, and the unremitting attention to the patients." The board particularly remembered "the three Sisters of Charity from Charleston, who have so long and with such constant care, skill and kindness, taken charge of the hospital." Clearly, the aid provided by the diocese of Charleston made a lasting impression on the political leaders of Augusta. Catholics had served the city freely during its time of greatest need.[103]

Unfortunately, controversy caused by Mayor Cumming's letter spoiled the atmosphere of post-epidemic thanksgiving. Cumming's letter to

Bishop England about the sisters had included the following statement: "Guided by the Christian spirit of the Rev. Mr. Barry, in the midst of a panic-stricken community, whose pastors fled from their churches and their flocks, were scattered abroad, their disinterested devotion to the claims of suffering humanity, presented a beautiful moral spectacle, which made a deep and lasting impression upon the hearts of all who witnessed its exhibition."[104] In the context of the honor culture of the South, Cumming's letter impugned the reputation of the Protestant ministers of Augusta and contrasted their supposed cowardice with the bravery of Catholic women. The negative connotations of Catholic nuns at the time made the letter even more striking. Four Protestant ministers—A. N. Cunningham (Presbyterian), E. E. Ford (Episcopal), Augustus Longstreet (Methodist), and C. W. Key (Methodist)—protested the mayor's charge. They sent Bishop England letters explaining their conduct during the epidemic and demanded that he print them. England complied in the December 21, 1839, edition of the *Miscellany*.[105]

In their joint letter, the four pastors explained that they had not abandoned their churches during the epidemic. All four had been out of the city when the yellow fever struck, either on personal leave or on church business. All four returned during the epidemic and worked in the city. Two had battled the fever as well. In their letter, they denied wanting to diminish the praise of the Catholics but protested that Catholics would not "consent that a factitious lustre should be cast upon their virtue by means of a *contrast* unjustly disparaging to others." In the individual letters, however, the ministers indicated that they had resided in the Sand Hills during the epidemic. In a prefatory note to the letters, the editor of the *Miscellany* wrote that "the Sand Hills are a pleasant and healthy summer retreat, about two or three miles from the city, considerably elevated, and upon which a large number of the more wealthy citizens have excellent cottages or mansions."[106] Thus while the paper allowed the ministers to vindicate their reputations, the introduction to the letters invited further comparison. The Protestant ministers catered to the rich in the safety of the Sand Hills while Father Barry and the sisters ministered to the poor amid the dangers of the city. The *Miscellany* did not comment on the four letters, but the editor's implication regarding the Sand Hills defended the reputation of Catholics during the epidemic, establishing their reliability to Augusta's leaders. Perhaps the very fact that the ministers demanded the publication of their letters in the *Miscellany* showed that Catholicism had increased significantly in stature.

While measuring the decline of cultural prejudice is difficult, some evidence suggests that Bishop England's strategy enjoyed long-term success. In 1850, the Catholic hierarchy divided the Diocese of Charleston into two, transferring Georgia to the new Diocese of Savannah. In 1853 the Sisters of Our Lady of Mercy established a community in Augusta, where their reputation was already well known. They opened a school that served both as a public and a private school. In 1854 Augusta suffered from another yellow fever epidemic. The sisters again ran a makeshift hospital at the Holy Trinity rectory. They also operated an orphanage for girls. During the Civil War, the sisters nursed wounded soldiers in the city. In 1871 the city council paid the sisters to oversee the City Hospital.[107] The Sisters of Our Lady of Mercy thus became a major fixture in nineteenth-century Augusta. Catholics seemed also to have won the respect of at least one of Augusta's Protestant ministers. Augustus Baldwin Longstreet, the Georgia writer and Methodist minister, befriended Father Barry and worked in Augusta during the epidemic. In 1856, in the midst of the Know Nothing movement, Longstreet wrote a pamphlet defending Catholics from the charges of the nativists.[108] Bishop England's strategy of using charitable activities as a means to dispel cultural prejudice took a long time to bear fruit but seems to have been the most successful part of his plan.

As Bishop England had often noted, the geographic expanse of the South hampered efforts to spread Catholicism. The bishops of Charleston continually struggled to marshal the resources necessary to maintain their far-flung institutions. A brief snapshot of one such effort—Bishop Ignatius Reynolds's first visitation of the Diocese of Charleston in 1844—reveals the challenges, challenges their evangelical neighbors shared.

Reynolds became the second bishop of Charleston in 1844. Fr. Jeremiah O'Connell, who was ordained in 1844 and served under Reynolds, remarked that no one wanted the episcopacy of Charleston "because of the poverty of the diocese, the intolerance of the natives, the institution of slavery, and the eminence of the first bishop." Because of his dedication, O'Connell appreciated Reynolds greatly. When he was in good health, Reynolds, O'Connell remarked, imitated Bishop England "in toil and missionary labor." He "visited the entire region, frequently administering Confirmation, reconciling difficulties, opening new missions, encouraging the clergy by word and example."[109] O'Connell also praised Reynolds's skill as a preacher and public speaker. When the bishop died in 1855, the congregation at St. Mary's Church, the Catholic parish in the heart of Charleston, noted that Reynolds's "whole episcopate was devoted to his people."[110] In particular, Ignatius Reynolds won his reputation by his travels over his far-flung diocese.

In fact, church law demanded that Bishop Reynolds travel his diocese regularly. The Council of Trent in the sixteenth century restored the practice of bishops visiting the parishes in their dioceses to perform the sacrament of confirmation and to police them. In addition, bishops would interact with the people they ruled. The Council of Trent required these canonical visitations annually or, when that was impossible, every two years.[111] Bishop Reynolds set out for Georgia two months after arriving in Charleston.

Georgia's human and physical geography presented a challenge to anyone attempting to travel the state. Georgia is the largest state east of the Mississippi River, measuring nearly 320 miles at its "greatest length" and 260 miles at its "greatest width."[112] According to the U.S. Census of 1840, Georgia had 691,392 people, and of these 280,944 were enslaved. By 1850 Georgia's population had significantly increased, to 906,185. Both the white and enslaved populations grew during the decade. In 1850, however, the population density of the state was only 15.4 people per square mile; its urban population was small, only 38,994, while its rural population was 867,191.[113] Besides Savannah, on the Atlantic coast, Georgia's most important inland cities lay along the fall line, the ancient coastline of Georgia that divides the coastal plain from the piedmont region. The geographer Edward Sell mentions that at the fall line there is "an abrupt drop in the surface level" where "there are rapids and waterfalls in the streams which cross the line and flow south and southeast." In early Georgia "this was as far as boats could travel to trade with the Indians, so the early trading posts which later became . . . modern cities grew up here."[114] The fall-line cities of Columbus, Macon, Milledgeville, and Augusta were centers of trade, usually handling cotton coming from upriver and shipping it down to ports on the Atlantic or the Gulf of Mexico. The populations of fall-line cities, however, were small. Most of Georgia's population was dispersed over a wide rural landscape.

Southern Catholics shared their evangelical neighbors' laments of few clergy and long travel in distant, remote areas. The 1844 edition of the *Metropolitan Catholic Almanac* listed five Catholic priests stationed in Georgia parishes along with one missionary priest. Each of the priests bore responsibilities for missions surrounding his parish.[115] All Christian groups, therefore, could benefit from better transportation networks.

South Carolina played an important role in the internal improvement movement that sought to reshape the national economy after the War of 1812 by facilitating commerce between the interior and the coasts. Nationally, John C. Calhoun advocated for a new system of internal improvements that could diminish the potentially destructive forces of sectionalism by forging economic connections among the states.[116] On the state level, South Carolina took the lead during the 1830s in constructing railroads. Stung by the economic depression that began in 1819 and lasted through most of the 1820s, merchants and politicians in Charleston devised schemes to increase trade to the city. They hoped that the city's economic fortunes could improve by siphoning off business from Savannah, its rival, and connecting western farmers to Charleston. To that effect, a group of citizens asked the state legislature in December 1827 to consider financing a railroad between Charleston and Hamburg, South Carolina, a new town situated opposite Augusta on the Savannah River. The railroad, they hoped, would be able to carry cotton and other agricultural goods from the river to Charleston instead of having to be sent downriver to Savannah.[117] The legislature chartered the South Carolina Canal and Railroad Company early in 1828.[118] The company surveyed a site in 1829, and construction began the following year. The 136-mile line finally opened in September 1833. "When completed," the historian U. B. Phillips noted, it was "the longest railway in the world."[119] Trains could run between "16 and 21 miles an hour" carrying both passengers and cargo. Traffic increased on the railroad throughout the 1830s, and South Carolinians began expanding the lines in order to connect to Columbia. The Columbia branch opened in 1842, joining the state capital to both Hamburg and Charleston.[120]

Georgia politicians and businessmen, jealous of the success of the South Carolina Canal and Railroad Company, decided to charter several railroad companies to compete with their neighboring state. Georgia too had eagerly developed infrastructure plans following the War of 1812.

Georgia politicians in the 1820s envisioned river improvements, canals, and a series of turnpike roads that would bring goods "to the water courses."[121] Assistance to steamboat companies had increased river traffic on the Savannah River and done wonders for Augusta's economy.[122] But with the opening of the Charleston to Hamburg line, Governor Wilson Lumpkin, a strong advocate of a statewide system of internal improvements, promoted railroad development. Businessmen in Athens wanted a line to connect them to Augusta. In 1833 the state legislature chartered the Georgia Railroad Company to build the line, and construction accelerated in 1836.[123] Financially successful, the Georgia Railroad Company ultimately connected its lines with the Western and Atlantic Railroad Company's lines at Terminus (the future Atlanta) in the fall of 1845 and to Chattanooga, Tennessee, in 1849.[124] The state legislature also chartered the Central of Georgia Railroad Company in 1833. The company sought to build a line connecting Savannah to Macon, which the directors believed would be the future center of the cotton trade in Middle Georgia.[125] The line would also cross several rivers, which could allow the company to build ports to divert river traffic to Savannah. After seven years of labor, 190 miles of Central's lines reached Macon on October 13, 1843. Passengers could ride the line for three cents per mile.[126] By 1847 the line from Macon to Atlanta was open. In 1853 a rail line connected Columbus, a city on the fall line of the Chattahoochee River on Georgia's western border, to Macon. The next year a rail line joined Augusta with Savannah.[127] Georgia's rail system connected important cities to Savannah and created an easier way to traverse the state.

Catholic clergy in the Diocese of Charleston understood well the benefits of an improved transportation network: it would facilitate access to the widely dispersed Catholic population and provide jobs to Irish immigrants. Rev. Jeremiah O'Connell, reflecting on his years in the Georgia missions, remarked, "With the slow and expensive mode of travel then prevailing, the visitation of the several outlying stations was both difficult and laborious, and scarcely performed in less than six or eight weeks." "Modern improvements in travelling," he continued, "serve God's purpose, and are advantageous to religion." He called the railroad "the modern missionary."[128] Bishop England included news of meetings of the South Carolina Railroad Company and the progress of its lines in the pages of the *United States Catholic Miscellany*. For example, on

November 5, 1831, England reported in the *Miscellany* that after reading the report of the superintendent of the South Carolina Railroad Company, "we are led to hope that the great work which is to produce such extensive and permanent benefit to our Southern section of the Union, will be soon in full operation."[129] The railroad promised easier trade and more rapid travel, thus increasing the ability of clergy to visit southern Catholics, and hired Irish laborers to build track, giving jobs to Catholic immigrants and increasing their number in the Diocese of Charleston. O'Connell related numerous accounts of ministering to the families of Irish railroad workers. He also discussed the efforts of Father O'Neill, Catholic pastor in Savannah, who worked with the Central of Georgia Railroad Company and Savannah officials to quiet labor disputes and riots among Irish workers.[130] In an indirect way, transportation improvements enhanced the status of the clergy and allowed them greater freedom of movement, a privilege Ignatius Reynolds would exploit in 1844.

Bishop Reynolds commenced his first five-week-long visitation of Georgia on the morning of Friday, June 7, 1844. The *Savannah Daily Republican* noted the bishop's arrival "per steam packet Beaufort District, from Charleston" in its Saturday edition.[131] According to an advertisement in another Savannah paper, the Savannah and Charleston Steam Packets made the journey between the cities in a day's time for a six-dollar fare. The steamer leaving Charleston departed at nine o'clock in the morning and would arrive in Savannah the "same evening."[132] The June 15 edition of the *Miscellany* carried a letter to the editor describing Reynolds's arrival and visit. The bishop first enjoyed "a brief repose at the City Hotel" before going to "the residence of the Pastor" of the Church of St. John the Baptist. The correspondent noted that the church was crowded on Sunday (June 9) with those who "wished to see and to hear the successor of the illustrious Bishop England." Reynolds did not disappoint. After mass, Reynolds gave a speech about the sacrament of confirmation. He then conferred the sacrament on fifty-nine people. The bishop performed the visitation "according to the rites prescribed in the Pontifical." He asked "the usual questions," the correspondent noted, and the pastor had complaints about lax mass attendance on holy days and low participation in "catechism and religious instruction" for children.[133] The bishop addressed the congregation on these matters before the main event, preaching.

Religious preaching, particularly oral debates, served as an important source of entertainment in antebellum America, demonstrating the allure of theology to ordinary Americans of the time.[134] Antebellum Catholics appreciated the same phenomenon. Father O'Connell, for example, wrote that "sermons preached in court-houses, and all places of civic gatherings, are generally well attended by all classes." Despite the "indifferentism" of many southerners, O'Connell continued, they showed "outward respect for the Christian religion, no matter by whom professed."[135] He also commented that Bishop England and Bishop Reynolds were excellent preachers and understood that their audiences would sometimes be mixed. In fact, in Reynolds's 1844 visitation of Georgia he frequently spoke to crowds of both Catholics and Protestants. Although both groups probably perceived the bishop's speeches at least in part as entertainment, the clergy saw their preaching in a more serious light. O'Connell commented that doctrinal sermons on a controversy were often effective teaching tools for both Catholics and Protestants.[136] For this reason, Bishop Reynolds would often speak on controversial topics at great length during his visitation.

For example, the Savannah correspondent to the *Miscellany* noted that Bishop Reynolds preached to a great crowd on the Catholic doctrine of the Eucharist, taking the Gospel of John, chapter 6, as his text. He began with "natural philosophy," wrote the correspondent, and refuted philosophers' "objections to the doctrine of the real presence." The correspondent believed that the sermon was particularly powerful in its logical rigor, for he mentioned conversing with several Protestants in the audience afterwards. One, a lawyer, said that "he would positively feel embarrassed, were he called on to refute the arguments of Bishop Reynolds, in defending the negative protestant doctrine on the Eucharist." He also mentioned that he had never heard anyone explain the doctrine previously. Indeed, this was part of the strategy of the visitation. Reynolds not only visited the Catholic population but also sought to dispel the prejudices of Protestants who came to hear him. He did so not by avoiding differences in religious doctrine but by providing lengthy, and apparently entertaining, treatments of Catholic teachings that Protestants found troubling. By refusing to dodge controversial topics, the bishop also played to the southern sense of honor. By appearing combative, but in a respectful way, the bishop demonstrated that he did not shrink from his neighbors. He sought their respect. The correspondent to the *Miscellany* believed Reynolds had won what he sought: "The Bishop has given great satisfaction, as well in his official as in his social relations, to the Catholics, and to those of our Protestant fellow citizens who have been introduced to him."[137] Reynolds would repeat his performance several times in the following weeks.

The *Miscellany* reported that Bishop Reynolds left Savannah on Wednesday, June 12, and reached Macon later that evening to make his visitation of St. Joseph's Church, founded in 1841. Macon, a fall-line town in Bibb County, was established at the request of the legislature in 1823. Many believed that its central location made it a prime location for the cotton trade, as it could receive cotton from farmers in the Georgia Piedmont, above the fall line. The Central Railroad completed its line connecting Savannah and Macon in 1843. According to an advertisement in the nearby *Milledgeville Federal Union*, the distance between the two cities was 190¼ miles. The train ran each day of the week except Sunday and could make the trip in twelve hours.[138] Presumably, Reynolds arrived by train. The *Miscellany* published a letter from "Z" that detailed the bishop's visitation. "Scarcely had the Bishop arrived in the city," the correspondent wrote, "when he was requested to deliver lectures each evening during his stay, in the explanation of our doctrines." He began on Thursday, June 13, and preached to a full church, which "Z" noted could hold five hundred people. Many non-Catholics attended.[139]

As in Savannah, Bishop Reynolds preached on doctrinal controversies that divided Catholics and Protestants. The correspondent related that Reynolds began his first address by insisting on "the necessity of brotherly love and harmony among all, but especially those bearing the name of christians." The bishop then spoke on the topic of *sola scriptura*, a central doctrine of the Reformation. The correspondent did not relate the specifics of the address but noted that the bishop denied that the Bible was the sole rule of faith, a topic he returned to on Friday night. On Sunday, the bishop confirmed "17 or 18 persons" during mass. Then he preached "for more than an hour and a half." The correspondent noted that he had "never heard the Bishop so happy or so eloquent in his delivery as on this occasion." On Monday, June 17, "Z" reviewed the church accounts. He mentioned that the bishop was "a little hoarse from his continual preaching" but that he was able to visit numerous people. The bishop, thought "Z," "succeeded in dispelling whatever prejudices may have lurked in the bosoms of his audience against Catholicity." The correspondent's assessment of the visit repeated all of the themes already mentioned in the accounts of the Savannah visitation, and Bishop Reynolds left Macon having achieved his purpose.[140]

Reynolds departed Macon on Tuesday, June 18, for the westernmost parish in the diocese, Saints Philip and James, founded in 1837, in Columbus. Columbus lay below the fall line on the Chattahoochee River, which forms part of the western border of Georgia and empties into the Gulf of Mexico at Apalachicola, Florida. The Georgia legislature founded Columbus in 1828 and made it the seat of Muscogee County. Columbus was a cotton town and had a thriving cotton mill industry during the antebellum period. The town, however, was rather isolated; it was not connected by railroad to Macon until 1853.[141] Father O'Connell described the journey:

> The distance between Columbus and Macon . . . was one hundred miles, the road steep and rugged, sandy or clay-bottomed, intersected by many streams and rivers unspanned by a bridge. I have frequently accomplished the journey in fourteen hours on horseback, at the penalty, however, of very shallow genuflections for a week after.[142]

Although the *Miscellany* does not say so, Reynolds probably made the trip to Columbus by stage—what O'Connell called the "republican vehicle." O'Connell complained that the stage was usually crowded and passengers suffered "excessive jolting over bad roads." He related a story of Bishop Reynolds and Father O'Neill of Savannah traveling on the stage from Milledgeville to Columbus when the vehicle overturned, injuring both men. That trip, however, must have taken place after 1844. Columbus's Catholic population was small in the 1840s, according to O'Connell only seventy-five persons in 1845. O'Connell noted that the Catholic population was made up of Irish, Italians, Germans, an Englishman, a native of Massachusetts, and three slaves from Maryland, including a man named Brooks, "who led the choir on Sundays."[143]

A correspondent to the *Miscellany*, "Senex," described the bishop's visitation in Columbus. Unsurprisingly, it sounded much like his previous two stops. Reynolds arrived in Columbus on the morning of Wednesday,

June 19, and soon commenced his busy schedule of public lectures and visitations. On Thursday, the bishop preached to a congregation of Catholics and Protestants "on the proper disposition to hear the word of God," according to the *Miscellany*. On Friday, he lectured on divine revelation and the need for an authoritative interpreter of revelation. The correspondent to the *Miscellany* maintained that the bishop stressed the chaos of Protestantism because of the lack of an authoritative interpreter of revelation. On Saturday Reynolds met with the vestry of the parish and examined their financial records. Then, on Sunday, June 23, according to Senex, he performed the ceremonial visitation, confirmed eighteen people, and preached for an hour and a half at mass "on the marks of the Church" to a "very numerous congregation." Senex noted that the bishop "thanked his Protestant brethren for their great attention and gentlemanly deportment in the Church." He then proposed a Total Abstinence Society for the parish and enrolled twenty-seven members.[144] The local newspaper, the *Columbus Enquirer*, commented favorably that Reynolds "delivered several discourses to large and intelligent audiences, who could not fail to have been well pleased and edified with the eloquence, as well as ability and urbanity which characterized his preaching."[145] Senex reported to the *Miscellany* that a few Protestants "have acknowledged themselves convinced of the truth of our doctrines, from the Bishop's discourses, and say, were he to remain with us a few weeks, they would become Catholics." He ended by noting that one Protestant "has entered a course of instruction."[146] Again, Reynolds had preached to large crowds on controversial subjects.

When Bishop Reynolds left Columbus for Milledgeville at six o'clock on the evening of Monday, June 24, he had been on the road for over two weeks but was only halfway through his travels. He probably took the stage on a 130-mile eastward trek to the state capital. Milledgeville, another fall-line city and the seat of Baldwin County, had been founded by the Georgia legislature in 1803. The legislature named it the state capital in 1804. The city was situated about 30 miles northeast of Macon. Milledgeville lacked a Catholic church until Sacred Heart parish church was built in 1874.[147] The *Miscellany* noted that Reynolds met local Catholics at a hotel. The meeting was apparently short. Reynolds informed the group that clergy from Macon would visit the city "every second month."[148] He left the city that evening, probably on the stage that ran between Macon and Augusta. On the morning of June 27 he arrived in Sparta, the seat of Hancock County, about 25 miles from Milledgeville. Sparta had been established in 1795 and was an important cotton town. Sparta too lacked a Catholic church; one would not be built there until 1869. But Reynolds met with a few Catholics and, according to a report in the *Miscellany*, "administered the sacrament of Baptism." The paper reported that he "promised the Catholics, that they should be occasionally visited by the clergyman stationed at Locust-Grove," Reynolds's next stop, about 30 miles northeast.[149] His stay in Sparta must have been brief because the *Miscellany* reported that he arrived in Locust Grove (present-day Sharon) on Thursday evening, June 27.

Locust Grove lay in Wilkes County, slightly northwest of Augusta, and was one of the oldest Catholic communities in Georgia. In the early 1790s a number of Catholic families from Maryland moved to the state and joined with a few Catholics in the area to found the Church of the Purification in 1792. Local historian of Wilkes County, Robert M. Willingham, notes, "In the 1790s the congregation was further strengthened by the arrival of several French families from Santo Domingo." In 1818 the Catholics founded Locust Grove Academy, which, according to Willingham, "was the first Roman Catholic school chartered in Georgia."[150] Bishop England had visited Locust Grove, and the *Miscellany* mentioned it regularly.

Bishop Reynolds resumed his busy schedule of public preaching in Locust Grove, replicating scenes from earlier in his episcopal visitation. The *Miscellany* received a letter from "O.A.L." detailing the bishop's visit. O.A.L. noted that the bishop arrived "considerably exhausted by the fatigues of travelling and the severe heat of the weather." After a day of rest, Reynolds, on Saturday, June 29, "examined the children in Catechism, who had been prepared by the Rev. P. Whelan." On Sunday, Reynolds confirmed nineteen Catholics at a well-attended ceremony. After mass, Reynolds preached. The crowd was too large to fit into the church, but someone opened the church doors so Reynolds could be heard outside. Again, he selected a point of controversy, the sacrament of Penance, to defend before his audience of Catholics and Protestants. The correspondent to the *Miscellany* wrote that some Protestants there mentioned that "though they believed Bishop England unsurpassable, they looked on the present Prelate as his equal." The visitation ritual was not novel, then, for Protestant citizens of Wilkes County had turned out before to see the spectacle and be entertained by the preaching.[151]

On Monday, July 1, Bishop Reynolds, accompanied by Rev. Peter Whelan and Rev. John Barry of Holy Trinity Church in Augusta, traveled 12 miles up the road to the town of Washington. There the bishop dedicated a new stone church, St. Patrick's. On Tuesday, "before a numerous and enlightened auditory," according to the *Miscellany*, the bishop recycled his sermon from Savannah, preaching on the Catholic doctrine of the Eucharist and John, chapter 6. On Wednesday, July 3, he offered mass and confirmed three people before returning to Locust Grove. On Independence Day 1844, Bishop Reynolds said mass at the Church of the Purification. The *Miscellany* noted that he told the Catholics there that it was good to celebrate July Fourth by attending mass and praying for their country. He hoped that the "liberties" they enjoyed "may be secured to our latest posterity." The correspondent to the *Miscellany* mentioned that "his remarks were impressive and full of feeling." He then celebrated July Fourth at the parsonage with Reverends Whelan and Barry. He set out for Augusta that evening.[152]

Bishop Reynolds arrived in Augusta on the morning of July 5 "by the Western cars," probably the railroad of the Georgia Railroad and Banking Company, which had a line reaching to Athens. Reynolds probably made a short trip south from Locust Grove to the railway. He then rode the line for about 50 miles to Augusta. The correspondent to the *Miscellany* noted that Reynolds offered mass on Friday, July 5, and "transacted a good deal of business."[153] In its Saturday morning edition, the *Georgia Constitutionalist* noted Reynolds's arrival in the city and announced that he would "preach in the Catholic Church to-morrow morning at half past ten o'clock, during High Mass."[154] On Sunday, July 7, the bishop confirmed thirty-three people, "some of whom were converts," according to the *Miscellany*. Then he held the visitation and preached on the "Providence of God" at High Mass. After mass he blessed a new addition to the church building. The correspondent to the *Miscellany* was very impressed with the new bishop. He stated that the bishop left by railroad for Columbia, South Carolina, on July 9.[155] The *Miscellany* announced his return to Charleston by rail on Tuesday, July 16.[156] Bishop Reynolds had been away for an exhausting five weeks of travel in the summer heat. Without the railroad, his journey would have taken even longer.

Lack of clergy, the problem of securing adequate funding, intellectual and cultural prejudices, and geographic expanse complicated the efforts of Catholics in the Diocese of Charleston by making it difficult to establish a permanent institutional presence in the South. The lack of an institutional presence meant fewer encounters of ordinary southerners with Catholicism. The record of Bishop Reynolds's visitation highlights the slight institutional presence and resources of southern Catholics. The people in Columbus, for example, told the correspondent to the *Miscellany* that they wished Reynolds would stay longer so that they could learn more about Catholicism. The small Catholic parish on the outskirts of town perhaps did not seem significant enough for non-Catholics to visit. People in Locust Grove compared Reynolds favorably to Bishop England, meaning that they had heard England preach. But the dispersed Catholic population and the rigors of travel made it difficult for men like John England and Ignatius Reynolds to follow up on the interest their preaching generated during their visitations. The *Miscellany* mentioned several times Reynolds's exhaustion during his journey through Georgia. Also, in several places, including the state capital, Catholics lacked a church. Infrequent visits from clergy meant that Catholicism would be hardpressed to take root and grow there. The lack of Catholic infrastructure in the state, a dearth of clergy, and cultural suspicion made Catholicism a harder sell in America's free market of religion.[157]

Southern Catholics and their evangelical neighbors faced similar problems during the early years of the nineteenth century. Nevertheless, the Methodists and Baptists had built an institutional presence in the South during the previous fifty years. They had confronted both the hostility of their largely unchurched neighbors and the same geographic expanse in their efforts.[158] But they had persisted, building the institutions—churches, schools, newspapers—that were necessary to plant their presence in the soil. Catholic and Protestant leaders realized that institutions could build cultural capital and allow their religions to grow. Both met the challenge of American culture in similar ways.

Common experiences and approaches strengthened the Jeffersonian nationalism of South Carolina Catholics and Protestants by bringing them together. But these common experiences did not always translate into amicable relations. For Catholics to stake their claim to being part of Calhoun's "assemblage of peoples" they would have to demonstrate their worth and defend themselves vigorously from attacks. To do this South Carolina Catholics would have to enter the contentious world of Christian apologetics and public debate.

CHAPTER THREE

Apologetics

Will the Real American Please Stand Up?

The Catholic strategy of building an institutional presence in the South as a means to spread Catholicism brought challenges and costs. Institution building required significant funds, which forced Catholic leaders in a region with few Catholics and much anti-Catholic bias to spend time raising money. But the Catholic plan demonstrated a devotion to place. Catholic leaders desired to expand their church and to convert others to Catholicism. In conjunction with these aims, Catholic churches, schools, and other charitable institutions made the church a substantial property holder, rooting it firmly in the community and furthering its claim to be part of the people of the state. Above all, the Catholic commitment to place necessitated friendly relations with non-Catholics and immersion in southern culture.

Traditional anti-Catholic prejudice complicated the Catholic strategy. American Catholics labored under deep suspicions, a legacy of the religious violence and controversies of the English Reformation.[1] In particular, many Protestants charged that Catholics could not be good citizens because their ultimate loyalty lay with the papacy. With the founding of the *United States Catholic Miscellany* in the 1820s, South Carolina Catholic leaders responded vigorously to such charges.[2] The Jeffersonian understanding of the Union did not demand cultural homogeneity but did expect dedication to republicanism. Goodwill among citizens fostered common sentiments. Public denials of Catholic acceptance of republican government mixed with base caricatures of Catholic belief, therefore, negated Catholic claims of affinity with their neighbors and implicitly threatened nascent Catholic institutions. Virtually every extant issue of the *Miscellany* contains some notice of religious controversy, revealing that accommodation was far from easy. Catholic leaders took seriously charges of an innate Catholic attraction to political authoritarianism and expended tremendous efforts refuting them. The debates, while tedious for the modern reader to follow, serve as important windows into the Catholic strategy of accommodation in the Diocese of Charleston.

Two debates, in which South Carolina Catholics battled John Bachman, pastor of St. John's Lutheran Church, illustrate these tensions. Bachman, an intellectual and well-respected scientist, had moved to Charleston from New York in his twenties. Like the Catholics in the city, Bachman was an outsider and leader of immigrants, in his case, Germans.[3] In 1838 Bishop England responded with twenty-one public letters to an anti-Catholic sermon that Bachman had delivered. Again, in 1852–53 several Catholics tangled with Bachman over nativism and the Protestant Reformation. This time Bachman first tried to force Charleston Catholics into an unwinnable contest by compelling them to choose between faith and country and then denounced them as beyond the pale of the community. Catholics, in turn, attempted to portray Protestantism as an unstable foundation for American liberty and to depict themselves, because of their faith, as the most devoted republican citizens.

Like many of antebellum South Carolina's Catholic leaders, John Bachman was not native to the state. Born near Rhinebeck, New York, to an ethnically Swiss family, Bachman grew up a devout Lutheran. He studied for the ministry in Philadelphia, but bouts with tuberculosis weakened him. In 1815, believing that a warmer climate would be more suitable for his condition, Bachman accepted the pastorship of St. John's Lutheran Church in Charleston.[4] An energetic pastor and preacher,

Bachman built Lutheran institutions in the city and state. He brought numerous blacks into the church, founded the Tract and Book Society for Lutherans in the state, and helped to found the Synod of the Lutheran Church in South Carolina in 1824. He served as president of the synod for the next ten years. Southern Lutherans, like southern Catholics, suffered from a dearth of clergy, so, in 1831, Bachman helped to found a Lutheran seminary in Lexington, South Carolina.[5] In fact, Bachman's dynamic plan of institution building closely resembled that of Bishop England and his successors.

Like many of the Catholic clergy in South Carolina, Bachman immersed himself in the life of his adopted city and state. In 1816 he married Harriet Martin of Charleston, who was related to St. John's former pastor, and became a fixture in the community. As did ministers of other churches, he founded Lutheran charitable societies to work with Charleston's poor. Having grown up in a slaveholding family in New York, Bachman showed no animosity to the peculiar institution and held slaves in Charleston. He also involved himself in the city's intellectual life. He joined Charleston's prestigious Literary and Philosophical Society and served as its president. In 1853 Bachman helped to establish the Elliott Natural History Society to discuss and encourage science. He also published on natural history and, in 1831, met the celebrated artist and ornithologist John James Audubon, who became a close friend.[6]

Bachman's first controversy with Charleston Catholics took place in the context of what James D. Bratt has termed the "reorientation of American Protestantism." Bratt argued that revivalism, which had defined American Protestantism since the 1740s, began to be replaced by new issues during the tumultuous decade of the 1830s. At this time, immigration, urbanization, the solidification of the second party system, and the rise of abolitionism reshaped American culture and elicited new responses from American Protestants. In particular, Bratt identified the Protestant-Catholic divide as a primary issue during and after the 1830s. He also noted that Protestants began to worry about the question of unity in the increasingly fractured religious climate. A vigorous print culture, sparked by technological advances that reduced the cost of printing, allowed for an information explosion. Protestants vigorously appropriated the new print culture to mark cultural boundaries and define themselves with greater doctrinal precision, highlighting their divisions.[7]

Lutherans in South Carolina mirrored these changes. John Bachman gave serious attention to the issue of Lutheran and Protestant unity, especially as the Lutheran Church dealt with the problem of schism. Southern Lutherans generally supported the institution of slavery in the face of attacks on its morality by northern Lutherans. Bachman despised abolitionists, for example. Lutherans quarreled about revivalism as well as the desirability of a stronger adherence to the Augsburg Confession, the major creedal statement of Reformation-era Lutheranism. In this context, Bachman advocated broad unity, stressing that disagreement on theological explanations, such as the doctrine of the real presence, were unimportant.[8] Bachman used his debates with Catholics to reinforce his positions.

At the same time, the 1830s witnessed a large increase in immigrants and a resulting explosion of religious polemics. In 1832 sixty thousand immigrants came to the United States, an annual number matched throughout most of the decade. Many of the immigrants were Catholic Irish, and anti-Catholic literature proliferated. Protestant polemics often aimed at building a united Protestant opposition to the growing Catholic presence. David Bennett believes that the aim was successful, for by the mid-1840s "American churches presented a virtually united front against Rome."[9] Thus in his debates with Catholics, John Bachman revealed himself to be a staunch nativist.

Bachman's 1838 public controversy stemmed from a sermon he gave in the city on November 12, 1837, to the Lutheran Synod of South Carolina that was subsequently published. On that day Bachman preached on "the doctrines and disciplines of the Evangelical Lutheran Church." The sermon stressed the general agreement of Protestants on doctrinal points and contained a strong anti-Catholic edge. In fact, it illustrated plainly a Protestant strategy of using anti-Catholicism to unify American Protestants. Bachman began with a defense of Luther. According to Bachman, Luther and his colleagues did not try "to establish a new religion till then unknown in the world" but instead "wished to reform, to purify the Church from corruptions in doctrines, and from useless ceremonies which had been accumulating for ages, and to bring it back to the purity and simplicity of the Apostolic days." Luther exhibited a "simplicity and purity" that allowed him to lead a "great moral revolution" that "has proved a blessing to the world." But Bachman praised Protestantism in general, not simply Luther. In extolling the Augsburg Confession, Bachman noted that it was "made the groundwork of the thirty-nine articles in the Episcopal Church, and which with some variations, contain the principles of all Protestant denominations."[10] In other words, Protestants stood, more or less, as one.

For Bachman the good side stood with Luther and the Reformers, while evil lay with Catholicism. If Luther restored Christianity, then the continued existence and growth of Catholicism represented an abomination. Bachman next attacked a small group of Lutherans in North Carolina, the "Hinkelites," for doctrinal errors that stemmed from the close resemblance of their views of baptism and the Lord's Supper to Catholic beliefs. From Bachman's point of view, proximity to Catholic teaching set them outside the pale of Protestantism. As he demonstrated the deviations of the Hinkelites from the Augsburg Confession, he not only attacked Catholicism as antithetical to reason and basic Christian doctrine but also labeled Catholics themselves as hopelessly deluded. Hinkelites apparently believed in the Catholic doctrine of transubstantiation, the belief that during the sacramental ritual of the Lord's Supper the bread and wine changed substantially into the body and blood of Jesus while retaining the appearance of bread and wine. Bachman noted, "If a man can once bring his mind to believe such a doctrine, he must have arrived at a state of credulity that will render him incapable of deciding between truth and error." Although Lutherans condemned transubstantiation, they had "ceased to agitate" on the question of the exact nature of the communion bread during the ceremony of the Lord's Supper, "leaving its members to follow the dictates of conscience agreeably to the light of Scripture."[11] Lutherans, therefore, tolerated differing Protestant explanations while universally condemning Catholic ones.

As a member of a minority Protestant church with stronger roots in the German states than in the Anglo-American world, Bachman was pleading for his fellow Protestants to accept Lutherans as brethren. He maintained that Lutherans had "never desired the aid of the State, in support of its ministers" and was, therefore, friendly to republican institutions. He objected to a recent publication that declared, "The Lutherans, of all Protestants, are said to differ least from the Romish Church." Catholics, he noted, believed in a powerful priesthood, "pomp and parade" in worship, an "over-grown hierarchy," and intolerance and possessed a "persecuting spirit." Lutherans rejected all of this. In addition, Lutherans defended the Bible, unlike Catholics, who withheld "the word of God from the common people." Bachman concluded that other Protestants should not attack Lutherans just because they "are attached to the altars where our fathers worshipped"—in other words, for their ethnicity. "The German does not easily forget his father-land," Bachman conceded, but German Protestants who maintained their native language and religion would always remember Luther's legacy and thus could be trusted to be good fellow citizens.[12] In this way, Bachman identified citizenship with Protestantism. The Lutheran Synod of South Carolina was, he assured his listeners, "willing to unite with every lover of the Gospel of Christ in producing the downfall of sectarianism, though not the obliteration of sects."[13] Throughout his sermon, Bachman presented Lutheranism selectively to emphasize its similarities with Protestantism in American culture.

Bishop John England responded to Bachman's sermon with twenty-one lengthy letters in the *Miscellany* between February and August 1838. England and Bachman knew each other, and their approaches to leading their churches and embracing their adopted city were remarkably similar. Both men involved themselves in similar institutions, such as the Literary and Philosophical Society, and local social reform movements, such as anti-dueling. But Bishop England viewed Bachman's sermon as an unprovoked, gratuitous attack on the city's Catholics, who had been working with Bachman toward similar civic goals and, given the strictures of southern honor culture, appealed to the community for vindication.[14] In spite of the provocation, Bachman did not respond to the bishop's letters. In February, just as the letters began, Bachman's mother died. He traveled to New York to settle family affairs, returning to the city in April. In early May, a great fire devastated Charleston, and Bachman ruined his fragile health by working for the city's relief. In June 1838 Bachman traveled to Europe, attempting to recover his health, and returned to the city in late December. Thus Bishop England had the freedom to attack Bachman's sermon without having to address replies.[15]

In his first published letter on February 1, 1838, Bishop England expressed disappointment in Bachman's portrayal of Catholics. England mentioned that he had "esteemed" Bachman as "not only quite free from every tinge of hypocrisy, and cant, but as possessing much candor and honesty of purpose." He doubted Bachman was a "bigot."[16] But the rest of the letter, while respectful in tone, demonstrated that the bishop's mind had been changed. England particularly objected to Bachman's claim that Catholics who believed in transubstantiation were irredeemably irrational. Bachman's charge excluded Catholicism from any serious discussion, implying that one would be as foolish to waste time listening to a Catholic as to a lunatic. Such charges could be used to disqualify Catholics from citizenship as well.

Instead, Bishop England argued that Protestantism, by dispensing with traditional church authority, had made Christianity into a prejudice rather than a knowledge and love of truth.[17] Protestants combined the doctrine of *sola scriptura*—the idea that scripture alone contained divine revelation—with the right of individual private judgment. The individual could read the Bible and decide for himself the meaning. But Bishop England depicted private judgment as a problematic concept. For example, Bachman attacked the Hinkelites for religious error, but they had followed, the bishop insisted, the same means "to understand the Word of God" as had Bachman, private judgment. Bachman claimed the Hinkelites had been misled and needed to pray to restore their faith. Bishop England commented, "Upon this principle [private judgment], which I apprehend you both hold in common, there is not, and there cannot be on earth, any tribunal to determine which of you correctly interprets the Divine Word." Bachman himself had no solid basis to be "assured" that his interpretation of the Bible was correct.[18] Both Bachman and the Hinkelites appealed to the Bible on the principle of private judgment. If the individual is the arbiter of biblical interpretation, then no individual could bind anyone else to his interpretation. This radical subjectivity in regard to doctrine made Christian belief mere prejudice—that is, according to the whim of the individual rather than any certain knowledge of the teachings of Jesus.

Bachman derived his error, the bishop believed, from the Reformers he celebrated. England explored Bachman's claim that Luther and the Reformers were not trying to found religions of their own but were restoring the original teachings of Jesus. If this was the case, then the Reformers "must have known with certainty the doctrine which Christ taught upon any particular point, before they could have correctly pronounced that any received teaching, on that head, was erroneous."[19] To illustrate his point the bishop used the example of transubstantiation, the

Catholic doctrine Bachman had condemned as irrational. He pointed out that the Reformers had disagreed vigorously with one another regarding the doctrine of the real presence and that some even refused to accept part of the Augsburg Confession because it "too openly favored the Catholic doctrine of transubstantiation." The bishop wrote that Bachman had unwittingly exhibited "what is historically true." Bachman had discovered the Reformers "first rejecting a doctrine which they" disliked and "then looking for a substitute; and so far from having ascertained what our Saviour taught, they differ among themselves, each striving to substitute his own opinion for that doctrine which all Christendom had held as coming from the Redeemer, but which they rejected." Bachman, like the Reformers, merely substituted "the private judgment or opinion of each individual, for the one unchanging testimony of an authoritative public tribunal," the witness of the church.[20]

In the next eight letters, Bishop England demonstrated, by appealing to the writings of the Reformers and the history of the Reformation, that Bachman's bold claim of Protestants' essential unity was mistaken. Examining the debates between Protestants and Catholics over the Augsburg Confession, the bishop noted that the Confession did not clearly condemn transubstantiation, a point that even the Reformer Melancthon understood.[21] He dove into medieval history to show that the heretics Bachman used to posit a continuity between Luther and the early church did not "hold exactly the same tenets that are now held by any division of Protestants." The bishop then referred to eucharistic imagery in the Old Testament and accused Calvin of distorting one particular passage that did not fit his theology.[22] England next explained the Catholic construal of New Testament passages on the eucharist, particularly John, chapter 6, and the various Last Supper narratives to demonstrate that the Catholic interpretation was sensible and based on a plausible reading of the biblical texts. Bachman had resorted to broad invective, but detailed analysis, England asserted, demonstrated his ignorance of Catholicism's actual claims and evidentiary appeals. England's explanation implied then that Bachman's 1837 sermon was merely crude propaganda.

Throughout his letters, Bishop England sought to add credibility to his argument by appealing to the written record. Facts could be checked. Claims could be substantiated. The bishop argued that Catholic teaching drew support from a "host of witnesses of the faith, from the days of the

Apostles."[23] The witnesses had left a record, like the Reformers had, that could be verified. For Bishop England the issue was a matter of fact, not unsubstantiated opinion. Because Catholicism based its authority on Christ and could demonstrate historically the continuity of its teachings, it alone could say what Christianity was. Conversely, Bachman's reliance on private judgment left him with nothing convincing. "Do you not, Sir, perceive," he concluded, "that if private opinion is an unalienable right, it belongs equally to all others as it does to you?"[24] If Bachman believed every Christian possessed private judgment, then he could not deny this right to Catholics. This left him with no solid ground on which to attack Catholics for their beliefs about biblical teaching. Instead of creating a unity of doctrine, England insisted, Protestantism established anarchy in religion, a condition that would eventually destroy faith and discredit Christianity as a credible source of social order.

The first part of Bishop England's response revealed his aggressiveness and bold style. Written during a period of intense anti-Catholicism, the bishop's letters demonstrated that Catholics in Charleston would not back down from attacks. In the honor culture of the South, this would certainly win sympathy. Bachman had cast aspersions on Catholics publicly, demeaning the reputation of the church. England answered publicly, questioning Bachman's expertise. Bachman had depicted Catholics as irrational and corrupt. Bishop England responded that Catholics were more rational than Protestants and possessed a stronger Christian faith and more plausible tradition.[25] Bachman had portrayed Catholics as different from the rest of the Christian community of the state and offered this as a reason to exclude them from civilized discourse. Bishop England embraced that difference as proof that Catholicism was a better religious system than the anarchy and irrationalism of Protestantism. Bachman, a leader of a small group of Protestants in the state, had attacked Catholics' reputations. England responded not simply to Lutherans, but to all Protestants.

By embracing Catholicism's differences as superior, the bishop seemed to accept Bachman's characterization of Catholics as outsiders to the state's Christian majority. Herein lay the tension for Catholics in public debates with Protestant nativists. If Catholics stressed the strengths of their doctrine against Protestant claims, they admitted their separate status, which could reinforce the Protestant community's suspicions. If they

emphasized their accommodation to the community, they seemed disin-
genuous for papering over their unique beliefs. Either way, Protestants
could reinforce the image of Catholics as outsiders. Bachman, as we shall
see, understood the dilemma of the Catholic rhetorical position well.
Bishop England, demonstrating perhaps that stereotypical Irish pluck,
simply responded aggressively. He did so, it seems, in order to attack in
his second round of letters to Bachman the most cherished myth of
nineteenth-century American nationalism, the intimate connection between Protestantism and America's republican liberty, and then posed a
dilemma of his own.

An editorial in the *Miscellany* on June 30, 1838, signaled the transition to the new theme. The editor apologized to the readers because the
paper had to "dip into, and wade through the disgusting libels, the foul
ribaldiry [*sic*], the miserable sophistry and heavy misrepresentations published by the directors of what is called the religious press of the United
States." The Protestant press not only attacked Catholic doctrine but also
"falsified our history, and sought to deny us the common name of Christians." Now the Protestants were combining "to destroy our rights as
citizens and to traduce us as enemies of our republican institutions." Although the power of the *Miscellany* was limited, the editor noted that
there was "honor" in being a "pioneer in the service" of defending the
faith in the United States.[26] Defending Catholics as republican citizens
was necessary to maintain an affinity with non-Catholic southerners. In
the next issue, Bishop England began an extended discussion of the history of the Reformation in northern Europe to deny that there was an
essential connection between Protestantism and republican liberty.

As the first target in his campaign, Bishop England exposed Bachman's distortions of Lutheran history. Bachman had claimed that Lutheranism was friendly to republicanism because, the bishop charged, he
wanted to appeal "to the fraternal affection" of "fellow Protestants by
showing how unlike to the Catholic despots were the republican Evangelical Lutherans." But, in 1838 there were "*seventeen reigning Sovereigns*"
in the Lutheran "communion." Like Catholics, Lutherans in Europe
lived under monarchies and church establishments. Thus when Bachman claimed Lutherans had never wanted state support for their ministers he correctly described the situation of American Lutherans but not
the history of Lutheranism in Europe.[27] In fact, Lutheranism had suc-

ceeded during the sixteenth century in direct relation to the coercion wielded by the state on its behalf.

Bishop England also argued that the history of the Reformation era demonstrated that Luther and the Reformers used force against their religious opponents and supported strong monarchies that violated the cherished principles of American republicanism: freedom of religion, protection of private property, and limited government. David Bennett has noted that nativists "repeatedly pictured themselves as libertarians and their adversaries as the enemies of freedom."[28] Bishop England recognized this tendency. To make his case, the bishop appealed to histories produced by Protestant and secular authors, such as Johann Mosheim and William Robertson. As he told Bachman near the end of the debate, "The records of history are open to us equally as they are to you."[29] This implied that all citizens could inspect those records as well.[30]

In his sixteenth letter, Bishop England appealed to the case of Luther and the Anabaptists. He quoted a lengthy passage from Mosheim, a staunch defender of Luther, to show that the Reformer "first urged these unfortunate fanatics to insurrection, by inspiring them with strange notions of Christian liberty," but then sought "their extirpation because they would not confine their notions of Christian liberty within the boundaries which he thought fit to prescribe." Not only did Luther violate his own principle of private judgment but he also showed a willingness to support state coercion of his enemies. Bishop England also noted, using Mosheim's work, that Lutherans formed armed leagues before being threatened by the Holy Roman Emperor. The Lutheran leagues then sought foreign support in order to establish Protestantism in Europe. Threats of violence against Catholic princes along with the extreme rhetoric of Luther himself, who called for the death of the pope, unsurprisingly produced violence. Protestant aggressiveness next led to violations of property rights. Lutheran princes, "by force, stripped the Catholics of their church-property." German Lutherans, Bishop England claimed, had initiated this persecution and violence.[31] Thus Lutherans had trampled on the religious liberty of others while hypocritically claiming the right of private judgment, initiated force against Catholics, and used the increased power of the German princes to confiscate Catholic church property. Protestants could not plausibly claim that their faith tradition was essentially libertarian. Therefore, nativists could not convincingly argue that Protestantism and republican citizenship were naturally linked.

While Bishop England did not claim that Protestantism essentially supported tyranny, he noted through numerous examples that historically there was a strong connection between the rise of Protestantism and the growth of despotic power. In arguing this way, he inverted the usual narrative of progress that characterized the Whig view of history.[32] Catholic corruption and tyranny inspired, so the narrative went, the heroic reformers to rise up and, against all odds, defend freedom from the hands of political and religious tyrants. During August 1838 the bishop, demonstrating his erudition, turned to the history of the Reformation in Prussia, Denmark, and Sweden, three bastions of Lutheranism, and showed that in each case Lutheranism had been established through the betrayal of traditional liberties and property rights. The Lutheran princes had used their power to persecute Catholics, denying them religious freedom. Lutheran apologists, like Mosheim and, by implication, Bachman, claimed that Lutherans had not stolen property but merely returned it to its true owners, the people. But Bishop England balked at these suggestions, noting that the church "had, by the sanction of law, been in quiet possession of the larger portion of this property, during upwards of two hundred years." American readers might have wondered what this barrage of historical minutiae had to do with them. In his August 9 letter, the bishop drew a parallel to American colonial history. Catholics in Maryland had created a colony that allowed religious toleration. Maryland had tolerated "the Puritan and the Protestant . . . when these men persecuted each other." The Protestants repaid Catholic toleration by capturing control of the colony and enacting "the penal code" of England. "And the American Protestant proclaims that the Catholic is intolerant!," exclaimed the bishop.[33] England admitted that Catholics too had "despots" in the church, but his point was to dispel Bachman's claim that Lutherans had always sat on the side of liberty.[34] Bachman might denounce tyranny publicly, the bishop maintained, but "the principles of your [Bachman's] religious changes" have "done more to encourage, to support, to flatter and to uphold it, than had been done in Europe for centuries before."[35] If Protestantism was not essentially on the side of liberty, then the nineteenth-century American anti-Catholic narrative was wrong.

Bishop England's challenge was crucial, since the subtext of both Bachman's sermon and Bishop England's letters concerned who could rightfully claim to be an American. The *Miscellany*, in its June 30, 1838, editorial, bluntly stated, "We call American, every one to whom the Constitution and the law extends the right of Citizen."[36] But England's letters to Bachman complicated this approach. The bishop ultimately confronted the nativist dilemma by simply posing one of his own. Many nativists claimed both that America stood for liberty and that Protestantism rooted and fed liberty in American soil. But England implied that these two propositions were not compatible. If America was essentially Protestant, then, based on the example of Protestantism during the Reformation, it was hostile to liberty and property. The original Protestants had turned to the coercion of government to instill their prejudices. If America cherished liberty and property rights, it need not yoke itself to Protestantism. Instead, other traditions, especially Catholicism, could offer their own support for American liberties. Catholics, as the bishop implied, could be better Americans than nativists who distorted history to serve their purposes and supported violations of their fellow citizens' rights on the grounds of religious and ethnic identity.

Bishop England closed his letters by appealing to the values of southern honor culture. First, he tried to shame Bachman. "Did you imagine," Bishop England asked, "that no one had read the history of those nations or of your own religion?" "Or," he continued, "is it possible that you never read those historians yourself?" Bachman's ignorance was no excuse for his public attack on Catholics. The bishop exclaimed, "And you, not only the President of the General Synod of the Evangelical Lutheran Church of the United States, but also the President of the Literary and Philosophical Society of Charleston, South Carolina!"[37] Appealing to honor culture demonstrated that Bishop England viewed himself—and wanted others to view him—as part of the community. He ultimately demanded the judgment of the community on his behalf. Despite his different set of religious beliefs, England appealed to a common social ethic. He probably suspected, however, that his aggressive posture would draw a response from Bachman. Thus, he ended his last letter on a conciliatory note: "Accept my apology, if any thing has escaped from my pen, that may be calculated to give you any personal offence, and be assured, that however I may feel myself obliged to differ from your religious opinions, there are not many who hold you in higher personal esteem."[38] In any event, Bachman did not respond to Bishop England's letters when he returned from Europe in December 1838. In fact, he delayed his response for fourteen years. By that time Bishop England had died. The next debate between Bachman and Charleston Catholics would be even more explosive and potentially problematic for Catholic goals in the city.

John Bachman's 1852–53 battle with Charleston Catholics came on the heels of a new flood of immigration. Sparked primarily by the Irish potato famine, over two and a half million people migrated to the United States between 1847 and 1854. Irish Catholics flooded eastern cities in unprecedented numbers.[39] Charleston's Irish population, though not all Catholic, also grew during the decade, causing a demographic shift in the racial makeup of the city. By 1860 Charleston had a white majority population. Most of Charleston's Irish lived in family units, but as a whole the population was transitory. Irish immigrants moved frequently in their search for jobs. Christopher Silver has calculated that "no more than 23 percent of the Irish enumerated in the 1850 census were present to be counted when the census" of 1860 was taken.[40] The changing demographics contributed to a feeling among many Charlestonians that their city was changing too fast, a sentiment exploited by the growing nativist movement.

Bachman's scrap with the city's Catholics occurred within a larger debate and covered the usual question of Catholicism's compatibility with republicanism. The debate was complex and a bit chaotic because of the various people who entered and exited the extended paper war. But there were four basic steps in the conflict. First, Catholics appealed to the ethic of honor, while their opponents invoked the rhetoric of liberal rights. In the second phase, Catholics charged that nativists' claims to liberalism and toleration were hypocritical given that they did not wish to tolerate Catholics. Bachman and the nativists responded that Catholics had no honor but comprised an evil religious system that spread corruption to the country. Third, Catholics responded that Protestantism, exemplified in the life of Martin Luther, led to moral corruption and thus formed an insufficient basis for republican virtue. Bachman and his nativist allies responded by defending Luther and calling for Protestant unity in the face of the Catholic threat. Fourth and finally, Catholics asked nativists to be accurate about Catholic beliefs and encouraged calm. Bachman denied that Catholics could appeal to reason and insisted that the non-Catholic public refrain from supporting or patronizing Catholic institutions in order to diminish Catholic influence in the city. Each step in the debate proceeded logically from the previous one and imparted a certain rhetorical coherence, even if those involved did not always follow the steps in an orderly fashion.

The debate began when a Protestant minister, Edward Leahey, arrived in Charleston in March 1852 and announced that he was "late a Monk of La Trappe" who wished to reveal the dark secrets of Catholicism. To that end he preached in Rev. Thomas Smyth's Presbyterian church as well as in at least one Methodist church. He then sought to give a public lecture at the Masonic Hall. Although other papers in the city refused to print it, the Charleston *Evening News* ran an ad for the lecture that read, in part, "A Lecture on the Unchristian treatment of Females in the Confessional by Popish Priests, according to the standard of Popish Theology, sold in this country to answer the use of members of the Roman Catholic Church, with the oath which Bishop Hughes has taken at his consecration." The ad promised that Leahey would make "awful disclosures" and thus announced that "Ladies and Youths are positively prohibited from coming to this Lecture." Admission was fifty cents, the proceeds going "to propagate the Gospel among the Catholics." The Masons ultimately withdrew permission for Leahey to use the hall, apparently concerned about the public controversy that would surely follow, and the lecture did not take place. But Catholics quickly responded to the insults and salacious implications in the advertisement.[41]

First, England's successor, Bishop Ignatius Reynolds, published a letter to Charleston Catholics in the *Mercury*, one of the leading secular papers in the city. In it he invoked the language of honor while cautioning restraint. "We shall make no comment on this announcement, so unjust and so insulting," he wrote. The advertisement, he noted, had insulted the clergy, the city's Catholics, and their "wives and daughters, dearer to you than life itself." Reynolds questioned the propriety of printing the announcement. He told his flock to pray for their persecutors and to show "evidence of your love of civil order" by obeying the law. Rumors had already swirled concerning the possibility of the city's Irish engaging in mob violence against Leahey.[42]

But while Reynolds counseled restraint, he had also acknowledged the slight to honor. Leahey's announcement implied that Catholic husbands and fathers knowingly turned loose a lecherous clergy on their wives and daughters. As David Brion Davis has noted, anti-Catholic literature frequently charged that Catholics endangered women, who enjoyed a special place as the culture's guardians of morality and civilization. By charging the city's Catholic population with a failure to protect their women, Leahey denied that they possessed any honor.[43] To those who abided by the culture of honor, Leahey's attack violated boundaries of common decency and sparked outrage.

The *Evening News* responded by appealing to libertarian ideals. The editor explained that he did not take a stance in the religious controversy, nor was he libeling anyone. Thus, there should be no protest to his running the ad. "We have nothing to do," he thundered, "either with points of doctrinal theology or the practices of any sect of religion." He also noted that a similar ad for Leahey had run in Baltimore papers with no protest. He acknowledged, however, that "several of our Catholic subscribers have withdrawn their patronage for doing what custom immemorial has enjoined on us." He even suggested that this was a form of "persecution."[44] Freedom of the press, he insisted, should reign.

Fr. James Corcoran, editor of the *Miscellany*, answered aggressively to protect Catholics' reputations. He called Leahey's announcement "offensive and indecent" and chided the *Evening News* for publishing it. He claimed that Leahey caused civil disturbances everywhere he went and should not be publicized. Corcoran also praised the *Mercury* for rejecting the ad. That paper was "pre-eminently the representative of all that is chivalrous and honourable in the spirit of the South" and would not print such an "illiberal, indecent attack on a body of Christian citizens." Corcoran then noted that some—a reference to the editor of the *Evening News*—defended the advertisement on the grounds that northern papers published similar ads. He called this a promotion of the "License of the Press" and trusted that the time had not come when "the people of Charleston are to learn their rights and duties from Northern example." Corcoran thus located Catholics alongside the southern honor culture and its defenders. He staked a claim to the community while implying that the editor of the *Evening News* had violated its sensibilities and the social order.[45]

Next, the editor of the *Evening News* charged the *Miscellany* with vi-
olating the standards of liberalism. He called Corcoran's March 20 editorial "virulent, illiberal and intolerant," protesting that he "knew nothing of the character or mission of the monk Leahey." This protest seems
flimsy, for the suggestive nature of the advertisement revealed Leahey's
purpose. Nevertheless, the editor accused Corcoran of playing "to the
passions of the uninformed and unreflecting." Corcoran was a dema-
gogue, the editor charged. Catholics had responded irrationally and now
attacked the very freedom of the press. The editor insisted that because
the *Miscellany* was a "religious paper," it should promote "peace and charity." But instead the paper was "incendiary in its character and aims." The
Miscellany sought to impose its own views on the city: "In fact, the Miscellany wants the largest liberty for itself; but it would erect itself into the
judge to determine when liberty becomes in others licentiousness."[46] The
editor, with seemingly no self-awareness that he was telling the editor of
the *Miscellany* what his place was, accused Catholics of trying to dominate the press of the city.

The first step in the debate, therefore, pitted two opposite ethics,
honor and liberalism, against one another. Catholics appealed to honor,
that is, to their public reputation, in a way that invoked commonly accepted values. In this they sought the support of the non-Catholic community, for example, the *Mercury*. On the other hand, the editor of the
Evening News invoked abstract rights of freedom of the press and toleration. The honor ethic judged the advertisement and the action of the
editor to publish it as dishonorable, inflammatory, and thus worthy of
public rebuke. The editor, after invoking an ethic of toleration to justify
his publication of the announcement, ended by calling Catholics illiberal
for denouncing him publicly and for cancelling their subscriptions to his
paper. He refused to apologize for his liberalism. As the debate began,
both sides appealed to different standards, actions sure to intensify the
disagreement.

On Tuesday, March 23, Charleston's city government became em-
broiled in the controversy. Denied other venues, Leahey now wanted to
speak at the American Hotel. One of the owners asked the city council
if the city would be liable "for any damages to the property, in case Rev.
Mr. Leahey were allowed to lecture in that hotel." Leahey was in attendance and argued that he simply wanted "to exercise that freedom of

speech which the constitution and customs of our country guarantee to every citizen." Two aldermen argued that Leahey should be allowed to speak and noted that the Catholic clergy should restrain any mobs that might form. One noted that Catholics themselves, including Bishop England, had given public lectures in which they had attacked Protestantism. The Catholics could not, then, protest Leahey's presence.

In response, the mayor interjected that the issue was not freedom of speech but public order. Leahey protested, but the mayor told him that the earlier announcement for the speech had promised "obscene" material "and would be offensive to the Christian denomination against whom the lectures were directed." Alderman Gilliland, a Presbyterian, noted that he was "in favour of the unrestricted right of speech." Another alderman sided with the mayor's contention that the real issue was public order. Leahey made his last push, arguing that Catholics were trying to "deprive an American citizen of his purchased right of freedom of speech." Catholics were running scared because he could expose all of the secrets contained in their prayer books and theological works. He promised that if the council refused to let him speak "he would denounce their illiberality to the whole country."[47] In effect, Leahey was threatening the reputation of the whole city and particularly its political leaders.

At this point Alderman John Bellinger arose to oppose Leahey. Bellinger had converted to Catholicism as an adult from the Episcopal church and had served as Bishop England's physician.[48] The *Courier* listed him in September 1850 as a new alderman representing the fourth ward of the city.[49] Bellinger took notes on the council's debate with Leahey and had them published in both the *Courier* and the *Miscellany*, and it was his speech that launched the paper war that followed.

First, Bellinger painted Leahey and his supporters as dishonest. He noted that Leahey's freedom of speech had not been threatened. Leahey had already preached in "three different churches" in Charleston. He also objected to the comparison drawn between Leahey and Bishop England. The bishop had not lectured on "topics that are not mentionable to the chaste ears of females and youths" as Leahey promised to do. Leahey's contention that he was exposing Catholicism by revealing secrets from their books was also ridiculous, Bellinger insisted. He noted that the books to which Leahey referred could easily be obtained in the city and read by anyone with a "liberal education." He concluded, "There is, then,

no necessity for these lectures—neither to vindicate the right of freedom
of speech, which has not been interfered with, nor to enlighten the Protestant portion of the community, for the means of information are within
every one's reach." Thus, Bellinger implied, Leahey's supporters really desired to spread anti-Catholicism in the city for nefarious purposes. Their
stated purpose for defending Leahey—their appeal to abstract rights—
did not stand up to reason. None of his rights had been violated. Bellinger
next warned that support of Leahey would wound "the harmony that has
so long subsisted between Catholic and Protestant in this community."
He maintained that while the clergy had warned Catholics against dis-
turbing the peace, not all would listen. The "gratuitous insult to the morality of their clergy and the world-renowned chastity of their women"
would lead some to "punish" the insult "in blood."[50] After all, silence was
not an option, for Catholics had to protect their honor.

Bellinger made another clever, subtle attack on his opponents' honesty
by referring to an earlier riot against abolitionists. In 1835, when the postmaster of Charleston discovered that abolitionists had mailed thousands of
antislavery pamphlets to South Carolina, a mob formed in the city and
burned the mail. During the riot, rumors circulated that the mob should
find Bishop England, who was suspected of antislavery views. A group of
Protestants and Catholics took up arms to protect the bishop and his
church from a possible mob attack. Bellinger referred to the cooperation
between Protestants and Catholics to protect the bishop without mentioning anything about abolitionists. His implication was subtle. Charlestonians were not civil libertarians. The city had violently suppressed the freedom of speech of abolitionists on the grounds of public order. None of the
aldermen would dare to oppose such action. The city council had—rightly,
in Bellinger's view—limited freedom of speech in the city on the grounds
of public order. Therefore, refusing to support Leahey's specious claims
was no different. The analogy also equated Leahey with the hated abolitionists. Both appealed to abstract rights to spread lies and foment discord.
In Bellinger's view good Charlestonians should oppose such men.[51]

In the end, several councilmen wished to prohibit Leahey from
speaking, but lawyers for the city denied that the council could do so.
They advised the mayor to "caution all persons taking part in the proposed proceeding" that the city council "would not hold itself responsible
in damages." The mayor should, however, deploy the police to the lecture

to preserve order. But Leahey did not speak, and there was no riot. Leahey eventually left town and tried to lecture in other cities. In May 1853
the *Courier* reported that Leahey was on trial in Wisconsin for murder-
ing a man he claimed was sleeping with his wife.[52]

Two things bothered Protestants who read Bellinger's account of the
city council's proceedings: Bellinger's cavalier attitude to freedom of
speech and a brief comment that he made about Martin Luther. Although Bellinger had argued that Leahey was a scoundrel and implied
that he was no different from the abolitionists, others continued to appeal to freedom of speech. Bellinger's willingness—for whatever reason—to prohibit the lectures of a Protestant minister speaking on Catholicism reinforced the Protestant charge that Catholics hated
republican government and threatened American liberties. When Bellinger objected to the comparison between Leahey's talk and Bishop England's sermons on Protestantism, he asked, "Did he [the bishop] ever
charge upon the present generations of Protestants, clergy and laity, the
immoral practices licensed by their chief reformer, the sanction for which
is extant in his writings? I aver, confidently, that he never did."[53] Bellinger maintained that Bishop England had not demeaned the morality
of Charleston's Protestants by imputing to them the sins of past Protestants. But he had indeed offered a gratuitous insult to Martin Luther's
reputation. Unsurprisingly, two old foes of Charleston's Catholics, Benjamin Gildersleeve and John Bachman, responded. The paper war now
began in earnest.

The Catholic attacks on their opponents' claims to liberality must
have stung because they responded by denying the legitimacy of Catholics to appeal to republican standards. Rev. Benjamin Gildersleeve had
long been an opponent of Catholics when he lived in Charleston. He had
edited a Presbyterian paper, the *Observer*, for many years but by 1852
lived and operated his paper in Richmond, Virginia. The *Evening News*
published an exchange between Gildersleeve and Bellinger. Here Gildersleeve reiterated the liberalism of Protestants while denouncing Catholicism as an evil system of corruption.

Gildersleeve first attacked Bellinger for blending his religious beliefs
with his civic duty as an alderman. He insisted that Bellinger's religious
faith compelled him to violate liberty. Gildersleeve noted that "the Alderman and the Catholic were inseparably blended together" and that it

was not "at all strange that it should be so." Bellinger's Catholicism was the problem. The Protestant aldermen had defended freedom of speech; the Catholic defended repression. Gildersleeve quipped, "Why, sir, you must have been dreaming that you were one of the committee of '*the Index*,' with power to suppress all utterances not in accordance with your standard of faith." Gildersleeve's charge was grave. Bellinger, he said, acted as a good Catholic in trying to suppress free speech. He further charged that the threat of violence by the Irish mob proved the corruption of Catholicism. Protestants, he thundered, did not threaten violence against Catholics when Bishop England preached against them. But Catholics in Charleston were "driven to a tempest by the storm of passion." "How can it be accounted for, except it be from the religious principles which respectively govern them?," he asked.[54] Ultimately, Gildersleeve answered Catholic charges of hypocrisy by forcing Catholics into an unwinnable dilemma. For Gildersleeve, a good Catholic was by nature a bad republican, indeed, a tyrant. Therefore, only a bad Catholic or a Protestant could be a good republican. Gildersleeve's charge, then, was that Catholics could not be trusted with public office because tyranny was in their very nature.

When Bellinger protested Gildersleeve's dilemma in his response, Gildersleeve refused to budge or acknowledge his objections. Bellinger pointed out again the hypocrisy of liberal appeals. Gildersleeve admitted that the Protestant aldermen in the debate spoke as Protestants. Bellinger protested, "If I, following in the same course, expressed mine as a *Catholic*, I am amenable to no censure therefor."[55] If Protestants could use their religious beliefs to make political decisions, then Catholics could do the same. Again, Bellinger pointed to the double standard of liberal tolerance. Anti-Catholics did not tolerate all. They decided who could receive and be denied toleration. Catholics in Charleston had committed no violence despite the slights to their honor. But in other cities Protestant mobs had burned down churches and convents, he pointed out.

Gildersleeve simply pressed on. "You [Bellinger] acted *consistently* with your principles as a Catholic," he wrote. "Always and everywhere—*semper et ubique*—you estop free inquiry when you can."[56] Catholicism, Gildersleeve thought, was an irredeemable system, and Americans were foolish to suffer it. Bellinger's loyalty to his faith "implies *subjection* to a priesthood, most of whom are of foreign origin, and all of whom, on their investiture with the insignia of their office, take an oath of allegiance to a foreign power, which Jesuitical casuistry alone can interpret as compatible with true fealty to our National and State governments."[57] Thus Catholics could not be republican citizens for Catholicism made them tyrants.

At the same time, Bachman echoed Gildersleeve's comments in five lengthy letters in defense of Luther. Speaking of Catholicism, Bachman remarked, "A system opposed to reason and the word of God cannot be permanent."[58] He then depicted Bellinger as a tool of the Catholic clergy of Charleston, those "who have possession of the minds, consciences and souls" of the laity. In portraying Bellinger as a tool, Bachman denied him any honor as an independent gentleman; he was merely the representative of an evil system. In Bachman's estimation, Catholics in Charleston hid behind the reputations of their women to deny freedom of speech to Protestants. Charleston's Catholics were "principally foreigners, who have fled from what they regard the oppression and poverty of their native country, and have sought an asylum in our own free and hospitable city." But these people were not free. Instead, Bachman wrote, "they are rigid Romanists, more under the influence of their spiritual teachers than any other denomination in our city." They were ungrateful to the "generous community" that welcomed them as they threatened the liberties of Americans through mob violence. Catholics were formed from the "principles" they "imbibed."[59]

By refusing to acknowledge Leahey's slight of Catholics' honor and by labeling Catholics unrepublican, Gildersleeve and Bachman placed them outside of the respectable community. Their comments further enraged Catholics, who demanded satisfaction for their wounded reputations. Instead, the Charleston *Evening News* printed other letters that painted Catholics as untrustworthy interlopers in the land of Protestant liberty.[60] These suggested that Catholics were only salvageable if they became Protestants. The refusal to take Catholic claims seriously led Catholics to their next tactic, describing Protestantism as insufficient for maintaining republican virtue. It was Protestantism, not Catholicism, that really endangered the American Republic.

In responding to Gildersleeve's charges about Catholicism, Bellinger initiated the third stage in the debate by making specific charges about Martin Luther and the deficiencies of Protestant moral theology. Instead of seeking to prove that Catholicism was not evil, Bellinger asserted that it was Protestantism that was a destructive religious system. To do this, Bellinger made two general points about Luther and the Reformation in the second half of his letter to Gildersleeve. First, he contended that Luther's doctrine of salvation by faith alone combined with his "denial of a Free Will in Man" promoted moral license.[61] As he pointed out, readers could perceive the negative effects of Luther's teachings in the Reformer's life and teachings. Second, Bellinger, quoting an English historian, argued that the Reformers were revolutionaries who encouraged popular excesses and succeeded due to the "tyranny of princes."[62] These points were similar to the charges Bishop England had made in his 1838 letters to Bachman. Both attacks portrayed Protestantism as deficient for supporting a Republic that counted upon the virtue of the citizenry for its vitality.

To enhance his argument, Bellinger attempted to give his discussion of Luther a learned patina. Beginning in early April, Bellinger collected secondary and primary sources to support the charges he would make in his April 22 letter to Gildersleeve. He cited two contemporary Protestant historians, Englishman Henry Hallam and D'Aubigne, who was Swiss, as well as two seventeenth-century writers on the Reformation, the French bishop Bossuet and the Lutheran historian Seckendorf. He also referred to the writings of the philosophe Pierre Bayle as well as to Luther's own writings. Bellinger had access to a 1550 edition of Luther's works but desired to examine another version, preferably in German, to "compare copies of various editions of Luther's works, in order to ascertain, to what extent alterations have been made in the later editions." On April 8 he wrote to John Bachman requesting permission to examine his copies of Luther's works. Bachman graciously complied with the request, although he told Bellinger that he had not appreciated his comment on Luther before the city council. Bellinger did not read German, so he hired a young Charleston student, a non-Catholic, who had recently returned from his studies in the German states, to compare passages from the German edition and his own edition. Bellinger satisfied his curiosity and then wrote his letter to Gildersleeve in which he paraphrased rather than translated Luther's works to support his contentions.[63]

In his letter, Bellinger made several specific claims about Luther. He began with a generalization: "So soon as one apostatizes from the Catholic faith, he slides rapidly down the plane of ill-manners and of general immorality, as Luther has taught us by his recorded self-experience." Bellinger charged that Luther was violent, intemperate, and condoned sexual immorality. He had given his "formal permission to the Landgrave of Hesse to take a second wife" and, in his sermon *De Matrimonio*, gave "plain sanction to what is commonly considered concubinage, polygamy, and adultery." Bellinger then paraphrased Luther regarding these issues. He concluded, quoting Hallam, that Luther's moral system threatened "*the foundations of religious morality*."[64] Luther's doctrines of salvation by faith alone and his denial of human free will made man no better than a beast and gave individuals no religious interest—because good works played no role in salvation—in doing good.

Bellinger then noted that Luther's teachings, repeated more or less by other Reformers, destroyed European society during the sixteenth century. Quoting Hallam again, Bellinger observed that the Reformers preached first to the "ignorant" and then capitalized on the popular excesses inspired by the Protestant message. Hallam had noted the "revolutionary spirit" of the Reformers that reveled in "destruction for its own sake." In addition, Hallam maintained, "Reform was brought about by intemperate and calumnious abuse, by outrages of an excited populace, and the tyranny of princes."[65] Bellinger charged, therefore, that the Reformation spawned a corrupt religious system, led by an immoral person, Martin Luther. In doing so, he turned the criticism of Gildersleeve back on the Protestants. From this point of view, the product of faulty doctrine and morality was social disorder and tyranny. Thus Protestantism, according to Bellinger, produced what Luther professed. Tyranny and popular immorality resulted not from abuses of Protestantism but from its very nature. It provided a flawed foundation for republican virtue.

Unsurprisingly, Bellinger's missive provoked outrage from Bachman, who responded with thousands of words of nativist invective mixed with a defense of Luther and the Reformation. Bachman was at his best in identifying the weaknesses in Bellinger's use of sources. But when Bachman defended Luther, especially in the case regarding the second marriage of the Landgrave of Hesse, he was less successful. Nevertheless, Bachman used the debate to further the case against Catholicism and to stress the importance of Protestant unity in the face of Catholic attacks.[66]

While Bachman did not critique all of Bellinger's sources on Luther, he did point out several problems with those he had used. For example,

Bachman reminded his readers that Bellinger could not translate German. Not only did this prevent him from reading much of Luther's writings but it also prevented him from reading German scholarship on Luther. Bachman referred to several scholars, Hengstenberg and Marheinke, for example, who had corrected faulty translations and paraphrases of Luther documents produced by certain Catholic writers. Before attacking Luther, Bachman insisted, Bellinger should have guaranteed the accuracy of his sources. But Bachman's larger point was that Bellinger, as a Catholic, was unable to think freely. Thus, the specifics of his attack on Luther were unimportant because the church dictated his conclusions. Bellinger, therefore, was dishonest because he had to discuss religion with "a bridle on his mouth."[67] Bellinger's research "was done for him," noted Bachman, by Catholic hacks who made careers defaming Luther's reputation.[68] Bachman's critique was a further use of the dilemma he and Gildersleeve had perfected. If Bellinger was a good Catholic, he would attack Luther in the dishonest fashion of his church. If he thought freely for himself and considered the evidence, not only would he see that Luther was a good man, but he would also be a bad Catholic for contradicting the judgment of the church.

Bachman also criticized Bellinger's reliance on Bossuet and Bayle, arguing they had made errors that later scholars had exposed, as well as his invocation of a spurious Luther sermon on marriage. Bachman called Bossuet dishonest and claimed that the seventeenth-century French bishop and writer was "incapable of judging fairly of his great opponent," Luther. "He garbles Luther's words, and tears them from the context," he wrote. He also elided some of the quotations he used from Luther to make their meanings change. In particular, Bachman accused Bossuet of "willfully" mistranslating a passage of Luther's writing in the case of the marriage of the Landgrave to disguise Luther's actual motivations.[69] In addition, Bachman charged that Pierre Bayle "did not consult Luther's works, but referred to the frauds of Luther's enemies." In fact, Bellinger had referred to Bayle in the discussion of the Landgrave's second marriage, but Bayle had not even addressed this.[70] Bellinger also referred to Luther's sermon De Matrimonio to argue that Luther had supported concubinage. Bachman asserted that the document could not be authenticated and had been disavowed by Luther himself.[71] Bachman noted that Bellinger could have consulted other sermons on marriage in Luther's

Works, but, because Bellinger could not read German, he did not do so. Bachman admitted that Bellinger did not always repeat the errors of his sources.[72] But he attacked the sources to discredit Bellinger's claims.

Bachman was not as convincing when he turned to defending some of Luther's actions. The second marriage of Philip of Hesse in 1539 had early become a stock incident in polemics against Luther. Philip supported Luther and the Reformation. He desired to divorce his first wife and marry another woman. In 1539 he sought the opinion of several Protestants, apparently with the threat that if they did not give their consent he would join the Holy Roman Emperor and the Catholic side. Luther and Melancthon secretly gave their consent to Philip marrying his paramour but not divorcing his wife, thus making Philip a bigamist. Philip's second marriage—to Margarethe von der Saale—became a scandal.[73] Catholic writers deemed Philip a bigamist and stressed that Protestants had sanctioned this outrage. Bellinger brought up the charge in his attack on Luther. Polygamy had become a political issue during the early 1850s due to the Mormon controversy. So Bellinger probably thought that he could further weaken the case for Protestantism by tying it to Mormonism. Bachman acknowledged, albeit begrudgingly, the facts of the case. Luther and Melancthon had supported Philip's second marriage. But Bachman reasoned that the Reformers' errors "may be easily traced to their previous discipline in the time-serving and persecuting church, in whose doctrines and disciplines they had been trained for so many years."[74] Bachman opined that Catholics could hardly criticize Luther given all of the crimes of Catholicism. The Reformers, he noted, "were reluctantly compelled to attend" to the duty of marriage advice and law because marriage had been a religious rather than state matter. Thus Luther had been placed in a tight situation, "and although he did not act wisely, he still acted conscientiously."[75] Judging by later letters to the papers, Bachman's defense did not convince contemporaries.[76]

Ultimately, Bachman characterized Bellinger's argument as merely an ad hominem attack, which led him to reiterate his contention that Catholicism was a corrupt system. "I cannot but think," Bachman charged, "that Roman Catholics have ventured on dangerous ground in endeavouring to prove that the Protestant religion cannot be true, because their Reformers were erring men." Of course, that had not been Bellinger's argument. Bellinger had used Luther as an example to argue that Protestantism insufficiently buttressed popular virtue. Bachman, however, decided to pursue the ad hominem angle. If Protestantism were false because the Reformers were imperfect, than "an exposure" of Catholicism would collapse the "whole system."[77] Bachman also used his opportunity to expound on the themes that Leahey had planned to discuss during his public lecture. Bachman cited Dens's *Theology*, a moral theology textbook used in some Catholic seminaries, and an American Catholic prayer book, *Garden of the Soul*, as evidence of Catholic immorality. Both books dealt with the Catholic sacrament of auricular confession. Bachman charged that both were indecent and allowed Catholic clergy to commit crimes against the chastity of women in the secrecy of the confessional. Bachman even referred to an edition of *Garden of the Soul* that contained an essay by Bishop England. Armed with his "smoking gun," Bachman assaulted Charleston Catholics, accomplishing Leahey's original aim in denouncing Catholicism as dangerous to the city.

Bachman closed his letters—and the third stage of the paper war—by calling for Protestant unity against the Catholic threat. Bachman also demanded that Bellinger retract his charges. If he had so attacked the reputation of "any living man in our community," he would have paid a legal penalty for libel and "his witnesses" would have been imprisoned "for the crimes of perjury, forgery, and fraud." But Catholics had no honor. Instead, they took advantage of the "free toleration of their religion by our laws" to spread their lies.[78] The Protestant public should unite "in protecting our institutions from foreign dictation and priestly intolerance." "Luther," he asserted, "must not be regarded as a sectarian." "He is the embodiment of Protestantism."[79] Luther's example of resistance to the pope could unify Charlestonians against the Catholics of the city. Bachman denied he had written for personal political gain, but even so his attack on Catholics gave comfort to nativists as another round of national anti-Catholicism emerged.

As Bachman's lengthy letters were being published, Catholics realized they were not faring well. Originally hoping to prevent Leahey from stirring up anti-Catholicism in the city, Bellinger, by arguing with Gildersleeve and Bachman, had given Protestants the opportunity to air Leahey's charges in a much larger forum, the newspapers. Bachman's reputation in the city and the length of the bitter paper war gave the issue a much longer life than one lecture by an itinerant preacher would have.

In response to this situation, Father Corcoran in the *Miscellany* became more strident. After Bachman's first letter in defense of Luther, Corcoran teased that the letter's "wandering and desultory character, its long and embarrassed sentences, its repetitions and confused jumbling of ideas" seemed to indicate Bachman's "senility."[80] But by August, after a long summer of Bachman's attacks on Catholicism, Corcoran referred instead to Bachman's "wounded pride and impotent arrogance" as well as his "calumnies" about Catholicism. He also charged Bachman with falsifying a quotation he took from the *Miscellany* in order to distort its meaning and place Catholics in the worst possible light, which suggested that Bachman was immoral as well.[81] The rhetoric escalated in part because Catholics originally framed the controversy as an affair of honor. But when Bachman refused to acknowledge Catholics' claims to honor no satisfaction was possible except through more extreme posturing. Corcoran's intemperate language would continue to stimulate Bachman's pen.

During the fourth stage in the paper war, other Catholic leaders counseled calm. In August 1852 Fr. Patrick Lynch, veteran of a lengthy paper war with the Presbyterian minister James Henley Thornwell during the 1840s, sought to clarify some errors Bachman made and moderate the rhetoric of the exchange. Lynch began, "I trust that neither you nor the public will suspect me of wishing to take part in the controversy now pending in regard to Luther."[82] Instead, he indicated that he wished to point out two mistakes Bachman had made in one of his attacks against Charleston Catholics. Lynch noted that Bachman did not understand Dens's *Theology* and had thus interpreted the book in a way opposite to the way it was intended. He provided Bachman and the public with an explanation of Catholic moral theology through an analogy to the law. Catholic morality could be divided into two classifications: common law and statute law. Common law, as the analogy went, represented the unchanging moral teaching derived from the natural law and divine revelation. The disciplinary laws of the church mimicked statute law. Dens's *Theology* could not be clearly appreciated, Lynch insisted, without this understanding. Bachman therefore had misunderstood what he had read. Dens did not teach that priests had free rein in the confessional. There were numerous church laws governing their conduct. In regard to the moral advice in Dens's *Theology*, Lynch identified its rigor: "Our moral teaching is far more strict and definite than many of our separated brethren have any idea of."[83] In particular, Lynch explained that Bachman had misread a passage in which advice was given for priests to counsel penitents about avoiding "the proximate occasion of sin," that is, to avoid places or circumstances that would tempt one to sin.[84] Bachman believed the passage in Dens allowed for a certain number of sins each month, whereas, Lynch pointed out, the passage advised clergy on how to direct penitents to identify places or circumstances that may have led them to sin by examining the frequency of their transgressions of the moral law. Bachman interpreted Dens as a book of horrors, but Lynch demonstrated that Bachman had no understanding of (or was willfully distorting) what he had read.

Lynch also corrected Bachman for writing that Bishop England had authored the prayer book *Garden of the Soul*. Like other Catholic devotional books, it contained a section for penitents preparing to confess their sins. Isolating items related to the sixth and ninth commandments, Bachman claimed the book was indecent for suggesting sexual perversions to women. Then he tied it to Bishop England. But Lynch explained that *Garden of the Soul* was an older Catholic prayer book. Several years after Bishop England's death, a New York publisher brought out an edition of the book and added an essay the bishop had written on the mass. Therefore, as a point of fact, Bishop England had not written the prayer book.[85] Certainly the point was a small one, but the paper war appealed to reputation. A writer who misinterpreted what he read and got simple facts wrong was not a credible source. Nevertheless, Lynch's tone was respectful and asked for peace and calm from Bachman.

Bachman's response demonstrated that he took Lynch's letter as a sign of Catholic weakness. Thus he pounced on his prey. Bachman first denied that he had made any errors, even defending his implausible claim that Bishop England wrote *Garden of the Soul*. He refused to allow Catholics to define themselves and their teaching, instead asserting that they could not be trusted and that he had correctly revealed their true beliefs. Bachman avowed that his attacks on Catholic prayer books "were the necessary consequence" of Catholics' "indecent boastings in the organ of their Church," the *Miscellany*, about Bellinger's performance during the paper war.[86] In addition, Bachman admitted that he would not argue with Catholic priests because they lived by a different moral code. This allowed them to lie, deceive, and persecute in the name of truth. For support of his assertion, he quoted the writings of a former Catholic priest. Bachman said that he preferred to debate with Catholic laymen "who are bound to observe the rules of conscience by which the Protestant community is governed." But he wrote that if Lynch wanted to debate him, he would do so in the pages of the *Miscellany* so that "Roman Catholics, for once, will be *able* to hear both sides."[87] In this attack, Bachman portrayed the Catholic clergy, in this case including Patrick Lynch, whom he knew well, as moral monsters outside of the boundaries of the community. By so situating him, Bachman indicated that no amount of reasoning or politeness would reach the clergy. They were simply evil. To his credit, Lynch responded patiently to Bachman's diatribe, pointing out that Bachman had elided parts of the title page of *Garden of the Soul* to assert falsely Bishop England's authorship. Bachman again responded by denying any errors and denouncing Lynch as two-faced and untrustworthy.[88]

By November 1852 the controversy seemed to have ended, but Bachman published the paper war as a massive book of over five hundred pages in April 1853 and included three new screeds that repeated and expanded on his previous charges against Catholicism.[89] This time Father Corcoran penned a lengthy editorial on the book, noting that the volume "has some value, as a record and expression of Dr. Bachman's psychological peculiarities," and that it revealed "No-Popery warfare in its latest form." But Corcoran believed that the book did not merit a serious response since Bachman constantly repeated falsehoods. "We consider that Dr. Bachman, by his letters and his book, has placed himself out of the pale of social courtesy," Corcoran wrote. Yet he promised to treat Bachman kindly in public.[90]

The book, however, reawakened the controversy because Bachman assaulted the Catholic strategy of institution building. In his new "Address to the Protestant Public," Bachman warned that Catholics used social institutions to spread their errors in society. He noted that the experience of England served as a warning. England, he maintained, was "an enlightened Protestant country" but accepted from Ireland "hordes of priests and labourers" every year. This in turn dramatically increased the number of Catholics in the country. English politicians, "by a strange infatuation," had relaxed the penal laws and allowed Catholics into Oxford and other universities. Bachman deemed that allowance "more dangerous to Protestantism than the bold unblushing pretensions of Popery itself." Americans, therefore, needed to guard their institutions from Catholics. "Formerly," Bachman noted, the Catholic population in the United States was small, forcing Catholics to depend "for their support on Protestants."[91] This had resulted in many Catholic converts to Protestantism. But Catholics, as their numbers grew, began to respond more aggressively by building institutions to consolidate their social position and maintain their numbers.

To drive home the current threat, Bachman attacked all Catholic institutions. Catholic leaders built "expensive churches" to make "the most imposing outside show." The large churches were expensive, "hence their poor priest-ridden people are taxed to an enormous amount." But Catholics were generally poor, so the clergy relied on raising money from "good easy Protestants," the same people they regarded as "heretics" doomed to hell.[92] Speaking of Charleston's Catholics' efforts to build a new cathedral in the city, he thundered, "Every block of granite we aid in adding to that Cathedral, will be an additional weight to sink us beneath the flood of Popish intolerance."[93] Catholics raised money in the city "by fairs, and raffles, and lotteries, to contribute to their charitable efforts," particularly orphanages. But Catholics did not support Protestant institutions and condemned Protestant heroes like Luther. Catholics constructed "boarding schools and colleges, where their people are instructed in the mysteries of Papacy." They also "have newspapers and other presses, exclusively devoted to the promulgation of their peculiar views." Catholics built these institutions to keep their own people in ignorance and to proselytize among the Protestants who might frequent them. Catholics constructed institutions "to build up the power of that worldly engine of ambition, intolerance and oppression, the Papal Hierarchy."[94] Though his characterization was distorted by prejudice, Bachman had correctly identified the central strategy of Charleston's Catholics.

Given their sinister purpose, Bachman advised Protestants to oppose both Catholic aspirations and institutions. Protestants should shun "apathy" and fight. They should oppose the attempts of Catholic immigrants "to control our elections, and intimidate us at our railroad depots and our lecture rooms, with threats of mob law." He also counseled Protestants to stop "aiding and abetting" Catholics "in rearing up institutions in the midst of us, that are dangerous to our liberties and injurious to public morals." He even demanded that Protestant parents pull their children from Catholic schools, which were "inferior to our own." Protestants should not place their daughters in "nunneries" and should boldly preach the Bible to Catholics. Protestants, "instead of disputing among themselves on unimportant points," should "labor by union and effort, by faith and prayer, to become the instruments" of God to bring down the Catholic Church.[95] He told Protestants not to listen to Catholic professions of republicanism, for if Catholics ever gained control, they would ban Protestantism. "Rome cares not what governments are established," Bachman contended, "provided she rules supreme."[96] According to Bachman, Catholicism brought vice, ignorance, and poverty, corrupting the American Republic. But Protestantism brought progress and virtue. In this way, Bachman again tied the debate to republican citizenship.

In the third of the new addresses, Bachman went even further and charged Charleston Catholics with bilking city funds for their hospitals, which they used to convert dying Protestants. In fact, in 1852 Charleston suffered a yellow fever outbreak, and Catholics had successfully petitioned the city council for use of part of Roper Hospital for the indigent who fell sick. Bachman asserted that the Catholics intended to treat "a few Protestants" in the hospital as "a cunning device" and a "show of liberality" so that they could ask the city to reimburse their costs. Outward good deeds during the epidemic, he warned, would help Charlestonians forget Catholic attacks on Luther and Protestantism. As it turned out, Dr. Bellinger and Father Lynch, Bachman's adversaries, controlled the hospital. Bachman claimed that Rev. Dr. W. Smith, a Protestant, told him that Catholics had forcibly "converted and baptized" a patient on his deathbed. But the patient had recovered and fled the hospital. He also charged that some Protestant patients felt "horror at the thought of being molested by the priests" as they lay dying.[97] He claimed that the Sisters of Mercy, the nurses at the hospital, blocked him from seeing patients and lied to him about the status of a Protestant so that he could not see him. But Bachman said that since the sisters "were machines moved by other agents," he was not angry with them. He predicted that Catholics would dispute these claims but said Catholic clergymen lived by a different "moral code" and should not be trusted. Clearly, his serious charges threatened the integrity of Lynch and Bellinger. Unsurprisingly, at the end of his address, Bachman implied that Catholic corruption demonstrated that they could not be republican citizens.[98]

Bishop Ignatius Reynolds waited until the July 9, 1853, edition of the *Miscellany* to respond to Bachman's accusations. Reynolds wrote that he had no desire "to enter into any controversy with" Bachman. Rather, he asked Father Lynch to investigate Bachman's charges and publish the findings. When he did, Lynch's letter was damning to Bachman's credibility. First, Lynch recounted that he wrote to Rev. W. Smith, the source of the story about a forcible baptism. Smith had been out of the city for a while. But, on returning, he told Lynch that Bachman had gotten the story wrong. The patient, Jacob Rutherford, had given his religion as "Protestant" when he entered the hospital. But then, while seriously sick, he told the sisters that his parents had been Catholic and he had been baptized a Catholic. He said that he had not lived a good life but wished to die as a Catholic. Reverend Smith had then come to see Rutherford. The sisters told him what had transpired and invited him to see Rutherford himself, which Smith declined. Lynch tracked down Rutherford, who had recovered, to verify the story, and he did so.

Bachman's other charges of being blocked from seeing patients turned out to be false as well. One incident stemmed from a misunderstanding. Bachman asked to see a Swedish patient who was a Protestant. The sisters said that he had left the hospital. Bachman had opened a door and there espied the man he sought. But, Lynch said, the patient in question was a Norwegian. When Bachman had asked to see the Swede, who had indeed left the hospital, the sister gave him an honest answer. So in this case Bachman had merely been confused. Lynch offered an apology to Bachman if the minister felt any of the staff of the hospital had been discourteous toward him. He also noted that every Protestant who "died in the hospital" had seen a Protestant minister before his death. Catholics had not interfered with the religious beliefs of any of the patients.

The charges of financial malfeasance also collapsed. Lynch stated that originally the plan was to treat twenty-five patients. But eighty-five patients had been crammed into the hospital. Some of Lynch's advisers told him to ask the city council for some reimbursement. The city council agreed and covered a third of the costs. The other two-thirds had been raised by benevolent societies in the city, including the St. Patrick's Benevolent Society, the Hibernian Society, the Irish Mutual Benevolent Society, and the donations of private individuals, many of them Protestants. Lynch concluded that he had responded thoroughly to Bachman because he did not want to leave his donors "under the impression that we had abused their trust, and acted with littleness and duplicity."[99] In the end, Lynch had succeeded because he was able to address the specific charges with the testimony of witnesses, both Catholics and Protestants. Bachman came off as a petty, dishonest bigot.

After this, Fr. James Corcoran, writing in the *Evening News*, tried to get the last word in the seemingly interminable paper war. The *News* announced it was closing its columns to the controversy unless the parties wished to pay for space.[100] Bachman had responded to Lynch's letter by denouncing him and demanding that the *Miscellany* open its pages to him so that he could debate Catholics. Corcoran ended his remarks by again framing the paper war as an affair of honor and defended his conduct. He acknowledged that he had been criticized for his aggressive language by those who wished he had used a more diplomatic tone toward Bachman. To this he responded, "I am by nature incapable of using such language. It is a constitutional peculiarity, which I am neither bound to account for, nor amend. I must call things by their true names, or take refuge in silence. It is impossible for me to feign respect, where I feel none. I am unable to smile and bow before what my heart loathes." Bachman had protested that Corcoran's language was not that of a gentleman. Corcoran replied, "I deny it, and I further deny his competency to pronounce on such matters."[101] Thus, he denied Bachman was a gentleman and worthy of honor. With this Corcoran declared victory in the paper war. From his perspective, Catholics had defended their honor successfully.

Catholics claimed victory, but it was a pyrrhic victory at best. Claiming honor demanded reverence for one's public reputation. But, as the paper war with John Bachman demonstrated, reputation involved a great deal of negotiation. Catholics wished to define themselves in certain ways, but they realized that their identity in the South's honor culture was partially dependent on the opinion of the non-Catholic majority. If the broader community accepted their claims to honor, then Catholics could assume they were part of the "people" of the state. Bachman had recognized this. He had, through his specific arguments, led Catholic writers to attack Protestantism, the religion of the majority, and to imply that it formed an insufficient basis for republican virtue. Catholics had uttered those words publicly and sincerely. Certainly, their Protestant neighbors would take issue with such sentiments. Catholics also had to respond to nativist charges, but, as Bachman's last thrust demonstrated, their responses, driven by the context of the debate, threatened to destroy their strategy of building an institutional presence and claiming affinity with non-Catholic southerners. Perhaps Bachman recognized the Catholics' weakness because he too was engaged in the same institution-building process from a minority position. In this sense, Bachman's attack demonstrated the gains Catholics had made.[102]

Bishop England, John Bellinger, Father Lynch, and Father Corcoran had also identified a formidable enemy, liberal nationalism.[103] Liberal nationalism, unlike the Jeffersonian form hailed by Charleston Catholics, celebrated cultural homogeneity and faith in the divine mission of America to spread liberty, often equated with Protestantism. This complicated both the Catholic presence in the United States and Catholic claims about reality. Increasingly, the nativists advocated this liberal nationalism, and their universal claims excluded certain groups, like Catholics, from a progressive future. South Carolina Catholics, laboring under this threat, longed for ways to celebrate both their republicanism and their separate religious identity.

CHAPTER FOUR

An Identity of Our Own Making

Public Representations of Catholicism in Charleston

As the prolonged and tedious Bachman paper wars demonstrated, public controversies were a two-edged sword. On the one hand, they served as a stage on which Catholics could demonstrate an affinity with southern culture by appropriating honor culture and language. On the other hand, this very demonstration required resorting to apologetics and an aggressive stance, which stimulated hostile sentiments that could threaten Catholics' attempts to build lasting institutions. In addition, by appealing to the South's honor culture, Catholics placed themselves in the hands of the community to validate their reputations.

Though they never renounced public debate, Catholics sought other opportunities to project an image of Catholicism and Catholic citizenship outside of the give-and-take of paper wars. The Jeffersonian view of union permitted cultural heterogeneity, so Catholics could identify themselves as possessing unique features that strengthened the community of citizens. In this paradigm, common sentiments, common historical experiences, and a common devotion to republicanism did not eliminate cultural contrasts. Thus Charleston's Irish Catholics used public holidays, particularly St. Patrick's Day, to highlight their differences from other citizens and simultaneously portray themselves as ideally suited for the nation. A close look at the context of three St. Patrick's Day celebrations emphasizes how Charleston's Irish Catholics promoted their ethnic identity while demonstrating their devotion to South Carolina.[1] Charleston Catholics also sought a lasting presence in the city by constructing an impressive Gothic Revival cathedral, the Cathedral of St. John and St. Finbar, during the 1850s. The cathedral claimed an identity for South Carolina Catholics and literally set it in stone. The diocese hired the leading practitioner of Gothic Revival architecture in the country, Patrick Keely, to design and build the church. When examined in the context of Charleston's architecture of the 1840s as well as religious controversy in the state, the decision to construct a large Gothic cathedral for a small, poor, and overwhelmingly immigrant population of Catholics demonstrates an aggressive challenge to southern Protestantism. In these public expressions, Charleston Catholics depicted themselves as loyal Catholics and patriotic South Carolinians, staking their claim as one of the "assemblage of peoples."

Many scholars have recognized the value of studying holidays and public celebrations. Holidays, as Amitai Etzioni defines them, are "days on which custom or the law dictates a suspension of general business activity in order to commemorate or celebrate a particular event."[2] Hanael Bianchi notes that holidays "typically reinforce values of participants, rely on symbols and arbitrary elements, have dramatic performances which communicate a narrative to the participants, and reaffirm common beliefs of those involved in the celebrations." In other words, holidays reflect cultural values. Bianchi, advocating a historical approach to considering public holidays, indicates that holiday celebrations change over time and thus can indicate broader shifts in society.[3]

Nineteenth-century Irish emigrant communities vigorously celebrated St. Patrick's Day (March 17). Mike Cronin and Daryl Adair maintain that the "St. Patrick's Day parade became an annual barometer of how potentially powerful (or at least numerous) Irish Americans were." "The parades," they continue, "allowed Irish Americans to project a set of be-

liefs and aspirations to both their cohorts and other Americans generally."[4] Kenneth Moss identifies St. Patrick's Day parades as major opportunities for Irish emigrants to develop an ethnic identity by linking
themselves to a common "Irish past." They formed an "imagined community" through their common celebrations.[5] The Irish in Charleston were
no different and participated in these events to highlight their ethnicity
and contributions to South Carolina and the United States.[6] In addition,
Irish Carolinians, especially members of the Catholic clergy, used the
celebrations to challenge nativist views of citizenship. While the focus of
the celebrations changed during the antebellum period based on the context of the time, each festival idealized the good citizen who practiced
virtue and proved willing to help and defend the community.[7]

Several Irish organizations played important roles in St. Patrick's Day
celebrations in Charleston; while not officially Catholic, they counted
important Catholic clergy and laymen among their membership. The
Hibernian Society of Charleston, founded in 1799, served a visible function in the city. Its first president was Dr. Simon Felix Gallagher, a
Catholic priest. Its third president, Col. Simon Magwood, a banker and
Protestant immigrant from Ulster, headed the society for thirty years.
Rather than a religious fraternity, the Hibernians were nonsectarian and
humanitarian in purpose. According to its 1801 constitution, the society
organized "for the purpose of true enjoyment" and "useful beneficence."
It sought to aid "distressed emigrants from Ireland." In 1841 it opened its
Greek Revival hall on Meeting Street, making a strong architectural
statement of belonging in the city. The society charged dues, consequently restricting its membership to prominent men in the city. Bishop
John England was an active member for over twenty years.[8]

Another group, the Irish Volunteers, a militia unit in Charleston, were
closely associated with the Hibernians.[9] The Volunteers formed in the
1790s, and political exiles from the failed 1798 Irish uprising further organized the company.[10] The unit operated in the War of 1812, the Semi-
nole War, and the Civil War. A number of Hibernians served in the Volunteers, including the society's second president, O'Brien Smith. During
the nullification crisis, the Volunteers pledged loyalty to Gov. Robert
Hayne and prepared to defend the state in case of a federal invasion. According to A. G. Magrath, a prominent member of the Volunteers, even
Bishop England's pleading could not sway the Volunteers from their

support of the nullifiers. Although commanded by elite Irish, the Volunteers were usually men of modest means.[11] The Irish Volunteers often marched in the St. Patrick's Day parades, displaying their martial valor.

The St. Patrick's Benevolent Society, founded in 1817 as an immigrant aid society, participated in the St. Patrick's Day festivities in Charleston as well. Capt. John Magrath, an exile from the 1798 Irish uprising, led the organization during most of the antebellum period. He also served in the Irish Volunteers. Like the Hibernians, the St. Patrick's Benevolent Society had both Catholic and Protestant members. Unlike the Hibernians, it included nonelites. The group provided aid and support to numerous Irish immigrants, especially during yellow fever epidemics.[12]

Across the United States, changing patterns of Irish immigration contributed to a surge of nativism during the 1830s. The historian Kevin Kenny notes that between 1783 and 1815 perhaps as many as 150,000 Irish migrated to North America, most of whom were Presbyterians. After the Napoleonic Wars, however, Irish immigration changed. Between 1815 and 1845 about a million Irish migrated to North America, half of them between 1835 and 1844. Kenny estimates that by 1840 the overwhelming majority of Irish immigrants to North America were Catholics.[13] Kerby Miller maintains that Catholic emigrants from Ireland began to outnumber Protestants by the early 1830s.[14] In the 1830s few Irish immigrants traveled to South Carolina, but those who did lived primarily in Charleston and other towns.[15] Religious hostility grew both in the British Isles and in the United States during the same time. Miller mentions that by the 1820s "conservative Anglican clergy and laymen launched a 'New Reformation' designed to" unify "Irish Protestants . . . in a holy crusade to eradicate Catholicism through a militant proselytism."[16] Protestant clergy in the United States responded similarly. The *United States Catholic Miscellany* during the mid-1830s reported a slew of nativist incidents, among them, the burning of the Ursuline convent in Charlestown, Massachusetts. In January 1835 Bishop England announced the formation of the Roman Catholic Missionary Society to convert Protestants and defend the Catholic religion.[17] On February 21, 1835, the *Charleston Courier* began running ads for Samuel F. B. Morse's nativist tract, *Foreign Conspiracy against the Liberties of the United States*.[18] "In Charleston, S.C.," Morse wrote there, "the Roman Catholic Bishop, England, is said to have boasted of the number of votes that he could control at an election."[19] Clearly, nativism fueled suspicion and worried the city's Catholics.

On St. Patrick's Day in 1835, in a national atmosphere of anti-Catholicism and specific charges against their bishop, South Carolina Irish Catholics enacted their roles as virtuous, patriotic republicans. The newspapers of Charleston briefly mentioned the day's festivities, and each of the papers printed roughly identical information, thus establishing a consistent representation of the events. The *Miscellany* noted that because the cathedral was under renovation the morning mass took place at the Ursuline convent chapel. Members of the St. Patrick's Benevolent Society, the paper reported, attended mass while the "Irish Volunteers, merely paraded, but did not attend church."[20] The militia parade was celebratory in nature but provided a show of Irish strength to the community.[21] At ten o'clock in the morning the Benevolent Society elected officers for the next year. Then the Volunteers and the Benevolent Society met for a banquet at Lege's Long Room on Queen Street.[22] According to a letter published in the *Southern Patriot*, the large kitchen fire that was needed to prepare food for the banquet briefly engulfed the roof of the building in flames before it was extinguished.[23] Bishop England also attended the banquet and gave an address. The Hibernian Society first elected its officers at St. Andrew's Hall and then commenced with its annual banquet at five o'clock in the evening.[24] The newspaper accounts usually included the toasts made at each of the gatherings, thus providing a glimpse of the ways the different groups portrayed themselves.

Significantly, the toasts at the banquet for the St. Patrick's Benevolent Society and Irish Volunteers conveyed a sense of patriotism and respect for liberty. The first toasts were official ones presented by the hosting organizations. A song followed each toast. Then individuals were free to offer random toasts. The official toasts began with tributes to Ireland and the Irish struggle for freedom from British rule. The sixth toast honored Bishop England: "The Patriot and the Scholar—Identified with the great struggle for Freedom in the land of his nativity, he could not fail to be admired in the land of his adoption." Three other toasts reflected the blend of Irish, American, and South Carolinian patriotism on display. One individual toasted the "struggles for freedom throughout the world." He noted that these struggles were "a cheering prospect for the philanthropist; the seal will soon be set upon the commandment, that

'Resistance to Tyranny is obedience to God.'" After a toast to the memory of George Washington, the participants toasted the United States as an "asylum for the oppressed." "Long may they remain uncorrupted and undivided," the participants celebrated, "to gladden the heart of the unfortunate exile, and sooth the anguish of the unhappy captive." After the brief nod to union, a toast celebrated South Carolina, making a vague reference to the recent willingness of the Irish Volunteers to support Governor Hayne during the nullification crisis. "South Carolina," the toast sounded, "The land of our choice—the home of our affections—in her prosperity are centered our fondest hopes—in her defence are prepared our strongest hearts."[25] Overall, the toasts celebrated a simple theme: Irish immigrants were loyal to their state and country. They hardly mentioned religion. Even Bishop England was recognized for his love of both Ireland and the United States rather than for his religious role. The toasts also indicated a devotion to liberty and a concern for those around the world seeking their political rights.

After the initial toasts, Bishop England spoke before another round. The *Courier* did not relate the contents of the bishop's address but noted that it was "one of the most excellent Addresses which has ever proceeded from him." The paper related that Bishop England expressed "the most deep and impassioned feelings towards the land of his nativity" and provided "the most touching allusions to the land of his adoption." The remaining toasts were informal, offered by individuals rather than by the gathering as a whole. They displayed the same themes, however. A toast by Captain Eude of the French Volunteers praised the Irish Volunteers, noting that "when South Carolina called upon her sons," the "Volunteers did swear to maintain her rights, and were ready to die for the freedom of their adopted country." In this case, "country" meant South Carolina. The Irish in Charleston had been divided on nullification (see ch. 5). Thus Major Van Rhyn, whom the paper identified as a committee member, made this toast: "Our adopted country: In the language of Lafayette, may she ever remain united and happy."[26]

The divergence in toasts actually served the Irish image well. Far from appearing as Samuel Morse's bloc of voters hostile to the interests of the state, the Irish, including the Catholic participants, seemed to share both common sentiments and divisions with their native South Carolina neighbors. In particular, the Irish Volunteers promoted their record of service to the state during the nullification crisis. Even though Bishop England had been a Unionist during nullification, he printed these toasts in the *Miscellany*, thus disproving charges of both a Catholic rejection of republican principles and of an Irish Catholic voting bloc in the city.[27]

The toasts at the Hibernian Society similarly stressed republicanism rather than religion. The society toasted Irish republican patriots such as Robert Emmet, Henry Grattan, and John Philpot Curran. Like the society itself, these men had supported civil and religious liberty despite their different denominational affiliations. The Hibernians likewise toasted the United States as "the *first* Hope of Man—the *last* abode of Liberty." After toasting the governor and the state of South Carolina, the Hibernians honored the U.S. Constitution as "the wisdom of ages practically illustrated." After the official toasts, individuals expressed sentiments of peace, liberty, and patriotism. For example, a Captain Tinkham toasted the "City of Charleston and its Prosperity: May they be commensurate with the hospitality of its citizens."[28] Thus, Catholics who participated in the Hibernian banquet displayed a broad-minded, nonsectarian patriotism. Again, they demonstrated their ability to collaborate with other citizens and promote civil and religious liberty.

Less than two weeks after the 1835 St. Patrick's Day celebrations, the *Courier* gave Morse's *Foreign Conspiracy* a negative review in terms that reflected for the most part the image conveyed by Charleston Catholics during the festivities of March 17. The writer in the *Courier* maintained that Morse had warned that Catholic immigrants from Europe, funded by European monarchs, sought to convert Protestants to Catholicism and wrest political power from solid American republicans. The *Courier* admitted that Catholics wished to convert Protestants. It also acknowledged Catholic political ambitions. But, the writer insisted, "we would combat only with the weapons of reason and charity—we would have neither political proscription nor social intolerance to mingle their bitterness with the strife." The *Courier* lamented that "an ill-advised production . . . dealing so much in *hyperbole* . . . should have made its appearance on the Protestant side of the question." The paper rejected Morse's implication that Protestants needed the protection of the state from Catholics. It noted that Morse's work showed "how easy it is for an excited fancy, and an impudent zeal, to lead perhaps even a good man into the very intemperance of folly." Morse, the paper reported, had sent a copy of his book with a note conveying a conversation Morse had had with a friend in which the friend indicated that no secular paper would give publicity to Morse's work, implying that the press was influenced by the Catholic threat. The *Courier* noted that it was an independent paper but that it would not "engage in a warfare of politico-religious intolerance against a respectable portion" of "fellow-citizens."[29] The *Courier*'s rejection of Catholic-baiting and its neutral portrayal of Catholicism matched the images cultivated during St. Patrick's Day. The paper did not see Catholics as seeking to wrest political control from other Americans. Instead, Catholics were fellow citizens deserving respect.

Bishop England, in the April 4 edition of the *Miscellany*, thanked the *Courier* for its "honest candor." He wished that the paper would have portrayed Catholics in a better light but appreciated its respect. Bishop England addressed directly Morse's charge that he controlled a bloc of votes in the city. He denied it, noting that South Carolina Catholics were divided in politics. The aim of the nativists, he wrote, was to provoke Catholic anger and encourage "riot." If Catholics resorted to violence, nativists would play the victim and win sympathy for their cause. Therefore, Catholics should stay away from direct confrontations.[30] In this light, the peaceful St. Patrick's Day celebrations had proven their worth for the Catholic image in the community.

Two events shaped the St. Patrick's Day celebrations in Charleston in 1847: the Irish famine and the Mexican War. News of the Irish potato famine and the massive starvation that accompanied it reached South Carolina newspapers in late 1846. Immediately, the Hibernian Society of Charleston initiated and organized a relief effort in the city and the surrounding areas. As Harvey Strum notes, relief efforts united South Carolinians of all creeds; even free blacks joined in the cause.[31] Charleston's St. Patrick's Day events that year were unusually somber, as Irish organizations dispensed with many festivities and raised money for relief instead. With regard to the Mexican War, John C. Calhoun began a speaking tour in the state in early March, warning South Carolinians of northern attempts to ban slavery in the western territories. Commentary on Calhoun's speeches consumed Charleston newspapers during March, pushing out extended coverage of St. Patrick's Day. Therefore, most of the coverage of St. Patrick's Day appeared in the *Miscellany*. While the festivities did not address directly Calhoun's political message, they amplified the anti-British sentiment sweeping the United States during the Mexican War, which many Americans viewed as a means of thwarting British ambitions in North America.[32] In addition, the Mexican War unleashed a new wave of anti-Catholicism.[33] Whereas a direct refutation of anti-Catholicism was the major message of the 1835 celebrations, Catholics in 1847 took an indirect approach, stressing their broad humanitarian efforts to assist a unique, important nation, Ireland. In doing so, they emphasized that the piety of the Irish made them important citizens and good republicans.

Famine relief efforts consumed the energies of the Hibernian Society in 1847. In its February 27 issue, the *Miscellany* reprinted a speech by Hibernian Alexander Black calling for vigorous efforts on behalf of the starving Irish. Black mentioned that "many of Ireland's favorite sons" were forced "by political and religious persecution" to flee to the United States. They should "send forth the voice of comfort and consolation," he opined, to their "famished brethren." Black moved that it was "wholly incompatible with the feelings, impulses and sympathies of generous hearts, that a period of such extreme national calamity and widespread human woe, should be indulged in as a time of feasting and rejoicing." Thus, the Hibernians agreed to forgo their annual St. Patrick's Day banquet and instead contribute the funds normally used for it to the cause of relief. The society agreed to meet on March 17 at noon to elect officers, as was customary. At five o'clock in the evening they would reconvene and devote their efforts to organizing famine relief.[34] Charleston's papers reported some of the gifts collected statewide and reprinted speeches by national figures such as Henry Clay on the subject of famine relief. In keeping with the nonsectarian tone, the Hibernians sent funds to the Irish Quakers to distribute to the needy.[35]

Likewise, the Irish Volunteers assembled at nine o'clock in the morning on March 17 and marched to "St. Patrick's Church on the Neck" to hear mass and a sermon by Bishop Ignatius Reynolds.[36] The *Southern Patriot* announced that the Volunteers would then take up a collection for famine relief before returning to the Half Moon Battery for their traditional shooting contests.[37] Again, March 17, 1847, was unusual due to the lack of feasting and customary toasts, but the Charleston papers found other events to report.

Concerns about the status of slavery in the western territories flooded South Carolina newspapers during 1847 as Calhoun pressed the issue in Congress. Although the Wilmot Proviso, which proposed to ban slavery from any territory gained from the Mexican War, failed in the Senate, Calhoun sought a permanent constitutional block to such a proposal in order to protect southern economic and political interests. In March Calhoun returned to South Carolina to reunite with his family and rally political support. On March 9 Calhoun spoke to a large crowd in Charleston. He told Duff Green that the meeting was "said to be the largest ever held here." He continued, "I find perfect unanimity here, including Whigs and democrats. I never have been received even here with greater unanimity and enthusiasm."[38] He told Thomas G. Clemson in another letter that "hundreds had to retire from the impossibility of getting" into the venue to hear his speech.[39] For two weeks the press was abuzz with reactions to the speech, pushing coverage of St. Patrick's Day festivities to the side.

Calhoun argued in his Charleston speech that southerners should reject partisan loyalties and unite. He blamed partisan competition and disregard for the Constitution for increasing sectional conflict over the slavery question. According to Calhoun, abolitionists, "the rabid fanatics, who regard slavery as a sin," and thus pressed to destroy it at all costs, made up no more than 5 percent of the northern electorate. But abolitionists enjoyed influence well beyond their numbers because they served as an important swing vote in states like New York where the Democrats and Whigs were evenly balanced. Both parties, in order to win presidential elections, catered to the abolitionist vote, Calhoun implied. Both parties, therefore, emboldened the abolitionists at the expense of the South. Calhoun's solution to the quandary was to unify the South into one party that would break from the national parties. Faced with the prospects of losing a huge southern voting bloc—and thus control of the levers of power—the parties would compete for southern votes. The new southern party could thus play kingmaker and demand disavowal of abolitionism as the price for the South's vote. Calhoun insisted, "It is thus, and thus only, that we can defend our rights, maintain our honor, ensure our safety, and command respect. The opposite course, which would merge them in the temporary and mercenary party struggles of the day, would inevitably degrade and ruin us." He warned that if his advice were not followed, the South would either be subjugated by the North or secede.[40]

Along with Calhoun's campaign, another current shaped the 1847 St. Patrick's Day celebration. Calhoun's call for southern unity seemed to encourage Irish attempts to portray themselves as loyal fellow citizens and thus stymie lingering anti-Catholicism.[41] On the other hand, the St. Patrick's Day commemoration of 1847 occurred during a serious shift in American engagement with the Irish. Scholars have noted a change during the antebellum period from an environmental to a biological explanation of ethnicity. Initially, it seems, Americans attributed national character to proper nurturing. Therefore, a free environment would train people to be free, thus allowing the Irish to Americanize over time. But by the mid-1840s, especially after the 1844 riots between nativists and Irish in Philadelphia, many Americans accepted that ethnic differences expressed deep-seated, immutable aspects of nature. Environmental explanations of ethnicity began to dwindle while essentialist arguments gained traction. As the famine drove more Irish than ever before to American shores, concerns about the Irish character became even more prevalent.[42]

This may explain why Bishop Reynolds addressed the issue of Irish character in his 1847 address on St. Patrick's Day. Two accounts of the speech appeared in the Charleston papers. The first ran in the March 25 edition of the *Mercury*, a week after St. Patrick's Day. The second account appeared in the *Miscellany* on March 27 in the form of an enthusiastic letter from someone who had listened to the speech. Although the accounts overlapped, the papers highlighted different themes in the oration.

The *Mercury* focused on the anti-British character of Bishop Reynolds's address, a theme that united Irishmen and Americans in 1847. The paper commented on the unusually "subdued tone" of St. Patrick's Day but insisted that Reynolds's speech was well attended. In fact, the writer for the *Mercury* admitted that he could not hear the opening of the speech because of noise in St. Patrick's Church. Reynolds, the *Mercury* stated, discussed St. Patrick's conversion of Ireland as a nonviolent spread of Catholicism. The English did not heed the peaceful example of St. Patrick, however. Whereas Ireland remained devoted to the "Ancient Religion," the English abandoned the faith out of a lust for power and then persecuted those who refused to follow their example. The Irish, Reynolds had noted, found themselves oppressed by "the most corrupt, powerful and opulent nation of earth." The British lion, he apparently quipped, should be replaced by a more fitting mascot, a fox or serpent.

The *Mercury* reported that Reynolds professed his love of America, "his own native land," but appreciated the land of his ancestors as well. He ended by encouraging famine relief efforts. The *Mercury* writer commented that the speech lasted for about two hours and was moving. He portrayed the speech as a typical St. Patrick's Day appeal to patriotism and respect for civil and religious liberty.[43]

In addition to the anti-British themes in Reynolds's address, the *Miscellany* highlighted the bishop's discussions of national character. In particular Reynolds had depicted Ireland as a "martyr nation," a fact that shaped Irish character significantly. For Reynolds a martyr nation was one that was "ever ready to die for the faith." Great Britain, the "Nero of nations," sought to devour Ireland much like a serpent surprises its prey. Persecution and perseverance characterized Irish history and shaped the Irish national character. The writer for the *Miscellany*, after discussing Reynolds's negative portrayal of Great Britain, wished that others could have seen "what an American Bishop, born upon American soil, and educated under the wings of her free institutions" thought of Great Britain. Reynolds's appreciation of freedom and his experience of free society, not his ethnic heritage, shaped his views. One accustomed to freedom could easily perceive tyranny at work. The writer continued that Bishop Reynolds's views were shared not only by many American Catholics but by "a large majority of the Protestant" population too. By stressing that national character had more to do with one's specific historical and cultural environments than some essential ethnic nature, the *Miscellany* rejected the rising trend of essentialist arguments regarding ethnicity used against Irish Catholic immigrants.[44]

Bishop Reynolds returned to the theme of nature later in his speech, expressing trust that Christianity could significantly reshape cultures and redirect selfish human nature to good ends. In this, he seemed to address the romantic notion of the nature of peoples. The writer for the *Miscellany*, summarizing part of Reynolds's discourse on the life of St. Patrick, maintained, "Nature had planted in the hearts of her [Ireland's] people a far different impulse from the one by which they were now actuated. Bravery was then inseparable from them; but it was the determined bravery of an unchristian age—it was the bravery of man against man—of nation against nation to the hilt." St. Patrick, he continued, worked to improve Irish nature. He "engrafted upon" the Irish "several branches of universal love," thus transforming their national character. Patrick did this not by obliterating their culture but by pruning "their more unrighteous propensities." Thus, Christianity had improved Irish national character. Irish bravery became Irish loyalty to the faith in the face of overwhelming odds. Reynolds implied that Catholicism, far from destroying cultures it encountered, made them better by directing them to universal ends. Given the context of rising nativism that perceived Catholicism as an alien force, his speech suggested that instead of being afraid of the Irish immigrants, Americans should welcome them. The Irish would not destroy American culture but, because of their own experience as a martyr nation, would help to improve the country through their example of loyalty to truth in the face of hostile opposition. In fact, Calhoun had demanded this kind of loyalty to the Constitution from South Carolinians only a week before. Reynolds did not address directly domestic political themes in the speech, but his attitudes reflected the immediate context. Character was not immutable, and just as St. Patrick improved the Irish national character, the Irish, Reynolds seemed to imply, could strengthen American national character. Catholics came to contribute, not to destroy.[45]

The St. Patrick's Day celebrations of 1860 garnered greater attention thanks to the changing demographics of Charleston. As the potato famine intensified emigration from Ireland, the United States absorbed hundreds of thousands of refugees.[46] Charleston experienced such an influx of foreign-born whites that by 1860 the city claimed a white majority. Christopher Silver has noted that by 1860 "Irish and German immigrants and their children, coupled with a smattering from other origins, accounted for nearly nine thousand inhabitants, or slightly less than 40 percent of Charleston's white population." Silver has shown that many of the Irish who came to the city during the 1850s traveled from New York, where unemployment was high, but did not remain for long. Silver wrote, "No more than 23 percent of the Irish enumerated in the 1850 census were present to be counted when the census takers took to Charleston's streets ten years later." Despite this, 70 percent of the Irish in Charleston lived in family units.[47] The older Irish societies, especially the Hibernians and the St. Patrick's Benevolent Society, assisted numerous Irish immigrants in the city, although Irish poverty remained a problem.[48] The

Irish took unskilled jobs and competed with both free blacks and slave labor. As Dee Dee Joyce has demonstrated, the political and social struggles resulting from the competition at the bottom of the city's labor hierarchy led the Irish to organize politically and press the city to enforce laws restricting the activities of free blacks and the hiring out of slaves. The growing number of Irish and their increasing political organization made them a significant minority in city politics.[49]

The sectional crisis also framed St. Patrick's Day in 1860. In October 1859 news of John Brown's raid on Harpers Ferry rocked the city and consumed public attention in the newspapers. The *Mercury* reprinted a story from the *Petersburg* (Virginia) *Express* whose opening line captured the mood of the city: "This Harper's Ferry affair is but a small eruption on the surface of a diseased body."[50] The paper predicted that the Union was finished. As Elizabeth Fox-Genovese and Eugene Genovese argued, "for many" the raid and the reactions to it in the North "either proved to be that last straw or put them in a frame of mind to reject Lincoln's election more firmly than they might have done."[51] The Charleston Irish during the St. Patrick's Day holiday addressed the crisis.

As usual, Irish Catholics portrayed themselves as loyal South Carolinians on March 17, 1860. The *Mercury* and the *Courier* provided extensive coverage of the St. Patrick's Day festivities, a testament to the growing importance of the Irish to the city. For instance, the newspapers reported the contents of three major speeches and gave summaries of a fourth. They also reprinted the many toasts at St. Patrick's Day dinners and highlighted the activities of the various militia units. Much of the rhetoric and many of the toasts resembled earlier St. Patrick's Day celebrations in blending religious and secular themes, but sectional concerns also intruded. The participants professed love for the Union and their devotion to state sovereignty. But they also made it clear that their primary political loyalty was to South Carolina. While the anti-British rhetoric echoed that of past celebrations, the speakers drew new, subtle analogies. The North's attitude resembled British arrogance, while the South took after persecuted but honorable and faithful Ireland.[52]

The bad weather did not diminish the festivities of the day. Rev. P. O'Neill sang High Mass at St. Patrick's Church, followed by a sermon on the life of St. Patrick from Rev. F. J. Carr of the Cathedral of St. John and St. Finbar. Interestingly the *Mercury* but not the *Miscellany* reprinted

Carr's sermon. According to its minute book, the St. Patrick's Benevolent Society met at the Masonic Hall and marched at nine o'clock in the morning to the Hibernian Hall, escorted by the "Irish Volunteers Meagher & Montgomery guards."[53] There Michael O'Connor, a Catholic lawyer and state legislator, gave a rousing oration that was reprinted in the city's newspapers. The Hibernian Society held its usual festivities and had a Catholic celebrity on hand, the outspoken Archbishop John Hughes of New York. Bishop Patrick Lynch of Charleston escorted Hughes to various functions throughout the day. The Irish militias, despite the rain, marched through the city, demonstrating their public spirit.

Rev. Felix J. Carr's sermon about St. Patrick stressed the steadfast, loyal nature of the Irish. Carr was born in Chester, South Carolina. His mother brought him to Charleston as a boy, and eventually he entered Bishop England's seminary. Showing great intellectual promise, he finished his seminary education in Rome. Upon returning to South Carolina, he served at the cathedral.[54] Carr emphasized that Irish loyalty to the Catholic faith proved their credibility and effectiveness as missionaries. St. Patrick, who persevered through countless trials, sought "to enroll under the banner of the Church a generous and high minded people . . . to render them as celebrated for their virtues as they had hitherto been for their vices." Like St. Patrick, Ireland had to endure great suffering. Carr thundered: "Persecution, servitude, the most inhuman and unheard-of barbarities, have been in vain adopted against her. The fair name of Religion has been used to sanction the grossest injustice." Carr rendered the obligatory condemnation of English bigotry and warned that England would continue its mission to corrupt Ireland. But Irish perseverance had spread Catholicism throughout the world. This remained the Irish charge, Carr noted. A loyal and steadfast people not only made good Catholics but, he implied, good citizens as well.[55]

The lengthiest address that day was delivered by Michael O'Connor of the St. Patrick's Benevolent Society. O'Connor was born in Beaufort, South Carolina. His father, an Irish immigrant, had planted Catholicism in Beaufort and attracted the friendships and acclaim of many of his fellow citizens.[56] O'Connor showed great promise and traveled to New York, where he was educated at St. John's College, the school founded by Archbishop John Hughes. Upon returning to South Carolina, he read law in Charleston and practiced in the city. In 1858 he won

election to the state legislature. There he earned a reputation for his ora-
torical skills. He vigorously opposed efforts to reopen the transatlantic
slave trade and warned against secession, arguing that disaster would
result from a breakup of the Union.[57]

O'Connor assured his audience that the Carolina Irish's loyalty lay
primarily with their state. He noted that the theme of his speech was
"the entire history of a great and ubiquitous people."[58] While he mean-
dered through Irish history, O'Connor praised Irish character in the
usual fashion, highlighting the Irish love of liberty and their steadfast-
ness in defending their faith. He accused the potato famine of driving
"millions into exile." The Irish in America, he insisted, "cannot entirely
break asunder that tie of nature, which binds you in fond and enduring
recollection to the land of your nativity." They had been forced from their
homeland. There was something dishonorable, he implied, about turning one's back on one's people. Yet he stressed that while the Irish honored their ancestors, they also possessed "an unchallenged fidelity and
unswerving devotion" to the Constitution of the United States. He
maintained that the United States was home to many peoples, "merged
into a common nationality."[59] But the Carolina Irish knew that if the
federal government "betrays its high and solemn trusts, and commits
treason against the people, the adopted sons of South Carolina will be
the first to trample it in the dust." O'Connor reiterated to his audience
that "your first allegiance is due to the State." He counseled the Irish to
"stand faithfully to your posts, and vindicate the institutions of our common mother."[60] O'Connor admitted that the Irish in America had dual
affections but denied that they possessed dual and conflicting loyalties.
South Carolina came first.

O'Connor aimed for sympathy by subtly identifying Ireland with
South Carolina and the South. At the conclusion of his speech, he
warned that "the political heavens are dark with evil portents of coming
disasters—while storm and tempest and the surges of fanaticism are
sweeping away the ramparts of the Constitution, and threatening to en-
gulf the Union."[61] This guided listeners' minds not only to the immediate
context of 1860 but back to O'Connor's portrayal of portents, disasters,
and fanaticism in the Irish history he had just recounted. Several connections emerge. When O'Connor mentioned Henry II's annexation of
Ireland, he noted that Ireland's "coffers enriched the British Treasury."

Two generations of South Carolinians had complained that through the tariff the federal government had milked the wealth of the state and relegated South Carolina to subordinate status. O'Connor portrayed Henry VIII as a fanatic who "established the unnatural union of Church with State." During the long Reformation, English Protestants plundered Ireland, leading to the regime of Cromwell, which "was marked by deeds of perfidy and cruelty." To South Carolinians remembering John Brown's raid, warnings of fanaticism seemed especially prescient. The southern press had portrayed Brown and the abolitionists as fanatics who would stop at nothing to achieve their goals. For them the violence of the Harpers Ferry raid confirmed this. The last line of the speech counseled the Irish to defend South Carolina. O'Connor did not have to connect the dots for his audience. His suggestions fell upon their ripe ears, which is certainly why the *Mercury*, *Courier*, and *Miscellany* praised his address. South Carolinians could learn from Irish history, O'Connor implied. The best citizens to help them were the Irish themselves who now viewed the state as their adopted "mother."[62]

Archbishop Hughes and Bishop Lynch also gave brief addresses that the newspapers reported, and both affirmed the connection between Ireland and the South. The similarities between the Irish and American environments meant that Irish immigrants shared a national character with the citizens of their adopted land. Hughes spoke at the Hibernian Society dinner. After praising southern hospitality and professing his love for the United States, he compared the United States and the relationship between Great Britain and Ireland. He observed that when the queen signed her name, she did so "as the Queen of Great Britain and Ireland," a recognition of Irish sovereignty. Speaking of sovereignty, Hughes added that "every State possesses [sovereignty] here." "The Sovereignty of Ireland," he exclaimed, "has never yet been extinguished." This implied, of course, that the U.S. government could not extinguish the sovereignty of the states either. Like O'Connor, Hughes warned that "the happiness of a people may be overturned by the efforts of a few fanatics, whether in religion or politics."[63]

Lynch's speech was shorter and less formal. He responded to the official Hibernian toast to civil and religious liberty. "It speaks of Ireland and of South Carolina," he said. "Of Ireland, which for centuries has yearned for civil and religious liberty, and of South Carolina, where, thanks to God, we have it." He counseled that peace would remain if the government refrained from treading on church affairs and the church did not "undertake to tell me how I shall vote." Lynch ended by toasting, *"The Sons of Ireland in Carolina.—Nowhere are they more at home."*[64] By identifying Ireland and South Carolina, Lynch confirmed the identity promoted by Charleston Catholics during the St. Patrick's Day festivities. If Ireland and South Carolina were related in character, then Irish South Carolinians were not aliens but instead knew their adopted state well, having experienced similar trials in Ireland. The Irish Catholics, therefore, not only claimed to be worthy citizens; they also claimed to be the best citizens South Carolinians could imagine. The message of 1860 was not that Irish Catholics could contribute to South Carolina as honored guests but that they were indeed South Carolinians and understood their adopted state intimately.

The St. Patrick's Day festivities in Charleston played an important role in Catholic self-definition. The meanings and actions of Irish Catholics changed over time in response to the perceived demands of the moment. In 1835, when Catholics confronted an outburst of nativism, St. Patrick's Day afforded Irish Catholics in Charleston an opportunity to demonstrate their ability to cooperate with Protestant citizens and proclaim their republican credentials. In 1847, when the potato famine rocked Ireland and sent thousands to the United States, St. Patrick's Day allowed Irish Catholics to demonstrate their willingness to help others in need. Catholics also used the day to reject essentialist interpretations of Irish character and affirm the national hostility to Great Britain. In 1860, thanks to the growth in the Irish population of Charleston during the previous decade, Catholics used the St. Patrick's Day celebrations to assert their compatibility with native South Carolinians and to present themselves as stalwart citizens of the state who shared both a political and cultural understanding with their non-Irish and non-Catholic neighbors. The increased press coverage in 1860 and the appearance of Archbishop Hughes demonstrated not only the growing importance of the holiday but also the importance of Irish Catholics in the city's politics and cultural life. St. Patrick's Day offers historians, therefore, an important window into the ways that Catholics portrayed themselves and indicates the values they proclaimed. By 1860 South Carolina Catholics projected themselves as worthy Carolinians, as strong in their patriotism and devotion to republican principles as their neighbors. They were part of the "assemblage of peoples."

On January 17, 1846, the *Miscellany* ran a letter from Bishop Reynolds announcing his plans to build a new cathedral and "residence for the Bishop" and seminarians in Charleston. He painted a dismal picture of diocesan infrastructure. Reynolds noted that Bishop England had died unexpectedly, leaving about $14,000 in unpaid debt. Due to the small number of Catholics in the diocese—Reynolds estimated 12,000, including "children, slaves, and coloured persons"—resources remained extremely scarce. Charleston, he claimed, had three churches but "not Catholics enough to form one numerous congregation." The current cathedral, "sinking into decay beyond the possibility of repair," would not suffice. Reynolds praised the generosity of those in his diocese and encouraged the clergy to raise money for the new cathedral by stressing the great legacy of Catholic architecture in Europe and the need to have a building worthy of "the inspiring grandeur of our Ritual." Theologically, the cathedral church, by symbolizing the teaching authority of the bishop, was "the most important church" of the diocese, Kevin Decker notes. Building a new cathedral required tremendous labor and resources, but it gave the bishop a unique opportunity.[65] Reynolds could oversee a Catholic structure in the important southern city of Charleston that could help define Catholic identity in the city and the South.

The *Miscellany* hinted at the form the new cathedral would take a month earlier when it reprinted two articles from a New York newspaper on Christian architecture. The articles, penned anonymously by "Varro," discussed the proper style of church buildings. In travels throughout the United States, Varro wrote, "I have seen but few places of worship calculated to inspire the slightest degree of veneration, reverence, or awe." Catholic churches, he declared, were "*exteriorly* the most unsightly." Catholics had once been "the most excellent of church builders" and needed to recover their tradition. The church building, Varro argued, existed for people to "commune with their Maker on heavenly things" and thus required special design. Churches were not structures where people simply sit "quietly at their ease and reckon up their weekly accounts" as if they were in a "tavern." Varro insisted that the great mistake in building churches in the United States had been "a departure from the

Gothic or Christian style." The Gothic style used symbols drawn from Catholic doctrine to teach the people. "Ordinary minds," Varro added, "are wholly governed through the eye and ear, and therefore the strongest impressions reach them by those channels." Properly built and ornamented churches would attract the young and revive the faith. Varro concluded in his second article that "it is almost only in the Christian style of architecture that objects can be embodied capable of inspiring pious and beautiful trains of thought." Varro advocated, therefore, what scholars call the Gothic Revival in architecture.[66]

Scholars debate the origins and scope of the Gothic Revival of the nineteenth century, but they agree that Anglicans initially promoted the movement in the English-speaking world. Undoubtedly, desire for Gothic Revival architecture stemmed from the intellectual and cultural currents associated with Romanticism. Interest in history, especially medieval history, grew during the century. According to Kenneth Clark, the novels of Sir Walter Scott heightened an interest in medieval history, which was necessary for the Gothic Revival. In addition, the Oxford Movement in the Anglican Church promoted the revival by seeking to ground Anglican doctrine and practice in Christian history.[67] Several Anglicans formed the Cambridge Camden Society to advocate the building of Gothic-ornamented churches on the grounds that they would facilitate true worship of God. The Gothic style also claimed an old historical identity for the English church, before the supposed corruptions of "Romanism." Other scholars have added that Gothic Revival grew in response to the destruction of many churches during the French Revolution and increasing secularist hostility.[68] The historian Ryan K. Smith, tracing the growth of the revival in the United States, argued that anti-Catholicism sparked the explosion in Gothic architecture among Protestant congregations. Protestants wished to appropriate "Roman Catholic power," Smith claimed, and thus constructed Gothic churches. Smith noted that Gothic architecture concerned laying "claim to religious tradition" and answering "the allure of sanctified Catholic church space."[69] The competition for souls and social position drove the Gothic Revival in the United States.

By far the most influential Catholic promoter of the Gothic Revival in the Anglo-American world was the British architect Augustus Welby Northmore Pugin. Pugin's father designed and constructed buildings, teaching his brilliant son the craft. In 1834, the twenty-two-year-old Augustus decided to convert to Catholicism and in 1836 published his first book on Gothic architecture. Many others would follow. Catholic Emancipation, which passed Parliament in 1829, meant that a Catholic architect and builder would have many opportunities to build new churches in Britain.[70] In his 1841 *True Principles of Pointed or Christian Architecture*, Pugin noted that those who designed and built churches needed to "*follow*" those who came before. "We may indeed," Pugin noted, "widen the road which our Catholic forefathers formed, but we can never depart from their track without a certainty of failure being the result of our presumption."[71] Pugin believed that architecture possessed a moral component.[72] Thus, his designs and recommendations deliberately promoted Catholic imagery and principles. He criticized Catholics for their ignorance of their own liturgical and architectural traditions, but he saved his most potent venom for Anglicans, especially those who advocated the Gothic style. He compared the two groups: "The [Anglican] Establishment are the many who, converted by political intriguers, avaricious and ambitious men, abandoned the faith of their fathers, and received parliamentary enactments for the decrees of the church. The English Catholics are the few who remained witnesses of the truth, under the severest trials of persecution."[73]

While Pugin praised the Cambridge Camden Society for its work in Gothic Revival, he refused to compromise with Protestantism. The Anglicans, he wrote in 1842, liked to blame the iconoclasm of the Reformation on the Puritans, but they too had destroyed Catholic art and architecture in their revolt against the old religion. Pugin insisted that the English Reformers had "wrought such a debasement of feeling among the people of this land, that nothing but the almighty power of God can restore the blessing of reverence among" the people. Anglican reformers of the nineteenth-century, Pugin noted, were wasting their time building in the Gothic style to revive the Church of England, "for unless the old faith and rites be restored, the deep chancels of antiquity would be no better than the other architectural masquerades of the day." But Catholics possessed the old religion and could use Gothic architecture to reinforce and reinvigorate the faith. For example, Pugin wrote, "a Catholic cathedral is no bad atmosphere wherein to imbibe a thorough detestation of Protestantism; for the contrast between the majesty of the building and the meagerness of the modern rites, appeal at once to the evidence of the senses."[74] For Pugin, Gothic architecture aggressively promoted Catholicism.

Pugin's appeal to beauty resonated in Charleston. Pugin maintained, "Let then the Beautiful and the True be our watchword for future exertions in the overthrow of modern paltry taste and paganism, and the revival of Catholic art and dignity."[75] Beauty became a vehicle for other ideas. The South Carolina author William Gilmore Simms, writing in 1842 about the use of romance and poetry to convey a sense of history, noted, "As in the gorgeous rites of the Catholic Church, the [*sic*] God first enters the mind through the medium of the eye. The passion and the agony of Christ, having a lively representation to the sight, imparts, in turn, a vivid conviction to the heart."[76] He thus made Pugin's point: an experience of beauty can transform the mind.[77] In 1845 Simms wrote an account of the architecture of New York City for the Charleston paper, the *Southern Patriot*. He noted that New York displayed "a most astonishing progress in Church-architecture," namely, the Gothic style. He particularly admired the still unfinished "steeple of Trinity" Episcopal church, recently designed by Richard Upjohn, the foremost Protestant practitioner of Gothic architecture in the United States.[78] Simms condemned the use of Greek Revival buildings as unsuited to the American climate and landscape. Like Pugin, Simms believed that the forms of culture embodied principles and a sense of history. Form mattered greatly.

The first Gothic architecture in Charleston appeared during the 1840s. Edward Brickell White, who first learned Gothic style in the North, built the first Gothic church in the city, the Huguenot Church, for an Episcopalian congregation.[79] He completed the church in 1845, and the building was dedicated that May. The *Courier* noted that when finished the church would be "an ornament to the city."[80] White also constructed two other Gothic-style churches in the state. In 1847 he finished Trinity Church in Columbia. The *Mercury* noted of the building, "A mind at all imbued with religious associations, cannot view it, without having its feelings of reverence confirmed and exalted." Confirming the effect of form on the mind once again, the paper continued, "Its quiet Abbey-like appearance invites to contemplation, whilst its towers, its arches and pinnacles, pointed upward to the skies, significantly remind the spectator of Heaven, as his only haven of rest."[81] In 1847–48 White built Grace Church in Charleston to wide acclaim.[82] The Gothic style had begun its march across the state.

As elsewhere, Episcopalians drove the Gothic Revival in the city and promoted the style for theological reasons. At the dedication of the Huguenot Church in May 1845, Rev. Charles Wallace Howard claimed in his sermon the antiquity of Calvinist beliefs. After describing the new structure as "our modest but beautiful edifice," Howard asserted, "We have this day revived the regular service of an ancient, pure and truthloving church; a service which had long fallen into disuse, but which is now revived as we fervently trust, to flourish even unto the end."[83] The remainder of the sermon recounted the history of French Catholic persecution of the Huguenots and celebrated John Calvin. At the same time, the sermon made use of two contexts. First, many Charlestonians had read long-running debates between Catholics and Protestants over the antiquity of the Catholic Church. This had been a favorite topic of Bishop England. In 1843 Fr. Patrick Lynch and Rev. James Henley Thornwell debated, in part, this topic.[84] Second, 1844 witnessed a resurgence of anti-Catholicism, especially in the wake of the Philadelphia riots, that harped on themes of Catholicism as a persecuting religion. Thus when Wallace claimed in the new Gothic structure that his church was "ancient, pure and truth-loving," the setting reinforced his message. The *Courier*, reporting on the sermon, noticed this message, pointing out that the Huguenots "even preceded Luther."[85] The Gothic setting lent credibility to the claim that Protestantism was "ancient," a tactic that Pugin had recognized and condemned in his writings.

In this context, Bishop Reynolds's decision to build a Gothic cathedral was a claim to Catholic significance and antiquity. The bishop had little respect in private for Episcopalian claims. In an 1850 letter to the archbishop of Cincinnati, John Purcell, Reynolds criticized Bishop England's earlier approach in the diocese: "He adopted the language and manners of Protestantism, especially Episcopalianism as far as he could. I think it necessary to guard the faith of the few and poor Catholics of my diocese by a clear line of demarcation."[86] The letter reveals much about Reynolds's approach in South Carolina. While he was not openly combative, he rejected accommodation to Protestant forms and modes to gain social acceptance. His desire for a new, grand Gothic cathedral would draw a "clear line" between Catholics and Protestants. Instead of using the *Miscellany* and public debate, Reynolds wished to challenge Episcopalian historical and theological claims by the presence of the new cathedral.

After announcing his intention to build a new cathedral, Bishop Reynolds spent several years raising money for the project. Naturally, he used the *Miscellany* to promote the endeavor. For example, on November 13, 1847, he published a letter to clergy detailing progress to that point. He wrote that he had collected $9,200 and acknowledged the generosity of the people, noting that they had also contributed greatly to relieve the sufferings of Irish famine victims during the same time frame. Reynolds maintained that it was time for "renewed exertions." He had asked for a census of the diocese in 1846 and now wished his clergy to use the information to solicit funds. He also defended his wish to delay construction until more funds had been raised. "Debt," he counseled, "is always one of the miseries of life, and often a *sin*, when contracted without a reasonable certainty of the means of payment."[87]

Reynolds's appeals marshaled the resources of all the Catholics in the diocese. The diversity is reflected in the lists of donors printed in the *Miscellany*. For example, in August 1848 the paper noted a generous contribution from Dr. John Bellinger of $1,000 as well as a number of $1 donations by numerous individuals, most with Irish surnames. The "St. Paul's Colored Society," a group of black Catholics, contributed $7.37. Ladies of the diocese held fairs in Charleston to raise money for the cathedral. The *Miscellany* also affirmed in 1853, perhaps remembering the old canard that foreign monarchists were funding immigrant Catholics to destroy America, that most of the money for the cathedral had been raised in the diocese.[88] Decker has argued that contributions to church building projects manifested the "religious devotion" of the people and that the "parish and cathedral churches" funded by these donations "were a visible manifestation of their religious and ethnic pride."[89] In other words, the cathedral would be a visible sign of Catholic identity in the diocese.

On May 18, 1850, Reynolds announced in the *Miscellany* that he had hired "Mr. P. C. Keely, of Brooklyn" as the architect and that the "Cathedral will be a gothic church of what is called the 'Ornamented English style,' 156 feet long and 72 broad on the exterior, and with a tower and spire 200 feet high." The dimensions were impressive. When completed, the cathedral would be the largest church in the city.[90] This would be an aggressive statement of Catholic identity, especially given that the Catholic population of the city was small and largely poor. Patrick Keely had recently won a reputation for his Gothic Revival churches in New York. An Irishman and devout Catholic, Keely came to the United States in 1842. The *Mercury* reported in 1850 that Keely was the "pupil (the only one in the United States) of the celebrated Pugin." Keely had not studied under Pugin, but by linking the two men the *Mercury* assumed that the cathedral would be at the forefront of the Catholic Gothic revival. By hiring Keely, Reynolds had linked himself to a broader intellectual and architectural movement. The paper concluded about the cathedral, "It will be an ornament to the Queen City of the South."[91]

The Cathedral of St. John and St. Finbar served primarily as an elaborate setting to stage public religious worship—what Reynolds referred to as "the inspiring grandeur of our Ritual"—but secondarily to attract the interest of non-Catholics. In July and August 1850, Charleston papers reported on Bishop Reynolds's elaborate ceremony at the cathedral site to lay the cornerstone. The *Courier* reported on the "imposing ceremony," which lasted three hours. It described the blessing of the cornerstone and noted the Gregorian chant performed by the assembled clergy. Then the paper relayed the highlights of the ninety-minute address by Reverend Moriarty. Moriarty, invoking the Old Testament, spoke of the need to build a worthy temple for God. The structure conveyed a religious sense, he said. The person worshipping in the new cathedral would be "aided" by the architecture "to shut out worldly distractions, and to feel himself in the presence of God." The *Mercury* reported that Moriarty also touched on "that disgrace of our times—Church debt." The *Courier* even asked Charlestonians to contribute to the cathedral project.[92] In their descriptions of the ceremonies, the secular papers of the city conveyed their appreciation of the proposed building and validated Reynolds's task of presenting Catholicism positively to the whole community.

Pugin had noted in 1841, "The vertical principle, emblematic of the resurrection, is a leading characteristic of Christian architecture, and this is nowhere so conspicuous or striking as in the majestic spires of the middle ages."[93] Decker has noted that Irish American Catholics particularly appreciated spires because the English penal laws had long prevented Catholics from worshipping in a building "possessing a bell or steeple."[94] A mixture of theological symbolism and ethnic pride combined to plan a large steeple for the cathedral. But non-Catholics also commented, both positively and negatively, on the messages conveyed by the cathedral's architecture as it neared completion. The *Courier* commented on the progress of the cathedral in May 1853. "Workmen," the paper informed, "have been busily engaged in covering in the skeleton of the steeple" that had been "secured upon its massive stone tower." "The men engaged in this apparently perilous employment, when viewed from the street, looked little larger than pigmies," concluded the paper.[95] Obviously the height impressed some observers.

Others were not so impressed. Presbyterian minister Benjamin Gildersleeve, long a resident of the city but by the 1850s living in Richmond, attacked the Gothic Revival style in his newspaper. Reporting on the dedication of a Gothic-style Episcopal church in Greenville, South Carolina, Gildersleeve mentioned that the dedicatory sermon insisted that the architecture of the church building would encourage prayer. Gildersleeve proclaimed, "For we know many Episcopalians in South Carolina and elsewhere, who are deeply pained at the Romanizing spirit of not a few in their communion. And indeed, the tendency of the age seems to be to the revival of formalism in its countless modifications—and all incompatible with the simple and effective teachings of the gospel."[96] After the dedication of the Cathedral of St. John and St. Finbar, Gildersleeve whined, "For ourselves we have often been surprised at the encouragement which they have received from Protestants of every denomination."[97] Clearly, the cathedral conveyed messages that some in the non-Catholic community could not ignore.

Bishop Reynolds dedicated the new cathedral on April 6, 1854, in an elaborate ceremony. The dedication was a major civic event. Reynolds brought Archbishop John Hughes from New York to preach the opening sermon. On March 22, 1854, the *Mercury* included a full description of the new cathedral, supplied to the paper by Fr. Patrick Lynch.[98] On April 7, the paper described the dedication of the building. After some initial prayers outside, the paper reported that "the doors of the Cathedral were thrown open." "The sight presented to the gaze," the *Mercury* continued, "was truly magnificent, as the beautiful proportions of the gorgeous temple of God were exhibited under the influence of the noonday sun, and the vast concourse of people, filling every available inch of ground, added greatly to the interest of the scene." After High Mass had been offered, Archbishop Hughes spoke at length. The *Mercury*'s correspondent appreciated the sermon. He concluded that the ceremonies, "for gorgeousness and completeness of design," had "never been excelled in any previous religious celebration in our city."[99] Bishop Reynolds must have liked the high praise, for the *Miscellany*, instead of giving its own report of the ceremony, merely reprinted the *Mercury*'s.[100]

The construction of the cathedral, while costly, did increase both the sense of Catholic distinctiveness and the interest of and acceptance by much of the non-Catholic community. But Bishop Reynolds had to spend his remaining days as bishop raising money to pay off the cathedral debt. When he died in March 1855, the *Courier* contributed a lengthy obituary. It praised Reynolds for his religious devotion and also for his two great tasks as bishop, the publication of Bishop England's writings and the construction of the cathedral.[101] The Cathedral of St. John and St. Finbar became an instant landmark in the city because of its great size. In June 1857 Simms published a long article on Charleston's architecture for *Harper's New Monthly Magazine*. The magazine printed a sketch of the cathedral. Simms noted that the "structure occupies a fine situation at the west end of Broad Street." He called the style "graceful and imposing."[102] He did not treat the cathedral—and the Catholics who built it—as exotic creatures; rather, he matter-of-factly included them and their new "structure" as citizens of the city. Catholicism had become part of the landscape. When Patrick Lynch became bishop of Charleston in 1858, the *Courier* reported on his consecration in the cathedral:

> We feel that we have given but a faint and feeble description of the imposing ceremonial of yesterday. The gorgeous vestments, the solemn chant of the clergy on the altar, the magnificent swell of the organ, pealing in glorious unison with the bird-like sweetness of female voices, formed a spectacle at once too solemn, imposing, grand and affecting to be noted on paper. . . . All we can say is, that never before in Charleston have we witnessed the like—a ceremonial worthy, indeed, of the stern, Gothic magnificence of the edifice in which it was performed.[103]

If possible, Bishop Reynolds and Pugin as well would have smiled in their graves.

The St. Patrick's Day celebration of 1860 and the reactions to the Cathedral of St. John and St. Finbar by secular writers during the late 1850s demonstrated that Catholics had become a significant force in Charleston.

While their numbers afforded them minimal influence, their cultural strategies had placed them squarely within the life of the city. They had become one of the "peoples" of the state. As Catholics gained greater prominence in Charleston, their presence became more common in other areas of South Carolina. Whereas vigorous public debates with hostile Protestants and nativists showed their willingness to fight publicly for their faith, Catholics presentations of their loyalty and religiosity in public settings won the respect of many in the community. The marches on St. Patrick's Day and the large, Gothic-style cathedral showed boldness, not reticence, on the part of Catholics. They sought to draw, in Bishop Reynolds's words, a "clear line" between themselves and their Protestant neighbors while at the same time showing themselves to be trustworthy, virtuous, and loyal citizens. Detractors would always find an audience, but by 1860 Catholics in South Carolina had claimed membership in the broader culture, a position many non-Catholics recognized and appreciated. Even so, Catholic advances on this front did not guarantee victory in their fight for respect and recognition. Gaining cultural credibility was one thing, but navigating the treacherous waters of antebellum politics would prove to be equally challenging.

CHAPTER FIVE

Republicanism and
Common Sentiments

South Carolina Catholics and Politics

Building church institutions, celebrating ethnicity, and defending the faith from attacks allowed South Carolina Catholic leaders to claim inclusion in the nation by emphasizing their devotion to republicanism, their common sentiments with their neighbors, and their similar historical experiences. Although each of these claims was heavily contested, Catholic leaders plausibly could erect a common front as they sought to be among the assemblage of peoples. But the world of politics presented a tougher challenge. If nationalism was a vision of an imagined community, the world of politics revealed the fissures and divisions papered over by romantic notions of united peoples. Politics required taking sides. Taking sides produced allies and enemies as well as feelings of unity and division. For the Catholic minority struggling to overcome historical prejudices against their religion, politics was particularly treacherous. In early nineteenth-century America, nativism lurked in the background of many political debates.

Although nativists rarely succeeded in promoting their agenda during the few times they gained limited power, their rhetoric threatened the common sentiments among Catholics and their neighbors that were necessary for the Jeffersonian view of the Union to thrive. Catholic political strategies, then, had to consider nativism and anti-Catholic prejudice.[1]

Catholic leaders in the Diocese of Charleston grappled with political strategies to navigate the two most stressful moments in antebellum South Carolina, the nullification crisis and the political turmoil of the 1850s. The nullification crisis of the late 1820s and early 1830s placed South Carolina on a collision course with the Jackson administration, while the sectional politics of the 1850s led the state to secede from the Union in December 1860. During the nullification crisis, Bishop England emphasized common republican sentiments to forge alliances with South Carolina political leaders. Although the bishop opposed nullification, he successfully navigated the crisis and refuted charges that Catholics somehow threatened republican politics. At the same time, he lectured his flock to apply Catholic moral principles when discerning the proper political action. On the other hand, during the 1850s Catholic leaders viewed national politics through the lens of the Revolutions of 1848 in Europe. Catholics in South Carolina, like Catholics in the North, feared that the revolutionary radicalism that drove Pope Pius IX from Rome would come to American shores.[2] The rise of the Know Nothing Party during the 1850s made real these fears. Catholic leaders in Charleston pledged support to southern conservatives in a battle with radicalism that both groups feared was sweeping the nation. Although their focuses were different, both Carolina Catholics and southern conservatives viewed the North as the locus of American radicalism and took refuge in Jeffersonian conceptions of both the Union and the Constitution. Both crises revealed a common strategy. South Carolina Catholics sought to build alliances with non-Catholics, claiming membership in and loyalty to their community in order to neutralize anti-Catholicism while at the same time offering religious justifications for their particular positions.

The 1820s were a particularly tense time in southern history as the Jeffersonian Republican Party, which had dominated the South since 1800, began to fracture. Both nationally and in South Carolina, two factions competed for power: the national Republicans and the Old Republicans.

The national Republicans usually endorsed a more expansive view of the role and powers of the federal government and blasted Old Republicans as unrealistic idealists.[3] The Old Republicans called for Jeffersonians to stay true to the original understanding of the Constitution as a limited grant of power that respected state sovereignty and the strict division of powers between the general and state governments. They greatly mistrusted national Republicans. In South Carolina, U.S. Secretary of War John C. Calhoun led the nationalist faction while Sen. William Smith led the Old Republicans. As elsewhere, politics turned vicious as the two groups competed for power and influence.[4]

The two Republican factions clashed during the presidential election of 1824. The Calhounites supported Andrew Jackson for president, whereas many of the Old Republicans rallied behind Georgia's William Crawford. Crawford, however, suffered a stroke that left him partially paralyzed and fared poorly. Jackson won more votes than any other candidate but failed to secure a majority in the electoral college. In the end, John Quincy Adams became president by a vote of the House of Representatives, giving rise to the charge that he and House speaker Henry Clay had sealed a "corrupt bargain" that secured Adams the White House and Clay the position of secretary of state in the new administration. The fallout from the election led to a reorganization of national politics, with New Yorker and former Crawford supporter Martin Van Buren leading efforts to create the Democratic Party to support Jackson in 1828. But Calhoun, Adams's vice president, opposed the president's nationalist agenda. Thus, by the middle of Adams's term, South Carolina politicians united in support of Andrew Jackson and the new Democratic Party.[5]

Earlier, the economic downturn caused by the Panic of 1819 and concerns about slavery had helped unify South Carolinians politically. After a brief boom and rise in cotton prices after the War of 1812, cotton prices dropped by two-thirds in the early 1820s. Farmers who had expanded their operations during the postwar boom now faced difficult economic circumstances.[6] At the same time, South Carolina's slave population grew more quickly than the white population after 1810, ensuring that the state would possess a black majority throughout the antebellum period. Meanwhile, the Missouri debates between 1819 and 1821, particularly Rufus King's antislavery speeches in the U.S. Senate, worried South Carolinians that the federal government might hinder slaveholding. In 1822 a violent plot, led by Denmark Vesey, among Charleston slaves and free blacks to seize a ship and sail to the Caribbean came to light. Vesey supposedly had read King's antislavery speech to some of the plotters. As concern about the safety of slavery grew in the state, many believed that the federal government, through its economic policies and antislavery discussions, threatened South Carolina's status quo.[7]

Political tensions skyrocketed in April 1828 when Democrats in Congress, led by Martin Van Buren, passed a protective tariff in order to draw support from the states of New York and Pennsylvania to Andrew Jackson's campaign for president.[8] The "tariff of abominations," as it was known in South Carolina, led to a vigorous antitariff movement in the state. Having suffered through an economic depression for most of the 1820s, South Carolinians blamed the new tariff for compounding their misery. In December 1828, after Jackson's election to the presidency, Calhoun, who would serve as Jackson's vice president, released anonymously the "Exposition and Protest," which condemned the protective tariff as unconstitutional and a danger to republican government. Calhoun invoked the Virginia and Kentucky Resolutions of 1798 as supplying a strategy for South Carolina. He proposed that the state legislature should declare the tariff unconstitutional and then call for a special convention of the people of the state to decide whether or not to nullify the tariff. In December the legislature fulfilled one part of Calhoun's wishes. It protested the tariff as "unconstitutional, oppressive, and unjust."[9] Over the next four years, as Lacy Ford put it, South Carolinians would divide into two parties, the nullifiers and the unionists, over the question of "whether nullification was a proper remedy for the ills which plagued the American experiment in republicanism or whether it was a cure that was far worse than the disease."[10]

Jackson's first term also worried South Carolina politicians. The year 1829 saw major infighting in his cabinet, which led to the marginalization of Calhoun. Then, in January 1830, Robert Y. Hayne of South Carolina debated Daniel Webster of Massachusetts on the floor of the Senate over the issue of nullification. Hayne, a faithful Calhoun lieutenant, attacked the protective tariff as unconstitutional and promoted nullification as a proper, peaceful, and constitutional remedy, while Webster defended a nationalist interpretation of the Constitution that denied the legitimacy of nullification. The debate brought national attention to the issue of nullification and further influenced the formation of political factions in South Carolina.[11]

The nullification crisis functioned primarily as a debate between different versions of states' rights theories rather than a contest between states' rights and nationalism.[12] Because both the proponents and opponents of nullification in South Carolina shared many similar views of the Constitution, their bitter disagreements concerned strategies rather than principles. The bickering presented a problem in South Carolina for those dedicated to ideological unity in the state. Disunity and party factionalism, even if it concerned strategies rather than principles, nevertheless worried those wedded to the republican ideology of the early republic.

In Charleston, Bishop John England viewed the tumultuous political events of the 1820s through a republican lens, stressing the importance of both virtue and ordered liberty.[13] Scholars have shown that the republican ideology, revived during the early modern period in Europe to celebrate civic order and self-government rather than monarchy, influenced Anglo-American thought greatly, especially in its insight of a perpetual battle between power and liberty.

John England developed his republicanism during his early clerical career in Ireland. As his biographers Peter Guilday and Patrick Carey have noted, the Veto Controversy of 1808–16 significantly shaped England's republican views. The controversy concerned two issues: the desire for Catholic Emancipation in Ireland and the attempt of the English government to control the Catholic Church in Ireland. Politicians presented bills in the House of Commons to guarantee emancipation for Irish Catholics as well as state salaries for Catholic clergy in return for the power of the English government to "veto nominations of bishops to Irish Sees." England vociferously opposed the veto. As Carey maintained, the Irish church had a "practical separation" of church and state and existed as a voluntary association with no state funding. If Irish bishops accepted the veto, the church in Ireland would secure a stable source of funding, an attractive option as it depended on contributions from its extremely poor members.[14]

John England argued in newspapers that the voluntary nature of the Irish church bound clergy and laity in more intimate bonds than would be the case in a religious establishment. Also, voluntaryism preserved the independence of the church from its greatest institutional threat, the state. England believed, Carey has written, that supporters of the veto "had underestimated the weakness of human nature and the power of the state." Catholicism, England maintained, should be maintained by reason, not coercion. England celebrated the defeat of the veto legislation but found himself shipped to Charleston in 1820, an exile of sorts. His Irish background, with its focus on voluntaryism, separation of church and state, and a vigorous, public defense of Catholicism, shaped his views of American politics.[15]

Like other republican thinkers, John England perceived acute tension between human reason and human passions. As he told Congress in 1826, human beings "do not always act as we have determined" and are tempted by the "allurements of the world." Thus people must "regulate our affections and desires" in order to "keep our passions in subjection to our reasonable determinations." Concupiscence and the limitations of the human intellect made such a task difficult. As he explained in an 1828 speech to the Anti-Dueling Society of Charleston, "Reason almost instinctively tells us that this injury of others for the gratification of our own pride . . . is bad," but "we labor to create sophisms for its justification." "So it is," he continued, "that the children of Adam are led by the impetuosity of passion against the admonitions of the understanding: and then to silence the voice of conscience, they compel or they suborn the intellect, to appear as the advocate of that which in its free and unsophisticated moments it condemned." Ultimately, it was England's appreciation of fallen human nature that made him suspicious of power.[16]

Bishop England believed that when power threatened liberty, the proper remedy was popular virtue. According to a correspondent to the *Charleston Mercury*, he told a Charleston crowd on July 4, 1826, that the "practice of virtue" was the "only certain and enduring basis of the republic."[17] In a later address, England warned a gathering of southern Catholics that if republicanism lost its "energy" because of popular corruption, it would become "the vision of an idle dream." England defined the concept of virtue as being the willingness of the individual to prefer the good of the whole above his "private interest." "Regarding the private good of each and not the public good of all," he continued, would "destroy the institutions of republicanism." England also believed that social institutions, especially the family and the church, were responsible for building popular virtue. As he put it:

Religion teaches man to love his neighbour as himself, and, consequently, to uphold himself those institutions which confer the most happiness on the whole—to transmit to others blessings which have been secured to him. And if it teaches him this—then indeed by religion we can bind a man stronger than by any bond this world exhibits; for his fate for eternity is bound up with his due discharge of his duty as a citizen.

Religion, therefore, was "the great conservative principle of republicanism." By teaching virtue, it kept the republic alive. Far from undermining American liberty, Catholicism, the true religion according to Bishop England, strengthened republicanism and staved off political decline.[18]
When viewed through a republican lens, political parties were dangerous to both virtue and liberty. In his July 4, 1826, address, Bishop England "particularly warned against the allurement of party feeling" and said that "the only feeling of the citizen should be for the welfare of his country." The good republican should not work politically to secure the "interest of an individual or a party," he argued. England envisioned a community of republican citizens devoted alike to virtue. In this, he differed little from South Carolina politicians such as William Smith and John C. Calhoun, who also idealized a republic of united, virtuous citizens. By including Catholics as part of the virtuous community, Bishop England assaulted nativist notions of Catholic disqualifications for republican inclusion. The bishop himself applied for citizenship in 1826 to prove his devotion to the American republic. The *Mercury*, describing the bishop's 1826 Independence Day address, noted that Bishop England was "one of the happiest illustrations of our free Constitution" and would soon "be a citizen equally concerned with the highest or the humblest, in sustaining the institutions and character of the country."[19]
The republican lens also celebrated the harmony of citizens. Bishop England publicized his affirmation of republicanism and demand for inclusion by building alliances with a diverse group of citizens to achieve shared political and social goals. In this way, Catholics would work with their fellow citizens toward common republican purposes. During the early phase of the nullification crisis, Bishop England utilized this approach to advocate for Catholic Emancipation in Ireland, a cause long dear to him.

The major political issue in Ireland after the Acts of Union in 1800 (which united the Kingdom of Great Britain and the Kingdom of Ireland in January 1801) was Catholic Emancipation. British penal laws excluded Catholics from Parliament and restricted Catholic social activities, particularly in education.[20] For thirty years Irish Catholics negotiated with various British politicians to secure permanent relief from the penal laws. Emancipation was finally achieved in 1829 after Irish activists, led by Daniel O'Connell, built a massive popular movement in Ireland to pressure Parliament.[21]

In his support for Catholic Emancipation in Ireland, Bishop England hoped to demonstrate the republican credentials of the Catholic community of his diocese while building close relationships with important southern politicians. This tactic, he hoped, could build affinity between Catholics and southerners. For example, on March 19, 1827, England participated in the formation of a voluntary association, "the friends of civil and religious liberty, residing in the city of Augusta."[22] By 1828 similar organizations had sprung up in Savannah and Charleston, and Bishop England devoted most of his energies to the Charleston chapter. The September 20, 1828, edition of the *Miscellany* announced an upcoming organizational meeting of the society. "We find the genuine spirit of Carolinian liberality in full vigor regarding the state of Ireland," the article started. The intendant (mayor) of Charleston, John Gadsden, had agreed to preside over the meeting, which was "to be conducted not by Irishmen, but by a host of native talent, liberality and honor." The paper noted that "the descendants of the exiled Huguenots" would be "advocating the cause of Catholics." This was "the true mode of crushing bigotry."[23]

The meeting occurred at City Hall in Charleston on September 22. After Bishop England greeted the distinguished group, those assembled elected a committee of fifteen to steer the association. These included prominent Charleston businessmen and politicians such as William Drayton, Alfred Huger, Hugh Legare, and James Petigru. The bishop read a set of resolutions that stated in part, "Our sympathy for the Roman Catholics of Ireland is chiefly excited by their adherence to the great principle, to which we are ourselves so firmly attached[,] . . . that principle which gives no civil ascendency to any man for his religious profession, and imposes no civil degradation upon any man, because of his peaceably following the dictates of conscience." He then read the official address of the organization. He declared that many of those who were assembled had experienced the "bitterness of persecution" but that they had also experienced the "blessings of that Religious Freedom which South Carolina so advantageously maintains." Thus the group could appreciate the importance of Catholic Emancipation.[24] After the initial meeting, the Charleston chapter of the Friends of Civil and Religious Liberty (renamed the Friends of Ireland) met frequently and the *Miscellany* regularly published the minutes of their meetings.

Above all, the religious diversity of membership in the Friends of Ireland helped achieve Bishop England's political goals. Article 2 of the organization's constitution stated, "Any person of whatever national, political or religious denomination, may be a member of the Association."[25] The *Miscellany* detailed the reality of this provision. For example, U.S. Senator Robert Y. Hayne sent a letter to Bishop England pledging his support for the Friends of Ireland.[26] Senator Hayne's brother, Col. A. P. Hayne, who had served under Andrew Jackson at the Battle of New Orleans, announced his support as well.[27] Neither was Catholic. On November 29, 1828, the *Miscellany* published a letter of support from Solomon Levy, a Charleston Jew, who appreciated O'Connell's attempts to remove political restrictions on Jews in England.[28] The Friends of Ireland also published an appeal for aid in French on December 6, 1828, hoping to solicit support from French-speaking citizens of Charleston, many of whom had been refugees from Haiti.[29] Other supporters included Henry L. Pinckney, editor of the *Charleston Mercury*, a radical states' rights paper, and anonymous donors listed as "a Presbyterian, born North of Ireland" and a "Unitarian of Charleston."[30] Bishop England even published a poem celebrating Irish freedom by the young Carolina poet, soon to become the most famous southern writer of the antebellum period, William Gilmore Simms.[31] The Friends of Ireland successfully united Charleston citizens in a cause favorable to Catholics, demonstrating Catholics were important members of the community.

Bishop England celebrated the success of the organization during the final meeting of the Friends of Ireland on June 4, 1829. In his opening remarks, the bishop thanked the "liberal Protestants of Ireland" for their support as well as the Friends of Ireland associations in the United States. He noted that the Americans had demonstrated a powerful republican principle: united effort can bring success. The early Irish movements for emancipation had been fraught with factionalism and strife. But, England noted, "when they learned to make and to receive mutual concessions without the dereliction of principle, when they placed confidence in each other, they became powerful in their union and they who previously despised and oppressed them became their suitors and their friends." "Public opinion," informed by a unified movement, assisted in turning the tide. In particular, the bishop extended his gratitude "to the Protestant friends" who had aided him in the Charleston organization. He insisted that the members should "respect the feelings of their fellow citizens who had differed from them upon the important topic which had engaged their attention, and always to bear in mind what they owed to the honor of the land of their birth, and the rights and liberties of the land of their adoption." With that the Friends of Ireland dissolved.[32] The organization had been a great success for Bishop England's plans for Charleston Catholics. He had shown that Catholics were good republican citizens who could unite on the side of liberty with non-Catholics. He hoped to capitalize on the goodwill that had been created by the brief but effective movement.

Unfortunately, the increasing political agitation caused by the nullification crisis threatened to overturn the success of Bishop England's strategy. The bishop had wanted a united community to make it easier for Catholics to coexist peacefully with the Protestant majority. Thus he had tried to avoid party politics. But nullification brought passionate political divisions to the fore. At first, England seemed to argue that because nullification involved intricate theories of constitutional interpretation, not morality or nativism, it did not threaten Charleston Catholics. Thus during the early stages of the crisis, he chose a politics of loyalty, supporting publicly those with whom he had formed good relationships during the Friends of Ireland movement rather than taking sides on the issues at hand.

Bishop England also displayed his loyalty by defending Robert Hayne. In March 1830 England commented on the Webster-Hayne debate in a nonpolitical fashion. The *Miscellany* printed a two-paragraph chastisement of Webster for misrepresenting the Catholic doctrine of indulgences during one of his speeches against Hayne. Webster had said, "Sir, if at this day any one feels the sin of Federalism lying heavy at his conscience, he can easily obtain remission. He may even have an indulgence if he is desirous of repeating the same transgression." Bishop England corrected Webster's faulty understanding of indulgences and then concluded, "It is below the dignity of a man of such a grade of intellect, and so extensive a range of information to sanction with his name a calumnious imputation."[33] The bishop insisted that he was making no comment on the political issues in the debate. But, in Charleston, an attack on Daniel Webster signaled sympathy for Hayne.

Other Catholics also criticized Webster's remarks, but some saw the bishop's criticisms as veiled Catholic support for Hayne. For example, the *Miscellany* published a letter from the *Baltimore Republican* attacking Webster's comment on indulgences.[34] A week later the *Miscellany* contained a letter to the editor of the *Baltimore Republican* claiming that Catholic criticism of Webster was excessive and implied wrongly that Webster was anti-Catholic. Politically, such a charge would turn Catholics away from Webster. The writer then turned the tables and accused Hayne of making anti-Catholic remarks.

The *Miscellany* responded by denying interference in political questions and reaffirming Catholic loyalty to South Carolina. The paper stated, "We have political opinions which agree with some held by Mr. Webster and others in accordance with those held by General Hayne, but we respect each of the eloquent and learned senators too highly to sit down contented with the injury that either might do to our religion." It did not state its specific political position but claimed concern only with religion. It noted, however, that Hayne and Bishop England "sincerely esteem each other." Hayne, who had supported the Friends of Ireland, had recommended Bishop England for the position of "chaplain to the Brigade which General Hayne then commanded." In addition, Hayne and Gov. James Hamilton of South Carolina had invited Bishop England "to preach in the Hall of Representatives." The paper defended Hayne as a man of "uniform steady and conspicuous liberality" in "his public and private conduct." It concluded, "If at any time it became fashionable in South Carolina to wage a private but an active warfare against catholics; Mr. Hayne's spirit was too high and his soul too honest to be drawn into the confederacy."[35] Thus the *Miscellany* defended Hayne's public reputation—a significant gesture in a political culture in which honor played an important role—without necessarily endorsing his policies.

This demonstrated Catholics were loyal South Carolinians without expressing overt sympathy for Hayne's message.

After the Webster-Hayne debate, political parties began to form in South Carolina, to the consternation of republicans like Bishop England. In July 1830 many Calhoun supporters met in Charleston to argue about nullification. At this point, men who were Bishop England's good friends and who had participated in the Friends of Ireland Association separated politically. In addition, Charleston Catholics divided over the issue.[36] By October, nullifiers and unionists battled in the state legislative elections. As William Freehling noted, 1830 brought a two-party system to the state. In Charleston, the unionists held the city government, but party competition increased in 1831. Unionists had hoped that the U.S. Congress would offer tariff relief during the spring legislative session but were disappointed, as might be expected. Congress's failure to reduce the tariff encouraged the nullifiers' political activities. Nullifiers formed the States' Rights and Free Trade Association in July and worked to spread it across the state in preparation for fall elections. The unionists failed to match the organizational efforts of their rivals.[37]

As nullifiers became more outspoken and aggressive, Bishop England, a unionist, wanted to reveal his position without exposing Catholics to partisan sniping. By September 1831, Bishop England became more worried about the divisiveness of the partisan politics that had overtaken the state. He decided to print a lengthy lecture in the *Miscellany* on the duties of a republican citizen in regard to voting. He urged unity around republican principles, thus reinforcing the requirements of the Jeffersonian view of the Union.

Bishop England began by casting the morality of citizenship in secular, republican terms. During the city elections of 1830 the unionists had won control of city government by a razor-thin margin.[38] Rumors of political corruption were rampant, which greatly bothered Bishop England. He stressed that he did not address his flock in these matters with a special religious authority: "I neither possess nor do I claim, nor ought you to concede to me, either as your pastor, or as your fellow-citizen, any greater power in this respect, than what I derive from the constitutions and laws of this state and of the United States." He then lamented the "party spirit" that had "unfortunately divided" the state.[39] He noted that Catholics should keep "altogether aloof from the intrigues, the cabals, the allurements, the promises, the expectations, and the other corrupting inducements which undoubtedly . . . exist at present among us."[40] He especially asked Catholics to reject the partisan feelings that led to demonizing the opposition and justifying acts of injustice. Such political corruption, he argued, rejected the moral duties of citizenship and divided the community, destroying the possibility of a united, virtuous republic. In addition, England counseled his flock, "a large portion" of which were "adopted citizens" from Ireland, to vote "solely as a Carolinian: as an American." In this he rejected attempts by parties to view Irish Catholics as a foreign ethnic voting bloc. Rather, he upheld the ideal of independent, equal, free republican citizens.[41]

Bishop England did not allow his emphasis on loyalty and accommodation to prevent him from speaking as a pastor to souls. He first insisted that there was "nothing in the present contest which directly or indirectly affects, either our faith, our discipline or our religious freedom." Thus he claimed to resist the urge "to enlist" his flock's "religious feelings on either one side or the other." But then the bishop turned from secular republicanism to scripture to warn about the possible moral pitfalls of nullification. He recognized, citing St. Paul in Romans, that Christians were "bound to adhere to" the legitimate governmental authority. He understood that the political question at stake in South Carolina was "whether our general government has acted unconstitutionally: and if so, whether either our state government or the state itself has the power to use a certain process to restrain the usurpation." These could be moral questions because of the allegiance owed by the Christian citizen.[42]

England noted that there was "another question in which morality and religion are also deeply concerned": secession.[43] Radical nullifiers, often invoking the American Revolution as precedent, had argued that if the federal government would not accept nullification, secession would be the only option to preserve liberty.[44] Even the Old Republicans, who usually rejected nullification, accepted the possibility of secession.[45] Bishop England, like other unionists, recognized the seriousness of the question. Unionists typically appealed to pragmatism when warning that secession would lead to bloodshed and the loss of public happiness. But here Bishop England raised an argument drawn from Revelation, something unique to Christians. He implied that because secession affected the question of a citizen's allegiance to government, his Catholic flock should consider the Christian faith when deciding how to vote. England counseled his flock to moderation, noting that "these questions perplex the minds of the wisest statesmen."[46] Still, the bishop's strategy appealed to both the republican ideals of the community and to his religious commitments.

After the unionists lost in the Charleston city elections in September 1831, Bishop England wrote in the *Miscellany*, "I am no advocate for the notion of *nullification*," thus breaking his public silence on the issue and jeopardizing his politics of loyalty.[47] The threat of renewed nativism occasioned the bishop's comments. In July 1831 a Protestant paper, the *Southern Religious Telegraph*, published "The Republic in Danger," warning of several threats to the republic: intemperance, Catholics, gambling, and Sabbath breaking. The paper, placing Catholics outside of the republican community, urged politicians to solve these problems. In July Bishop England responded to the nativists in a series of twelve letters. In the ninth and tenth letters, published in September after nullifier victories in the city elections, England both announced his rejection of nullification and offered his interpretation of the U.S. Constitution. While he seemed to alter his approach to politics by taking sides publicly on nullification, he reaffirmed his acceptance of a Jeffersonian interpretation of the Constitution to assure his neighbors, the non-Catholic majority, that he understood their sentiments.

In his letter published on September 17, 1831, Bishop England wrote, "The governments under which our affairs are administered derive their powers from conventions of the people, in which alone the sovereignty, properly and strictly speaking, resides." John C. Calhoun constantly stressed this very point. The conventions, the bishop noted,

have expressed the popular will in written constitutions; the legislatures derive their powers from the people, through those constitutions, and only to their extent: in many of them are to be found declarations of rights, in others of them restraining clauses and principles are found, and in some of our constitutions a combination of both exists; and where the legislative power is thus restrained by the popular will, any effort to violate, or to evade the restraint, would be an act of palpable usurpation.

Based on these principles, the bishop also rejected Protestant attempts to use the power of the U.S. government to establish certain temperance and

Sabbatarian laws. Their attempts rested on the general welfare clause of article I, section 8, of the Constitution, the "elastic clause" condemned by South Carolina republicans. "The broad construction of general welfare," he maintained, "is one which no good republican can admit." Broad construction would destroy any checks on government and institute a tyranny by allowing government to exercise powers not delegated to it. Even though he rejected nullification in the letter, the bishop assured his audience that he, like many of his non-Catholic fellow citizens, supported a Jeffersonian interpretation of the Constitution. In addition, by rejecting Protestant attempts to use government to forward a religious agenda, he assured Americans that Catholics would eschew using government to promote their own religious commitments.[48]

In the letters reponding to the "Republic in Danger," Bishop England tried to convince his South Carolina audience that Catholics in the state were no threat to the political order, regardless of his position on nullification. In this way, he continued to stress Catholic loyalty to the republican political culture of the state. His ability to use the constitutional language of his non-Catholic neighbors as well as his stance against the mixture of Protestantism and politics demonstrated that he was no threat to republican institutions. In fact, his strategy claimed a place for Catholics within the state as good neighbors.

Bishop England realized there were difficulties with his position. He wrote privately to his friend, clergyman Simon Bruté, in October 1831:

I am attached to the American Constitution, but I am not blind to its great imperfections nor am I reckless of the inordinate ambition & gross corruption which I fear will at an early period produce its ruin. I do not think our Confederation is likely to last a great many centuries. But my duty is whilst I live under it to live according to its principles.[49]

But many Americans, including his neighbors and his flock, disputed what these principles demanded, exacerbating his problem. The acrimony of the nullification debates made England's hope for a united, virtuous, republican citizenry seem like a hopeless dream. During the crisis, South Carolina, to paraphrase the states' rights radical Thomas Cooper, had calculated the value of the Union.[50] The nullifiers' intransigence had put the state on a collision course with the federal government. Bishop England felt pressured to articulate his opposition, knowing that his stance might alienate some of his former allies. Thus England's politics of loyalty had refuted nativist charges of Catholic incompatibility with republicanism by uniting Catholics with their fellow citizens in common causes. But loyalty had unintended implications. The bishop, by identifying closely with his non-Catholic neighbors, had made their dangerous fights and problems—problems that did not relate directly to his articulated religious mission (see ch. 2)—his own. In this way, Catholicism in South Carolina became tied to the political future of the state.

Bishop England missed the heat of the battles when, in December 1832, the people of South Carolina, in convention, nullified the tariffs of 1828 and 1832 and dared President Jackson to stop them. In July 1832, he sailed for Europe and did not return for fifteen months. Then, between 1834 and 1836, he spent much of his time outside of his diocese attempting to negotiate a concordat between the papacy and the Haitian government, which previously had not allowed the Catholic Church to operate freely.[51] The *Miscellany* reported news of the party maneuverings regarding nullification but refrained from editorializing about the situation.[52] In 1837, Bishop England wrote the Pastoral Letter after the Third Provincial Council of Baltimore, a gathering of the bishops of the country to discuss the condition of the church. In it he urged a renewal of zeal regarding religious duties and, as the historian Michael Pasquier has argued, hoped that Catholics would "disengage" somewhat from politics.[53] Disengagement, however, would not last for long.

American historians have usually explained the crisis of the Union during the 1850s as the result of agitation on the slavery issue. But the European Revolutions of 1848 also significantly colored American Catholic understandings of politics in the decade before the Civil War.[54] The European revolutions began in France in February 1848, just after news reached Washington that the Treaty of Guadalupe Hidalgo had been signed with Mexico.[55] The acquisition of millions of acres of new territory in the Southwest exacerbated tensions over the future of slavery in the country while the European revolutions, particularly those in Italy that displaced Pope Pius IX from the Vatican, led many American Catholics to fear that revolutionary radicalism would spread to American politics at their expense. In South Carolina, Catholic leaders, dreading political radicalism

and nativism, constructed an antiradical alliance with conservative southerners, worried about the future of slavery, to resist the Know Nothings
and the Republican Party of the North. When the secession crisis came
in December 1860, South Carolina Catholic leaders followed the logic of
their alliance and embraced the breakup of the Union.

In 1848, political turmoil seemed to erupt everywhere in Europe.
France, the German states, Italy, and the Hapsburg Empire, as well as
peripheral regimes such as Poland and Ireland, witnessed political unrest.
Liberal nationalists, and in lesser numbers socialists, demanded new free-
doms and rights from conservative governments. In Italy, nationalists
wished to drive the Austrians out of the north and the House of Bourbon
out of the south. They had hoped that the new pope, Pius IX, who had a
reputation for liberal sympathies, would support their cause. But when
Pius refused to support war on Austria, the liberals turned on him. On
November 15, radicals assassinated Pius's prime minister, Count Rossi.
On November 24, fearing for his life, the pope fled Rome. By February 9,
1849, Italian radicals had declared Rome a republic. At this point, Peter
D'Agostino notes, "the Republic declared the end of the pope's temporal
power, secularized Church property, and instituted freedom of worship."
Pius responded on February 18 by asking France, Austria, Naples, and
Spain to intervene to restore his rule of the city.[56]

Initially, popular opinion in the United States generally supported the
Revolutions of 1848, with one important exception: Catholics. American liberals believed that the revolutions revealed the progress of liberty
around the globe while anti-Catholics, especially after Pius IX fled Rome
at the end of 1848, celebrated the revolutionary attacks on the papacy. For
example, New York newspapers reported extensively on the revolutions.
Margaret Fuller, the Transcendentalist intellectual, reported from Europe for Horace Greeley's *New York Tribune* with what Larry Reynolds
calls "unbounded enthusiasm" for the revolutionaries' cause.[57] In contrast,
the flight of Pius IX and the revolutionary violence of the summer and fall
of 1848 worried many American Catholics. While Fuller's reports in the
Tribune defended the assassination of Count Rossi and portrayed the
Roman Republic as a peaceful, tolerant regime, Catholic opinion, led by
Archbishop John Hughes of New York and Orestes Brownson, counter-
attacked. In January 1849 Hughes preached a sermon in New York on the
sufferings of Pius IX at the hands of radical revolutionaries.[58] Brownson,

in the pages of *Brownson's Quarterly Review*, attacked the revolutions as well. He affirmed that democracy could be a good form of government if it respected law and the social order but said that he preferred "any thing to Red Republicanism." Brownson also feared the spirit of the revolutions was invading the United States. "Wild and reckless fanaticism is at work with our institutions, undermining law, and preparing the way for anarchy and despotism," he wrote.[59] Both Hughes and Brownson, who enjoyed national reputations thanks to the explosion in Catholic publishing during the late 1840s that brought their names and words to Catholics throughout the country, warned of the destructive nature of modern revolutions and attacked the revolutions' defenders as violent, dangerous people who assaulted all who questioned them.[60]

In South Carolina, the *United States Catholic Miscellany* followed the lead of northern Catholics Hughes and Brownson in denouncing the Revolutions of 1848. In a February 24, 1849, editorial, the *Miscellany* denounced Italian revolutionaries as threatening social order and peace. Modernity was advancing with "railroad speed to the utter dissolution of society, and with it the ruin of every thing worth living for," the editor wrote. Modern revolutionaries "use the sacred name of liberty solely for the destruction of order." The paper did not lament the fate of European tyrants overthrown by the revolutions but believed that the revolutionaries were "miscreants" and "fools whose aim is licentiousness not liberty." By persecuting the pope, the revolutionaries attacked the friend of true liberty. The editorial admitted that the Papal States were not essential either to the Catholic religion or to the papacy itself. Still, it praised Catholics who fought to defend the pope "against every invader and every rebel."[61]

The *Miscellany* also published several articles that described various crimes of European revolutionaries and insisted that Catholics could not support liberal aims. The August 4 edition of the paper reprinted a lengthy piece from the *Catholic Telegraph* of Cincinnati that noted that the European revolutionaries had demanded that Catholics support them. "We Catholics must kneel at no altar but a democratic one, if we wish to please them," the writer complained. "We must renounce our religion to secure their favour." Catholics, however, the writer asserted, should reject "red-republicanism" based both on the conduct and on the stated beliefs of republicans. The article also detailed cases of plunder in

Rome where republicans pilfered valuable objects from churches and sold them. They used assassins, killed priests, drove nuns "from their Convents," and desired to overthrow religion itself. The article then quoted Pierre-Joseph Proudhon, leader of the "red-Republicans" in France, on his atheism. Proudhon, the paper stated, called "Property *theft* and Capital a *nuisance.*" Like other republicans, Proudhon would "dissolve society, abolish individual freedom, destroy domestic rights, eradicate the Christian Faith and dethrone the Almighty God."[62] Stories of republican excesses flooded the *Miscellany.* The paper considered the leading republicans no better than common thieves and murderers.[63] By January 1850, however, the paper assured its readers that in condemning European republicanism, it was not condemning American republicanism, which preserved social order and ruled by law.[64]

The failure of the revolutions and the vocal opposition to revolutionary aims by Catholics enraged liberals. On February 13, 1850, Margaret Fuller, in her last dispatch to the *New York Tribune*, declared war on Catholicism. She warned that the "barbarities of reaction" had taken over Italy. They would ravish the land until "the wishes of Heaven shall waft a fire that will burn down all, root and branch, and prepare the earth for an entirely new culture." Fuller promised that the "next revolution, here and elsewhere, will be radical." "Not only Jesuitism must go," she thundered, "but the Roman Catholic religion must go." She concluded, "The Pope cannot retain even his spiritual power. The influence of the clergy is too perverting, too foreign to every hope of advancement and health."[65] In 1851 the *Tribune* continued to attack Archbishop John Hughes and the Catholic newspapers of the city for their illiberal attitudes, using their responses to the Revolutions of 1848 to question their commitment to religious freedom and a free press.[66]

The antipathy between liberals and the church placed Catholics in a dangerous place. Fuller and the *Tribune* exemplified the revolutionary mind-set that the *Miscellany* and other Catholic papers around the country had feared. It seemed clear that revolutionaries sought to destroy the social order and the Catholic Church. When Pope Pius IX returned to Rome in the early summer of 1850, Catholic papers warned that revolutionary assassins would threaten his peace.[67] But by invoking their own moral principles to oppose the revolutions, Catholics, in the eyes of liberals, identified themselves as enemies of modern progress.

The man who would be most responsible for shaping the public Catholic response in South Carolina to the secession crisis of 1860, Fr. James Corcoran, assumed editorial responsibilities of the *Miscellany* on July 20, 1850. Born in South Carolina to Irish immigrants, Corcoran had been educated by Bishop John England and then completed his seminary training in Rome. He was a devoted southern conservative, well read and well versed in southern constitutionalism. The Revolutions of 1848 energized him. Corcoran produced a string of editorials on radicalism and liberalism (he often used the words interchangeably) and the Revolutions of 1848 that revealed the lens that he would employ during the decade to interpret political events. Corcoran was neither subtle nor scholarly in his editorials.[68] He predicted that radicalism had found its home in the United States in the North and would, if unchecked, destroy the American constitutional order.[69]

Corcoran feared that the American press, particularly in the North, promoted radicalism in its coverage of the Revolutions of 1848. He asserted that Americans welcomed news of the revolutions because they "love liberty." But Americans "are not philosophers" and understood little about "the institutions and requirements of European society," he observed. The press should lead by explaining complex situations and correcting "popular errors." Instead, American editors aped the European liberal press by praising socialism and elevating "knaves and assassins to the rank of patriots and godlike heroes."[70] Corcoran also warned that European revolutionaries were migrating to the United States, where they were feted by the northern press. American newspaper editors refused to reveal the aim of the radicals. Corcoran bellowed, "*They thirst for blood. They long for the reign of the guillotine.*" Overall, Corcoran found hypocrisy at the center of radicalism. Northern editors like Horace Greeley, Corcoran claimed, condemned Pius IX while covering up the crimes of radicals and justifying violence against those they deemed tyrants. The Greeleys of the country celebrated radicals who profess that "all men are brothers, but practically [exclude] all from the brotherhood save the black slaves of the South, and the Red Republicans of Europe." Liberals preached liberty for themselves and their favored groups while justifying violence and theft against conservatives.[71]

Corcoran believed that European radicals' notions of liberty would produce disastrous results if applied to the United States. In a September

28 editorial Corcoran noted that "in the social and civil state there can be no absolute liberty." Those who made that a goal were only cloaking "the most diabolical and hideous licentiousness." "All liberty," he continued, "must be tempered: in the natural man by reason, in the social and civil man by law." Corcoran believed that the "perfection of political liberty consists in the maximum of individual freedom, tempered with the minimum of controlling law." But he rejected the existence of an "absolute standard" that could judge the limit. An abstract, universal standard would result in a situation in which the "Hottentot, or the subject of the King of Dahomey, might justly demand the same privileges, that the American citizen now considers his special birthright." He also perceived that liberalism would attack any restraint on individual will. Under liberalism, he predicted, "the victim of public justice would mount the scaffold with the conscience of a martyr."[72] Ten years later, John Brown would fulfill Corcoran's prediction.

Like other southerners, Father Corcoran believed that the North was the locus of American radicalism. He linked the increase in mob violence and disregard for constitutional limits on power to the revolutionary example of 1848. In an October 12, 1850, editorial, he argued that the growth of radicalism in America obliterated "daily that love and reverence for the Law and Constitution, which were once the proudest boast of American citizens." Radicals endorsed "mob-law," the immediate gratification of radical desire. He warned that mob law would punish whatever the mob and its leaders declared evil: "One day it may be the support of a virtuous candidate for office, the payment of due taxes, or the enforcement of legal decisions: the next it will be slave-holding, anti-socialism, or any other relic of conservative principles." He noted that "any one acquainted with the present state of Northern fanaticism, and the progress of Radical theories in that quarter" could perceive the danger that lay ahead for the South. Catholics should also beware. "By countenancing disorder and violation of law," Catholics "are guilty of a grievous sin against the precepts of their religion." Catholics needed to realize that the Constitution was the "safeguard" of the church in the United States. Catholics would be safe "as long as law and order hold their sway." But if "our Northern fanatics" succeeded in destroying constitutional restraints, Catholics would be victimized by violent mobs.[73]

The visit of the Hungarian revolutionary Lajos Kossuth became the first major national event to evoke sustained national commentary on the legacy of the Revolutions of 1848. Involved in the revolt against Austria, Kossuth eventually fled to the Ottoman Empire as his forces faced a united Russian and Austrian opposition. In 1851 he asked to travel to the United States. As the historian Michael Holt notes, Kossuth's arrival in New York in December 1851 "ignited almost unprecedented excitement and adulation from celebrity-worshipping Americans."[74] Thousands crowded the streets to get a glimpse of Kossuth. Scholars have pointed out that Kossuth's reputations as a revolutionary and an anti-Catholic played heavily in his reception.[75] Kossuth sought U.S. support for his fight against Austria and publicly denounced the American tradition of nonintervention in foreign affairs. But many Americans did not appreciate Kossuth's hectoring. As the scholar John Komlos wrote, "Kossuth's clever, but dogmatical, pronouncements produced a strong reaction against his mission." The two groups that most strongly opposed Kossuth were southerners and Catholics. Southern Congressmen overwhelmingly voted against measures to offer encouragement and aid to Kossuth. Catholics, particularly Archbishop Hughes in New York and Orestes Brownson, denounced Kossuth as a dangerous revolutionary. Komlos noted that the Catholic dislike focused on Kossuth's "well-known collaboration with Mazzini," the Italian revolutionary.[76] Irish Americans, particularly Catholics, disliked Kossuth because earlier in 1851 he had stopped in London and refused to support the Irish cause.

Even before Kossuth arrived in the United States, Corcoran attacked him vigorously, indicating that the Hungarian was part of a plot to encourage the development of European revolutionary radicalism in the United States. In a November 8, 1851, editorial, Corcoran noted that Kossuth was on his way across the Atlantic in order to "gather friends for starting another war in Hungary." Kossuth, he promised, would never settle in the United States because he "would be at too great a distance to carry out his revolutionary plans in Europe." Corcoran predicted that radicals in New York would lavish Kossuth with adulation when he arrived. The radicals wished "to link the constitutional, law-observing Republicanism of America, with the law-destroying Socialistic, Red-republican, Liberalism of Europe." Corcoran also noted that radicals had already "made no small progress at the North," as evidenced by "Free

Soilism, Abolitionism, Fourierism, and many other *isms*" that were celebrated in the region.[77] In a December 20, 1851, editorial Corcoran
gloated that Kossuth's reception in New York City had proven him correct. Kossuth, a "foreign agitator," wished "to show us that the advice
given and the rules laid down by Washington, Jefferson, and other
founders of our government" were "to be cast aside as the swaddling
clothes and bib and tucker of our infancy." In particular, Corcoran
scorned Kossuth's audacity and praised Catholic papers in the country
for opposing him.[78]

Again, in January 1852, Corcoran warned South Carolinians that
Kossuth's principles would produce disorder in the United States. On
January 3 Corcoran repeated his earlier warnings about that "Apostle of
disorder and revolt." He warned that Kossuth's advice to the United
States was inimical to its traditions. Scheming politicians would embrace
Kossuth's message so that they could distract the population with foreign exploits while they usurped liberty domestically. Southerners, who
had an "unfeigned reverence for the traditions of the past," needed to
stop patronizing "that spirit of radicalism" that Kossuth represented.
Soon, "the whirlwind of trouble and disorder, which alone can be reaped
from the sowing of windy theories amongst ignorant and wicked masses
of men," would sweep through the South. When that happened,
Corcoran predicted, disaster would follow.[79]

A few weeks later Corcoran ridiculed Kossuth's invocation of states'
rights during his tour as "the Devil quoting Scripture." Corcoran pointed
out that European radicals hated the decentralized government that
states' rights protected. The revolutionaries in Switzerland in 1848 tried
"to break up the single republics of Cantons, which, like our own States,
formed one confederation, to destroy their nationality, abolish the constitution, and in its place introduce one consolidated central despotism,
in which everything is controlled by the will, and, when necessary, by
the bayonets of the General Government." Corcoran quipped, "We
should as well like to hear Proudhon defending the rights of Property, or
Mazzini declaiming against Assassination." More ominously, he predicted that American radicalism would produce the same results as its
European parent.[80]

Although the Revolutions of 1848 were initially praised by many southerners, by 1852 a growing segment of the region had turned against

them. So Corcoran's editorials tapped into southerners' growing discontent with the perceived influence of European radicalism in the United States, especially as it related to slavery. On February 17, 1852, the *Miscellany* reprinted an editorial from the *Charleston Mercury* condemning Kossuth and radicalism in terms very similar to Corcoran's. The *Mercury* noted that Louis Napoleon had become the emperor of France, putting a final end to the republic. The paper believed that Napoleon III was better than the anarchy of radical rule. "But as conservators, anti-communists, and, above all, Southerners," it maintained, "we have a deep interest in the career of this man—He has dealt a fearful blow to the best allies of fanaticism at the North." The *Mercury* insisted that "socialism, abolitionism, and red-republicanism, are but different developments of the same infernal spirit." As proof, the paper exhibited Kossuth. On his way to the United States, the red republicans of Marseilles had greeted him in the same "hearty manner" as the "free soil and free negroes" of New York did. Kossuth represented those who believed that "law, time-honored customs, property, all must yield before the progress of democracy." Radicals destroyed any government they deemed an imperfect form of "ideal republicanism." This utopianism brought chaos, inviting tyranny to bring order. Such was the lesson of France's recent history.[81]

In the July 1852 edition of the *Southern Quarterly Review*, William Gilmore Simms attacked Kossuth for his arrogance as well. Abandoning the tradition of nonintervention would bring disaster, Simms predicted. "The right of intervention is an aggressive principle." Intervention "furnishes" to ambitious politicians "the opportunity or pretense for invasion and conquest." Kossuth grounded his appeal in his revolutionary principles of popular government, but Simms would have none of it: "No power is more exacting than a popular government—none more relentless in the exercise of power or remorseless in oppression." Thus Simms counseled southerners to demonstrate a good example to the world rather than revolutionize their politics.[82] Though different in their rhetoric, both the *Mercury* and Simms resisted Kossuth for trying to radically change the United States.

Conversely, Catholic opposition to revolutionaries like Kossuth risked reinforcing the idea that Catholics opposed republican governments and were thus un-American. Catholic opposition to the Italian revolutions and unification "separated Catholics from their American neighbors,"

Peter D'Agostino notes. "By contrast," he adds, "American liberals and Protestants celebrated the unification of Italy as a progressive realization of liberal and millennial hopes."[83] One way to discourage this opinion was for Catholics to gain non-Catholic political allies who could vouch for their loyalty. Bishop England had done just that with his Friends of Ireland movement. Now southern opposition to Kossuth offered Catholics an opportunity to form another political alliance.

By the mid-1850s, some South Carolinians repeated Corcoran's themes in other contexts, suggesting a common political interest. The potential threat of northern and foreign radicalism proved useful to South Carolina politicians in Congress during the 1854 debates over the Kansas-Nebraska Act. Senator A. P. Butler, for example, harped on northern radicalism in a February 24, 1854, speech in the U.S. Senate. Attacking northern abolitionists, Butler compared them to the radicals of the French Revolution. If abolitionists proclaimed the equality of whites and blacks, Butler claimed, "the horrors of the French Revolution, in all their frantic ferocity and cruelty, will be nothing compared to the consequences which must flow from such a state of things." Only radicals would enjoy such a situation, he held. During debate the next day, Butler attacked the "various *isms* at the North." He linked northern antislavery sentiment to other reform movements such as temperance, feminism, and female fashion fads, proclaiming that from "Abolitionism, to Maine-liquor-law-ism, to Strong-minded-woman-ism, Bloomerism, and all the *isms* which now pervade some portions of the North" none "infuse into the social system anything like a healthful action."[84] Ultimately, Butler predicted, northern radicalism would destroy the country. Butler certainly did not derive his ideas from Corcoran. Rather Corcoran adapted a certain contemporary conservative discourse to his own needs. The common message intimated a political affinity between Catholics and conservative southerners.

Throughout the remainder of the 1850s, the national and state political environments reinforced the Catholic-southern affinity. After the Kansas-Nebraska Act destroyed the Whig Party, the Know Nothings emerged to take their place. The Know Nothings, initially a secret society, seem to have originated in New York in the early 1850s from an organization called the Order of United Americans, one of many nativist groups protesting the social costs of massive immigration and the growing Catholic political presence.[85] In South Carolina, traditionally a one-party state, the Democratic Party had functioned as an independent entity, divorced from the national party. But by 1855 some Democrats in the state argued that South Carolina Democrats should integrate into the mainstream of the national Democratic Party.[86] In addition, the Know Nothings emerged in South Carolina in 1855. In April, a Know Nothing candidate won election as mayor of Columbia. Anti-Catholics organized in Charleston as well, using the *Charleston Evening News* as their mouthpiece.[87] In July, C. E. Kanapaux, Esq., a Catholic, ran for sheriff in Charleston against Col. J. E. Carew, a Protestant. The Know Nothings organized to campaign against Kanapaux. Before the election, therefore, Father Corcoran again promoted a Catholic-southern alliance.

The *Miscellany* used the familiar tactic in southern politics that the historian William Cooper has called the "politics of slavery" to indicate its southern sympathies.[88] The March 10, 1855, edition reprinted a story from a Columbia paper linking the Know Nothings in the North to abolitionism. Beyond the other issues that connected Know Nothings to each other, the story claimed, the "war against slavery" bound them together.[89] A few weeks later, the editor of the *Miscellany* noted that Sen. Henry Wilson from Massachusetts had been "attacked with apoplexy . . . whilst engaged in delivering an antislavery lecture." "It is very likely," the *Miscellany* opined, "that Mr. Wilson's lecture was not without its spice of anti-Popery. For how could a Know Nothing speak in public, *as such*, without dragging in this theme?" The *Miscellany* attributed the event to "God's providence" and noted that the famous anti-Catholic evangelical Lyman Beecher, who had helped to incite a mob that destroyed the Ursuline convent in Charlestown, Massachusetts, in 1834, had been "stricken with apoplexy in the middle of one of his no-Popery harangues."[90] In this case, the *Miscellany* used the same tactic against the Know Nothings as southern Democrats did, branding the party with the abolitionist label in order to drive away southern support.[91]

As the election for sheriff neared in Charleston, the *Miscellany* made its case for a Catholic-southern alliance against radicalism. In late June, the *Miscellany* reprinted the new Know Nothing platform that emerged from the party's national convention in Philadelphia. The paper also reprinted critiques of the platform from southern states' rights perspectives.[92] Southern papers accused the Know Nothings of advocating consolidated national government and a vigorous role for the federal government in economic affairs, a program similar to that of the defunct Whig Party.[93] By printing these articles, Charleston's Catholic newspaper implied that southern Democrats and Catholics shared a common enemy in the Know Nothings.

C. E. Kanapaux, the Catholic candidate for sheriff of Charleston, lost the election, receiving only 42 percent of the vote. Afterwards, in a lengthy editorial, the *Miscellany* denounced the Know Nothings for underhanded tactics. The paper acknowledged that Colonel Carew, the victor, was well respected and received support from many not aligned with the Know Nothings. But the "Know Nothing faction brought the religious question into the field and made it an issue of Catholic and Protestant." Know Nothing support for an immigrant over a native South Carolinian on the basis of religion—Carew was an Irish-born Protestant; Kanapaux was a native South Carolinian—made it clear to the *Miscellany* that anti-Catholicism rather than hostility to foreign immigration was most dear to their cause. Know Nothings used "all those implements that form an essential part of anti-Catholic warfare" in their attack on Kanapaux, especially "*forgery and falsehood*." They spread rumors that Fr. Patrick Lynch, administrator of the diocese, had preached a sermon of support for Kanapaux. They even claimed that the pope had sent Kanapaux money and that the Sisters of Our Lady of Mercy in Charleston had been raising campaign cash for him. Even Protestant ministers, the paper claimed, "went round to their flocks, and cautioned them against the horrible sin of voting for a Catholic."[94] It seemed in July 1855 that the Know Nothings in South Carolina were gaining ground. So Catholics would have to intensify their opposition.

In August 1855 South Carolina Know Nothings, emboldened by successes during the summer, planned to run candidates in the Charleston city elections in November, worrying both Catholics and Democrats. Many Democrats, fearing a strong, viable second party in the city and state, attacked nativism. The *Miscellany* joined the fray by criticizing Know Nothings for their views of the expanded authority of the state.

Catholics, tapping into southern fears of an expansive federal government, argued that Know Nothings gave the state too much control over religious and moral affairs. In the August 25, 1855, edition of the *Miscellany*, Father Corcoran reprinted a letter signed "A Protestant Citizen" from the *Charleston Mercury*, the leading states' rights paper. Corcoran wrote, "It is one of the clearest and most rational expositions of the case [against Know Nothings], that it has ever been our fortune to see from a Protestant pen." The crux of the letter concerned the Know Nothings' acceptance of a powerful liberal state. "A Protestant Citizen" set up a hypothetical dilemma to make his point. The state "proposes a law, or adopts a policy, involving a grave moral question for one of her citizens." Three men, a "Catholic, a Baptist, and a Deist[,] . . . have to determine upon their votes." Each discerns in his own way. The Catholic "consults his priest, the Baptist goes on his knees and communes directly with his God, the Deist refers the matter to his reason." Each citizen agrees that the law is immoral and that "they cannot, in conscience, obey." The law passes, and "the State punishes the disobedience in each." The state does not care, says the writer, "how they arrived at their conclusion." The Know Nothings, however, take the power of the state to a higher level. They condemn the Catholic for how he made his decision. "A Protestant Citizen" concludes, "In other words, this principle claims for the state the right to determine how moral truths shall be learned by its citizens, and it thus erects itself into the only and infallible church." The implication is that the state would then enforce its claims with religious zeal.[95]

Antinativist southerners agreed that religious freedom shielded citizens from the universal moral claims of a powerful, centralized state. In fact, "A Protestant Citizen" defended religious toleration as a limit on state authority. He noted that the "state does not profess to teach men their moral duties; it leaves them free to learn from God, through whatever teachers they may select." The Know Nothings want to punish citizens "for the selection of their teachers." By setting itself up as an arbiter of acceptable methods of religious teaching, the state places itself in judgment of religious claims. "A Protestant Citizen" contended that "if the State has the right to forbid this, because political questions are controlled by their moral elements, and therefore, it alone can decide upon the moral truth involved, we will be subject to a worse tyranny than the union of church and state; for the State, irresponsible, unreflecting, mastered by bad men, or government by selfish ones, will be the Church."[96]

In the context of this controversy, Father Corcoran assured South Carolinians that Catholics would be loyal. "Many Protestants," he predicted, "will discover that the Catholic religion not only *happens* to be always on the right, conservative side of all social questions, but is at the same time always an object of hatred and persecution to the wicked."

Know Nothings were no different from other persecutors. Corcoran's comments along with his decision to reprint the article from the *Mercury* were efforts to reach out to South Carolina Democrats who simultaneously were attacking Know Nothings in the state. South Carolina Protestants, he hinted, should see that Catholic Carolinians stood by them in the fight against abolitionism and the growth of state power.[97] Catholics were part of the southern community.

In the end, Corcoran's affinity for southern conservative Democrats paid off. The Know Nothings unsuccessfully ran a slate of candidates in the November 1855 city elections in Charleston. The defeat of the Know Nothing candidates and the public condemnations of nativism by prominent South Carolina politicians such as Lawrence Keitt indicated to Father Corcoran the success of his strategy.[98] South Carolina Catholics now had their southern Democratic neighbors as allies. During the 1856 presidential election, Corcoran reminded southerners of this Catholic loyalty. The Know Nothings ran Millard Fillmore, and the new sectional party, the Republicans, ran John Fremont. In an August 16, 1856, editorial, Corcoran noted that it was a "well-known fact that most of the prominent leaders of the Black-Republican party in several Northern States were elected on the double ground of Abolition and Anti-popery." For Republicans, he added, "Slavery and Popery . . . were the two cardinal evils of the Republic." Obviously, neither Catholics nor southerners could vote Republican. But Corcoran held that Catholicism posed other religious objections to the Republican agenda as well. He tied this to Catholic support for law and constitutionalism. Catholics, he maintained, were "the only religious body in the Union, who as such, are bound by the Constitution." Catholics rejected the lawless radicalism of red republicanism and its equivalent, abolitionism, in "Black-Republicanism." Corcoran believed that abolitionism disregarded constitutional limits and was thus "sinful."[99] Republicans, by coddling both nativists and abolitionists, were the new representatives of the European radicalism that had exploded in 1848. As the Know Nothings faded as a party after 1856, Republicans became the primary opposition to Democrats and picked up many of the nativist voters. The stage was now set for Corcoran's approach to secession in 1860.

The revival of the Italian unification movement in 1859 reinforced the lens through which Catholics in the United States viewed the politics of

1859–60. Italian liberal nationalists, led by Camilio Cavour, prime minister of Sardinia Piedmont, attacked Austria and annexed part of the
Papal States. In May 1860 Garibaldi and his thousand Redshirts, in the
presence of British naval vessels, invaded Sicily and took the island. By
August Garibaldi had landed on the Italian Peninsula and begun his
march north. In early September he took Naples. Cavour, fearing Garibaldi would next capture Rome and thus invite Austrian and French
military action, invaded the Papal States, claiming he was preserving
them from Garibaldi. By the end of September, Cavour's troops had de-
feated the papal army and annexed the rest of the Papal States. In November, Garibaldi and Victor Emmanuel II met and joined the conquered
Kingdom of the Two Sicilies to the much-expanded Sardinia Piedmont.
In March, Victor Emmanuel proclaimed the Italian Kingdom. Rome,
however, was still under papal control, thanks to French protection.[100]

American Catholics responded to the Italian ordeal of 1860 just as
they had done in 1849, with shows of sympathy for Pius IX and condemnations of European liberalism. As expected, the *Miscellany* supported
Pius IX and his claims to temporal authority over the Papal States. For
example, Corcoran insisted that the pope needed the Papal States "for the
proper exercise of his spiritual power." The states provided the pope with
the means to be "independent of all earthly powers." The pope, Corcoran
insisted, "must be either a sovereign or a subject." The "enemies of the
Church" knew this, "and that is the very reason why infidels and Atheists,
backed by the applause and funds of their Protestant friends, are doing
their utmost to destroy his temporal power."[101] The Diocese of Savannah
sent money to Pius IX in September 1860, and the Diocese of Charleston
followed in October.[102] Corcoran also printed expressions of sympathy
from Catholics elsewhere in the South. He ran statements from Catholics
in Mobile, Alabama, and Natchez, Mississippi. The Natchez paper,
Corcoran wrote, reported that "many Protestant sympathizers" had
signed a statement proclaiming that Italians operated under a "bastard
liberty" that cloaked "their schemes of infidelity and spoliation."[103] In his
April 15, 1860, editorial Corcoran noted the support from all over the
world for Pius IX. Everywhere Catholics mobilized their resources and
voiced their opposition to the liberal Italian regime. Corcoran concluded
by calling for southerners to recognize the moment: "If there is a people
in the world, who ought to know the difference between liberty and its

anarchical counterfeit, it is the people of the South, who have every opportunity to see it, not exactly among themselves, but across our immediate border."[104] The North, not Catholicism, was the threat.

In the case of Italian unification, Corcoran again equated northern
politics with European radicalism. Both proceeded in similar ways. In an
October 1, 1859, editorial, Corcoran insisted that Italian liberals achieved
their goals through intimidation, force, and robbery. Liberals in the Ro-
magna had confiscated church property and harassed Catholic clergy.
Liberals won their elections in the Papal States by stationing armed "free-
booters" at the ballot boxes to ensure compliant voters.[105] Italian radicals
displayed a lust for power that caused them to transgress all limits and
violate all traditional authority. Corcoran also connected John Brown's
October 16, 1859, raid on Harpers Ferry to northern and European radicalism. In a January 14, 1860, editorial, Corcoran responded to a story in
a Virginia Presbyterian newspaper that claimed that one of John Brown's
band had recently converted to Catholicism, thus implying Catholic sympathy for Brown's abolitionism. In response, Corcoran quoted seven
northern Presbyterian ministers who had supported John Brown. These
men had thus proclaimed "lying, stealing, house-breaking, arson, murder, treason *no sins at all*, but good and holy actions, deserving not only of
God's heavenly reward, but the endless gratitude and veneration of men."
As Corcoran pointed out, numerous Protestant clergy in the North had
declared Brown a martyr while the Catholic papers had condemned
Brown's actions.[106] On April 7, 1860, Corcoran also reprinted a story
from a Chicago newspaper about election day violence. Republicans, celebrating the election of their candidate, John Wentworth, as mayor, went
to a German Catholic neighborhood and hanged the parish priest in ef-
figy. The Republican mob then fought with the police. The *Miscellany*
multiplied stories such as these, drawing an equivalence between northern Republicans and European revolutionaries in their violence, disdain
for social order, and hatred for Catholicism.[107]

Finally, equating northern and European radicalism shaped Corcoran's presentation of Lincoln's election to the presidency. Given the
tremendous importance of Lincoln's election, it is stunning to note that
the majority of the November 10, 1860, issue of the *Miscellany* contained news about Italy. Only one small editorial predicted Lincoln's
election. Corcoran exclaimed, "Long years of menace, insult, outrage

and unconstitutional aggression have been at last, brought to a close by an event,—the election of a Black Republican President—which, though not yet officially announced, has reached the appalling degree of moral certainty." He hoped that political wisdom and the "sympathy of our sister commonwealths, the Sovereign States of the South," would allow South Carolinians to meet the crisis "with firm unwavering dignity."[108] Corcoran believed that the "Black Republicans" would act similarly to the European Republicans. Throughout the decade the paper had detailed continuous violations of law and political violence in Europe. Presumably, such situations would now repeat themselves in the United States. As Corcoran wrote in a December 1, 1860, editorial, "If we had amongst us some few dozen of Yankee traders, peddlars, agents, & c. banded together by secret oaths, for the purpose of creating disaffection and revolt; and should these men finding that the police laws of the state cripple their designs, invoke federal coercion or Northern raids of armed invaders on their behalf, South Carolina would occupy exactly the position of the Pope and of the King of Naples."[109] It was best, therefore, that South Carolina secede and avoid being ruled by those who, like the cutthroats of Europe, would satiate their lust for power at the expense of the South.

Corcoran was not the only American Catholic to draw on the Italian political situation for domestic political commentary. Taking the opposite interpretation, a Philadelphia Catholic newspaper compared South Carolina secessionists to radical revolutionaries like Garibaldi. Corcoran protested this characterization as "wanton, insulting assertion and nothing more." He insisted that the South's cause was conservative: "We are neither brigands nor professional revolutionists. We meditate neither the invasion nor the subversion of other sovereignties, but merely the maintenance of our own." Corcoran added that if the "Federal Government or our Northern neighbors" attempted to invade the state or blockade the Carolina coast, they would be "best entitled to the name of brigands and Garibaldists." Again, he noted that the South's cause was analogous to that of the pope.[110] The next week Corcoran furthered his complaint by invoking the example of John Brown. "Good Victor Hugo," he wrote, "most appropriately calls Garibaldi the John Brown of Italy." The South was in the same position as the Papal States in Italy, a victim of radical violence. For Corcoran the South shared the conservative cause with the pope, whereas northerners shared their radicalism with Garibaldi. If

Corcoran had known that Brown's band and supporters included several radical veterans of the 1848 revolutions, he could have made his argument even more forceful.[111] The Philadelphia paper responded a few weeks later, noting that it did not characterize all southerners as Garibaldians but only compared some southern extremists to those of revolutionary Europe.[112] It then noted that it supported the right of peaceful secession and abhorred the idea of war.[113] But the damage had been done. Catholics had divided publicly over politics, calling each other's religious loyalty into question.

At the same time, other northern Catholic papers attacked the South on theological grounds, denying the morality of secession. Corcoran responded by endorsing the southern conservative view of the Union as a means rather than an end in itself. He noted that one northern Catholic paper compared national union to the sacrament of matrimony, implying that secession was the equivalent of divorce and thus immoral. But Corcoran supported "a more worldly and business-like view of the matter." States, he insisted, formed a union to obtain the power to advance "their mutual interests." The Union, therefore, was only a means. If the Union failed to achieve its ends, the parties could dissolve the agreement and return to a separate existence. Corcoran believed that South Carolina had been wronged in the Union and thus secession was a proper, not immoral, remedy. As in a business partnership, if one or more of the parties breaks the agreement, the violated party is not obligated to remain in the partnership. Corcoran noted that the northern states had broken the agreement repeatedly during the 1850s, particularly in nullifying "by formal legislation, the Fugitive Slave-Law."[114] Northern radicalism, particularly on the slavery issue, had destroyed trust in constitutional solutions. Corcoran thus blended the Catholic critique of radicalism with southern concerns. From this perspective, secession was the remedy if the parties in the Union could not get along.

In response to northern Catholic criticism, Corcoran consistently associated the southern position with conservatism. For example, the *New York Freeman's Journal*, long a supporter of Archbishop Hughes and the Catholic cause against European radicalism, stated its opposition to secession. Corcoran affirmed the editor's observation that "Southerners as a general rule speak of their State, of belonging to it, and owing allegiance to it, whereas Northerners in a similar case would speak of themselves as

Americans, belonging to the Federal Government and owing to it their allegiance." But Corcoran believed that southerners held the better position because the nationalists had been the ones attacking the Constitution during the brief history of the United States. Those who held to state sovereignty had protected the Constitution. Catholics, he implied, need to support the South.[115] In the next issue of the paper, Corcoran reprinted an argument from a Louisiana Catholic newspaper, *Propagateur Catholique*, which defended state sovereignty and the morality of secession. He then answered charges of the *Freeman's Journal* that the *Miscellany* promoted secession. Corcoran lamely protested that he had not counseled secession but only defended the morality of secession against northern attacks.[116] A week later, the arguments became moot. South Carolina seceded from the Union on December 20, 1860. Other states followed over the next few months.

Corcoran also warned that northern Catholics would soon discover that the revolutionary principles of the Republicans would turn against the church. In March 1861, he printed part of a debate between two Cincinnati papers concerning secession. One paper had printed an article by a Republican who identified himself as a Catholic. The article criticized the *Catholic Telegraph* of Cincinnati for being too soft on the South and secession. It then warned the archbishop of Cincinnati that supporting the South would bring the wrath of the government down on him. Corcoran read the column as a threat. He warned that the "Black Republicans will commence an anti-popery war" once they tired of the antislavery campaign. This would cause Catholics to flee to the Confederate States of America, where they could enjoy liberty.[117] In this Corcoran returned to the theme he had proclaimed since 1856: Republicans were radicals and nativists. Like their ideological kin in Europe, they would use force to destroy their opposition and ordered liberty with it. Catholics would find themselves victimized by this violence just as Pope Pius IX had.[118] But, of course, Corcoran's tactic failed. As historians have noted, northern Catholics overwhelmingly supported the Union while southern Catholics endorsed the Confederacy. In Charleston, for example, Catholic politicians like Michael O'Connor, who had been moderate on secession, supported the Confederacy. Irish militia units in the city eagerly volunteered for Confederate service.[119] Sectional loyalty rather than a common Catholic approach to politics won out.

Nullification and secession demonstrated the strengths and weaknesses of the South Carolina Catholic leadership's attempts to solve the difficulties of political engagement. Bishop England found during the nullification crisis that the politics of loyalty could not always settle important issues, forcing him to choose sides publicly. Speaking on divisive public issues, however, came with risks. If the bishop endorsed the losing side, the church might be punished by the victors. If he appealed to his flock's religious identity, he seemingly endorsed the anti-Catholic canard that the clergy controlled voting blocs. In either case, Catholicism became entwined with local politics. Bishop England hoped that as times of crisis ended, a common devotion to republican virtue could again unite the community. This view, given the greater crisis looming in the future, would prove to be naive.

James Corcoran recognized during the 1850s that a new American nationalism demanding one people under a stronger central government endangered the Catholic presence in the United States. The new nationalists, whether nativists or liberals, usually supported the Revolutions of 1848 and celebrated the trials of Pope Pius IX. Corcoran realized that if these nationalists had their way, Catholics would no longer be counted among the "assemblage of peoples" Calhoun had identified. So Corcoran sought to attach Catholicism publicly to southern conservatives, who viewed both the Republican Party as evil and secession as a conservative, rather than radical, solution to the intractable problems of the Union. Ultimately, many non-Catholic South Carolinians did defend Catholics against the nativists and did recognize them as a loyal part of the community. But Catholic loyalty came at a high cost. Corcoran's alliance linked the success of the church to the political fortunes of the South, a region in which the church's influence was negligible. Thus the Civil War would prove to be a reckoning for both South Carolina and the Diocese of Charleston.[120]

South Carolina Catholics during the nullification crisis and secession argued both as southerners and as Catholics. In the end, however, Catholics had to hope that their non-Catholic neighbors would recognize their goodwill and loyalty. In fact, their posturing demonstrated that they engaged the political world from a place of profound weakness and dependence. This recognition, in part, shaped Catholic approaches to the issue that caused much of the sectional strife that ignited the war: slavery.

CHAPTER SIX

South Carolina Catholics
and Slavery

The slavery issue more than any other contemporary problem challenged South Carolina Catholics' strategy of building affinity with the culture of the Old South while maintaining a Catholic identity.[1] Many interpretations have condemned South Carolina Catholic clergy for craven accommodation to racial bondage.[2] But these interpretations have often ignored that there was not one uncontested position on slavery in the state to which to capitulate. Instead, there was a debate. On one side stood the slavery traditionalists, who wished to limit the autonomy of slaves and resisted any weakening of the master's authority. On the other side stood the evangelical paternalists, who wished to convert slaves to Christianity and ameliorate their conditions.[3] The Jeffersonian nationalism espoused by South Carolina's Catholic leaders allowed for cultural heterogeneity but stressed common sentiments. On issues like slavery the broader community divided, leaving the Catholic minority with difficult choices. They could choose sides, in which case selecting the winning side was important in order to escape retribution. They could also maintain an independent course that still respected the order of their community. In this case, they could celebrate their unique perspective while at the same time refuse a path of radical change. Bishop John England took that approach. He crafted a careful message on slavery that sought to guard his understanding of the Catholic faith as well as the common sentiments of the community in which he claimed citizenship. He located his message within the historical tradition of Catholic engagement with slavery and the specific context of the debate over slavery in South Carolina. His nuanced position was not strictly a pro-slavery argument. It blended Catholic insights and community sentiments, demonstrating both Catholic affinity with other southerners and a challenge to certain public opinions regarding the institution.[4] His outspoken position provoked the suspicions of some in the state about Catholic loyalty on the slavery issue.

After Bishop England's death, South Carolina Catholics gradually lost the nuances of the bishop's positions on slavery. In the 1840s and 1850s the *Miscellany's* statements on slavery rejected the most radical pro-slavery arguments. But Catholic writing on the issue, particularly by Bishop Patrick Lynch, dropped its emphasis on ameliorating the condition of slaves with the goal of future emancipation and accepted some of the racial justifications for the institution. Lynch's positions moved closer to majority thinking about slavery in South Carolina just as the institution collapsed during the Civil War. When appreciated in the context of South Carolina's engagement with slavery during the nineteenth century, Catholic leaders' approach to the slavery issue looks very much like their postures regarding other antebellum issues. They sought to maintain both their Catholic principles and their southern affinities.

The Catholic Church created the Diocese of Charleston in 1820 at a volatile time in the state both socially and economically. Demographically, South Carolina was in flux. White migration to the colony in the eighteenth century combined with the loss of slaves to the British during the Revolution had swung the state from a black majority population to a white majority during the early years of the nation. The census of 1820, however, indicated that South Carolina once again possessed a black majority.[5] The brief reopening of the transatlantic slave trade between 1803 and 1808 contributed to the increase.[6] During most of the antebellum period, Charleston was a black majority city.[7] Not all individuals, of course, were aware immediately of demographic trends, but economic fluctuations affected everyone and invited much comment. Cotton production boomed in South Carolina and the Lower South during the first two decades of the nineteenth century. Slavery took root firmly in the Upcountry as South Carolinians turned to cotton production. But the Panic of 1819 depressed cotton prices significantly and cast the state into a decade-long depression.[8] The Panic in turn contributed significantly to migration out of the state as farmers sought opportunities elsewhere.[9] Scholars have also designated 1820 as the year in which the Lowcountry's economy peaked. Between 1820 and 1860 the Lowcountry faced economic decline and slowly lost its dominance of the state's agricultural economy.[10] Meanwhile, the interconnected demographic and economic changes exacerbated concerns about slavery.

In 1822 a plot among free blacks and slaves in Charleston, the Denmark Vesey incident, rocked the city and state. Vesey was a free black carpenter in Charleston who had been a member of Charleston's "African Church," part of the African Methodist Episcopal (AME) Church founded in Philadelphia by Richard Allen. Vesey had been a slave but had purchased his freedom. A literate man, Vesey held gatherings in his home where he read and discussed the Bible, particularly Old Testament passages promising deliverance for slaves and retribution for injustice. Some of Vesey's followers may have been angry over white authorities' harassment of the AME congregation and its minister, Morris Brown.[11] By 1822 Vesey had convinced others to join him in a violent plot to wreak havoc in the city by revolting and seizing a ship. Vesey would then pilot the ship to Haiti and freedom. At the end of May 1822, a slave informed authorities about the plot and implicated some of the most trusted slaves in the city, including one of Gov. Thomas Bennett's house servants. The authorities initially discounted the warning, only to be informed again in mid-June of the plot. The intendent of Charleston, James Hamilton Jr., decided to act and made arrests. The city also created special secret courts to investigate and try the accused. The courts sentenced thirty-five persons, including Vesey, to death and sold thirty-seven men out of the state as dangers to the peace of South Carolina. The brand new *United States Catholic Miscellany* carried news of the executions in its July 17, 24, and 31 issues.[12]

The Vesey plot brought to the forefront of public attention the rising paternalist movement led by southern evangelicals. Lacy Ford has shown that paternalism before the late 1830s was an "insurgent" ideology that sought to overturn older justifications for and practices of slavery.[13] Paternalists demanded that slaves be recognized as human beings and treated fairly and with "affection." Masters, paternalists argued, must act as good stewards of their families, both white and black. Doing so would allow a more humane and Christian society to develop.[14] As the Charleston Baptist minister Richard Furman taught, slaves "became a part of his [the master's] family, (the whole, forming under him a little community) and the care of ordering it, and of providing for its welfare, devolves on him."[15] Ford maintained that paternalists challenged "masters about their stewardship obligations, which included fair treatment, adequate provisions, respect for family, and the nurturing of Christianity among slaves."[16] Paternalist evangelicals, particularly the Methodists and Baptists, brought thousands of slaves into their churches. A number of evangelicals supported teaching free blacks and slaves to read so that they could study the Bible. Some, like Charles Colcock Jones, a Georgian, created the mission to slaves in order to spread Christianity. Other Charleston evangelicals supported black preachers and, after the War of 1812, the formation of the AME congregation in Charleston.[17] All of these activities and proposals, though stopping short of endorsing emancipation, offered more autonomy to enslaved African Americans.

In their campaign, evangelicals battled an opposition that was more skeptical about the black population. Whereas evangelicals appealed to the consciences of both master and slave to keep order, slavery traditionalists relied on unflinching coercion applied by the master and the government to control the black population. Slavery traditionalists positioned the state, not the Gospel or the church, as the final arbiter of slavery. Traditionalists remained highly skeptical of black literacy, black preachers, and black churches and turned to the state government to ban all of them in the wake of the Vesey plot. A group of citizens in Charleston, for example, petitioned the state legislature to restrict the actions of the evangelical paternalists. Their memorial complained that South Carolina slaveholders, "under the influence of mild and generous feelings," had "extended many privileges to our negroes" in order to exult "in what they termed the progress of liberal ideas upon the subject of slavery." But the plan had not worked. Numerous slaves had plotted to murder their masters and the people of Charleston. Therefore, the memorialists noted, the state needed to firmly restrict black autonomy. One reform they asked for was "prohibiting under severe penalties, all persons from teaching negroes to read and write."[18] Such a law, of course, would limit the activities not just of blacks but also of the white paternalists advocating reforms to the institution of slavery.

Slavery traditionalists articulated their disgust with evangelical paternalism in newspapers and pamphlets. In 1822 Edwin Holland, a Charleston newspaper editor, wrote an extended attack on those he argued had encouraged the rebellion, mostly northerners but also some southerners. He insisted, "It is nevertheless indispensable to our safety to watch all their [blacks'] motions with a careful and scrutinising eye— and to pursue such a system of policy . . . as will effectually prevent all secret combinations among them, hostile to our peace." Holland believed that the "general spirit of insubordination among our slaves and free negroes" came from "the relaxation of discipline on the part of the whites." Harsher discipline and new laws, particularly ones that would drive free blacks from the state, were needed. Holland maintained, "We look upon the existence of our FREE BLACKS among us, as the greatest and most deplorable evil with which we are unhappily afflicted." Free blacks encouraged dissatisfaction and restlessness in slaves. Holland closed by reminding readers that the black population was a danger to the state and needed close policing.[19] Holland's message was clear: strong laws and state enforcement of them, not evangelical paternalism, was the solution to South Carolina's racial problems.

The chief spokesman of the opposition to evangelical paternalism was Whitemarsh Seabrook, a planter and future governor of South Carolina, who published a pamphlet in 1825 ridiculing evangelical attitudes toward the slave population. "Our history has verified the melancholy truth," Seabrook wrote, "that one educated slave, or coloured freeman, with an insinuating address, is capable of infusing the poison of insubordination into the whole body of the black population."[20] In 1822 the city of Charleston had published a pamphlet on the Vesey plot that contained some of the testimony of the conspirators. One man, Rolla, testified that he had gone to a meeting at Vesey's house and described the following scene: "At this meeting, Vesey said, we were to take the Guard-House and Magazines, to get arms; that we ought to rise up against the whites to get our liberties. He was the first to ride up and speak, and he read to us from the Bible, how the *children of Israel were delivered out of Egypt from bondage.*"[21] From Seabrook's perspective, this proved that Vesey had used his literacy to foment rebellion.

While Seabrook blamed northern clergymen for polluting the minds of Vesey and his followers, his comments applied equally to southern evangelical paternalists. Sounding like an Enlightenment philosophe, he noted, "History confirms my assertion, that the Clergy have in all ages exercised an almost boundless sway over the minds and actions of mandkind [*sic*]. . . . Although from the general diffusion of knowledge, and the ascendant power of education, their influence has been considerably diminished, it is yet of vast and potent magnitude." When clergy confined their comments to their "legitimate sphere, the revolutions of the sacred wheel of truth and religion," they would be a good influence on society. "But," he concluded, "whenever some direful cause shall propel it beyond its proper orbit, its characteristic traits will be obliterated, and obedience to its admonitions shall cease to be a virtue."[22] He also warned in his tract that the American Colonization Society would cause worse problems if it agitated further on slavery. Seabrook also denounced British abolitionists and the press for fomenting sectional discord and seeking the disunion of the states over the slavery issue. Seabrook's point was clear: the government was responsible for keeping the people safe from slave insurrections and should not tolerate any interference in its duty, particularly from clergy.

For their part, evangelical paternalists faced several problems in their battles with slavery traditionalists. First, evangelicals were a minority in the state and had limited influence on lawmaking. Charles Irons, examining evangelical activities in nineteenth-century Virginia, recognized that disestablishment hindered the effectiveness of evangelical efforts at reforming the institution of slavery. The state claimed that certain issues were part of its domain and thus religious groups could not interfere, rendering them essentially powerless. Irons pointed out that this allowed evangelicals to disclaim responsibility for the continued existence of slavery while at the same time placing "profound ideological obstacles in the way of evangelical action against slavery."[23]

Second, South Carolina religious groups quarreled among themselves, limiting the possibility of united action to influence legislation. For example, in the wake of the Vesey plot, Episcopal minister Frederick

Dalcho wrote a pamphlet arguing for better treatment of slaves as well as less autonomy for all blacks. Near the end of his pamphlet, he gloated that *"none of the Negroes belonging to the Protestant Episcopal Church were concerned in the late conspiracy."* He speculated that it was "because in the sober, rational, sublime and evangelical worship of the Protestant Episcopal Church, there is nothing to inflame the passions of the ignorant enthusiast." Dalcho contrasted his church with the black preachers who influenced the Vesey conspirators, but white evangelicals as well would have bristled at his demeaning tone toward non-Episcopalians.[24]

Third, lacking power and unity, white ministers, Ford asserted, "knew that the future of the entire mission to the slaves depended on maintaining the support of skeptical civil authorities who worried that slaves instructed in the gospel often became slaves unlikely to accept permanent subordination."[25] The state could shut down access of the churches to the black population. Thus, ministers had to tread carefully, affirming their loyalty to the state and opposition to abolition in order to preserve their access to souls.[26]

In the wake of the Vesey plot, Bishop England steered an independent course on slavery. Born into a nonslaveholding society in Ireland, Bishop England learned about slavery firsthand when he arrived in Charleston in 1820. He disliked the institution and expressed his opinion publicly. But the bishop found himself squeezed in the middle of a debate, with threats on either side. The evangelical paternalists included groups, particularly Charleston's Presbyterians, vocally opposed to Catholicism in the United States. The slavery traditionalists, however, elevated the state to a place that threatened the freedom of Christian efforts to improve society. Bishop England's public statements navigated between both groups, winning him few allies.

Like the evangelical paternalists, Bishop England sought black converts. Soon after arriving in Charleston in December 1820, England undertook a tour of his diocese, bringing him into contact with African Americans. As his diary indicates, he treated African Americans similarly to the whites he encountered. For example, in January 1821 he arrived in Locust Grove, Georgia, where a community of Catholics who had migrated from Maryland lived. In his diary entry for January 30, England remarked, "In the Evening I gave instruction to the Negroes amongst whom I found some intelligent and well instructed." A few days later, England recorded, "Baptized Anne, an adult slave of Mr. Bradford Thompson, her Sponsor, Anne, slave of Mr. Thompson Senr. and rehabilitated the marriage of that same women with Edward, a slave also of Mr. B. Thompson, it having been invalid on account of Cultus disparitas [one partner being unbaptized]." Before leaving Locust Grove, he noted on February 4, "I then baptized two black persons, Nathaniel, and Mary, the first a slave of Squire ———, the second free. I then conversed with some persons who sought explanations, and in the evening baptized three black adults, and married two couple [*sic*]."

England continued his work among African Americans as his tour progressed. While visiting the Catholic jurist William Gaston in New Bern, North Carolina, in May 1821, England wrote, "Celebrated Mass and had one Communicant—gave an exhortation, afterwards gave private instruction to a coloured man, servant to Mr. Gaston. . . . Heard Confessions and preached at night." While in North Washington, North Carolina, a couple of weeks later he noted, "After breakfast saw and conversed with two women and a black man who were desirous of instruction in order to learn whether they should become Catholics, also gave instructions to the Catholics who were preparing for the Sacraments. Heard confessions and preached at night." A week later he explained, "Saw some persons of colour who were desirous of instruction, conversed with them for a considerable time. One of them became a Catechumen, two others had favourable impressions made on them, but took time to consider what they should do." The next day he "baptized James Selby an adult free man of colour."[27] Such events occurred repeatedly throughout England's career.[28]

Scholars have recognized Catholic efforts in Charleston to convert African Americans. Suzanne Krebsbach, using surviving baptismal records from the cathedral, uncovered a large number of baptisms of slaves that suggest several patterns. She noted that during the 1840s the "number of black baptisms at the cathedral . . . exceeded that of whites." Krebsbach found black converts sponsored by their owners, but she also found that "the majority of slaves baptized at the cathedral were owned by non-Catholics."[29] In other words, Catholics pursued black converts who were not necessarily tied to church members. She also noted that black converts had white sponsors, often from "the prosperous middle class." Black Catholics in Charleston participated in "their own charitable organizations" as well. She concluded, "In Charleston, and perhaps in other southern cities, practicing Catholics worshipped with their slaves and participated in the sacraments with slaves and free persons of color."[30] Catholics in South Carolina, then, like their evangelical neighbors, sought to convert African Americans. Like the Protestant churches of the state, the Catholic Church in South Carolina had both enslaved and free persons in its congregations.

While Bishop England's efforts to win black converts mimicked those of the evangelical paternalists, he antagonized his Protestant neighbors by criticizing the Protestant mission to slaves. In 1828 the *Miscellany* criticized Charleston's Episcopalians for inconsistency due to their failure to teach their black church members to read the Bible. At the time of the short piece, Bishop England was debating Episcopalian Bishop Bowen, also of South Carolina, over Catholic understandings of tradition and revelation. The *Miscellany* reported that the Episcopalian minister who ministered to slaves at St. Stephen's Chapel in Charleston had published a report of his activities in which he insisted that it was not giving blacks Bibles that would convert them but teaching them orally according to the Episcopal catechism. The paper joked, "Why, this is really coming to the old mode of popery. Why not give the Bible to the blacks and let them find out Protestant Episcopalianism? Why give them the word of the expounder, the word of man, for the word of God?" Episcopalians acted toward Charleston's black population the same way that Bishop Bowen accused Catholics of acting toward everyone, restricting access to the Bible. In essence, the writer hinted, the Episcopalians established one Christianity for blacks and one for whites. The paper then quoted a French bishop who argued that the Bible needs an interpreter, the church, in order to save Christians from a cacophony of voices, each touting their own specific interpretation of the scriptures. The piece aimed to defend the Catholic understanding of the teaching authority of the church, but it also implied that if Episcopalians were consistent they would have to teach Charleston's blacks how to read the Bible for themselves.[31] The implication of the passage was incoherent. On the one hand it implied that the Catholic faith did not require literacy and was thus safer; on the other, it encouraged Protestants to teach blacks literacy in order to maintain their consistency.

In 1834 the *Miscellany* again antagonized the evangelical paternalists by provoking a dispute with the Presbyterians over the mission to slaves. In the July 12, 1834, edition of the paper, a letter from "A Catholic Observer" critiqued the Presbyterians and Charleston Catholics' old nemesis Benjamin Gildersleeve for failing to teach slaves how to read. The argument was similar to the one made against the Episcopalians in 1828. "A Catholic Observer" insisted that the "Protestant rule of faith" demanded that each individual could "judge for himself" the meaning of scripture. But the Presbyterians, by writing a catechism for blacks, effectively said that blacks "must give up their private judgment, and follow the dictate of Mr. G[ildersleeve]." This created a two-tiered Protestantism: an elite who interpreted the Bible and the people who were supposed to follow their lead. "A Catholic Observer" asserted that "if you wish to make a protestant of him [the slave], you must first teach him to read." The Presbyterian mission to slaves, then, demonstrated that "there is something defective in the protestant rule of faith." The faith of the slave must come, following the logic of the catechism for slaves, from the authority of the writer of the catechism. Thus, ironically, Gildersleeve and his Presbyterian colleagues in the mission to slaves claimed an "infallibility" for themselves in their presentation of the faith. The whole mission to slaves insulted blacks by not teaching them to read and interpret the Bible, which, as Protestants, the Presbyterians said was necessary. Catholics needed no such dodging. The writer gloated, "They [Catholic bishops] compose Catechisms for people of *all colours*. The Catechisms which they [Catholic bishops] compose, contain the doctrines which the Apostles taught, and which the scriptures teach when interpreted, not according to the fancy of any individual; but by the unanimous judgment of the whole body—when they catechize they act consistently." In response, Gildersleeve's *Charleston Observer* howled in protest, starting an exchange of letters that lasted a month.[32] Clearly, Bishop England had not made the evangelical paternalists his close allies.

Like the slavery traditionalists, Bishop England strongly attacked abolitionism as disruptive of the social order. The August 26, 1826, edition of the *Miscellany* reprinted a story from the *Dublin Register* about an antislavery meeting in Cork, Bishop England's hometown. The editor inserted commentary before the reprinted article, noting that the Irish abolitionists were the same men who kept the Irish Catholic peasants "in slavery of mind and body." Denying that the *Miscellany* was touching the "question of slavery," the editor asserted that there was "more real physical misery amongst the Catholic tradesmen and labourers of the county and city of Cork, than among all the slave population of all the Southern States of this Union." He concluded that this "hypocrisy ought to be exposed."[33]

Echoing the slavery traditionalists, the *Miscellany* also used the bloodiest slave revolt in the United States, Nat Turner's 1831 rebellion in Virginia, to attack Protestantism and abolitionism for threatening social peace. The editor reprinted a lengthy article from a northern Catholic paper, the *United States Catholic Intelligencer*, on opposition in New Haven, Connecticut, to a new college for blacks founded in part on abolitionist principles. The *Intelligencer* prefaced the story by decrying the "angry workings of the nullifying storm" as well as the "insurrectionary movements of the swarthy Moors, who, stimulated by the infectious influence of the fanaticism of the *Reformation saints*, are now scattering desolation and death through the South." The *Intelligencer* blamed Nat Turner's revolt on his Protestant fanaticism, a criticism echoed by southern slavery traditionalists. The paper also accused abolitionists of provoking violence. The editor praised the citizens of New Haven for recognizing that talk of abolition only served to stir up slaves in the South with the "maddening spirit of Revolution." Once unleashed, that spirit would "with all its brute, ferocious force present to the eyes of the astonished world, a more bloody spectacle than St. Domingo ever displayed."[34] The northern paper argued that slavery was a legal and political matter. Abolitionist rhetoric would create more Nat Turners and destroy national unity. By reprinting the article, the *Miscellany* further attacked evangelical paternalism while defining its position on abolitionism more clearly.

Bishop England, however, continued to antagonize slavery traditionalists by making public statements critical of slavery. For example, the October 20, 1832, edition of the paper published part of William Gaston's address to the University of North Carolina. Here Gaston boldly told the students, "On you too, will devolve the duty which has been too long neglected, but which can not with impunity be neglected much longer, of providing for the mitigation, and (is it too much to hope for in North Carolina?) for the ultimate extirpation of the worst evil that afflicts the Southern part of our Confederacy." He insisted that "slavery . . .

more than any other cause, keeps us back in the career of improvement."
Slavery, Gaston continued, "stifles industry and represses enterprize—it
is fatal to economy and providence; it discourages skill; impairs our
strength as a community and poisons morals at the fountain head."[35]
Gaston also denounced sectionalism in his address. That Bishop England would publish the address in Charleston demonstrated his distance from the slavery traditionalists and his unwillingness to defend
slavery in the abstract.

Also in 1832, Bishop England, traveling in Ireland to raise money for
the Diocese of Charleston, published in Dublin a pamphlet on Catholicism in his diocese. Although his Charleston neighbors were not aware
of the pamphlet in 1832, Bishop Reynolds included the piece in the
Works of John England, which he published in 1849. In the pamphlet, the
bishop stated that "no greater moral evil could be brought upon any
country than the introduction of slavery." But he also noted that emancipation involved "a very different question," that of social order and law.
The bishop assured his Irish readers that southern slavery was usually
mild, but he concluded, "It is a state of things which should never be
created, but which, when existing, cannot be easily removed."[36] England
repeated these sentiments to the cardinal prefect of the Propaganda in
Rome in 1833, calling slavery *"the greatest moral evil that can desolate any
part of the civilized world."*[37] In 1833 the *Miscellany* complained that the
lack of clergy in Liberia prevented more Catholics from emigrating
there, and wished for Rome to send priests to minister to American
blacks who had been settled there by the American Colonization Society
(ACS).[38] The ACS, as Seabrook's 1825 pamphlet demonstrated, was
very unpopular in South Carolina, and writing openly about the desire
to send missionaries there again laid bare the bishop's sympathies.
Whether in public statements or in private letters, Bishop England's antislavery and antiabolitionist positions were clear.

Bishop England further alienated slavery traditionalists by agreeing
to serve as a papal diplomat to Haiti. Pope Gregory XVI made John
England his representative to Haiti in order to negotiate an agreement
between the Catholic Church and the Haitian government to secure as
much autonomy as possible for the church, which had suffered greatly in
the aftermath of the Haitian Revolution. England did not want the assignment for several reasons. First, he would have to leave his diocese
during a time of increasing political turmoil. Not only was the nullifica-

tion controversy dividing South Carolina, but nativism was growing in strength nationally. Bishop England realized that his diocese needed strong leadership to avoid the factionalism that had plagued it before his arrival. Second, England feared that departing for Haiti would lead some southerners to question his loyalty to slavery and the South. After all, Whitemarsh Seabrook had just noted in his 1834 pamphlet that no clergyman who was suspect on the issue of slavery should be allowed to talk to blacks without white witnesses to report any irregularities in his message.[39] Such sentiments could place the bishop in a bind.

Bishop England described vividly the opposition to his mission to Haiti from abolitionists. He told his friend Dr. Cullen, "Northern sectarians published that the Pope gave me privately a commission to establish the Inquisition in the United States" and "appointed me his legate to Hayti, so as to enable me to establish relations of amity with the negroes who had achieved their freedom, and facilitate the abolition of slavery of negroes in the South." They did this to "render me odious to my own district especially, and to the citizens of the Union generally," acknowledged England. The charges were not true but hurt his standing in the South.[40] Later, England wrote in the *Miscellany* that a group of New York abolitionists had presented a petition to President Boyer of Haiti "requesting that no communication should be held with me as envoy from this same Pope Gregory XVI, upon the ground that he was not averse to southern slavery, and that I was an enemy to Daniel O'Connell, and an enemy to negroes." England claimed that Boyer had revealed this incident to him in a conversation. Boyer, who had "more common sense than most of the abolitionists," refused to take the bait, and by most accounts enjoyed an amicable relationship with Bishop England.[41] To England, the fact that New York abolitionists would try to sabotage his mission to Haiti, which had nothing to do with U.S. foreign policy or the interests of the state of New York, revealed that they were anti-Catholic fanatics and had little genuine concern for the black people of Haiti. The incident only furthered his dislike of abolitionists.

For all these reasons, Bishop England occupied a unique position in the fray over slavery in the state. While he denounced abolitionists as dangerous—the majority position in South Carolina—he managed to antagonize both the evangelical paternalists and the slavery traditionalists on a host of other issues. Their hostility became a badge of his independence. But the bishop's desire to maintain an independent position on slavery ensured that he would have few allies during the tumultuous abolitionist mail campaign of 1835.

Scholars have long recognized that the 1835 American Anti-Slavery Society's abolitionist mail campaign significantly shaped the debate over slavery during the antebellum period, but it also had a tremendous effect on the battles between traditionalists and evangelicals. The controversy began on July 29, 1835, when a ship from New York delivered the mail to Alfred Huger, postmaster of Charleston. After some of the mail was delivered, bothered customers began to return items to the post office. The mail contained abolitionist tracts, addressed to clergy and important citizens in the city. Huger locked the rest of the mail in the post office and refused to release it. While waiting for instructions from the postmaster general, Amos Kendall, Huger sorted the mail and isolated the abolitionist literature. That night, a small mob entered the post office and stole the abolitionist pamphlets; they burned them publicly the next day. As Ford noted of the incident, "The panic that swept Charleston and the vicinity in the aftermath of the seizure of the abolitionist mail surpassed even that of the Denmark Vesey insurrection scare."[42]

An episode in 1833–34 in the running battle between evangelical paternalists and the slavery traditionalists provided an important piece of the context of Charleston's response to the 1835 crisis. Energized by Nat Turner's revolt and perhaps worried by recent British emancipation in the West Indies, the slavery traditionalists, led by Whitemarsh Seabrook, attempted in the fall of 1833 to push through the legislature a bill eliminating black literacy and restricting severely the efforts of paternalists to ameliorate slavery by educating blacks. One proposal stated, "No Clergyman, although a slave-holder, who believes in the illegitimacy of personal servitude, or who advocates directly or indirectly the doctrine of emancipation, to be allowed to officiate." Another penalized teaching any black person in the state how to read. Yet another prohibited black preachers. When the legislature voted to defer consideration of the bill until the next year, Seabrook published a pamphlet to identify the dangers of paternalism.[43] He argued that "abstract opinions on the rights of man" should not be "allowed in any instance to modify the police system of the plantation." Masters should take care of their slaves' basic needs but should also police their slaves closely. Clergy, Seabrook wrote, were "the most useful class in society when they keep rigidly within the limits of their station." But clergy were usually "deficient in their practical knowledge of mankind" and prone to "abstract notions." He thought that the paternalists were causing "discontent" among slaves by preaching reform. Clergy instead, insisted Seabrook, should teach slaves "on points essential to his salvation" but realize that the "mind of the negro is not prepared for the refinements and subtleties of the evangelical school."[44] He maintained that the Nat Turner rebellion was fomented by black preachers, revealing the danger of the paternalist program. The paternalists, he feared, sought to establish church oversight and discipline for the "practical exercise of the master's authority" and thus endangered the safety of all. Seabrook closed his pamphlet with a letter from a correspondent in Virginia describing the aftermath of Nat Turner's rebellion. The letter blamed evangelical women for teaching slaves to read and causing discontent on the plantation.[45] Charleston clergy of various denominations held meetings in the fall of 1834 to press their paternalist message, but Seabrook and his allies succeeded in December in passing a bill prohibiting teaching slaves, but not free blacks, literacy. The slavery traditionalists had won an important battle against the evangelicals.[46]

During the abolitionist mail crisis of 1835, slavery traditionalists capitalized on their recent gains. Immediately following the burning of the mail, local politicians called a public meeting and appointed a committee of five, which included Robert Hayne, to govern the city during the crisis. Not willing to let a crisis go to waste, as the saying goes, the committee forced the city's schools for blacks to close, which had long been a goal of traditionalists like Seabrook. The city also announced that it would criminalize the willful transportation into and reception of abolitionist literature in Charleston.[47] Furthermore, the committee demanded that northern states recognize slavery as a domestic affair for each state to handle without outside interference. The *Courier* even declared slavery a "blessing" and argued that citizens of other states did not have the right to denounce slavery in South Carolina. The paper insisted that northern states legally punish abolitionists on the grounds that their rhetoric stirred up slaves to revolt and violated the Constitution's designation of slavery as a state issue.[48] Popular antiabolitionist meetings popped up all over the state, and threats of extralegal activity silenced any potential opposition.[49] The paternalists were reeling. The traditionalists demanded unity on the question of slavery and used the crisis to declare certain topics outside the boundaries of accepted speech.[50]

Bishop England found that his independent course on the slavery issue isolated him during the crisis. The best account of the crisis's effects on Catholics' efforts in Charleston comes from a February 1836 letter that Bishop England wrote to his good friend Paul Cullen, who was then rector of the Irish College in Rome. Describing the mob in front of the post office on July 29, England wrote, "Whilst they were at the Post-office, two or three of my flock, who were mingled in the crowd and whose religion was not suspected, overheard them arrange that as soon as they concluded at the Post-office they would come to the Seminary and give me (I lived there) the benefit of Lynch's Law, tear down the buildings and the church, &c." The bishop had been fingered as an abolitionist. He quickly mobilized his flock, including members of the Irish Volunteers, to guard the church. "We kept guard for two nights," he wrote, "and no attempt was made to molest us." During the second day, "several of the most respectable citizens of all religions sent to have their names enrolled on our guard; and the city officers said they were ready with their whole force to come to us should we need their assistance," the bishop continued.[51]

Clearly, the threat was gone, but civil leaders sought their pound of flesh from the bishop: the closure of his school for free blacks. This would be a blow to England's strategy of building institutions. Without an institutional presence in the black community, the Catholic Church would lose influence with African Americans. Bishop England published a letter on the matter in the *Courier* on July 31, 1835. He denied receiving any abolitionist pamphlets and professed his disdain for abolitionism. He also addressed a public letter to the South Carolina Association, an institution formed in the wake of the Vesey plot to police Charleston blacks, noting that his school for free blacks did not violate state law. He maintained that he would close the school but would not be singled out on sectarian grounds. He wrote, "If it be the wish of the citizens that they [schools for blacks in the city] should be discontinued, let that wish be signified to all indiscriminately by the City Council, or by the South Carolina Association, and I shall not be found backward in sacrificing my opinion to their advice."[52] By the middle of August all the schools for free blacks in the city had closed.

While some have condemned Bishop England for cowardice under pressure and for abandoning the free blacks of the city, the reality was murkier.[53] The bishop recognized that without the goodwill of non-Catholic citizens, Catholics would have no chance of survival, much less success. He therefore made a prudential decision to close the school for the meantime. Even the Protestant missionary Charles Colcock Jones, as Ford relates, scaled back his mission to slaves in the wake of the 1835 hysteria before accelerating it again in the late 1830s.[54] The incident demonstrated the lack of power that the evangelical paternalists and Bishop England had in the state by 1835.[55] Traditionalists had emerged triumphant and suppressed for a time the paternalist insurgency. Most scholars have missed, however, that Bishop England planned to reopen his school later. Peter Clarke noted that in Bishop England's speech to the second convention of the diocese in 1840, he expressed a desire to reopen his school for free blacks. "I trust," he said, "that we may now be permitted to resume that instruction, which the irritation of the moment required us to suspend, and that our fellow-citizens will feel convinced that in the discharge of this duty, we feel ourselves answerable to God to avoid anything that can disturb the peace and good order of society, or violate the laws of those states whose exclusive jurisdiction on this subject we religiously acknowledge."[56] The *Miscellany* reported the following on January 2, 1841: "The Bishop has been occupied during the past week in conducting the exercises of a Spiritual Retreat for the Sisters of Our Lady of Mercy, preparatory to selecting from that congregation a new community, who will have the charge of giving to the free female children of color such an education, as permitted by the laws of South Carolina."[57] Bishop England had retreated for a time but had not accepted his defeat as permanent.

Punishment of Bishop England would continue during the legislative session in November and December 1835, revealing the political clout of the slavery traditionalists. Charleston Catholics held a series of public meetings in September to ask the bishop to create a new parish on the Neck, the northern end of the city. The *Miscellany* reported a large crowd at the cathedral in mid-September, which presented a petition to the bishop prepared by "nearly fifty catholic families, besides a number of individuals and a considerable number of coloured persons belonging to the church, residing on the Neck," for a parish closer to their homes. The bishop agreed to consider the matter and noted that the people would have "to procure an act of incorporation, from the legislature," and come up with money to build the church.[58] In October Bishop England decided to pursue the matter and thus headed to Columbia to secure a charter for his new parish church, which would be opened in 1837 as St. Patrick's Church.

But Bishop England was blindsided by opposition from the legislature. He described his trip to Columbia to "get some acts of incorporation passed for the Convents and Churches" to Paul Cullen. The bishop traveled with three prominent politicians with whom he was friends, former governors Robert Hayne (who had overseen the Committee of Five) and James Hamilton Jr. (who had served as intendant of Charleston during the Vesey scare) as well as his legal counsel, James L. Petigru (a dedicated unionist during the nullification crisis). The men criticized him for serving the pope in Haiti. Along the way, Bishop England related, the men "endeavored to impress upon me the mischief that I would do to the Catholic Religion, not only in my own Diocess, but through the whole Southern country, by going then to Hayti, and affording the opponents of our Religion so plausible a pretext for creating prejudices amongst the slave-holders against our Church."[59] England reminded his companions that he was not an abolitionist and had defended himself and the church quite well.

When the bishop arrived in Columbia, however, he immediately sensed trouble. The legislature, which usually invited England to preach to them when he was there, did not allow him to preach. Then he found "the petitions for incorporating the Catholic institutions delayed in Committees." Puzzled, England approached some of the committee members in private to determine the cause of the delay. "I was told confidentially," he continued, "that they had for me personally as much respect as ever; but that they were prejudiced against Convents & c., and wished to show their disapprobation of my going to Hayti." England eventually succeeded in getting the bills through committee and then spoke for two hours in front of the legislature to "remove prejudices" against him. England explained the principles of Catholic Church governance and the efforts of Catholics in South Carolina. He also played to the sectional pride of the legislators. "I besought them," he maintained, "as they valued their good name, not to degrade Carolina by placing it by the side of Massachusetts," which had been the scene of recent nativist violence. England said that he "had them in tears" and that his bills passed. He departed for Charleston to make preparations for returning to Haiti, when his vicar, Dr. Clancy, who revealed to the bishop that he was an abolitionist, begged him not to leave. Clancy feared that the Haitian mission would destroy the "good" that the bishop "had just effected, and endanger Religion here at such a critical moment."[60] Nevertheless, England decided later in 1836 to go to Haiti. As he told Cullen in another letter, "I know the cry here will be very unpleasant; but to lose Hayti without a struggle would be worse."[61] The slavery traditionalists had shown Bishop England that they were firmly in charge, yet he persisted in his unpopular mission to Haiti. While eschewing radicalism, he charted his own course on the slavery issue rather than simply accommodating the opinion of the majority in the state.

Bishop England's most famous and controversial writings on slavery were his eighteen public letters in the *Miscellany* in 1840–41 addressed to Secretary of State John Forsyth of Georgia. The letters became famous during the antebellum period as they were republished after the bishop's death in 1842 and recommended by Charleston clergy as the proper Catholic approach to the slavery issue. The letters won Bishop England acclaim from non-Catholics and political conservatives in the South for his rejection of abolitionism. Many scholars have interpreted the letters as pro-slavery in their thrust, but when examined in the context of the bishop's running debate with the slavery traditionalists in South Carolina, a more complex interpretation emerges.

There are two pieces of context needed to explore the letters to Forsyth more clearly. The historian John Quinn has expertly explained the first: Pope Gregory XVI's condemnation of the slave trade in 1839 and Bishop England's immediate reaction to it. The second is the contentious presidential campaign of 1840, in which both the Whigs and the Democrats played on the rising anti-Catholicism of the late 1830s to score victories with voters. Those two events, along with the debates about slavery in South Carolina, demonstrated that Bishop England's intention was not to promote the institution of slavery but again to offer a uniquely Catholic approach to the issue.

Pope Gregory XVI's 1839 condemnation of the slave trade, published with encouragement from the British, added energy to the debate over slavery in the Anglo-American world. The British wished to suppress the transatlantic slave trade and hoped that a papal declaration would carry weight with the governments of Spain and Portugal, which were still shipping Africans to Cuba and Brazil as slaves. Gregory's statement made no mention of British influence but built on earlier papal teaching to condemn reducing people to slavery and selling them for profit. Scholars have debated whether or not *In Supremo* condemned the institution of slavery outright, but it certainly contained a clear indictment of the slave trade.[62] The document energized abolitionist sentiment in Ireland and the United States.

Bishop England printed *In Supremo* in the *Miscellany* on March 14, 1840, and offered comments denying that the pope had called for the abolition of slavery in the United States. One can imagine that, given his recent experiences following the abolitionist mail crisis, the bishop wished to deflect suspicions that Catholics wanted to attack southern slavery. The *Miscellany* praised Gregory's statement for two points. First, Christians should not "reduce into slavery those who have their natural freedom, and to inflict upon them all the consequent evils of bondage." Second, Christians should not treat slaves "with cruelty or with undeserved harshness oppression or injury,—and that not only their physical but moral necessities, should be liberally provided for by those to whom they belong." The paper insisted that the situation of slavery in the United States was different from that described by the pope because U.S. participation in the transatlantic slave trade had ended in 1808. Slavery was part of the national fabric, and "it is impossible," the paper maintained, "that it should be abolished for a considerable time to come" because of the certain damage to "society." Then, dismissing further sermonizing, the paper asserted, "Of the moral effects of a state which admits of no immediate change it is useless to treat."[63] South Carolina would not be emancipating its slaves, and thus talk of abolition would be futile. Slaves, the paper concluded, were generally well treated in the South.

The *Miscellany* distinguished abolition from abolitionism, to borrow Cuthbert Allen's phrase. The bishop did not praise or recommend slavery. In other words, he did not deny the benefit of abolishing slavery in the distant future. He opposed abolitionism, however, which he described as threatening the social order through violence. The *Miscellany* observed that "no truth is to us more evident than that intermeddling of northern abolitionists has tended to retard the generous and human efforts which the southern proprietors were spontaneously making for the increase of the comforts and the amelioration of the moral condition of the slave."[64] In other words, abolitionist agitation had empowered the slavery traditionalists to restrict the paternalist insurgency. Abolitionists and slavery traditionalists were the two extremes that needed one another to function. The paper implied that Catholics and others who attempted to help enslaved African Americans had gotten squeezed in the middle and their efforts made ineffective. This only made the lives of slaves worse.

Partisan attacks on Catholicism during the presidential election of 1840 provided the second piece of context for framing Bishop England's letters on slavery. Since the burning of the Charlestown convent outside of Boston in 1834, the country had witnessed a rising tide of nativism. Naturally, the political parties tapped into the popular mood. First, the Whigs' attack on Bishop England came from a national source with South Carolina connections. Calhoun ally Duff Green, whose daughter had married Calhoun's son, edited a pro-Harrison newspaper, the *Baltimore Pilot and Telegraph*, that accused Bishop England of building a political machine to assist Democratic president Martin Van Buren in his reelection effort. Green identified a letter the bishop had written to a Democratic Party operative in Columbus, Georgia, in July 1840 as evidence of England's pernicious influence.

Bishop England, treasuring his independence, had tried to stay outside the political campaign in 1840. But the Democratic Party of Muscogee County, Georgia, had invited Bishop England to speak at a barbecue. The bishop declined but sent a letter to John H. Howard, head of the county party, with his thoughts on the election. He called for citizens to eschew partisanship and endless wrangling and come together for the common good. He wished that all citizens would lay aside "unkind feelings, bitterness, strife, and mere partisan attachments" in order to return "habits of good Republican simplicity" and zeal for the country's welfare. He hoped voters would select those they deemed "the best qualified to promote the general good." He also told the Democrats of Muscogee County that a mere election would not solve their economic woes resulting from the Panic of 1837. "I think," he wrote, "that the best remedy for our present unfortunate position is to be found in preferring industry to speculation, labour to cabal, economy to ostentation, patient and persevering frugality to dissipation." The bishop also mentioned that he did not believe that the federal government had caused the Panic and did not think that it had the power "to alleviate that distress" that the people felt. In this point, he repeated President Van Buren's opinions on the Panic, but the tone of his letter was decidedly antiparty, playing on earlier themes in American republicanism.[65]

Duff Green accused Bishop England of "putting aside his priestly robes, and entering the field of politics," and attempted, like the slavery traditionalists had, to silence the bishop. Green argued that Bishop England used his spiritual power to influence Catholics to vote for Van Buren. Thus, while acknowledging that the bishop's words might be "correct of themselves," they would be read in a partisan fashion and lead Catholics to vote Democrat. Green's letter reflected the same attitude as the pamphlets of Whitemarsh Seabrook toward the South Carolina clergy. While Green sought to prevent Bishop England from commenting on politics, he freely opined on the Catholic Church. Green said that the "Catholic monarchies" in Europe were arranging a plan to "revolutionise our government" by sending Catholic immigrants. Catholics in America, he claimed, had been founding schools and collecting money to revolutionize society and government. Bishop England, Green noted, was rumored to be the "Inquisitor-General of the United States." Green designated himself as a believer in "toleration in politics as well as in religion," but this claim covered thinly what his writing revealed to be an aggressive statism that sought to keep the churches under the thumb of the state, to prevent clergy from speaking on political matters, and to render churches impotent in secular affairs. Like Seabrook, Green viewed the clergy as powerful, dangerous, and unrealistic. Thus he used the rhetoric of toleration against Bishop England. Clergy could not speak on political matters, but laymen could speak on religious and political matters. Green's inconsistency belied a prejudice, the *Miscellany* thought. The *Miscellany* asked rhetorically, "But suppose the Bishop had 'put aside his priestly robes, and entered into the field of politics,' as Mr. Green asserts he has done in this instance, why does the General [Duff Green] again clothe him in those robes? Why not assail him without thus covering him with what he had put off? Is it not manifest that the object was to mangle the robes under the pretext of merely wounding the politician?"[66] In other words, Green's agenda was to silence Catholics, not to defend toleration or other liberal virtues. Like Seabrook, Green saw the power of the churches as potentially dangerous to his ends. Bishop England seemed to realize that opponents such as Green and Seabrook wanted churches docile to the wishes of the state. Seabrook had supported legislation in South Carolina designed to limit the freedom of clergy to interact with African Americans. At the same time, Seabrook's proposals had stipulated that clergy who held slaves and believed that slavery was good and beneficial could have some access to slaves. He could claim to be friendly to religion, but he wanted clergy who took their orders from the state. Green was no different. The *Miscellany* pointed out in the October 17, 1840, issue that numerous Protestant clergy had spoken at Harrison rallies. Green, however, had been silent regarding these clerical intrusions on politics.[67] Thus Green appeared to be a bigoted hypocrite. The paper also pointed out that Green's real agenda was to strip Catholic clergy of their right to speak on public issues, thus silencing a church that he did not like.[68] The *Miscellany* exposed the fact that Green was planning to edit a nativist paper after the 1840 election and reprinted the prospectus from Green's new paper.[69]

Bishop England and the *Miscellany* engaged Duff Green simultaneously with another attack on Catholics, this time by John Forsyth, secretary of state in the Van Buren administration. Forsyth gave an address to Georgians on August 29, 1840, encouraging their support for Van Buren in the election. He played the "politics of slavery," as William J. Cooper Jr. has called it, by arguing that abolitionists had been involved in the nomination of William Henry Harrison. Harrison, Forsyth charged, was "forced upon the southern portion" of the Whig Party "by the combination of anti-masonry and abolitionism." Much of the speech was partisan boilerplate, but Forsyth suggested that Catholics had joined with the abolitionists to support Harrison. He noted that Pope Gregory XVI had been pressured by the British to publish *In Supremo* and that Daniel O'Connell was collaborating with abolitionists to strengthen the movement in the United States. A Harrison presidency would thus endanger slavery in the United States.[70] While much milder toward Catholics than Duff Green, Forsyth had suggested that Catholics were in league with abolitionists, a charge Bishop England rose to refute.

Bishop England's eighteen letters in response to John Forsyth addressed the slavery traditionalists of South Carolina more than the nebulous charges of the secretary of state. The bishop had been deprived by popular opinion and political pressure from responding systematically to the abolitionist mail crisis, and, in many ways, the letters to Forsyth make more sense when viewed as Bishop England's rejoinder to the hysteria following the summer of 1835. After all, the *Miscellany* had already framed an interpretation of *In Supremo* in March 1840, and the bishop had condemned and disavowed abolitionism frequently. In addition, both Green and Forsyth, by making the church a political scapegoat and using nativist suspicions for political gain, recalled the tactics of the slavery traditionalists. The letters to Forsyth, then, expounded on the bishop's continuous strategy to articulate a Catholic approach to the slavery issue.

In fact, Bishop England dismissed Forsyth's specific charges rather quickly. He reiterated his own opposition to abolitionism and noted that abolitionists both in Britain and in the United States tended to be vicious anti-Catholics, making the idea of a Catholic-abolitionist alliance far-fetched. He reminded his audience that he had scolded O'Connell publicly for attacking southern slaveholders. He denied that the pope took orders from the British government and again distinguished the slavery the pope condemned in *In Supremo* from "domestic slavery," that of the United States. None of this information was new to the *Miscellany*.[71]

Bishop England expanded his approach to slavery, however, in subsequent letters by first examining the issue philosophically. He began with natural law. He argued that because "life and its preservation are more valuable than liberty," slavery, under certain conditions, did not violate natural law. Natural law did "not establish slavery," he wrote, "but it does not forbid it." Citing St. Augustine of Hippo, Bishop England maintained, "Slavery is an evil and is also a consequence of sin." Because the institution was not natural, it had to be "established by human law." Slavery was thus fundamentally a political institution. The bishop declared, "I am not in love with the existence of slavery," and promised, "I would never aid in establishing it where it did not exist." When read in light of the slavery traditionalists' demands for a solidly pro-slavery clergy, Bishop England's philosophical treatment of slavery seems subversive. He did not celebrate slavery but justified it under certain circumstances rather than universally. If, as Fox-Genovese and Genovese have suggested, the trajectory of slavery discourse in the South was to defend it in the abstract, Bishop England had refused to follow.[72]

In his third and fourth letters Bishop England examined the Bible on slavery, a common tactic of the evangelical paternalists, and again found justification for slavery under certain circumstances. Like many evangelical defenders of slavery, the bishop pointed out that the divinely inspired Mosaic law allowed for slavery, thus proving that the institution was not intrinsically immoral. But he highlighted a number of important qualifications on Old Testament slavery. First, under Abraham and the patriarchs, slaves formed part of the household and were "treated with parental care." Second, Mosaic law permitted slavery but subjected the institution to numerous regulations governing who could become a slave, the process of enslavement, and treatment of slaves. Again referring to St. Augustine, the bishop summarized Old Testament slavery as paternalistic. The master had "the right and obligation . . . to restrain his slaves from vice, to preserve due discipline, to govern with firmness and yet with affection." The master could discipline slaves "with moderate, corporeal chastisement" in part because he had a "public duty" to maintain "peace" and "good order" in society. When he turned to the New Testament, Bishop England found that Jesus did not condemn slavery, but Christian teaching demanded the transformation of human relations and thus affected pagan slavery. The bishop denied that New Testament teaching endorsed social egalitarianism but allowed that by invoking charity and spiritual equality it imposed moral restrictions on master and slave. Masters had to act with "tenderness, affection, and charity," while slaves had "to be faithful, patient, obedient and contented." Bad masters might escape immediate punishment but would be judged by God for their behavior. Christian teaching rendered "the master merciful, and the slave faithful, obedient, and religious."[73] True freedom for the Christian, the bishop opined, came only in heaven. The bishop's treatment of the Bible and slavery thus aligned with evangelicals' accounts.

While Bishop England's brief tour of the Bible on slavery resembled similar efforts of the evangelical paternalists, the rest of his letters, which explored slavery during Christianity's first millennium, challenged the slavery traditionalists in significant ways. The letters are long and much of their content obscure to contemporary readers, but they contain three central points that distinguish the bishop's position on the issue. First, the church had always supported amelioration of the conditions of servitude. Bishop England noted that "as Christianity made progress, the unnatural severity with which" the slave "was treated became relaxed, and as the civil law ameliorated their condition, the canon law, by its spiritual efficacy, came in with the aid of religion to secure that" Christians "should give full force to the merciful provisions that were introduced." Citing Augustine, the bishop said that the state should pass laws to regulate slaves while the Church "was to plead for morality and to exhort to practise mercy."

Second, the church supported the manumission of slaves and foresaw a gradual end to the institution. In the early church, the bishop claimed, "Christians had, from motives of mercy, charity, and affection, manumitted many of their slaves in the presence of the bishops." Clergy also ransomed slaves. Bishop England noted that an early French bishop had "sold the plate belonging to the church, and used glass for the chalice, that he might be able by every species of economy to procure liberty for the enslaved." The church had supported manumission "by lawful means permitted by the state," a subtle shot by England at the abolitionists who endorsed, he thought, violent means of emancipation.

Finally, Bishop England stated that the church supported means of amelioration, manumission, and emancipation enshrined in the state's law. This point was important. The bishop pointed out that Christians had not merely appealed to the goodwill of the masters—the approach of the evangelical paternalists—but had pressed the state to codify protections for slaves. For example, he pointed out that the law should recognize slave marriages, "for marriage is one of those natural rights which is not conveyed away by the subjection of the slave." He noted that slaveholders sometimes separated enslaved married couples, a "galling affliction" of slavery. As Christians became more prominent, they demanded "that some restraint should be placed upon that absolute power which the owners had." When the state did not protect slave marriages by restricting the ability of owners to split couples, slaves preferred "concubinage to wedlock." The bishop asserted, "This is one of the worst moral evils attending slavery, where no restraint of law effects its removal."[74] Clearly, Bishop England was speaking to the South Carolina of his day as much as he was reviewing history.

His final letter on slavery, when placed in context, again reveals the slavery traditionalists to be his main target. On February 25, 1841, Bishop England wrote a note to be published in the *Miscellany* indicating that he would have to suspend his letters on slavery. He decided to answer a question that had been posed to him: was he supportive of slavery and its continued existence? The bishop answered, "I am not—but I also see the impossibility of now abolishing it here. When it can and ought to be abolished, is a question for the legislature and not for me."[75] His response echoed his earlier claim that slavery was a political issue and thus he would offer no specific proposals either to reform or to abolish the institution. The state, not the church, had established slavery. The responsibility for slavery's existence, therefore, was the state's, not the church's. In 1841 the legislature of South Carolina was considering whether or not to close certain loopholes to prevent further manumissions of slaves in the state.[76] That fact sheds more light on the bishop's answer. He had just claimed in his letters that openness to manumission was part of the Christian influence on secular law. His argument suggested that he would support broader manumission. But slavery traditionalists controlled the legislature, and they closed the loopholes. By implication, then, Christian influence had waned in the state. Janet Duitsman Cornelius has argued that South Carolina religious leaders, instead of uniformly accommodating to slavery to maintain peace, never won the trust of the masters and did not embrace "all of the proslavery argument."[77] While Bishop England's treatment of slavery left much to be desired, he did not capitulate to the slavery traditionalists. He did not denote slavery as natural or beneficial and continued to call the institution an evil in public forums well after the abolitionist mail hysteria had stifled public debate. Bishop England presented an approach informed by philosophy, history, and Christian revelation. His conclusion, given the context of 1841, was that the forces of secularism ruled the government, making legal reform of slavery doubtful.

After Bishop England's death in 1842, the slavery issue became more important in national politics, but South Carolina Catholics commented less on slavery in the *Miscellany* and did not treat the institution in any systematic fashion. Part of the reason for this lay in the status afforded Bishop England's letters to Forsyth as a quasi-official diocesan statement on slavery. For example, the *Miscellany* editorialized on December 9, 1843, about charges circulating that Catholics were supposed to support abolition and that the American hierarchy had suppressed *In Supremo*.

The editor stated that both propositions were false, identifying the exact date *In Supremo* had been published in the *Miscellany* and noting its approval by the American bishops at their provincial council. He referred to Bishop England's letters to Forsyth as clearly interpreting the papal letter by distinguishing domestic slavery from the slave trade. The editor admitted, "Catholics may and do differ in regard to slavery, and other points of human policy, when considered as ethical or political questions." But, he noted, "our Theology is fixed." The editor added, citing Bishop England, that slavery was not intrinsically immoral.[78] In 1844 William George Read, a convert to Catholicism and friend of Bishop England, gathered the letters to Forsyth into one volume for publication in order to refute Daniel O'Connell and the Irish abolitionists.[79] In December 1845 the *Miscellany* commented on the debate over slavery between two Protestant ministers, Richard Fuller of South Carolina and Francis Wayland of Rhode Island, which had recently been published. In its review, the paper appealed to England's letters: "The Bishop announced what is Catholic doctrine." The case was closed.[80] Even as late as 1858 in the midst of the growing sectional crisis, a letter to the editor of the *Miscellany*, written under the name "Viator," invoked Bishop England's letters on slavery as a sensible statement on the contentious subject. "Viator," however, related his discomfort in reading the last of the Forsyth letters, in which Bishop England wished for an end to slavery. After wrestling with the thought, "Viator" concluded by claiming to have heard a story about Bishop England that occurred at the end of England's contentious negotiations with the Haitians. "Viator" asserted that the bishop, on the failure of his mission to Haiti, had finally realized that slavery was a way to elevate the black race.[81] In this case, Bishop England's letters came to support arguments that the deceased bishop had not explicitly made.

South Carolina Catholics also continued in the tradition of Bishop England by condemning abolitionism for encouraging violent revolution, sectional tension, and disrespect for social order. In the June 1, 1850, edition of the *Miscellany*, the editor reprinted a short piece from a New Orleans paper reporting on a pro-slavery speech given by a Protestant minister in New York. The New Orleans paper noted that the lecture was refreshing because usually "evangelical ministers have been disgracing their professions, by engendering bad feelings, and perverting the sacred cause of religion to the unholy purpose of fomenting party and sectional strife."[82] In a December 1854 editorial on northern Episcopalians becoming abolitionists, the *Miscellany* stated that abolitionism in the churches reflected the Protestant principle of private interpretation of Revelation. "Religion," the paper said, "when based on such a shifting standard as private interpretation, must necessarily accommodate itself to the progress of the age, and our age prides itself on the title of Humanitarianism."[83] Like Bishop England, South Carolina Catholics continued to use abolitionism as a weapon against Protestantism. Fr. James Corcoran, when editing the *Miscellany* in 1859, declared, "For no man . . . can be an Abolitionist and a Catholic together. He might as well expect to remain in her communion and at the same time be allowed to profess Protestantism." Corcoran's point, repeated numerous times in his editorials, was that abolitionism counseled disorder. One did not have to profess love for slavery, but, by calling slavery intrinsically evil, abolitionism rejected Catholic moral teaching.[84] South Carolina Catholic spokesmen, then, continued the antiabolitionism message of Bishop England but did not seek to enact the reforms England had envisioned in his letters to John Forsyth.

At the same time, like Bishop England, Catholics continued to deflect suspicion that they were abolitionists. The *Miscellany* frequently printed assertions that Catholicism was incompatible with forms of political radicalism, of which abolitionism was one. For example, in June 1853, the *Miscellany* reprinted with approval a short notice from the *New York Freeman's Journal*, Archbishop Hughes's diocesan paper, which read, "American Abolitionism and European Red Republicanism are essentially the same." The piece also repeated a rumor that the Vatican had placed *Uncle Tom's Cabin* on the index of prohibited books. The story noted that whether or not that particular claim was true, "the doctrines of the Catholic Church and the principles of social order and political harmony are always in unison."[85] The paper also highlighted the anti-Catholicism of abolitionists to further distance Catholics from abolitionism.[86] Despite repeated protests, papers continued to claim that Catholics were secretly abolitionists. For example, in October 1856, Father Corcoran responded to a story in the *Due West Telescope* that invoked *In Supremo* as evidence of Catholic sympathy for abolitionists and insisted that the *Miscellany* thus lied about its devotion to the South. Corcoran responded that Catholics were loyal primarily to Catholic doctrine and saw it as their duty to be good citizens. Catholicism rejected "revolutionary attempts" to remake society and, hence, abolitionism.[87] The continued suspicion of Catholicism, particularly during the Know Nothing campaigns of the mid-1850s, intensified the *Miscellany's* condemnations of radicalism and abolitionism.

The *Miscellany*, echoing Catholic teaching, also upheld Bishop England's insistence on the unity of the human race, rejecting the intellectual movement that saw blacks as an inferior, separate species of humanity. Bishop England, in an address on classical education in 1832, had recommended the study of medicine to his audience. He noted that all men throughout the world, on every continent, could be served by a doctor because all were "equally a child of Adam."[88] Despite the new racial theories arising in the 1850s, the *Miscellany* held firm to this view. For example, the paper, commenting in 1851 on an article on polygenesis published in the *Southern Quarterly Review*, noted that "we cannot of course assent to the positions of the writer, who combats the Unity of the human race."[89] Even though John Bachman battled Catholics in the Charleston papers, the *Miscellany* agreed with his defense of the unity of the human race.[90] In this position, they rejected the growing pro-slavery racialism.

The *Miscellany* also opposed radical pro-slavery measures of the 1850s such as the efforts in South Carolina to reopen the transatlantic slave trade and southerners' imperialist adventurism—"filibustering"—in Latin America.[91] In February 1857 the paper reprinted a speech by the governor of Georgia, Herschel Johnson, against reopening the slave trade. Johnson argued that agitation on the subject would only antagonize the South's allies in the North and thus be counterproductive.[92] In August 1857 the paper reprinted notes from a debate in the House of Commons in which British politicians renewed their opposition to efforts to reopen the slave trade. Such stories suggested that political efforts to open the trade would be futile.[93] A few weeks later, Father Corcoran commented positively on the defeat at the Southern Convention of measures designed to support William Walker's filibustering in Nicaragua and to reopen the transatlantic slave trade. Walker, a Tennessean, briefly took over the government of Nicaragua and reinstituted slavery. His supporters hoped to annex other Latin American countries to the United States as slave states.[94] In September 1857, the *Miscellany* reprinted a story from a New Orleans paper detailing the folly of Walker's expedition to Nicaragua. Again, the *Miscellany* refused to endorse pro-slavery radicalism.[95]

While the public positions of the clergy of the Diocese of Charleston up until secession continued to support Bishop England's main points regarding slavery, during the Civil War Bishop Patrick Lynch expressed a different perspective on the institution. Thanks to the efforts of David Heisser, Lynch's 1864 pamphlet on slavery has been recovered and reprinted. Lynch's family owned slaves, and during the war Lynch managed over ninety slaves given to the diocese by the estate of William McKenna, the most prolific slaveholding Catholic in antebellum South Carolina.[96] In 1864 the Confederate States sent Lynch to Rome to seek diplomatic recognition of the Confederacy from the Vatican. His mission failed, and Confederates believed that Pope Pius IX refused to support the Confederacy because of slavery. In 1864, to gain broader European support, Lynch wrote and published a pamphlet on slavery in several languages. The pamphlet differed from Bishop England's writings some twenty years before and revealed that the gradual "ideological reconfiguration of slavery," to use Ford's phrase, had influenced Charleston's third bishop.[97]

The pamphlet began in a fashion similar to Bishop England's writings in identifying slavery as an unfortunate institution but one subject to the moral law. Lynch noted, "To say that *freedom is better than slavery*, is to my mind very much like saying that *health is better than sickness*."[98] But, like sickness, slavery would be a permanent feature of human affairs. Lynch claimed that he did not seek to defend slavery in the abstract but to describe its operation in the United States. He took for granted, however, that slavery was not intrinsically immoral. Thus he could offer his experience with slavery as a credible source of knowledge about the institution. Speaking of himself in the third person, Lynch wrote, "He has spent all his life,—near, half a century—in a slave holding state. For twenty four years he exercised the Ministry among all classes. He has seen the working of the system of Slavery in its daily routine."[99] Lynch characterized the moral ideal within slavery to be paternalism, or as he called it, "patriarchal."[100] The slave was bound to give the master "the produce of his reasonable life long labour under the owner's direction," while the master was "bound in return to give to the slave a reasonable support according to his condition." Slavery involved "mutual claims and obligations" subject to the moral law. There were abuses of the system, but these reflected sinful human nature and did not invalidate the institution of slavery.[101]

One difference in Lynch's pamphlet was his use of racial arguments to support slavery's continued existence in the Confederacy. Ford has argued that by the 1840s the intellectual reconfiguration of the ideology of slavery led its defenders to stress that "slavery as it existed in the South was justified by racial differences."[102] This argument did not have an important place in England's letter to Forsyth, but Lynch relied on essentialist arguments about black people. For example, in describing the necessity of the master's oversight of his slaves, Lynch noted that the master had to counteract "a negro's natural inclination to waste."[103] In describing religion among slaves, Lynch wrote, "Essentially a sensuous race, loving the excitement of an hour, and having generally good voices, and a natural sense of music, the negroes love to join in prayer meetings or assemblies of their own." Speaking of morality among blacks, he asserted, "The negroes are, as a race, very prone to excesses, and, unless restrained, plunge madly into the lowest depths of licentiousness." He rejected the environmentalist argument that slavery might be responsible for this, pointing to the free black populations in the Caribbean for support of his claim. He noted that blacks did not work hard and were "incapable of" any "Self Government."[104] Lynch's argument for the continued existence of slavery rested, then, on the idea of black inferiority. Slavery must continue, he thought, because blacks were suited to little else.[105]

The second major difference between Bishop England and Lynch related to the question of amelioration of the conditions of slavery. England, in reviewing the history of the Catholic Church's interaction with slavery, argued that the church supported ameliorating the slaves' conditions through law and, eventually, eliminating slavery. In this, England stood against the slavery traditionalists, who opposed such talk as dangerous and foolish. But Lynch came down on the side of the slavery traditionalists. For example, Bishop England had begun his school to educate free blacks and by 1840 tried to revive it. But Lynch, in his pamphlet, defended the restriction of education to whites. Repeating the arguments of the slavery traditionalists, he noted that the abolitionists had tried to entice slaves and free blacks to revolt. The laws against black literacy were enacted "to destroy the mode by which evil agents could most artfully and secretly work among them from a safe distance." He concluded, "The propriety of such laws depended on the question, whether the whites were right in endeavouring to protect themselves."[106] The tone of the passage strongly suggests that Lynch believed they had been right.

Another difference between England and Lynch involved the question of slave marriage. In the letters to Forsyth, Bishop England had indicated that laws prohibiting the breaking up of slave marriages by sale of a spouse were one example of Christian ideas making their way into law in order to improve the conditions of slaves. Bishop England did not make a specific policy reference for South Carolina, but his implication was clear: Christianity historically supported protections for slaves under the law. Lynch examined the question but rejected a legal route for amelioration. Instead, he trusted the consciences of the masters and defended the English way of allowing "custom and usage to regulate matters freely so long as they do so tollerably [sic] well."[107] This was exactly the argument of Whitemarsh Seabrook and the slavery traditionalists regarding slave management in general: leave it to the masters and keep the church out of it. Lynch added that the religious diversity of the South would make it impossible to establish marriage tribunals to police slave marriages as had been done in Spanish colonies. Thus it was better left to the masters. He believed that while separations happened, they were not the norm. The church, by teaching both masters and slaves, would do more good than additional laws.[108]

The fourth difference between England and Lynch regarded slave manumission. In the letters to Forsyth, England identified a trend to manumit slaves, highlighting the work of clergy who ransomed and freed slaves. In his last letter, written while the legislature was considering closing loopholes on manumission, the bishop had recorded his desire to see slavery ended. He did not make specific policy recommendations but claimed that manumissions had played a role in the Christian movement to end slavery gradually. Lynch, however, rejected manumissions as impractical and dangerous, again reflecting the attitudes of the slavery traditionalists of the 1830s. Lynch noted that manumissions were once frequent in the South but had declined. He wrote, "But as the number of free negroes increased and the libertinism and viciousness of that class, and their evil influence on the slaves became more evident, the governments of the several states made laws on the subject."[109]

The slavery traditionalists had advocated for an end to manumission to limit the number of free blacks, an increase of which they perceived, especially after the Haitian Revolution, as a wedge to break apart slavery. Lynch also stressed the positive dimensions of laws against manumission. Such laws, for example, tried to prevent masters from freeing old or decrepit slaves in an effort to shirk their duties to care for their slaves. Finally, Lynch noted that, in the context of laws that required free blacks to leave the state—and thus leave behind their families and friends—manumission was for many blacks increasingly unattractive. Thus Lynch tried to justify the declining rate of manumissions.

Lynch and England also differed on the gradual end to slavery. Bishop England had acknowledged the seeming intractability of slavery but in his letters to Forsyth noted that Christianity gradually worked to end the institution. Lynch, at the end of his pamphlet, considered various schemes of emancipation, rejecting each one as dangerous. A general emancipation, he predicted, would increase racial "antagonism" and start a race war. "The atrocities of San Domingo would be reenacted," he wrote.[110] Financial difficulties would cripple the South as well under a general emancipation. He next considered a period of apprenticeship for blacks to prepare them for freedom, as well as plans for colonization of blacks either in Africa or in the western parts of the Confederacy. But he rejected these schemes as impractical and costly.[111] He concluded that the race of American slaves presented the greatest obstacle due to racial antagonism. "If the masters and slaves were of the same race, as was the case in Europe, with regard to the Slavery of the first eight or nine centuries of Christianity, this Antagonism of course would not exist," he wrote. "A freed man would soon be undistinguishable from one always free." Race, however, persisted, and "the members of one can never pass into the other and be lost in the mass."[112] Thus Lynch concluded that slavery would have to continue indefinitely. He could foresee no circumstances in which emancipation would work for the benefit of either whites or blacks. He had begun by stating that he did not seek to defend but describe slavery as it existed. But, in the end, his pamphlet defended slavery as a necessary system of racial control.

The scholar Mark Noll has noted that both Catholics and Protestants in the South fell prey to the racism intertwined with American slavery.

This prevented many sincere Christians from envisioning a world without slavery or even making strong efforts to reform the institution through law. South Carolina Catholics, like their Protestant neighbors, worked to evangelize blacks and, despite the intellectual limits of their views, enjoyed some success. For much of the antebellum period, South Carolina Catholics, especially Bishop England, had tried to maintain a distinctive position on the slavery issue to portray themselves as both faithful Catholics and loyal Southerners. As the Civil War approached, however, other forces, particularly nativism and the spirit of modern revolution, worried white Catholics more than the slavery issue.[113] Indeed, by characterizing abolitionism as part of modern revolutionary thought and by classifying "domestic slavery" as morally permissible, Catholic leaders relegated slavery to the status of a secondary issue. They devoted much more time to attacking nativism and modern revolution. Catholic leaders, then, were unable to maintain their devotion to finding a unique way to approach the issue. It is not surprising that Patrick Lynch's slavery pamphlet, the final public expression of South Carolina Catholics on the issue, adopted the dominant racial justifications of slavery and repeated the reasoning of those slavery traditionalists against whom Bishop England had fought so long. In this important case, the South Carolina Catholic leadership failed to maintain an independent course, eventually capitulating to the position of the dominant culture in which they lived.

Conclusion

The Secession Winter of 1860–61 proved to be a heady time for South Carolina Catholics. On December 29, 1860, Fr. James Corcoran altered the title of his newspaper to the *Catholic Miscellany*, dropping "United States." He explained, "All we could do for the present was to expunge those two obnoxious words, which being henceforth without truth or meaning, would ill become the title of a paper, that, apart from all motives of patriotism, professes to be an advocate of the Truth."[1] Whereas prior to secession the *Miscellany* had largely ignored domestic politics, the 1861 issues covered extensively the buildup to war and its early prosecution. The paper examined the reactions of northern Catholic papers to secession and called to task northern Catholic intellectuals like Orestes Brownson for opposing the South's course of action. The *Miscellany* had long reprinted columns from *Brownson's Review* but now chastised the famous convert for his support of the Union. Father Corcoran noted ironically that Brownson "has discovered and proclaims it to the world that Abe Lincoln is 'an honest man.'" Brownson praised other Republicans as well, leading Corcoran to exclaim, "What a pity that some of Mr. Brownson's strong faith could not be knocked into our hard-headed Commissioners at Washington!"[2]

He referred, of course, to failed Confederate attempts to secure a peaceable transfer of Fort Sumter to Confederate hands. A week later, with "the booming of cannon all over our harbor," at Fort Sumter, Father Corcoran bid the North goodby. "May God in his mercy," he wrote, "protect our homes, avenge a righteous cause, and put to speedy flight the hirelings who already occupy, or are on the point of invading, our soil!"[3] South Carolina Catholics thus proclaimed their loyalty to the Confederate States of America.

Throughout the war, southern Catholics supported the Confederacy with their southern neighbors. Historians have demonstrated that while the Catholic Church in the United States, as a national institution, did not divide during the war, northern Catholics supported the Union and southern Catholics supported the Confederacy.[4] For South Carolina Catholics, the decades of pledging loyalty to the South and her institutions paid off during the war. South Carolina Catholics volunteered for military service and offered prayers for their new nation, showing that they could be trusted as good southerners and republicans. They demonstrated their loyalty to the end.

Non-Catholic southerners appreciated the loyalty of their Catholic neighbors, recognition that antebellum Catholics had craved. One of the most striking examples comes from the South Carolina writer William Gilmore Simms's 1865 pamphlet, *Sack and Destruction of the City of Columbia, S.C.* In January 1865, Gen. William Tecumseh Sherman unleashed his army on the population of South Carolina, resulting in the burning of the capitol in February. Simms produced a gripping narrative of the city's destruction, using many eyewitness accounts. Simms, who had known Bishop England and corresponded with Bishop Lynch, recounted the suffering of Catholics in Columbia in the face of Sherman's terror.

For Simms, Sherman's army treated the citizens of Columbia—of all religious persuasions—equally bad, allowing them to suffer together. In the introduction to his pamphlet, he laments that "six temples of the Most High God have shared the same fate" as did "the schools of learning." "Shrines equally of religion, benevolence and industry," he continued, "are all buried together in one congregated ruin."[5] Simms later wrote, "Our people felt all the danger."[6] The possessive "our" referred to all who suffered together, Catholics and non-Catholics. Everyone's property was threatened. "The negroes," Simms insisted, "were robbed equally with the whites of food and clothing."[7] Quoting the supposed words of one of Sherman's generals, Oliver Howard, "It is only what the country deserves. . . . We will not leave woman or child," Simms stressed that the Yankees treated all they encountered as equally deserving of pain.[8]

In particular, Simms told the story of the destruction of the Ursuline convent in the city as well as the sisters' St. Mary's College, which had been founded by the tireless missionary priest, Rev. Jeremiah Joseph O'Connell. Simms began by mentioning that Sherman had left his "Irish Catholic troops" outside of the city, depriving the Catholics of Columbia of any hope of protection by their coreligionists. The Ursuline convent, Simms wrote, was "under the charge of the sister of the Right Rev. Bishop Lynch" and served as "an academy of the highest class." There the Ursulines educated "the daughters of Protestants of the most wealthy classes throughout the State."[9] Although the nuns had hoped, given their status and occupation, to be spared, they learned from Union officers that Sherman intended to destroy the city. Simms mentioned that the "Mother Superior had clung to her house to the last possible moment" in order to protect the school, which had a prized art collection, musical instruments, and a large library. In addition, many people, fearing the worst from the Union Army, had sent "much treasure" to the convent "for safe keeping."[10] But, as night fell, the nuns abandoned the convent, seeking shelter in St. Peter's Church, the Catholic parish in the city. After barely making it there, the nuns and their students had to spend the night in the graveyard after soldiers attempted to set the church building on fire. Simms mentioned that a similar scene occurred at the Presbyterian graveyard, which also held refugees seeking protection.[11]

In his pamphlet, Simms noted sadly the destruction of the convent and school, quoting from a letter by Rev. Lawrence O'Connell. Father O'Connell wrote that St. Mary's College "was robbed, pillaged and then given to the flames." Not only did the art collection burn, but so did the "excellent library," which had been "selected with great care, and with no limited view to expense." Some of the priests who taught at the college lost personal libraries and their "notes taken from lectures of the most eminent men in Europe." These treasures were "not often valued by the vulgar, but to the compiler they are more priceless than diamonds."[12] Simms undoubtedly shared Father O'Connell's desolation. His own extensive library at his plantation, Woodlands, suffered the same fate at the hands of Sherman's soldiers.[13]

Simms pointed out that Catholics also suffered grave insults to their religion. The Union Army arrested one priest who begged in vain to save religious objects from the burning convent. "A sacrilegious squad drank their whiskey from the sacred chalice," Simms recounted. "The sacred vestments and consecrated vessels used for the celebration of the mass— all things, indeed, pertaining to the exercise of sacerdotal function— were profaned and stolen."[14] When some of the nuns protested to a Union officer about the destruction of their convent as well as a small replica of the Cathedral of Charleston, the man "muttered bitterly" that he wished "the same fate to befall every cathedral in which *Te Deum* had been performed at the downfall of our glorious flag."[15] Simms explained that Bishop Lynch had sung the *Te Deum* after the surrender of Fort Sumter and hinted that the Union officers knew that the bishop's sister headed the Ursulines in Columbia.[16] Thus the Union Army had plotted and executed its revenge.

In Simms's view, the crucible of suffering melted together the people of Columbia. Catholics took their places in Simms's narrative beside Presbyterians, Episcopalians, and Freemasons, all of whom had lost property during the sack of the city. In one sense, Simms's pamphlet echoes book 2 of Virgil's *Aeneid* on the Sack of Troy. The survivors of the horrific destruction formed the Roman race that went on to greatness; Simms hoped history would repeat. His vivid portrait of common suffering fulfilled the longings of all who followed Bishop England's strategy. Catholics, declared the South's preeminent man of letters, were loyal southerners too.

Not all South Carolina Catholics, however, took comfort in their new-found acceptance. Father O'Connell, who served as a missionary in the Diocese of Charleston for over thirty years, wrote the first history of the diocese in 1879 during his retirement at a Benedictine monastery in North Carolina. O'Connell had been in Columbia when it burned and made references to Simms's *Sack and Destruction* in his narrative. But he saw the Civil War as a tragedy for the church in South Carolina because it had destroyed all progress made since the formation of the diocese in 1820.

Like Simms, O'Connell employed images from the *Aeneid* to explain the difficulties southerners faced. In 1833 Bishop England had written to Rome about his overwhelming task, "My diocess is one of the largest, and perhaps it is the poorest, in all Christendom."[17] O'Connell depicted John England as Aeneas: "He was chosen to be the apostle of the new Continent and transferred from the banks of the River Lee, a Catholic Ilium, to the distant shores of Carolina, with a new St. Finbar's whose free and merry bells would sound happier and sweeter on the placid streams of the Ashley and Cooper."[18] Just as Virgil highlighted Aeneas's burden or labor (Latin *molus*) in founding Rome, O'Connell commented of Bishop England, "The establishment of the diocese was a worldwide labor, and consumed all the days of his life."[19] Whereas Aeneas's charge—the Roman mission to pacify and govern the world—was secular, O'Connell described Bishop England's charge as religious: "It was Bishop England who overthrew all error in the land, refuted calumnies, rebuked falsehood, disarmed prejudice, broke down opposition, established sees, built the Church, conquered enemies, founded religion, and won respect for both classes of the hierarchy, not only in the diocese of Charleston, but all over the United States."[20]

O'Connell's account of the difficulty of Bishop England's charge emphasized that the main problem he faced was Catholicism's location on the periphery of southern culture. Southern Catholics, he lamented, had made few converts. O'Connell estimated that only "about fifty influential families ha[d] joined the Church" since 1820 in the three states that had originally composed the diocese. On the other hand, Catholics had more success with those of lower status. "Many individuals, poor people and negroes," O'Connell commented, "have been converted, children baptized before death, and the Faith preserved among the adults or immigrants generally."[21] Most Catholics in South Carolina were, like Father O'Connell, Irish immigrants. Quoting from an article in the *Catholic Review*, O'Connell corroborated the prejudice against the Irish and pointed out that the immigrants were usually "the poorest and least educated class of their native country."[22] It was virtually impossible to construct a permanent, respectable institution in southern culture on the foundation of the poor, working-class Irish.

Near the end of his lengthy narrative, Father O'Connell also lamented the lack of social status the Catholic Church possessed in the South. Whereas northern bishops worked "to provide churches for their constantly growing numbers," southern bishops and their paltry number of missionary priests worked hard "to obtain a Catholic at all."[23] He noted that a "few persons of intelligence and social position had the courage to brave public opinion and profess the faith," but "their influence in society was limited by universal condemnation." "They," O'Connell continued, "were branded as crazy people or fools, and would not be elected to fill the most paltry offices of the State."[24] Catholics endured "constant struggle" and "unconsolable labor" along with "unmitigated poverty" in their work to establish their faith.[25] O'Connell's narrative in part blames the slow progress of the faith in the South on its inability to provide sufficient institutions that could render a Catholic culture in the South plausible.

Ultimately, O'Connell blamed the Civil War for halting the progress made building Catholic institutions in the South. The bishops of Charleston had labored, particularly in the field of education, to build institutions that would cater to southerners and help to dispel prejudice. O'Connell himself had worked to found St. Mary's College in Columbia. Bishop Reynolds and Bishop Lynch had constructed a beautiful cathedral church in Charleston. O'Connell noted several cases of anti-Catholic prejudice in Confederate South Carolina but admitted that the "Church was at last popular." "But her outward glory," he lamented, "was short-lived and evanescent as the bloom of the morning flower which vanishes at eve; it perished with the Confederacy."[26] The great Charleston cathedral burned down in a fire that ravaged the city in December 1861.[27] The fire also destroyed the bishop's residence and "the extensive diocesan library." Due to a clerical error, the diocese had allowed its insurance policy on the cathedral to lapse. All was lost.[28] More damage occurred under the brutality of Sherman's army as it destroyed much of Columbia's Catholic institutional presence. O'Connell commented, "The destruction of our religious and educational institutions . . . threw the congregation back into its normal state, and retarded the progress of our holy Faith many years."[29] O'Connell compared Columbia under Sherman to "Rome under Nero" and "Paris under Robespierre."[30] The war had returned the diocese to "the same position in the United States as at the consecration of Archbishop Carroll, in 1790."[31] In the aftermath, Bishop Lynch resorted to begging among the Yankees in order to rebuild his shattered diocese.[32]

The prospect of restarting efforts to build up the Catholic Church in southern culture seemed daunting. O'Connell, who hated the institution of slavery for its moral effects on whites and blacks, hoped emancipation would help the church in its mission, but he knew that Catholics in South Carolina had suffered a heavy blow.[33] Despite much labor, Catholics had made little progress. While non-Catholics like Simms might welcome Catholics as loyal southerners, such attitudes did not rebuild infrastructure or make converts. The war deprived South Carolina Catholics of a stronger institutional presence in which they could concentrate their cultural and religious efforts. For Catholicism to grow in the South, Catholics needed plausible institutions patronized by both Catholics and non-Catholic southerners that provided access to the cultural mainstream. Until this occurred, Catholics would have to use secular or Protestant institutions to gain cultural credentials and acceptance. Access to southern cultural centers could be a sign of diminishing anti-Catholic prejudice, but it meant that Catholics would engage non-Catholic southerners primarily on secular or Protestant grounds. While this could encourage a common purpose and identity as southerners—as Simms's narrative suggested—it made the Catholic task of converting southerners and winning acceptance as Catholics (not just as southerners) much more difficult. Despite decades of effort by both clergy and laity, the dependence of Catholics on secular culture was the legacy of antebellum Catholicism in the diocese of Charleston. The Civil War, which destroyed the South, reduced clerical dreams of a southern Catholicism to ashes. Postbellum generations would have to build anew.

Introduction

1. In 2009, the historian Kevin Levin posted to his Civil War Memory blog the story of the crown of thorns and then a few weeks later a retraction. In his first post—"So It Was a Holy Cause After All" (September 10, 2009)—Levin included on his blog a picture of Pope Benedict XVI standing next to President George W. Bush, waving to a crowd. In the background are two flags, one of which is the Confederate Battle flag. Levin commented, "Apparently, Pope Benedict is continuing the Catholic Church's tradition of sanctifying the Confederate cause. So, it looks like the Myth of the Lost Cause wasn't a myth after all. I had no idea." Commenters on the blog quickly pointed out that the pope was standing on a stage lined with state flags. The Confederate flag in the picture was part of the state flag of Mississippi. The pope's appearance had nothing to do with either the Civil War or the South. (See http://cwmemory.com/2009/09/10/so-it-was-a-holy-cause-after-all/.) Levin's immediate reaction to the image reflects an idea that can be found in scholarly circles as well: the natural affinity between the Old South and Catholicism. Levin, on September 27, 2009, wrote "Update on Jefferson Davis's Crown of Thorns," in which he demonstrated that the "crown of thorns" had been made by Varina Davis (http://cwmemory.com/2009/09/27/update-on-jefferson-daviss-crown-of-thorns/).

2. Curran, "Rome, the American Church, and Slavery," 33.

3. For one example, see *The Liberator* (Boston, MA), December 12, 1851. During the controversy over Louis Kossuth's visit (discussed in ch. 5), Garrison's *Liberator* ridiculed Kossuth for failing to come out against slavery. But the abolitionist paper also attacked Archbishop Hughes and Orestes Brownson for rejecting Kossuth. The writer, calling himself "Sharpstick," asserted, "I firmly believe that

Romanism is a deadly and unscrupulous enemy of the rights of mankind." The paper attacked Catholics and southerners and sometimes linked them together.

4. William Kurtz includes in his book an 1870 Thomas Nast political cartoon picturing simian Irish Catholics and Confederates firing on Fort Sumter. The cartoon protested Catholic attempts to gain public funding for Catholic schools in New York and used the comparison to Confederates to suggest disloyalty to the United States. *Excommunicated from the Union*, 137.

5. Wallace, *Catholics, Slaveholders, and the Dilemma of American Evangelicalism, 1835–1860*; Franchot, *Roads to Rome*.

6. Genovese, *The Southern Tradition*, 14–15, 25; Fox-Genovese and Genovese, *The Mind of the Master Class*, 321–24; Faust, *A Sacred Circle*, 66.

7. Stern, *Southern Crucifix, Southern Cross*, 17.

8. Gleeson, *The Irish in the South*, 194.

9. Thompson, *The Church, the South and the Future*, 93–94; Haddox, *Fears and Fascinations*; Giemza, *Irish Catholic Writers and the Invention of the American South*. See Eugene Genovese's comment in *The World the Slaveholders Made*, 190: "That the South was Protestant rather than Roman Catholic proved to be unfortunate, as Fitzhugh appreciated in his day and perhaps only Allen Tate has appreciated in ours."

10. Miller, "A Church in Cultural Captivity," 14. Miller has written a number of other essays on Catholics in the South that should be read as well. Miller, "Catholics in a Protestant World; Miller, "Roman Catholicism in South Carolina."

11. See Clark, "The South's Irish Catholics"; Joyce, "White, Worker, Irish, and Confederate." For other treatments of the Irish in South Carolina, see O'Brien, "The Irish in Charleston, South Carolina"; Gleeson and Buttimer, "We Are Irish Everywhere."

12. Jenkins, *The Lost History of Christianity*, 245.

13. Quigley, *Shifting Grounds*, 41–49. Some of the other works on southern and Confederate nationalism that I consulted are Faust, *The Creation of Confederate Nationalism*; Rable, *The Confederate Republic*; McCardell, *The Idea of a Southern Nation*; Bernath, *Confederate Minds*; Walther, *The Fire-Eaters*; Heidler, *Pulling the Temple Down*; and the classic treatment, Potter, "The Historian's Use of Nationalism and Vice Versa."

14. Quigley, *Shifting Grounds*, 16–86; Anderson, *Imagined Communities*.

15. Quigley, *Shifting Grounds*, 35–41.

16. Gutzman, *Virginia's American Revolution*, 101.

17. Kastor, *The Nation's Crucible*, 22.

18. Thomas Jefferson to Dr. Joseph Priestley, January 29, 1804, in Jefferson, *Thomas Jefferson: Writings*, 1142.

19. Calhoun, "Speech on the Veto Power," February 28, 1842, in Lence, *Union and Liberty*, 493.

20. Genovese, *Southern Tradition*, 44. Taken in a constitutional sense, Calhoun's "assemblage of peoples" refers to the people of the separate states being the components of the Union. But Genovese seems to expand that sense to cover a broader meaning about the various peoples that made up the South. I follow Genovese's implication when using this phrase.

21. Anderson, *Imagined Communities*, 36.

22. Quigley, *Shifting Grounds*, 56–63; Carpenter, *The South as a Conscious Minority*, 7–41.

23. Miller, Introduction to *Catholics in the Old South*, 6.

24. Gjerde, *Catholicism and the Shaping of Nineteenth-Century America*, 14, 174. See also Tate, "The Power of Historical Narrative."

25. Quoted in Quigley, *Shifting Grounds*, 43. The quotation appears in Simms, *The Wigwam and the Cabin*, 4. Unless otherwise noted, all emphases appear in the original sources. See also Moltke-Hansen, "Southern Literary Horizons in Young America," esp. 6.

26. The historian of southern Catholicism Michael J. McNally remarked in a 1987 article, "Secondary material on Catholicism in the Southeast is scarce, especially material on the lower states. The availability of primary sources also presented difficulties." His comment is still true, although the secondary literature has grown significantly. "A Peculiar Institution," 122.

27. Gleeson, *The Irish in the South*, 82.

28. Anderson, *Imagined Communities*, 79–80.

29. Gleeson discusses Irish Catholics and the Lost Cause in the conclusion to *The Green and the Gray*, 222–24.

CHAPTER ONE. *The Context of Catholicism in Antebellum South Carolina*

1. Gleeson, "The New Americanism in Catholic Historiography." For various narratives and arguments, see Hennesey, "Roman Catholicism," 284. See also Hennesey, *American Catholics*; Casanova, "Roman and Catholic and American," 83; Dolan, *In Search of an American Catholicism*, chs. 1 and 2; Dolan, *Catholic Revivalism*; Chinnici, "American Catholics and Religious Pluralism"; Carey, "American Catholic Romanticism, 1830–1888"; O'Brien, *Public Catholicism*, chs. 1 and 2. On the Ultramontanes, see McGreevy, *Catholicism and American Freedom*, 19–42. See R. Laurence Moore's perceptive work, *Religious Outsiders and the Making of Americans*, 3–21, 48–71, for a persuasive challenge to the contours of the traditional historiographical debate about nineteenth-century Catholic immigration. With keen insight, Moore explains the strength and consequences of the Americanist perspective in interpreting the history of Catholicism in America.

See Carroll, *American Catholics and the Protestant Imagination*, 1–61, for a challenge to the traditional characterization of the Irish.

2. Scholars have debated the exact nature of South Carolina culture before the Civil War. Banner, "The Problem of South Carolina." See also Weir, "The South Carolinian as Extremist"; Sinha, *The Counterrevolution of Slavery*. Lacy K. Ford Jr. has offered a different interpretation in his seminal *Origins of Southern Radicalism*, 101–2.

3. Edgar, *South Carolina*, 269.

4. Ford, *Origins of Southern Radicalism*, 12, 14.

5. Freehling, *Prelude to Civil War*, 25–48.

6. Ford, *Origins of Southern Radicalism*, 244, 43.

7. Dodd and Dodd, *Historical Statistics of the South*, 46.

8. Edgar, *South Carolina*, 276–77, 288.

9. Fraser, *Charleston, Charleston*; Pease and Pease, *Web of Progress*; Bellows, *Benevolence among Slaveholders*; Strum, "South Carolina and Irish Famine Relief."

10. Ford, *Origins of Southern Radicalism*, 36–37.

11. Ibid.,102, 94–95. Ford focuses on the idea of personal independence.

12. Bartlett, *John C. Calhoun*, 30–31; Ford, *Origins of Southern Radicalism*, 92–95.

13. Smith, "Remembering Mary, Shaping Revolt"; Basil, "South Carolina Catholics before the Roman Discipline," 791–93.

14. Miller, "Roman Catholicism in South Carolina," 86.

15. I derived my account from Basil, "South Carolina Catholics before the Roman Discipline"; Guilday, *Life and Times of John England, First Bishop of Charleston*, 1:164–282; Gillikin, "Competing Loyalties"; Madden, *Catholics in South Carolina*, 17–29.

16. The national population in 1820 has been estimated at 9,618,000. In 1850, the estimate is 23,261,000. Austin, *Political Facts of the United States since 1789*, 461. New England's population in 1820 was 4,359,916 and in 1850, 8,626,851. Anderton, Barrett, and Bogue, *The Population of the United States*, 27.

17. Dodd and Dodd, *Historical Statistics of the South*, 18, 38, 46.

18. Dolan, *Catholic Revivalism*, 8.

19. Woods, *History of the Catholic Church in the American South*, 260, table 8.3. The statistics on churches that follow come from Woods's book.

20. *The Metropolitan Catholic Almanac and Laity's Directory, for the Year of Our Lord 1851*, 118.

21. McNally, "A Peculiar Institution," 124, 129.

22. Woods, *History of the Catholic Church in the American South*, 258.

23. Gleeson, *Irish in the South*, 16–17, 23–25.

24. Lowman, "James Andrew Corcoran," 71–81.

25. See Basil, "South Carolina Catholics before the Roman Discipline"; Guilday, *The Life and Times of John England*, 1:164–282; Gillikin, "Competing Loyalties," 146–60; Krebsbach, "Black Catholics in Antebellum Charleston"; Silver, "A New Look at Old South Urbanization"; Bell, "Regional Identity in the Antebellum South"; Gleeson, *Irish in the South*. These works contain tidbits about the various groups of Catholics mentioned.

26. Campbell, "Bishop England's Sisterhood," 18–20.

27. "Statistics," *United States Catholic Miscellany* (Charleston, SC), August 1, 1829.

28. *Metropolitan Catholic Almanac and Laity's Directory, for the Year of Our Lord 1851*, 116–17; Stern, *Southern Crucifix, Southern Cross*, 13.

29. O'Connell, *Catholicity in the Carolinas and Georgia*, 602.

30. Heisser and White, *Patrick N. Lynch*, 7–14; O'Connell, *Catholicity in the Carolinas and Georgia*, 170–74.

31. O'Connell, *Catholicity in the Carolinas and Georgia*, 606, 357, 342.

32. Silver, "A New Look at Old South Urbanization," 149–51; Gleeson, *Irish in the South*, 29.

33. Not all Catholics, including specifically the Irish, were confined to urban areas in the North. See the excellent work by Emmons, *Beyond the American Pale*.

34. Woods, *History of the Catholic Church in the American South*, 249.

35. Carey, *An Immigrant Bishop*, 7, 60. The biographical data come from Carey (3–97); and Clarke, *Lives of the Deceased Bishops of the Catholic Church in the United States*, 1:271–309.

36. Kearns, "Bishop John England and the Possibilities of Catholic Republicanism." The best work on John England and republicanism is unfortunately unpublished; see Devanny, "Bishop John England and the Rhetoric of Republicanism."

37. England, "Report of Bishop England to the Cardinal Prefect of Propaganda."

38. Ibid., 319. On the trustee issue, see Basil, "South Carolina Catholics before the Roman Discipline"; Guilday, *Life and Times of John England, First Bishop of Charleston*, 1:164–282; Carey, "The Laity's Understanding of the Trustee System, 1785–1855"; McNeil, *Recovering American Catholic Inculturation*.

39. England, "Report of Bishop England to the Cardinal Prefect of Propaganda," 319–20.

40. Ibid., 322.

41. Ibid., 321.

42. Ibid., 322.

43. Ibid., 323.

44. Ibid., 325.

45. Mathews, *Religion in the Old South*, 82, 97.

46. My reading of Bishop England's intention comes from the theory of cultural change outlined by the sociologist James Davison Hunter of the University of Virginia in a 2002 talk, "To Change the World," presented to the Trinity Forum. http://71513.netministry.com/images/TO_CHANGE_THE_WORLD_HUNTER.pdf (pp. 3–13).

47. Clarke, *Lives of the Deceased Bishops of the Catholic Church in the United States*, 2:291–309. O'Connell, *Catholicity in the Carolinas and Georgia*, 112–13, provides some personal details about Reynolds as well. See also Guilday, *A History of the Councils of Baltimore*, 140.

48. Reynolds wrote a long letter to Lynch about his (Lynch's) finances, January 31, 1847, Box 5, Folder H, Archives of the Diocese of Charleston, Charleston, SC. See Reynolds's letter to his clergy announcing his plans to build a new cathedral and commenting on the financial state he discovered when he took over in 1844: *United States Catholic Miscellany*, January 17, 1846. And see Reynolds's letter to Lynch about his desire to keep the *Miscellany* running: June 11, 1845, Box 5, Folder C, Archives of the Diocese of Charleston: "I have great anxiety about the Miscellany, and one of my principal objects in writing you, is to entreat you to make a powerful and unyielding effort to sustain that paper."

49. See Tate, "Catholics and Southern Honor."

50. The biographical details come from Heisser and White, *Patrick N. Lynch*, 4–56.

51. The letters are excerpted in Zanca, *American Catholics and Slavery*, 242–47.

52. Heisser and White, *Patrick N. Lynch*, 57–125. See also Heisser, "Bishop Lynch's People."

53. Heisser and White, *Patrick N. Lynch*, 126–91.

CHAPTER TWO.   *Spreading the Word*

1. England, "Address to the First Convention of the Diocess Held at the Cathedral at Charleston, November 1839," in Messmer, *Works*, 7:252, 253, 258, 259–60.

2. Ibid., 261, 260.

3. Shaw, *American Church*, 3–5; McGreevy, *Catholicism and American Freedom*, 19–42; Dolan, *In Search of an American Catholicism*, 65–70; Byrne, "American Ultramontanism"; McAvoy, "Americanism and Frontier Catholicism," esp. 293–94; Spalding, "The Catholic Frontiers"; Tentler, "How I Would Save them All." More recent scholarship has questioned the assumption that the frontier environment promoted the ideological Americanization of nineteenth-century Catholics. See Dichtl, *Frontiers of Faith*, 3–7, 187–91. See also Pasquier, *Fathers on the Frontier*, 152; ch. 2 lays out the difficulties of missionary priests on the frontier. Other

accounts focused on various cultural and ideological factors, e.g., O'Connell, *Catholicity in the Carolinas and Georgia.* O'Connell wrote the first history of the diocese of Charleston and harped on the influence of nativism throughout (see, e.g., 408–10). Another work focused on Catholic theological trends as either attracting or repelling Southern Protestants is Buttimer, "Turning Away from Georgia and Toward Rome." Randall Miller focused on a number of important material factors in Catholicism's struggles in the South: R. Miller, "A Church in Cultural Captivity," 38, 42, 44–45. My conclusions in this chapter support in general the perspective of Stern, *Southern Crucifix, Southern Cross,* 2–17.

4. England, "Address to the Fifth Church Convention in South Carolina, November 1827," in Messmer, *Works,* 7:87.

5. England, "Address to the Twelfth Church Convention in South Carolina, November 1835," in Messmer, *Works,* 7:141.

6. Loveland, *Southern Evangelicals and the Social Order,* 45–47.

7. Heyrman, *Southern Cross,* 82–83; Hatch, *The Democratization of American Christianity,* 60–61, 79, 195–200.

8. England, "Address to the Eighth Church Convention in South Carolina, November 1830," in Messmer, *Works,* 7:106.

9. England, "Address to the Eighth Church Convention in Georgia, May 1835," in Messmer, *Works,* 7:244.

10. England, "Address to the Society of St. John the Baptist, First Anniversary, 1836," in Messmer, *Works,* 7:282.

11. England, "Address to the Second Church Convention in Georgia, April 1827," in Messmer, *Works,* 7:207.

12. England to Petit De Villers, Esq., May 27, 1829, in England, "Letters from the Right Reverend John England, D.D., to the Honorable William Gaston, LL.D., continued," 119–20.

13. Scholars have commented on the tensions between the French and Irish clergy in the United States. See Guilday, *Life and Times of John England,* 1:221–24, 275, 481–82; McAvoy, "The Formation of a Catholic Minority in the United States 1820–1860." On French priests in the antebellum South, see Pasquier, *Fathers on the Frontier.*

14. England to Dr. M. O'Connor, February 25, 1835, in England, "Papers Relating to the Church in America, Third Series," 201.

15. England, "Address to the Seventh Church Convention in South Carolina, November 1829," in Messmer, *Works,* 7:97.

16. England, "Address to the Second Church Convention in South Carolina, November 1824," in Messmer, *Works,* 7:80.

17. England to William Gaston, February 18, 1822, in England, "Letters from the Right Reverend John England, D.D. to the Honorable William Gaston, LL.D.," 380.

18. O'Connell, *Catholicity in the Carolinas and Georgia*, 165.

19. England, "Address to the Fifteenth Church Convention in South Carolina, November 1838," in Messmer, *Works*, 7:184.

20. See Carey, "Voluntaryism," 49–62. Carey, *An Immigrant Bishop*, 5–81.

21. England, "Address to the First Convention of the Diocess Held at the Cathedral at Charleston, November 1839" in Messmer, *Works*, 7:256–57.

22. England, "Undated Manuscript," in England, "Papers Relating to the Church in America, Fourth Series," 304, 303, 305.

23. Ibid., 303. On different types of republicanism, see McDonald, *Novus Ordo Seclorum*, 70–71. See also Kearns, "Bishop John England and the Possibilities of Catholic Republicanism."

24. England, "Undated Manuscript," in "Papers Relating to the Church in America, Fourth Series," 307–8.

25. England to Simon Bruté, June 9, 1827, Box 3, Folder B, Archives of the Diocese of Charleston. Bruté would later serve as the first bishop of the Diocese of Vincennes, Indiana.

26. See Pocock, *The Machiavellian Moment*, 506–49, on the dialogue between virtue and corruption in the American republican tradition.

27. England, "Address to the Fifth Church Convention in South Carolina, November 1827," in Messmer, *Works*, 7:86.

28. "Philosophical and Classical Seminary of Charleston," *United States Catholic Miscellany*, June 12, 1822.

29. England, "To the Public," *United States Catholic Miscellany*, August 14, 1822.

30. England to William Gaston, September 21, 1822, in England, "Letters from the Right Reverend John England, D.D. to the Honorable William Gaston, LL.D.," 381–82.

31. England to William Gaston, December 18, 1824, in England, "Letters from the Right Reverend John England, D.D. to the Honorable William Gaston, LL.D., continued," 102.

32. England, "Address to the Second Church Convention in South Carolina, November 1824," in Messmer, *Works*, 7:81.

33. England to Francis Lieber, October 27, 1835, Box 3, Folder S, Archives of the Diocese of Charleston.

34. England, "Address to the Society of St. John the Baptist, Second Anniversary, November 1837," in Messmer, *Works*, 7:291.

35. Bratt, "The Reorientation of American Protestantism," 67.

36. See Guilday, *Life and Times of John England*, 1:474–516. The opening of the seminary is described: "Charleston," *United States Catholic Miscellany*, January 26, 1825.

37. Billington, *The Protestant Crusade 1800–1860*, 121.

38. England, "Address to the Tenth Church Convention in South Carolina, November 1833," in Messmer, *Works*, 7:122, 124.

39. England, "Address to the Twelfth Church Convention in South Carolina, November 1835," in Messmer, *Works*, 7:142. See Guilday, *Life and Times of John England*, 1:522–40, for background to his travels during these years.

40. Morse, "Imminent Dangers to the Free Institutions of the United States through Foreign Immigration and the Present State of the Naturalization Laws," 9–10.

41. England, "Address to the Twelfth Church Convention in South Carolina, November 1835," in Messmer, *Works*, 7:143; see also 7:241–42.

42. England, "Address to the Society of St. John the Baptist, First Anniversary, 1836," in Messmer, *Works*, 7:280.

43. "Missionary Society," *United States Catholic Miscellany*, January 24, 1835.

44. England, "Address to the Society of St. John the Baptist, First Anniversary, 1836," in Messmer, *Works*, 7:281.

45. Ibid., 7:283, 281.

46. England, "Address to the Eighth Church Convention in South Carolina, May 1835," in Messmer, *Works*, 7:245.

47. Tocqueville, *Democracy in America*, 600, 601, 603–4.

48. Appleby, *Inheriting the Revolution*, 99–100. All statistics are from Appleby.

49. Moore, "Religion, Secularization, and the Shaping of the Culture Industry in Antebellum America," 219.

50. John, "Recasting the Information Infrastructure for the Industrial Age," 58–59. John connects the growth of newspapers to congressional legislation.

51. Ibid., 60–61.

52. Ibid., 68. See also John, *Spreading the News*, for more background on the transfer of information in the early republic. See Pasley, *"The Tyranny of Printers,"* for the political side of the newspaper business.

53. Ratner and Teeter, *Fanatics and Fire Eaters*, 8.

54. Hatch, *Democratization of American Christianity*, 145–46.

55. Moore, "Religion, Secularization, and the Shaping of the Culture Industry in Antebellum America," 218. See also Zboray, *A Fictive People*, 89–92.

56. Nord, "Religious Reading and Readers in Antebellum America," 242–45, quotations on 242, 245. See also Nord, "The Evangelical Origins of Mass Media in America."

57. American Tract Society, "The American Colporteur System," reprinted in *The American Tract Society Documents, 1824–1925*, 17. The ATS established a Depository (branch) in Charleston in 1822. *The American Tract Society Documents*, 93.

58. John Wolffe, "Anti-Catholicism and Evangelical Identity in Britain and the United States, 1830–1860." Wolffe details the extent of anti-Catholic organizing and mentions the large quantity of publications aimed at Catholics.

59. Carey, *An Immigrant Bishop*, 20.

60. England, *Diurnal of the Right Rev. John England, D.D., First Bishop of Charleston, SC*, 45.

61. England to Gaston, February 18, 1822, in England, "Letters from the Right Reverend John England, D.D. to the Honorable William Gaston, LL.D.," 380.

62. Foik, "Pioneer Efforts in Catholic Journalism in the United States (1809–1840)," 265.

63. England, "Report of Bishop England to the Cardinal Prefect of Propaganda," 325.

64. *United States Catholic Miscellany*, June 5, 1822.

65. "Prospectus," *United States Catholic Miscellany*, June 12, 1822.

66. England, "Address to the Twelfth Church Convention in South Carolina, November 1835," in Messmer, *Works*, 7:149.

67. "United States," *United States Catholic Miscellany*, June 5, 1822.

68. O'Connell, *Catholicity in the Carolinas and Georgia*, 560.

69. "Address before the Sixth Church Convention of Georgia, March 1831," in Messmer, *Works*, 7:227.

70. England, "Report of Bishop England to the Cardinal Prefect of Propaganda," 325–26.

71. "To Our Subscribers and to the Public," *United States Catholic Miscellany*, July 22, 1826.

72. John England to Simon Bruté, August 28, 1825, Box 2, Folder K, Archives of the Diocese of Charleston.

73. See the *Miscellany*, November 10, 1849, for an announcement of the sale of *The Works of Bishop England* and praise for Reynolds that he exhumed Bishop England writings "from the pages of an obscure paper at great labor and risk."

74. Ignatius Reynolds, Preface to *The Works of the Right Reverend John England*, 1:v–vii. There are various letters in the Archives of the Diocese of Charleston concerning the *Works*. In Box 11, Folder D, there are reports from two people regarding subscriptions to the *Works* in Charleston and Augusta, Georgia.

75. "Bishop England," *Charleston Courier* (Charleston, SC), October 23, 1849.

76. "From the N.O. Bulletin," *United States Catholic Miscellany*, January 5, 1850.

77. "Writings of Bishop England," 96, 97.

78. "Compiled from the Boston Pilot," *United States Catholic Miscellany*, December 29, 1849.

79. Kenrick, "The Works of the Right Rev. John England First Bishop of Charleston, collected and arranged under the immediate Advice and Direction of his immediate successor, the Right Rev. Ignatius Aloysius Reynolds." Carey, *An Immigrant Bishop*, 215, lists Bishop Francis Kenrick of Philadelphia as the author.

Gallicanism refers to the French Catholic religious movement that stressed the rights of the French government over French bishops at the expense of papal control.

80. O'Connell, *Catholicity in the Carolinas and Georgia*, 117.

81. "Bishop England's Works," *United States Catholic Miscellany*, January 20, 1855.

82. Walters, *American Reformers*, 3–4, 24–37.

83. Bellows, *Benevolence among Slaveholders*, 27.

84. Campbell, "Bishop England's Sisterhood," 11–14; "A Southern Teaching Order."

85. England, "Address to the First Convention of the Diocess Held at the Cathedral at Charleston, November 1839," in Messmer, *Works*, 7:258–59.

86. Humphreys, *Yellow Fever and the South*, 1, 3.

87. Pierce and Writer, *Yellow Jack*, 55.

88. Humphreys, *Yellow Fever and the South*, 49.

89. Heath, *Constructive Liberalism*, 232. On the outbreak, see Foster, "Nightmare on Broad Street"; Jones and Dutcher, *Memorial History of Augusta, Georgia*, 254–62.

90. "Board of Health," *Georgia Constitutionalist* (Augusta, GA), August 29, 1839.

91. "Health of Augusta," *Charleston Courier* (Charleston, SC), August 26, 1839; and *Charleston Courier*, August 30, 1839.

92. "Health of Augusta," *Georgia Constitutionalist* (Augusta, GA), September 5, 1839. Notice of Dr. Antony's death appeared in the October 10, 1839, issue.

93. *Georgia Constitutionalist* (Augusta, GA), September 5, 1839.

94. *Tri-Weekly Chronicle & Sentinel* (Augusta, GA), November 11, 1839.

95. "Health of Augusta, &c.," *Georgia Constitutionalist* (Augusta, GA), October 24, 1839.

96. "The Fever," *Southern Banner* (Athens, GA), September 27, 1839; *Charleston Courier* (Charleston, SC), September 10, 1839.

97. *Tri-Weekly Chronicle & Sentinel* (Augusta, GA), November 12, 1839. Edward J. Cashin estimates the population in *The Story of Augusta*, 85.

98. "Health of Augusta," *Georgia Constitutionalist* (Augusta, GA), November 12, 1839.

99. "Mayor's Office," *Georgia Constitutionalist* (Augusta, GA), October 3, 1839.

100. "Board of Health," *Charleston Courier* (Charleston, SC), October 5, 1839.

101. *Chronicle & Sentinel* (Augusta, GA), November 19, 1839. See also Alfred Cumming's obituary in the *Augusta Chronicle* (Augusta, GA), October 25, 1873, for more information.

102. See "Sisters of Our Lady of Mercy" and the letters that follow, *United States Catholic Miscellany*, November 16, 1839.

103. Ibid.

104. Ibid.

105. "The Mayor of Augusta," *United States Catholic Miscellany*, December 21, 1839.

106. Ibid. On Sand Hills or Summerville, as it came to be called, see Cashin, "Summerville, Retreat of the Old South." Cashin mentions on p. 48 that Summerville was a retreat from fever outbreaks in Augusta.

107. Callahan, "Development of the Roman Catholic Society of Augusta and Richmond County during the Nineteenth Century," 10–12.

108. "Judge Longstreet's Letter," *United States Catholic Miscellany*, March 1, 1856.

109. O'Connell, *Catholicity in the Carolinas and Georgia*, 105–6, 112–13.

110. "Tributes to the Memory of Our Deceased Prelate," *United States Catholic Miscellany*, March 24, 1855.

111. Meehan, "Canonical Visitation," in *Catholic Encyclopedia*, 15:479–80. The article includes a description of the ceremony.

112. Sell, *The Geography of Georgia*, 8.

113. Dodd and Dodd, *Historical Statistics of the South*, 18. In order to place Georgia's population density in 1850 in context, the listings of the population density of several other states for that year are as follows. Southern states: South Carolina, 23.87; Kentucky, 26.07; Virginia, 23.17; Alabama, 15.21; Mississippi, 12.86; Louisiana, 12.52. Northern states: Connecticut, 78.06; Massachusetts, 137.17; New York, 67.33; New Jersey, 71.46; Pennsylvania, 49.19; Rhode Island, 122.95; Vermont, 39.26. "Midwestern" states: Ohio, 49.55; Michigan, 7.07; Illinois, 15.37; Indiana, 29.24. It is not surprising that the states in the Northeast have produced more research and possessed more, and more stable, Catholic institutions in the nineteenth century. They all had population densities three to seven times greater than those in the South and upper Midwest. In terms of the South, Georgia's population density was on the low end in 1850. I have taken the numbers here from the chart in *The Seventh Census of the United States: 1850*, xxxiii.

114. Sell, *The Geography of Georgia*, 9.

115. *The Metropolitan Catholic Almanac and Laity's Directory for 1844*, 117. The *Almanac* listed the following clergy: John Barry, Augusta; Jeremiah F. O'Neil, Savannah; Peter Whelan, Locust Grove; Thomas Moloney, Columbus; Thomas Murphy, Macon; Gregory Duggan, missionary to northwestern Georgia.

116. The national story of the political fights over internal improvements has been told by Larson, *Internal Improvement*, 39–107; and "Bind the Republic Together."

117. See, e.g., the 1828 speech by Albert Horry, a South Carolina railroad enthusiast. Horry, *An Address Delivered in Charleston before the Agricultural Society of*

South Carolina at the Anniversary Meeting, on Tuesday, the 19th August 1828, 30. See also Goodrich, *Government Promotion of American Canals and Railroads, 1800–1890*, 104–7.

118. Phillips, *A History of Transportation in the Eastern Cotton Belt to 1860*, 136–37.

119. Ibid., 153.

120. Ibid., 149, 174; Grinde, "Building the South Carolina Railroad"; Ward, "A New Look at Antebellum Southern Railroad Development."

121. Heath, *Constructive Liberalism*, 238.

122. Ibid., 252, 278.

123. Phillips, *A History of Transportation in the Eastern Cotton Belt*, 221–33; Gagnon, *Transition to an Industrial South*, 141–62; Wood, "The Georgia Railroad and Banking Company," 544–46.

124. Phillips, *A History of Transportation in the Eastern Cotton Belt*, 243; Wood, "The Georgia Railroad and Banking Company," 549.

125. Phillips, *A History of Transportation in the Eastern Cotton Belt*, 255–58.

126. Ibid., 263, 292.

127. Ibid., 280–84.

128. O'Connell, *Catholicity in the Carolinas and Georgia*, 244.

129. "Domestic News," *United States Catholic Miscellany*, November 5, 1831. He also printed news reports of how many passengers used the line. He reported on a public meeting from Columbia, SC, demanding a line to tie into the Charleston-Hamburg line. July 13, 1833; July 20, 1833. The paper also reported railroad accidents. See "Domestic News," October 12, 1833.

130. O'Connell, *Catholicity in the Carolinas and Georgia*, 515–16. See the excellent book by Marrs, *Railroads in the Old South*, 55–83, 189. See the letters testifying to O'Neill's effectiveness with railroad workers: *United States Catholic Miscellany*, November 23, 1839. For a broader perspective about the Irish and their participation in internal improvement projects in South Carolina, see Silver, "A New Look at Old South Urbanization."

131. "Passengers," *Savannah Daily Republican* (Savannah, GA), June 8, 1844.

132. "Savannah and Charleston Steam Packets," *Savannah Daily Georgian* (Savannah, GA), July 9, 1844.

133. "Right Rev. Bishop Reynolds," *United States Catholic Miscellany*, June 15, 1844.

134. Holifield, "Theology as Entertainment," 500.

135. O'Connell, *Catholicity in the Carolinas and Georgia*, 241.

136. Ibid., 448.

137. "Right Rev. Bishop Reynolds," *United States Catholic Miscellany*, June 15, 1844.

138. "Central Rail Road," *Milledgeville Federal Union* (Milledgeville, GA), June 11, 1844. Simms, *Macon*, 17–25.

139. "Episcopal Visitation," *United States Catholic Miscellany*, June 29, 1844.

140. Ibid.

141. Phillips, *A History of Transportation in the Eastern Cotton Belt*, 281; Coleman, *A History of Georgia*, 159; "Columbus," in *Cyclopedia of Georgia*, 1:432–33.

142. O'Connell, *Catholicity in the Carolinas and Georgia*, 572.

143. Ibid., 427, 571, 573.

144. "To the Editor of the US Catholic Miscellany," *United States Catholic Miscellany*, July 13, 1844. On temperance in the South, see Tyrrell, "Drink and Temperance in the Antebellum South," esp. 490, for the importance of Georgia to the movement.

145. "Bishop of Charleston," *Columbus Enquirer* (Columbus, GA), June 26, 1844. The editor also noted the formation of the Total Abstinence Society.

146. "To the Editor of the US Catholic Miscellany," *United States Catholic Miscellany*, July 13, 1844.

147. Cook, *History of Baldwin County, Georgia*, 1–30, 117.

148. "To the Editor of the US Catholic Miscellany," *United States Catholic Miscellany*, July 13, 1844.

149. Ibid.; Shivers, *The Land Between*, 220.

150. Willingham, *The History of Wilkes Country, Georgia*, 37–38, 67.

151. "To the Editor of the US Catholic Miscellany," *United States Catholic Miscellany*, July 13, 1844.

152. Ibid.

153. Ibid.

154. *Georgia Constitutionalist* (Augusta, GA), July 6, 1844.

155. "To the Editor of the US Catholic Miscellany," *United States Catholic Miscellany*, July 13, 1844.

156. "The Bishop," *United States Catholic Miscellany*, July 20, 1844.

157. For the concept of the religious free market, see Hatch, *Democratization of American Christianity*.

158. Heyrman, *Southern Cross*.

CHAPTER THREE. *Apologetics*

1. Gjerde, *Catholicism and the Shaping of Nineteenth-Century America*.

2. A number of scholars have argued that clergy before 1820 shunned religious controversy as counterproductive. T. Spalding, "The Maryland Tradition"; Farrelly, *Papist Patriots*; Agonito, "Ecumenical Stirrings"; Chinnici, "American Catholics and Religious Pluralism, 1775–1820"; Curran, *Papist Devils*.

3. On Bachman, see Stephens, *Science, Race, and Religion in the American South*; Waddell, "Introduction: John Bachman's Works and Life"; [Catherine Bachman,] *John Bachman*. The 1852 debate with Charleston Catholics is covered very briefly and insufficiently both in Waddell's introduction to *John Bachman*, 16–17, 21, and in Heisser and White, *Patrick N. Lynch*, 40–44.

4. Stephens, *Science, Race, and Religion in the American South*, 11–13.

5. Ibid., 14; South Carolina Synod of the Lutheran Church in America, *A History of the Lutheran Church in South Carolina*, 165–75, 184. See also Bell, "Regional Identity in the Antebellum South."

6. Stephens, *Science, Race, and Religion in the American South*, 14–17, 31; South Carolina Synod, *A History of the Lutheran Church in South Carolina*, 224; Stephens, "The Literary and Philosophical Society of South Carolina"; Heisser and White, *Patrick N. Lynch*, 33–34.

7. Bratt, "The Reorientation of American Protestantism, 1835–1845," esp. 62. Both Catholics and Protestants used the print culture to define themselves with more precision. In 1837, Disciples of Christ founder Alexander Campbell and Bishop John Baptist Purcell of Cincinnati published a massive debate on the Protestant-Catholic divide. The *Miscellany* included debates and apologetics in its pages to define the doctrines of Catholicism clearly for its readers. For the nineteenth-century Catholic use of polemics, see Dolan, "Catholic Attitudes toward Protestants."

8. South Carolina Synod, *A History of the Lutheran Church in South Carolina*, 197–99, 213–14, 220, 242–45. See also Havens, "The Liturgical Traditions II"; Holifield, *Theology in America*, 397–414.

9. Bennett, *The Party of Fear*, 29, 52.

10. Bachman, "A Sermon on the Doctrines and Disciplines of the Evangelical Lutheran Church," in Messmer, *Works*, 1:58, 60–62.

11. Ibid., 67, 70. See also South Carolina Synod, *A History of the Lutheran Church in South Carolina*, 189; Holifield, *Theology in America*, 409–10. See Fenton, *Religious Liberties*, ch. 4, for a discussion of the issue of transubstantiation and anti-Catholic literature. Fenton summarizes the Protestant position on the issue: "Having been duped into believing that priestly words can change signifiers into signified, Catholics have forfeited the right to participate in representative governance" (99).

12. Bachman, "A Sermon on the Doctrines and Disciplines of the Evangelical Lutheran Church," in Messmer, *Works*, 1:73, 75, 76, 78, 77. Bachman's sentiments on Protestant unity fit with Nathan Hatch's comments in ch. 6 of *Democratization of American Christianity*, 162–89.

13. Bachman, "A Sermon on the Doctrines and Disciplines of the Evangelical Lutheran Church," in Messmer, *Works*, 1:78. See Griffin, *Anti-Catholicism and Nineteenth-Century Fiction*. Griffin notes that anti-Catholic narratives served "not merely as a means of attacking Rome, but as a flexible medium of cultural critique"

(17). Bachman's appeal for Protestant unity represents this trend. American Lutherans in the nineteenth century were anti-Catholic. Samuel Simon Schmucker, who E. Brooks Holifield calls "the most influential American Lutheran theologian of the era," wrote anti-Catholic pamphlets and knew Bachman. Holifield, *Theology in America*, 402. For one of Schmucker's anti-Catholic tracts, see *The Papal Hierarchy Viewed in the Light of Prophecy and History*.

14. Wyatt-Brown, *Southern Honor*; Tate, "Catholics and Southern Honor"; Freeman, *Affairs of Honor*, xvi, 105–58, describes these types of exchanges as "paper wars."

15. The *Courier* mentioned some of Bachman's travails and travels. *Charleston Courier* (Charleston, SC), February 13, 1838, announced his mother's funeral. "Ship News," *Charleston Courier*, April 18, 1838, announced his return from New York. *Charleston Courier*, December 29, 1838, announced Bachman's return from Europe. For the great fire, see Fraser, *Charleston! Charleston!*, 216–17. The *Miscellany* discussed the Charleston fire in its May 12, 1838, edition. In terms of Bachman's silence during the 1838 debate, I base my judgment on the evidence quoted from the *Courier* and the following. In the August 20, 1853, edition of the *Miscellany*, the editor published a letter signed "Up-Country Man," which commented on Bachman's new book. The letter writer noted, "Years ago, when Dr. Bachman was in his *prime*, and when the illustrious Bishop England wrote his Bachman letters, Dr. B., for aught I know, was ominously silent as a statue." I also checked the surviving copies from 1838 of Benjamin Gildersleeve's Presbyterian paper, the *Charleston Observer*, which frequently argued with the *Miscellany*, to see if it mentioned anything about Bachman responding to Bishop England in 1838. Emory University's archive has copies of the 1838 paper. Although a few issues are missing from that year, there was no reference in the surviving numbers to Bishop England's letters against Bachman or of any response by Bachman. In the 1852 controversy, Gildersleeve, then publishing his paper in Richmond, entered the fray against the Catholics of Charleston.

16. England, in Messmer, *Works*, 1:79.

17. See Nathan Hatch's discussion of sectarianism and *sola scriptura* among Protestants. He writes: "Protestants from Luther to Wesley had been forced to define carefully what they meant by *sola scriptura*. They found it an effective banner to unfurl when attacking Catholics but always a bit troublesome when common people began to take the teaching seriously." *Democratization of American Christianity*, 179. See also Holifield, *The Gentlemen Theologians*, 102–6.

18. England, in Messmer, *Works*, 1:80–81.

19. Ibid., 1:83.

20. Ibid., 1:90, 85.

21. Ibid., 1:107.

22. Ibid., 1:131, 155–56. Bishop England discussed Genesis 14:18–20 and Hebrews 6 and 7, which contain verses about the priest Melchisedech.

23. Ibid., 1:179.

24. Ibid., 1:185.

25. See Holifield, *Theology in America*, 415–33. Holifield notes several themes that appear throughout Bishop England's debate with Bachman, including Catholics' appeals to reason and history against Protestant polemics.

26. "To Our Readers," *United States Catholic Miscellany*, June 30, 1838.

27. England, in Messmer, *Works*, 1:219, 220, 223. On the importance of the principle of voluntaryism in nineteenth-century American Protestantism, see Adams, "The Voluntary Principle in the Forming of American Religion." But Bishop England also embraced this principle. See Carey, "Voluntaryism."

28. Bennett, *Party of Fear*, 54.

29. England, in Messmer, *Works*, 1:280.

30. The appeal to history was a mainstay of both nineteenth-century Catholic apologetics and nineteenth-century southern constitutional polemics, another tie of affinity. Dulles, *A History of Apologetics*, 112–13, 175–76, 184–89. The Oxford Movement shared this historical focus. Heisser and White, *Patrick N. Lynch*, 51, on Lynch's correspondence with John Henry Newman. The *Miscellany* editorialized about Newman's conversion to Catholicism: "Rev. J. H. Newman," *United States Catholic Miscellany*, November 15, 1845. On the Oxford Movement in general, see Conser, *Church and Confession*, 161–214. On history and southern constitutional polemics, see Tate, "A Historiography of States' Rights"; Quigley, "That History Is Truly the Life of Nations."

31. England, in Messmer, *Works*, 1:236, 239, 242, 244.

32. Colbourn, *The Lamp of Experience*; Butterfield, *The Whig Interpretation of History*.

33. England, in Messmer, *Works*, 1:266.

34. Ibid., 1:219.

35. Ibid., 1:286.

36. "To Our Readers," *United States Catholic Miscellany*, June 30, 1838.

37. England, in Messmer, *Works*, 1:268.

38. Ibid., 1:288.

39. Bennett, *The Party of Fear*, 62.

40. Silver, "A New Look at Old South Urbanization," 144, quotation on 154.

41. "Monk Leahey," *United States Catholic Miscellany*, March 20, 1852. On the general theme in nativist literature of Catholic attacks on the family and the chastity of women, see Pagliarini, "The Pure American Woman and the Wicked Catholic Priest." The Leahey affair was part of a national trend during the 1850s. See Anbinder, *Nativism and Slavery*, 28–30.

42. "Monk Leahey," *United States Catholic Miscellany*, March 20, 1852. The ad implied that Catholicism invaded the sacred home, a mainstay of nineteenth-century American Protestantism. See McDannell, *The Christian Home in Victorian America, 1840-1900*, 1–19.

43. On protecting women and the culture of honor, see the perceptive piece by Frank, "Between Death and Dishonor." See also Davis, "Some Themes of Counter-Subversion," 216–20.

44. Bachman, *Defense of Luther and the Reformation*, 2, 3.

45. "The Press of Charleston," *United States Catholic Miscellany*, March 20, 1852.

46. Bachman, *Defense of Luther and the Reformation*, 8, 9, 10.

47. Ibid., 12–16.

48. Heisser and White, *Patrick N. Lynch*, 40–41. See "Death of Dr. Bellinger," *United States Catholic Miscellany*, August 18, 1860, for Bellinger's lengthy obituary. The obituary refers to the controversy with Bachman.

49. "Proceedings of Council," *Charleston Courier* (Charleston, SC), September 4, 1850.

50. Bachman, *Defense of Luther and the Reformation*, 17–20.

51. Ibid., 21. See "From the Evening News, July 26," *United States Catholic Miscellany*, July 30, 1853, for the charge that Bachman's principles would welcome abolitionists. For the Riot, see Kelly, "Charleston's Bishop John England and American Slavery," 48–56.

52. Bachman, *Defense of Luther and the Reformation*, 22; *Charleston Courier* (Charleston, SC), May 2, 1853.

53. Bachman, *Defense of Luther and the Reformation*, 17.

54. Ibid., 24, 25, 28.

55. Ibid., 33.

56. Ibid., 254.

57. Ibid., 257.

58. Ibid., 67.

59. Ibid., 46, 49–50, 55; Kenny, "Race, Violence, and Anti-Irish Sentiment in the Nineteenth Century." Kenny discusses the Irish penchant for collective violence that blackened their reputation.

60. David Bennett notes that this was a common image of nativism. *The Party of Fear*, 2.

61. Bachman, *Defense of Luther and the Reformation*, 42.

62. Ibid., 37.

63. "From the Evening News of 14th inst.," *United States Catholic Miscellany*, May 22, 1852.

64. Bachman, *Defense of Luther and the Reformation*, 36, 39, 42.

65. Ibid., 37.

66. David Brion Davis, "Some Themes of Counter-Subversion," 215, notes of nativist literature, "The exposure of subversion was a means of promoting unity, but it also served to clarify national values and provide the individual ego with a sense of high moral sanction and imputed righteousness." Bachman illustrated well Davis's point.

67. Bachman, *Defense of Luther and the Reformation*, 110–11.

68. Ibid., 104.

69. Ibid., 108–9.

70. Ibid., 228.

71. Ibid., 200.

72. Ibid., 228.

73. Pettegree, *Brand Luther*, 288; Oberman, *Luther*, 236–39, 284–89; Dawson; *The Dividing of Christendom*, 106–7.

74. Bachman, *Defense of Luther and the Reformation*, 166.

75. Ibid., 186, 191.

76. A number of letters published in the *Miscellany* by both Catholics and Protestants show that some remained unconvinced by Bachman's defense of Luther. See "From the Evening News," *United States Catholic Miscellany*, August 14, 1852; "From the Evening News" and "From the Evening News of 18th inst.," August 21, 1852. Patrick Lynch also received several letters from family members who mentioned that they had read his rebuttals to Bachman in the *Miscellany*. See, e.g., Sr. Baptiste to Lynch, August 28, 1852, Box 7, Folder G, no. 1, and Mary Lynch to Patrick Lynch, September 20, 1852, Box 7, Folder G, no. 5, Archives of the Diocese of Charleston.

77. Bachman, *Defense of Luther and the Reformation*, 165–66.

78. Ibid., 233, 235.

79. Ibid., 250–51.

80. *United States Catholic Miscellany*, May 1, 1852.

81. Ibid., August 21, 1852.

82. Bachman, *Defense of Luther and the Reformation*, 314.

83. Ibid., 315–17; quotation on 317.

84. Ibid., 317. Davis pointed out nativists' obsession with Dens's *Theology*, "Some Themes of Counter-Subversion," 218.

85. Bachman, *Defense of Luther and the Reformation*, 319.

86. Ibid., 321.

87. Ibid., 323, 328.

88. Ibid., 329, 349. One way to understand such rhetoric is to recognize the language of conspiracy among the nativists. Gordon Wood identified several reasons why conspiratorial thinking was prevalent during the late eighteenth century and beyond. Wood, "Conspiracy and the Paranoid Style," 409, 420–21, 440.

89. The *Charleston Courier* advertised the book for sale in its April 18, 1853 issue (see the ad titled "Luther and the Reformation").

90. "Dr. Bachman's Book," *United States Catholic Miscellany*, April 23, 1853.

91. Bachman, *Defense of Luther and the Reformation*, 360, 361.

92. Ibid., 362.

93. Ibid., 437. Bachman's charges were not uncommon among Protestant anti-Catholics. See Smith, *Gothic Arches, Latin Crosses*, 99–100.

94. Bachman, *Defense of Luther and the Reformation*, 362, 364. See the comment by Robert Dunne, "When Irish Catholics began entering the country in significant numbers the mainstream responded as if its relatively stable existence was threatened." *Antebellum Irish Immigration and Emerging Ideologies of "America,"* 103.

95. Bachman, *Defense of Luther and the Reformation*, 366, 368.

96. Ibid., 418.

97. Ibid., 446, 448, 450. The Catholic Diocese of Charleston's archives have a couple of letters to Patrick Lynch from individuals discussing the heavy cost of running the hospital. One asks Lynch to press the city to contribute money. Alexander Allemong and William B. Ryan to Lynch, October 8, 1852, Box 7, folder H, no. 6. See also W. Wragg to Lynch, November 8, 1852, Box 7, Folder K, no. 3, Archives of the Diocese of Charleston.

98. Bachman, *Defense of Luther and the Reformation*, 452, 454, 504.

99. "Dr. Bachman and His Book," *United States Catholic Miscellany*, July 9, 1853.

100. Bachman apparently paid for space in the *Evening News*. The *Miscellany* printed his brief response to Corcoran in the August 6, 1853, edition (see "From the Evening News, July 30"). Corcoran noted in the *Miscellany*, August 27, 1853 (see "To Correspondents"), that he would not allow Bachman's friends to defend Bachman's book in the pages of the *Miscellany*. The paper war, therefore, ended.

101. "From the Evening News, July 26," *United States Catholic Miscellany*, July 30, 1853.

102. This picks up on the point made by Moore, *Religious Outsiders and the Making of Americans*, 70.

103. McGreevy, *Catholicism and American Freedom*, 68–118, 294–95, discusses the tensions between nineteenth-century American Catholics and nationalists. Davis notes that "nativists sought unity and moral certainty in the regenerative spirit of nationalism." "Some Themes of Counter-Subversion," 221.

CHAPTER FOUR.   *An Identity of Our Own Making*

1. In looking at three different St. Patrick's Day celebrations, I mimic the approach of Huff's "The Eagle and the Vulture."

2. Etzioni, "Holidays and Rituals," 6.

3. Bianchi, *St. George's Day*, 7. See also Sharpe, *Remember, Remember*.

4. Cronin and Adair, *The Wearing of the Green*, 35.

5. Moss, "St. Patrick's Day Celebrations and the Formation of Irish-American Identity, 1845–1875," 130. See also the helpful article by Litwicki, "Our Hearts Burn with Ardent Love for Two Countries."

6. Two scholars have examined St. Patrick's Day celebrations in Charleston: Joyce, "White, Worker, Irish, and Confederate," ch. 5; Guinn, "Among Kith and Kin." Guinn looks at the 1855 celebrations at the height of Know Nothing activity in the city.

7. Conzen et al., "The Invention of Ethnicity." The article focuses on a method that recognizes that ethnic identity is constructed and changes over time. A compelling case study of this process is Meagher, *Inventing Irish America*. I would also include Phillip Gleason's caveats about the ethnicization approach. Gleason, "American Identity and Americanization," 54.

8. Reprinted in Mitchell, *The History of the Hibernian Society of Charleston, South Carolina, 1799–1981*, 106. See also Gleeson, *The Irish in the South*, 55–73. "Hibernian" comes from the Latin name for Ireland, *Hibernia*. Cosgrove, "The Hibernian Society of Charleston, South Carolina."

9. Mitchell, *History of the Hibernian Society*, 51.

10. Mitchell, *South Carolina Irish*, 53–56; Salley, *History of Irish Volunteers Company from 1798 to 1836*, 1–3.

11. Gleeson, *Irish in the South*, 61; Salley, *History of Irish Volunteers Company from 1798 to 1836*, 1–15; *The Irish Volunteers Memorial Meeting and Military Hall Festival, October–November 1877*, 9–10.

12. Mitchell, *South Carolina Irish*, 56; Williams, *Shamrocks and Pluff Mud*, 52–53; Joyce, "White, Worker, Irish, and Confederate," 185–86.

13. Kenny, *The American Irish*, 45–46.

14. Miller, *Emigrants and Exiles*, 198.

15. Gleeson, *The Irish in the South*, 25–37.

16. Miller, *Emigrants and Exiles*, 231.

17. "Missionary Society," *United States Catholic Miscellany*, January 24, 1835.

18. "New Books—Just Received at the Depository," *Charleston Courier* (Charleston, SC), February 21, 1835.

19. Morse, *Foreign Conspiracy against the Liberties of the United States*, 94.

20. "St. Patrick's Day," *United States Catholic Miscellany*, March 21, 1835.

21. See the point made by Cronin and Adair, *Wearing of the Green*, 35–36.

22. "St. Patrick's Day," *United States Catholic Miscellany*, March 21, 1835.

23. "Letter from the Engineer's Department," *Southern Patriot* (Charleston, SC), March 18, 1835.

24. "St. Patrick's Day," *Charleston Courier* (Charleston, SC), March 19, 1835.

25. "St. Patrick's Day," *Charleston Courier* (Charleston, SC), March 20, 1835.

26. Ibid.

27. "America—Ireland. Celebration of St. Patrick's Day," *United States Catholic Miscellany*, March 28, 1835. See Higham, "Integrating America," 16.

28. "St. Patrick's Day," *Charleston Courier* (Charleston, SC), March 19, 1835. See Gjerde, *Catholicism and the Shaping of Nineteenth-Century America*, 89, for Catholic celebration of civil and religious liberty. See also Pasulka, "The Eagle and the Dove," esp. 310, on the persistence of republican rhetoric.

29. "Foreign Conspiracy against the Liberties of the United States," *Charleston Courier* (Charleston, SC), March 28, 1835.

30. "The Discussion," *United States Catholic Miscellany*, April 4, 1835.

31. Strum, "South Carolina and Irish Famine Relief, 1846–1847." The *Miscellany* began reporting stories about the famine in Ireland in the fall of 1846; see "The Potato Disease—Public Distress" and "Starvation Meetings in Cork," September 19, 1846; "Ireland," September 26, 1846; "Threatened Invasion of the City of Cork" and "Food Riots in Sligo," October 31, 1846.

32. On anti-British sentiment, see the excellent work, Haynes, *Unfinished Revolution*, 230–73.

33. Pinheiro, *Missionaries of Republicanism*.

34. "Relief of the Irish. Proceedings of the Hibernian Society," *United States Catholic Miscellany*, February 27, 1847.

35. "America. Relief of Ireland," "Meeting for Relief of Ireland," and "Provisions for Ireland," *United States Catholic Miscellany*, March 13, 1847. See the *Charleston Courier* (Charleston, SC), March 20 ("Relief to Ireland") and March 22 ("Relief to Ireland"), 1847. See the *Charleston Mercury* (Charleston, SC), March 10 ("Provisions for Ireland"), March 11 ("Relief to Ireland"), March 12 ("Relief to Ireland"), March 13 ("Provisions for Ireland"), and March 29 ("Irish Relief Meeting at Barnwell C.H."), 1847.

36. "St. Patrick's Day—Bishop Reynolds's Discourse," *Charleston Mercury* (Charleston, SC), March 25, 1847.

37. "Irish Volunteers," *Southern Patriot* (Charleston, SC), March 16, 1847.

38. John C. Calhoun to Duff Green, March 9, 1847, in Jameson, "Correspondence of John C. Calhoun," 718–19.

39. Calhoun to Thomas G. Clemson, March 19, 1847, in Jameson, "Correspondence of John C. Calhoun," 720. See also Bartlett, *John C. Calhoun*, 344–45.

40. John C. Calhoun, "Speech at the Meeting of the Citizens of Charleston," in Lence, *Union and Liberty*, 529, 536, 537.

41. Berlin and Gutman, "Free Men and Slaves," 1191, 1188; Rousey, "Aliens in the WASP Nest," esp. 158–59. Rousey comments, "The surprising numbers of northerners and foreigners who helped give diversity to southern cities were paralleled by remarkable concentrations of nonevangelicals, including a large propor-

tion of Roman Catholics" (158). See also Miller, "The Enemy Within"; Clark, "The South's Irish Catholics"; Doyle, "The Irish as Urban Pioneers in the United States, 1850–1870," 46, chart of South Carolina statistics.

42. Knobel, *Paddy and the Republic*, 68–103.

43. "St. Patrick's Day—Bishop Reynolds's Discourse," *Charleston Mercury* (Charleston, SC), March 25, 1847.

44. "Bishop Reynold's Oration on St. Patrick's Day," *United States Catholic Miscellany*, March 27, 1847. For the Catholic clergy's attempt to use the displacement caused by the famine to heighten religious practice among the Irish peasantry, see Miller, "Irish Catholicism and the Great Famine."

45. "Bishop Reynold's Oration on St. Patrick's Day," *United States Catholic Miscellany*, March 27, 1847.

46. Miller, *Emigrants and Exiles*, 280–344; Kenny, *The American Irish*, 89–130; Gleeson, *The Irish in the South*, 26–37.

47. Silver, "A New Look at Old South Urbanization," 144, 149, 151, 154; quotations on 144 and 154. On the mobility of Irish famine immigrants, see Miller, *Emigrants and Exiles*, 317–19. David Noel Doyle estimates over 4,800 Irish-born citizens (and their children) in Charleston in 1860. See Doyle, "The Irish as Urban Pioneers in the United States, 1850–1870," 47.

48. Klebaner, "Public Poor Relief in Charleston, 1800–1860," 219.

49. Joyce, "White, Worker, Irish, and Confederate," ch. 6; Gleeson, *The Irish in the South*, 35–36.

50. "The Harper's Ferry Conspiracy," *Charleston Mercury* (Charleston, SC), October 25, 1859.

51. Fox-Genovese and Genovese, *The Mind of the Master Class*, 643.

52. Conzen, "Mainstreams and Side Channels." Conzen's model of assimilation—as a river with side channels—in which immigrants both shape and are shaped by American cultures is important to consider here.

53. St. Patrick's Benevolent Society Minute Book, March 17, 1860, Archives of the Diocese of Charleston.

54. O'Connell, *Catholicity in the Carolinas and Georgia*, 456.

55. "Celebration of St. Patrick's Day," *Charleston Mercury* (Charleston, SC), March 19, 1860. Timothy L. Smith notes that uprooting and migration could become a "theologizing experience" rather than a force of secularization. This dynamic can be perceived in the clergy's speeches in 1860. Smith, "Religion and Ethnicity in America," 1181.

56. O'Connell, *Catholicity in the Carolinas and Georgia*, 170–75.

57. O'Connor, *The Life and Letters of M.P. O'Connor*, 1–23.

58. Ibid., 225.

59. Ibid., 238, 240.

60. Ibid., 240–41. Sheridan Gilley remarked of the Irish in America, "Simply by being republican and anti-British, they were from the first loyal to America and felt at home there." O'Connor's speech plays on this theme. Gilley, "The Roman Catholic Church and the Nineteenth-Century Irish Diaspora," 203.

61. O'Connor, *The Life and Letters of M.P. O'Connor*, 241.

62. Ibid., 231, 232, 233, 241. Jon Gjerde's point is appropriate here: "In this way, the Catholic viewpoint hewed to a complementary identity in which they not only claimed allegiance to state and ethnoreligous group, but argued that their membership in each enriched their allegiance to both." *Catholicism and the Shaping of Nineteenth-Century America*, 168.

63. Kehoe, *Complete Works of the Most Rev. John Hughes*, 2:756, 757. On Hughes during the Civil War era, see Kelly, "A 'sentinel(s) of our liberties.'"

64. "St. Patrick's Day," *United States Catholic Miscellany*, March 24, 1860.

65. "Letter of the Bishop to the Clergy of the Diocess of Charleston," *United States Catholic Miscellany*, January 17, 1846. See also Decker, "Grand and Godly Proportions," xiii. R. Miller, "Roman Catholicism in South Carolina," 90–91, briefly discusses the cathedral.

66. "Remarks on Church Building" and "Remarks on Church Building 2nd Article," *United States Catholic Miscellany*, December 6, 1845. Varro quoted Augustus Welby Pugin in one of his letters. His language sounds very similar to that of Pugin.

67. Clark, *The Gothic Revival*, 26, 94.

68. Waddell, Introduction to *Charleston Architecture, 1670–1860*, 1:21. See also Downs, "America's First 'Medieval' Churches"; Stanton, *The Gothic Revival and American Church Architecture*; McDannell, *The Christian Home in Victorian America, 1840–1860*. McDannell notes that Gothic style created a "sense of history" (30). This fits into the theme of Romanticism. Kilde, *When Church Became Theater*.

69. Smith, *Gothic Arches, Latin Crosses*, 9, 85. The Fox-Genovese and Genovese comment on both the sense of history among southern intellectuals and their ambivalence toward the Middle Ages. Their chapter "Coming to Terms with the Middle Ages" helps place the Gothic Revival architecture into a southern context. *The Mind of the Master Class*, 305–28.

70. Clark, *The Gothic Revival*, 164–75.

71. Pugin, *The True Principles of Pointed or Christian Architecture*, 9. For a brief discussion of Pugin, see Allitt, *Catholic Converts*, 45–51.

72. Clark, *The Gothic Revival*, 201.

73. Pugin, *Present State of Ecclesiastical Architecture in England*, 42–43. This volume contained two articles that Pugin had published in the *Dublin Review* in 1841 and 1842.

74. Pugin, *Present State*, 130.

75. Pugin, *True Principles*, 67.

76. Simms, *Views and Reviews in American Literature History and Fiction*, 54.

77. Davis, "Catholic Envy," 114–15.

78. "Correspondence of the Southern Patriot," *Southern Patriot* (Charleston, SC), September 12, 1845; on Upjohn see, Stanton, *The Gothic Revival and American Church Architecture*; the Simms reference came from Severens, *Charleston*, 128.

79. On White and his Gothic style, I consulted the following: Ravenel, *Architects of Charleston*, 183–95; Waddell, Introduction to *Charleston Architecture, 1670–1860*, 1:21–24; Poston, *The Buildings of Charleston*, 85, 100; Severens, *Charleston*, 128–34. Ravenel notes: "The Huguenot Church, built for a group of Episcopalians who decided to return to the faith of their French Protestant forefathers, was begun in 1844 and finished in 1845" (191).

80. "The Gathering of the Huguenots," *Charleston Courier* (Charleston, SC), May 13, 1845.

81. "Trinity Church, Columbia," *Charleston Mercury* (Charleston, SC), March 15, 1847.

82. Severens, *Charleston*, 133.

83. Howard, *A Sermon Delivered at the Re-Opening and Dedication of the French Protestant Church*, 3.

84. See Tate, "Catholics and Southern Honor." See also Bishop England's writings from the year 1826 in which he dwelled on this theme, for example, his numerous letters on the "Calumnies of J. Blanco White," in Messmer, *Works*, 2:213–562.

85. "The Gathering of the Huguenots," *Charleston Courier* (Charleston, SC), May 13, 1845.

86. Reynolds to Purcell, March 5, 1850, quoted in Madden, *Catholics in South Carolina*, 61. The letter comes from the Notre Dame Archives, Purcell Papers, II, 4, K. There is a photocopy of the letter in the Archives of the Diocese of Charleston.

87. "Letter of the Bishop to the Clergy of the Diocess—New Cathedral," *United States Catholic Miscellany*, November 13, 1847.

88. "New Cathedral," *United States Catholic Miscellany*, August 12, 1848; and "The Cathedral," *United States Catholic Miscellany*, November 5, 1853.

89. Decker, "Grand and Godly Proportions," 43.

90. "The New Cathedral," *United States Catholic Miscellany*, May 18, 1850. Waddell wrote, "When completed, the spire reached 220 feet in height, making it the tallest in the city. The overall length and width were 153 feet by 73 feet, and the seating capacity was 1,200. Considering that St. Paul's, Radcliffeborough, is 164 feet by 70 feet and that its seating capacity is the same, it seems to have been considered necessary to equal the largest church in the city. It surpassed St. Paul's

in being stone rather than brick and in having a spire, which inadequate foundations had made impossible for St. Paul's. The total cost of the Catholic cathedral was $103,000." *Charleston Architecture, 1670–1860,* 1:245.

91. "New Roman Catholic Cathedral," *Charleston Mercury* (Charleston, SC), August 1, 1850. On Keely, see Kervick, "Patrick Charles Keely, Architect"; McAleer, "Keely, 'The Irish Pugin of America'"; Decker, "Grand and Godly Proportions."

92. Reprinted in "New Roman Catholic Cathedral," *United States Catholic Miscellany,* August 3, 1850. The concern about debt was apt. The cathedral ran into serious construction overages. See the descriptions in "General Meeting of the Catholics of Charleston," *United States Catholic Miscellany,* November 8, 1851.

93. Pugin, *Present State,* 17–18.

94. Decker, "Grand and Godly Proportions," 35.

95. "St. Finbar's Cathedral," *Charleston Courier* (Charleston, SC), May 28, 1853.

96. *Richmond Watchman and Observer* (Richmond, VA), November 25, 1852.

97. *Richmond Watchman and Observer* (Richmond, VA), July 19, 1855.

98. Lynch had to oversee the project. Keely was rarely in the city to do so. "The New Cathedral of St. Finbar," *Charleston Mercury* (Charleston, SC), March 22, 1854. Richard C. Madden discusses Keely's absence: *Catholics in South Carolina,* 63.

99. "Consecration of the Catholic Cathedral," *Charleston Mercury* (Charleston, SC), April 7, 1854.

100. Consecration of the Cathedral," *United States Catholic Miscellany,* April 8, 1854.

101. "Death of Bishop Reynolds," *Charleston Courier* (Charleston, SC), March 7, 1855.

102. Simms, "Charleston, the Palmetto City," 15.

103. "Consecration of Bishop Lynch," *Charleston Courier* (Charleston, SC), March 15, 1858.

CHAPTER FIVE. *Republicanism and Common Sentiments*

1. Jon Gjerde notes what he calls the Catholic conundrum: "The Catholic conundrum, in contrast, was how the Church could be pluralistic and liberal, on the one hand, and particularistic on the other. If the Catholic leadership affirmed both that a spiritual dimension was central to the arrangements of the temporal and that these rights were vested in the ecclesiastical authority, Protestants perceived an inherent contradiction that only offered greater evidence of the gravity of their own puzzle." *Catholicism and the Shaping of Nineteenth-Century America,* 91.

2. See the nuanced discussion of Catholicism's encounter with liberalism: Steinfels, "The Failed Encounter." See also Gleason, "American Catholics and Liberalism, 1789–1960."

3. Freehling, *Prelude to Civil War*, 100.

4. The following works are helpful on the postwar period: Dangerfield, *The Era of Good Feelings*; Howe, *What Hath God Wrought*; Rothbard, *The Panic of 1819*; Ellis, *Aggressive Nationalism*; Risjord, *The Old Republicans*; Skeen, "Calhoun, Crawford, and the Politics of Retrenchment." The last point in the paragraph—that South Carolina followed national trends—is made by Ford, *Origins of Southern Radicalism*, 103. In my opinion, Ford convincingly answers historians who argue that South Carolina was unique throughout the early republic. For those opinions, see in particular, Banner, "The Problem of South Carolina"; Weir, "The South Carolinian as Extremist"; Greenberg, "Representation and the Isolation of South Carolina, 1776–1860"; Sinha, *The Counterrevolution of Slavery*, 20–61; Moltke-Hansen, "Protecting Interests, Maintaining Rights, Emulating Ancestors."

5. See Parsons, *The Birth of Modern Politics*, 39–108. Several historians cover the hostilities between the Old Republicans and Calhounites in South Carolina. See Ford, *Origins of Southern Radicalism*, 99–144; Freehling, *Prelude to Civil War*, 89–133. Freehling's book has been challenged by several historians, who point out problems in Freehling's research and data. His critics include Bergeron, "The Nullification Controversy Revisited"; Denney, "South Carolina's Conception of the Union in 1832"; Pease and Pease, "The Economics and Politics of Charleston's Nullification Crisis"; and Ochenkowski, "The Origins of Nullification in South Carolina."

6. Edgar, *South Carolina*, 273–75.

7. Ibid., 327–31; Robertson, *Denmark Vesey*, 120.

8. Remini, "Martin Van Buren and the Tariff of Abominations."

9. "Protest," in Lence, *Union and Liberty*, 365.

10. Ford, *Origins of Southern Radicalism*, 136.

11. On the Webster-Hayne debate, the following three pieces are helpful: Sheidley, "The Webster-Hayne Debate"; Melish, *Disowning Slavery*, 229–33; and Jervey, *Robert Y. Hayne and His Times*, 235–67. On Calhoun's life and his role in the events of nullification, see Bartlett, *John C. Calhoun*.

12. Ellis, *The Union at Risk*, ix.

13. I use the "lens" imagery in this chapter following the lead of Reynolds, *Righteous Violence*, 48.

14. Carey, "Voluntaryism," 52, 49. This paragraph and the next one are light revisions from my previously published article (reprinted by permission of the publisher), Tate, "Confronting Abolitionism," 373–404.

15. Carey, "Voluntaryism," 54, 56. On England's early life, see Guilday, *The Life and Times of John England*, 1:36–123. On England's seminary education, see

Holifield, *The Gentlemen Theologians*, 101–6; Saunders and Rogers, "Bishop John England of Charleston," 306; Smith, "The Fundamental Church-State Tradition of the Catholic Church in the United States," 489–91; Clarke, *A Free Church in a Free Society*, chs. 2 and 5; Madden, *Catholics in South Carolina*, 31; Kearns, "Bishop John England and the Possibilities of Catholic Republicanism"; Carey, *An Immigrant Bishop*. The political background of eighteenth-century Ireland that influenced John England and many of the Irish immigrants in the Diocese of Charleston can be appreciated in Wilson, *United Irishmen, United States*; Whelan, *The Tree of Liberty*, 99–130; and Connolly, *Political Ideas in Eighteenth Century Ireland*, 22–25.

16. England, in Messmer, *Works*, 7:12, 433; Kearns, "Bishop John England and the Possibilities of Catholic Republicanism," 59.

17. "The Rev. Dr. England," *Charleston Mercury* (Charleston, SC), July 8, 1826.

18. Messmer, *Works*, 7:68–69, 6:306; Kearns, "Bishop John England and the Possibilities of Catholic Republicanism," 53–54. See Rahe, *Republics Ancient and Modern*; Wood, *The Creation of the American Republic, 1776–1787*, 65–70; Pocock, *The Machiavellian Moment*, 507–13; Rodgers, "Republicanism"; Calhoon, *Dominion and Liberty*, 103–4. And see McDonald, *Novus Ordo Seclorum*, 70–77, on the republican debate over relying on constitutional mechanics or virtue. See also Ashworth, "The Jeffersonians."

19. "The Rev. Dr. England," *Charleston Mercury* (Charleston, SC), July 8, 1826; Formisano, "Political Character, Antipartyism and the Second Party System."

20. A. Jackson, *Ireland 1798–1998*, 23–68. See also Reynolds, *The Catholic Emancipation Crisis in Ireland, 1823–1829*, 1–65.

21. On the support for Catholic Emancipation in the United States, see Moriarty, "The Irish American Response to Catholic Emancipation." See also Sams, "The Cauldron of Enmities"; Codignola, "Roman Catholic Conservatism in a New North Atlantic World, 1760–1829." Codignola calls Catholic Emancipation the "turning point from survival to success" for Catholics in the British world (720).

22. "Civil and Religious Liberty—Meeting in Augusta," *United States Catholic Miscellany*, April 7, 1827.

23. "Meeting at the City Hall," *United States Catholic Miscellany*, September 20, 1828.

24. "Public Meeting in Charleston, on Monday, Sept. 22, 1828," *United States Catholic Miscellany*, September 27, 1828.

25. "Friends of Ireland," *United States Catholic Miscellany*, October 11, 1828.

26. "General Hayne," *United States Catholic Miscellany*, September 27, 1828.

27. "Friends of Ireland," *United States Catholic Miscellany*, November 15, 1828.

28. "Friends of Ireland," *United States Catholic Miscellany*, November 29, 1828.

29. "Friends of Ireland," *United States Catholic Miscellany*, December 6, 1828. I would like to thank my colleague at Clayton State, E. Joseph Johnson, for translating the address for me. For a discussion of French Catholics in Charleston before the establishment of the diocese, see the excellent piece by Gillikin, "Competing Loyalties."

30. "Friends of Ireland," *United States Catholic Miscellany*, February 7, 1829; "Friends of Ireland," February 28, 1829; "Friends of Ireland," March 7, 1829.

31. "Address," *United States Catholic Miscellany*, April 25, 1829.

32. "Friends of Ireland," *United States Catholic Miscellany*, June 6, 1829.

33. "Mr. Webster," *United States Catholic Miscellany*, March 6, 1830.

34. "Mr. Webster and the Catholics," *United States Catholic Miscellany*, March 13, 1830.

35. "The Senate and the Catholics," *United States Catholic Miscellany*, March 20, 1830.

36. Pease and Pease, "The Economics and Politics of Charleston's Nullification Crisis," 347.

37. Freehling, *Prelude to Civil War*, 177–259. See also Sinha, *The Counterrevolution of Slavery*, 38–40.

38. Pease and Pease, *The Web of Progress*, 74–75.

39. "Letter from the Right Rev. Doctor England, to the Roman Catholic Citizens of Charleston," *United States Catholic Miscellany*, August 27, 1831.

40. Ibid.

41. Ibid. John Devanny's comment here is appropriate: "This marriage of civic virtue to moral virtue is a key element in England's political thought. It serves a very practical as well as theoretical purpose for it places the self-interested individual, the violator of social order, at odds with society and with God." "Bishop John England and the Rhetoric of Republicanism," 58.

42. Letter from the Right Rev. Doctor England, to the Roman Catholic Citizens of Charleston," *United States Catholic Miscellany*, August 27, 1831.

43. Ibid.

44. See Pauline Maier's article "The Road Not Taken" on the ways in which nullifiers used Revolutionary history for precedents.

45. For one example, see Nathaniel Macon's exchange with Andrew Jackson in Freehling, *The Nullification Era*, 195–201.

46. "Letter from the Right Rev. Doctor England, to the Roman Catholic Citizens of Charleston," *United States Catholic Miscellany*, August 27, 1831.

47. "Letter IX," *United States Catholic Miscellany*, September 17, 1831. For a lengthy examination of Bishop England's "Republic in Danger" essays that stress his arguments against nativism, see Harvey Hill, "American Catholicism?"

48. "Letter IX," *United States Catholic Miscellany*, September 17, 1831. Bishop England's statements resemble many of Calhoun's points in his 1831 "Fort Hill Address." See Lence, *Union and Liberty*, 377, 382.

49. England to Bruté, October 31, 1831, Box 3, Folder G, Archives of the Diocese of Charleston.

50. Cooper is quoted in Sydnor, *The Development of Southern Sectionalism, 1819–1848*, 189.

51. Guilday, *Life and Times of John England*, 1:520, 532, 538.

52. Bishop England, of course, continued to comment on American politics during the last few years of his life. Most famous were his letters regarding Catholicism and slavery in the early 1840s. But he did not comment as widely on the U.S. constitutional order as he had in the early 1830s.

53. Pasquier, *Fathers on the Frontier*, 178. The *Miscellany* reprinted the bishops' letter in the June 10, 1837 issue. A brief discussion of the Councils and Pastoral Letters appears in Guilday, *The National Pastorals of the American Hierarchy, 1792–1919*, ix–xiii.

54. Scholars have long examined the reactions to the Revolutions of 1848 in the United States but, with few exceptions, have failed to integrate the story into a broader discussion of American politics during the 1850s. The literary scholar Larry Reynolds has traced the radicalizing effect of the Revolutions of 1848 on figures in the American literary renaissance. In a recent work, he demonstrated that the revolutions and their aftermaths wrecked the idea of nonviolence among many abolitionists, including John Brown and his band. Peter D'Agostino, in an excellent work, maintained that the Catholic Church's tenuous relationship with the movement for Italian unification became for American Catholics an important lens through which to view political events of the last half of the nineteenth century. A recent article by Miles Smith IV argued that the southern reactions to the Revolutions of 1848 revealed that the aristocratic ideal was deeply engrained in southern culture, a point neglected by some historians of the 1850s. Reynolds, *Righteous Violence*; Reynolds, *European Revolutions and the American Literary Renaissance*; D'Agostino, *Rome in America*; Smith, "From Savannah to Vienna"; Mize, "Defending Roman Loyalties and Republican Values." The Genoveses noted the great importance of the Revolutions of 1848 in the thought of the slaveholding intellectuals of the South. Fox-Genovese and Genovese, *The Mind of the Master Class*, 41–68. See also Farmer, *The Metaphysical Confederacy*, 155–56; Curti, "The Impact of the Revolutions of 1848 on American Thought"; Morrison, "American Reaction to European Revolutions, 1848–1852."

55. Reynolds, *Righteous Violence*, 18.

56. D'Agostino, *Rome in America*, 28; Stearns, *1848*, 123–39, 205–8.

57. Reynolds, *European Revolutions and the American Literary Renaissance*, 65; Spencer, *Louis Kossuth and Young America*, 1–27.

58. Marraro, *American Opinion on the Unification of Italy, 1846–1861*, 54; D'Agostino, *Rome in America*, 29.

59. Brownson, "Conversations of an Old Man and His Young Friends, No. II," 237, 240.

60. See Reynolds, *European Revolutions and the American Literary Renaissance*, 51; Mize, "Defending Roman Loyalties and Republican Values"; D'Agostino, *Rome in America*, 20.

61. "Papal Dominions," *United States Catholic Miscellany*, February 24, 1849. Luca Codignola argues that Catholics in the Atlantic world by 1829 "shared a political attitude based on an abhorrence of radicalism, a straightforward loyalty to the established government, and a delicate balance between deference and firmness concerning their political and institutional leaders." "Roman Catholic Conservatism in a New North Atlantic World, 1760–1829," 756.

62. "Catholics and Democrats," *United States Catholic Miscellany*, August 4, 1849.

63. "Atrocity of the Republicans," *United States Catholic Miscellany*, November 10, 1849.

64. "Roman Republicanism," *United States Catholic Miscellany*, January 26, 1850.

65. "Italy," Supplement to the *New York Daily Tribune*, February 13, 1850. Fuller drowned at sea on her return to the United States in 1850.

66. "The Roman Catholic Church and Religious Liberty," *New York Daily Tribune*, October 23, 1851. See also the July 1, 1851 ("The Destruction of Society"), and July 8, 1851 ("Archbishop Hughes and his late Sermon"), editions of the *Tribune* for more attacks on Hughes in light of his stand on the Italian question.

67. "His Holiness Again in Rome," *United States Catholic Miscellany*, May 25, 1850.

68. Steinfels, "The Failed Encounter," narrates the complexities that Corcoran ignored. The historian Owen Chadwick noted in his book on the papacy and the revolutions of the late eighteenth and early nineteenth century that revolution "pushed Catholicism toward that association with the political right which was not typical of its past." He continued, "The Popes knew that they stood for order, and that they were valued because they stood for order. As the twin forces of nationalism and liberalism began to overwhelm Europe, the papacy was seen less as a force for order than as a small additional dam against changes which could not for ever be resisted." *The Popes and European Revolution*, 610.

69. The only two works that consider specifically South Carolina Catholics and secession are Lofton, "Rev. Doctor James A. Corcoran and the *United States Catholic Miscellany* Concerning the Question of Slavery and the Confederacy"; and Heisser and White, *Patrick N. Lynch*. Heisser and White focus more on Bishop Lynch and his exchange of public letters in 1861 with Archbishop John Hughes

of New York. There is a broad discussion of secession and the Catholic press in Frese, "The Catholic Press and Secession, 1860–1861." See Fogarty, "Public Patriotism and Private Politics," for more about the common antebellum Catholic political strategy of refusing to comment on specific political events.

70. "Radicalism," *United States Catholic Miscellany*, August 17, 1850.

71. "The Aim of the Patriots," *United States Catholic Miscellany*, September 21, 1850.

72. "France," *United States Catholic Miscellany*, September 28, 1850.

73. "Mob Law," *United States Catholic Miscellany*, October 12, 1850.

74. Holt, *The Rise and Fall of the American Whig Party*, 692. Here is Albert Von Frank on Lincoln's Kossuth resolution: "How heady the enthusiasm was at this time might be indicated in the unguarded statement of an obscure ex-congressman from Illinois named Abraham Lincoln, who, in a series of resolutions supporting Kossuth, maintained that 'it is the right of any people, sufficiently numerous for national independence, to throw off, to revolutionize, their existing form of government, and to establish such other in its stead as they may choose.'" Von Frank, "John Brown, James Redpath, and the Idea of Revolution," 144–45.

75. Hanley, *Beyond a Christian Commonwealth*, 69.

76. Komlos, *Louis Kossuth in America, 1851–1852*, 90, 148.

77. "Kossuth," *United States Catholic Miscellany*, November 8, 1851. On Fourierism, see Guarneri, *The Utopian Alternative*. Guarneri recognized the "Fourierists' basic commitment to the ideals and values of northern society" (10). Corcoran is tying radicalism to the North.

78. "Kossuth," *United States Catholic Miscellany*, December 20, 1851.

79. "Our New Policy," *United States Catholic Miscellany*, January 3, 1852.

80. "Doings of Kossuth," *United States Catholic Miscellany*, January 24, 1852. Peter Stearns notes that the Revolutions of 1848 were most successful in Switzerland: *1848*, 6.

81. "Louis Napoleon and His Revolution," *United States Catholic Miscellany*, February 17, 1852.

82. [Simms], "Kossuth and Intervention," 230, 233. Fox-Genovese and Genovese discuss this article in *Mind of the Master Class*, 59. The *Southern Quarterly Review* published an article in 1853 that distinguished southern constitutionalism from contemporary understandings of "popular government." See "Political Philosophy of South Carolina." Corcoran expressed similar perspectives in his editorials as the *SQR* did on popular government.

83. D'Agostino, *Rome in America*, 11–12.

84. Speeches of Senator A.P. Butler, February 24–25, 1854, *Appendix to the Congressional Globe*, 33rd Cong., 1st sess., 233, 237. Schultz, *Nationalism and Sectionalism in South Carolina, 1852–1860*, 61. Andrew Stern recognizes the south-

ern Catholic interest in forming an alliance with Protestant neighbors, but focuses on issues other than those discussed here. "Southern Harmony."

85. Levine, "Conservatism, Nativism, and Slavery"; Laurie, *Beyond Garrison*, 274; Maizlish, "The Meaning of Nativism and the Crisis of the Union," 167–68. Other treatments of the Know Nothings include Gienapp, "Nativism and the Creation of a Republican Majority in the North before the Civil War"; Holt, "The Politics of Impatience"; Holt, *The Rise and Fall of the American Whig Party*, 836–985; Anbinder, *Nativism and Slavery*. A keen summary of Know Nothing scholarship and influence appears in Formisano, *For the People*, 198–215; Billington, *The Protestant Crusade, 1800–1860*; Knobel, *"America for the Americans."* See also Endres, "Know-Nothings, Nationhood, and the Nuncio." The only monograph on Know Nothings in the Old South is Overdyke, *The Know Nothing Party in the South*. Newer views have not been synthesized yet and appear in the article literature; see Alexander, "The Democracy Must Prepare for Battle"; Frederick, "Unintended Consequences"; Bladek, "Virginia Is Middle Ground"; Carey, "Too Southern to be Americans"; Broussard, "Some Determinants of Know Nothing Electoral Strength in the South, 1856"; Cantrell, "Southern and Nativist"; Ross, "Pulpit and Stump"; Smith, "The Know-Nothings in Arkansas"; Wallace, *Catholics, Slaveholders, and the Dilemma of American Evangelicalism, 1835–1860*, 94–99. This section of the chapter is revised from part of a previously published article, reprinted by permission of the publisher: Tate, "South Carolina Catholics and the Know Nothing Challenge."

86. Schultz, *Nationalism and Sectionalism in South Carolina*, 21, 52–100. See Heidler, *Pulling the Temple Down*, 111.

87. Guinn, "Among Kith and Kin," 2.

88. Cooper, *The South and the Politics of Slavery*, 322–69. I agree with Bladek that it is hard to judge the effectiveness of these appeals in the Know Nothing campaigns in the South. Bladek, "Virginia Is Middle Ground," 65.

89. "The New Party," *United States Catholic Miscellany*, March 10, 1855.

90. "A Know-Nothing Lecturer," *United States Catholic Miscellany*, April 7, 1855. On Beecher, see Schultz, *Fire and Roses*. Corcoran's rhetorical tactic might be distasteful, but he was well informed about the tendencies of the northern Know Nothings. Bruce Laurie, in his insightful book *Beyond Garrison*, notes, "The fact is, however, that the Know-Nothings outdid the Free Soilers on anti-Southernism and antislavery" (279). Laurie also writes, "Know-Nothings who had passed through Free Soilism and who were possibly political neophytes had no more respect for the plantation system of the South than they did for the Catholic Church. For them the two were similar, with comparable hierarchies of parasitic planters and prelates living off the labor of others—peasants in Old Europe and poor whites in the South" (282).

91. Overdyke, *The Know-Nothing Party in the South*, 150; Carey, "Too Southern to be Americans," 28; Bladek, "Virginia Is Middle Ground," 49.

92. "The American Platform" and "The K.N. Platform," *United States Catholic Miscellany*, June 30, 1855. On the convention and its effects in the South, see Bladek, "Virginia Is Middle Ground," 65–70.

93. The *Charleston Mercury* doubted the coherence of the new party and mentioned its confused approach to its platform; see "The Know Nothing Party—What Can It Accomplish?," October 3, 1855.

94. "The Late Election," *United States Catholic Miscellany*, July 14, 1855. See also "The Election," *Charleston Mercury* (Charleston, SC), July 12, 1855. James Marchio printed the election returns in "Nativism in the Old South," 45.

95. "Proscription of Catholics," *United States Catholic Miscellany*, August 25, 1855.

96. Ibid.

97. "The True Cause," *United States Catholic Miscellany*, August 25, 1855.

98. "Hon. L.M. Keitt," *United States Catholic Miscellany*, January 19, 1856. In May 1856 Keitt escorted Preston Brooks to the Senate chambers to beat Charles Sumner. He was censured for this. He also attacked a Pennsylvania Republican in Congress in 1858. Edgar, *South Carolina*, 347–48; Walther, *The Fire Eaters*, 180–81; Abrahamson, *The Men of Secession and Civil War, 1859–1861*, 36–38.

99. "Worth Remembering," *United States Catholic Miscellany*, August 16, 1856.

100. Smith, *Italy*, 14–25; Di Scala, *Italy*, 110–14; Marraro, *American Opinion on the Unification of Italy*, 299; Ridley, *Garibaldi*, 444–509.

101. *United States Catholic Miscellany*, March 10, 1860. See Marraro, *American Opinion on the Unification of Italy*, 268–71.

102. "Papal Fund," *United States Catholic Miscellany*, September 8, 1860, and "Papal Fund," *United States Catholic Miscellany*, October 6, 1860.

103. "Diocese of Mobile" and "Address," *United States Catholic Miscellany*, April 15, 1860.

104. "Sympathy for Our Holy Father," *United States Catholic Miscellany*, April 15, 1860.

105. "Italy," *United States Catholic Miscellany*, October 1, 1859.

106. "Richard Realf," *United States Catholic Miscellany*, January 14, 1860.

107. "A Black Republican Outrage," *United States Catholic Miscellany*, April 7, 1860. See also the following issues of the *Miscellany* for characterizations of northern radicalism: April 15, 1860; June 30, 1860; October 20, 1860. The *Miscellany* has similar stories of European radicalism in the following issues: March 17, 1860; April 21, 1860; May 11, 1860; May 25, 1860; June 9, 1860; July 14, 1860; August 4, 1860.

108. "It Has Come at Last!" *United States Catholic Miscellany*, November 10, 1860.

109. "Italian Affairs," *United States Catholic Miscellany*, December 1, 1860. Corcoran's views were not necessarily identical to Bishop Lynch's. But Lynch gave him free rein as editor. He wrote to John Mullaly, who edited the *Metropolitan Record* in New York, on January 6, 1861: "There is only one Editor of the Miscellany— Dr. Corcoran.... Dr. Corcoran writes as he pleases, I cannot say that his Editorials are not sometimes not to my taste.... —But he has said nothing 'contra fidem et mores.'" In Wright, "Some Wartime Letters of Bishop Lynch," 21–22.

110. "The Crisis," *United States Catholic Miscellany*, November 24, 1860.

111. "Italian Affairs," *United States Catholic Miscellany*, December 1, 1860. The historian Albert Von Frank writes, "Others of Brown's young associates had connections with European revolutionary movements, including English-born Hugh Forbes, the company's treacherous drill-master, who had fought under Garibaldi and was employed, when Brown first met him, as a reporter on the *New York Daily Tribune*; Charles W. Leonhardt, a Polish revolutionary now working as a Kansas journalist; and Charles Kaiser, a Bavarian, and August Bondi, a Vienna-born Jew, both of whom had served under Kossuth. This leaven of revolutionary experience, gathered entirely apart from but now brought to bear on the question of American slavery and made articulate in the work of the Kansas journalists, functioned as a rebuke to that cautious, overdetermined, and self-doubting strain in American antislavery thought increasingly characteristic, in Brown's view, of the now frankly disappointing 'Eastern people.'" "John Brown, James Redpath, and the Idea of Revolution," 148.

112. Fox-Genovese and Genovese, *Mind of the Master Class*, 50–51. The Genoveses have noted that the Italian example did inspire southern nationalists to push to create their own southern nation, a point that validates the Philadelphia editor.

113. "Voice of the Press," *United States Catholic Miscellany*, December 8, 1860.

114. "The Crisis," *United States Catholic Miscellany*, November 24, 1860.

115. "The Present Crisis," *United States Catholic Miscellany*, December 8, 1860.

116. "The Crisis," *United States Catholic Miscellany*, December 15, 1860.

117. "A Black Republican 'Catholic,'" *Charleston Catholic Miscellany* (Charleston, SC), March 23, 1861.

118. Lincoln offered Garibaldi, the famous Italian radical, a Union command. Marraro, "Lincoln's Offer of a Command to Garibaldi"; Ridley, *Garibaldi*, 521–24; "Lincoln and Garibaldi; Letter," *Times* (London), February 14, 2000. See also Stock, "Catholic Participation in the Diplomacy of the Southern Confederacy." The rhetoric Stock examines—conflating northerners, revolutionaries, and nativists—was exactly that of Corcoran during the 1850s.

119. Gleeson, *The Green and the Gray*, 10–40; Schultz, *Nationalism and Sectionalism*, 227; O'Connor, *The Life and Letters of M. P. O'Connor*, 1–23.

120. Heisser and White, *Patrick N. Lynch*, 153–91.

CHAPTER SIX.   *South Carolina Catholics and Slavery*

Some of the material on Bishop England and slavery in this chapter comes from a previously published article, reprinted by the permission of the publisher, Tate, "Confronting Abolitionism."

1. The scholarship on southern Catholics and slavery is massive. See Farrelly, "American Slavery, American Freedom, American Catholicism"; Guilday, *The Life and Times of John England*; Allen, "The Slavery Question in Catholic Newspapers, 1850–1865," 101–4; Cooley, "Bishop England's Solution to the Negro Problem"; Rice, *American Catholic Opinion in the Slavery Controversy*, 65–69, 73; Clarke, *A Free Church in a Free Society*, 389–413; Miller, "A Church in Cultural Captivity"; Miller, "The Failed Mission"; Miller, "Catholics in a Protestant World"; Miller, "Roman Catholicism in South Carolina," 95–96; Davis, "Black Catholics in Nineteenth-Century America"; Zanca, *American Catholics and Slavery*; Devanny, "Bishop John England and the Rhetoric of Republicanism"; Curran, "Rome, the American Church, and Slavery"; Kelly, "Charleston's Bishop John England and American Slavery"; Gleeson, *The Irish in the South*, 129; Stokes, "Catholics in Beulahland"; Quinn, "Three Cheers for the Abolitionist Pope!"; Capizzi, "For What Shall We Repent?"; Stern, "Southern Harmony," 171–76; McNeil, *Recovering American Catholic Inculturation*, 62, 201, 221, 224; Pasquier, "Though Their Skin Remains Brown, I Hope Their Souls Will Soon Be White"; Wallace, *Catholics, Slaveholders, and the Dilemma of American Evangelicalism, 1835–1860*, 120–28; Woods, *A History of the Catholic Church in the American South, 1513–1900*, 215–95; Panzer, *The Popes and Slavery*; O'Brien, *Conjectures of Order*, 2:1083–95; Clarke and Underwood, "Bishop John England and the Compatibility of the Catholic Church and American Democracy."

2. Stokes, "Catholics in Beulahland," 236; Curran, "Rome, the American Church, and Slavery," 40–41, 49. Curran picks up on the theme that the American Catholic hierarchy did not see slavery as a major issue and tried to downplay it to preserve peace. Curran thinks the costs of that strategy were great. Stern, "Southern Harmony," 175–76; McNeil, *Recovering American Catholic Inculturation*, 62; Kane, "The Supernatural and Slavery," 204.

3. Ford, *Deliver Us from Evil*; E. Clarke, *Dwelling Place*. See Ford's helpful discussion of Clarke's book: Ford, "A Paternalist's Progress."

4. McGreevy, *Catholicism and American Freedom*, 52–66. McGreevy expanded his comments in an exceptional piece, "Catholicism and Abolition." Stern, "Southern Harmony," 175–76, recognizes that southern Catholic discussions of slavery often reflected southern social ideals. Noll, *The Civil War as a Theological Crisis*, 125–55. Even after Bishop England's death, Catholics in the South were

often suspected of being weak on the slavery issue. Some scholars have examined this question. See, e.g., Rousey, "Friends and Foes of Slavery." In the North, many lumped Catholics and slaveholders together as partners in crime, a rhetorical tactic best explained in Wallace, *Catholics, Slaveholders, and the Dilemma of American Evangelicalism, 1835–1860.*

5. Edgar, *South Carolina,* 327.

6. Shugerman, "The Louisiana Purchase and South Carolina's Reopening of the Slave Trade in 1803."

7. Egerton, *He Shall Go Out Free,* 128.

8. Edgar, *South Carolina,* 269–75, 324–28; Freehling, *Prelude to Civil War,* 25–48; Ford, *Origins of Southern Radicalism,* 44–95.

9. Edgar, *South Carolina,* 276.

10. Ibid., 269–70.

11. Egerton, *He Shall Go Out Free,* 101–25.

12. "Domestic," *United States Catholic Miscellany,* July 17, 1822; "Convictions," *United States Catholic Miscellany,* July 24, 1822; "Convictions and Executions," *United States Catholic Miscellany,* July 31, 1822; Edgar, *South Carolina,* 328–29.

13. Ford, *Deliver Us from Evil,* 162. Ford built on solid scholarship: Olwell, *Masters, Slaves, and Subjects*; Chaplin, *An Anxious Pursuit*; Young, *Domesticating Slavery*; Young, *Proslavery and Sectional Thought in the Early South, 1740–1829.*

14. Ford, *Deliver Us from Evil,* 147.

15. Furman, *Exposition of the Views of the Baptists,* 10.

16. Ford, *Deliver Us from Evil,* 162.

17. Ibid., 170, 183–84. Three excellent works flesh out these themes through different interpretations: Cornelius, *"When I Can Read My Title Clear"*; Irons, *The Origins of Proslavery Christianity*; Clarke, *Dwelling Place.*

18. Reprinted in Commons et al., eds., *A Documentary History of American Industrial Society,* 2:103–4, 115.

19. Holland, *A Refutation of the Calumnies,* 82, 83, 86. See also Tise, *Proslavery,* 59–60.

20. Seabrook, *A Concise View,* 13.

21. Corporation of Charleston, *An Account of the Late Intended Insurrection among a Portion of the Blacks of This City,* 33.

22. Seabrook, *A Concise View,* 16–17.

23. Irons, *Origins of Proslavery Christianity,* 72.

24. Dalcho, *Practical Considerations Founded on the Scriptures,* 33, 34.

25. Ford, *Deliver Us from Evil,* 185.

26. I am not implying here that evangelicals were somehow really opposed to slavery but had to put on airs in order to avoid harassment. Yet it is not often admitted in regard to religious ministers that they—just as much as liberal

intellectuals and closet southern abolitionists—had no real freedom of speech. See Eaton, *The Freedom of Thought Struggle in the Old South*. Mitchell Snay points out in *Gospel of Disunion* that Protestant ministers in the South were sometimes examined by concerned secular authorities about their views on slavery (36).

27. England, *Diurnal of the Right Rev. John England, D.D.*, 10–11, 21–23.

28. For other incidents during the 1820s and early 1830s in which Bishop England revealed his actions among the black population of his diocese, see England to Gaston, June 13, 1821, and June 20, 1821, in "Letters from the Right Reverend John England, D.D. to the Honorable William Gaston, LL.D.," 371, 374; England to Gaston, May 27, 1829, in "Letters from the Right Reverend John England, D.D. to the Honorable William Gaston, LL.D., continued," 118. It should also be noted that according to the U.S. Census for 1830, a male slave between the ages of 24 and 32 lived at the residence of Bishop England. Four other people lived at the residence as well. Heisser writes that the slave was England's coachman. U.S. Census, 1830, Charleston District, Ward 4, South Carolina, Roll 170, 102; Heisser, "Bishop Lynch's People," 241; Clarke and Underwood, "Bishop John England and the Compatibility of the Catholic Church and American Democracy," 209; Thigpen, "Aristocracy of the Heart." Thigpen has an excellent discussion of Catholics and slavery in Savannah in ch. 12.

29. Krebsbach, "Black Catholics in Antebellum Charleston," 153, 149, 156. See additional figures in Woods, *A History of the Catholic Church in the American South*, 287–88.

30. Krebsbach, "Black Catholics in Antebellum Charleston," 154, 159.

31. "The Vaudois," *United States Catholic Miscellany*, August 16, 1828.

32. "A Catechism for Coloured Persons!!!," *United States Catholic Miscellany*, July 12, 1834.

33. "White and Black Slaves," *United States Catholic Miscellany*, August 26, 1826. This tactic of comparing the conditions of black slaves and Irish laborers became a common trope in pro-slavery discourse. See Giemza, *Irish Catholic Writers and the Invention of the American South*, 51–53.

34. "The Black College," *United States Catholic Miscellany*, October 15, 1831.

35. "Address Delivered before the Philanthropic and Dialectic societies at Chapel Hill, June 20, 1832—by the Hon. William Gaston," *United States Catholic Miscellany*, October 20, 1832.

36. England, "A Brief Account of the Introduction of the Catholic Religion into the States of N. Carolina, S. Carolina, and Georgia," in Reynolds, *Works*, 3:257–58.

37. England, "Report of Bishop England to the Cardinal Prefect of Propaganda," 328–29.

38. "Liberia," *United States Catholic Miscellany*, November 23, 1833.

39. Seabrook, *An Essay on the Management of Slaves*, 26. On Bishop England's mission to Haiti, see Guilday, *Life and Times of John England*, 2:270–313; Clarke, *A Free Church in a Free Society*, 434–40.

40. England to Dr. Cullen, February 23, 1836, in England, "Papers Relating to the Church in America, Third Series," 218.

41. England, in Messmer, *Works*, 5:189.

42. Ford, *Deliver Us from Evil*, 483. My summary of the incident comes from pp. 482–85 of Ford's book. Also see John, *Spreading the News*, 257–80, for a brilliant analysis of the crisis.

43. Seabrook, *An Essay on the Management of Slaves*, 26, 29.

44. Ibid., 6, 13, 14, 15.

45. Ibid., 24, 31.

46. Ford, *Deliver Us from Evil*, 467–73; Cornelius, *"When I Can Read My Title Clear,"* 39–42; Wilkins, "Window on Freedom."

47. "Great and Important Public Meeting," *United States Catholic Miscellany*, August 15, 1835.

48. "The Philadelphia Inquirer," *Charleston Courier* (Charleston, SC), August 22, 1835.

49. Wyly-Jones, "The 1835 Anti-Abolition Meetings in the South."

50. "Great Public Meeting," *Charleston Courier* (Charleston, SC), August 4, 1835.

51. England to Dr. Cullen, February 23, 1836, in England, "Papers Relating to the Church in America, Third Series," 220–21.

52. "To the Presiding Officer of the S.C. Association," *Charleston Courier* (Charleston, SC), July 31, 1835.

53. Kelly, "Charleston's Bishop John England and American Slavery," 56.

54. Ford, *Deliver Us from Evil*, 476–80.

55. Cornelius makes this point well: *"When I Can Read My Title Clear,"* 47–48.

56. England, in Messmer, *Works*, 7:276; Clarke, *A Free Church in a Free Society*, 411.

57. "School for Colored Children," *United States Catholic Miscellany*, January 2, 1841. Walter Edgar notes that antebellum visitors to Charleston commented on black children going to school in the morning, a sign that restrictions on black schools were inconsistently enforced. Edgar, *South Carolina*, 299.

58. "Charleston Neck," *United States Catholic Miscellany*, September 19, 1835.

59. England to Dr. Cullen, February 23, 1836, in England, "Papers Relating to the Church in America, Third Series," 221–22.

60. Ibid., 222–25. See Billington, *The Protestant Crusade*, 85–90. One effect of northern mobs attacking Catholic churches during the 1830s was that it made bishops, like England, very sensitive to public opinion.

61. England to Dr. Cullen, April 9, 1836, in England, "Papers Relating to the Church in America, Third Series," 237. In 1826 the United States Congress had exploded into debate over the issue of sending U.S. diplomats to Panama for a Latin American congress. Some southern congressmen opposed the mission because of the possibility of Haiti's participation. See Dangerfield, *The Era of Good Feelings*, 356–64; Dangerfield, *The Awakening of American Nationalism, 1815–1828*, 248–50. It is no surprise, then, that Bishop England received a hostile reaction to his mission to Haiti.

62. See Quinn, "Three Cheers for the Abolitionist Pope," 71.

63. "The Slave Trade," *United States Catholic Miscellany*, March 14, 1840.

64. Allen, "The Slavery Question in Catholic Newspapers, 1850–1865," 140; "The Slave Trade," *United States Catholic Miscellany*, March 14, 1840.

65. "Catholic Voters," *United States Catholic Miscellany*, September 12, 1840; Formisano, "Political Character, Antipartyism, and the Second Party System"; Saunders and Rogers, "Bishop John England of Charleston," 313–15. See Martin Van Buren's 1837 speech to the special session of Congress he had called to deal with the Panic of 1837: "Against Government Aid for Business Losses," in *Annals of American History*, 6:314–16.

66. "Catholic Voters," *United States Catholic Miscellany*, September 12, 1840.

67. "Catholic Voters," *United States Catholic Miscellany*, October 17, 1840.

68. "Catholic Voters," *United States Catholic Miscellany*, October 10, 1840.

69. "Danger to the Republic" and "Prospectus," *United States Catholic Miscellany*, October 31, 1840.

70. "Politics of the Day," *Niles National Register* (Baltimore, MD), September 26, 1840; Cooper, *The South and the Politics of Slavery, 1828–1856*, 98–148; Quinn, "Three Cheers for the Abolitionist Pope," 77–80; Murphy, *American Slavery, Irish Freedom*, 1–80; Riach, "Daniel O'Connell and American Anti-Slavery."

71. Messmer, *Works*, 5:183–90. See also Capizzi, "For What Shall We Repent," 778–82.

72. Messmer, *Works*, 5:193–95; Fox-Genovese and Genovese, *Slavery in White and Black*.

73. Messmer, *Works*, 5:196, 202, 210, 211.

74. Ibid., 5:215, 211, 219, 221, 229, 260. For a reading of the Forsyth letters similar to my own (but not considering the same context), see Haddox, *Fears and Fascinations*, 51–55.

75. Messmer, *Works*, 5:311.

76. Wikramanayake, *A World in Shadow*, 43; Powers, *Black Charlestonians*, 39–40.

77. Cornelius, *"When I Can Read My Title Clear,"* 48.

78. "The Catholic Church—Domestic Slavery, and the Slave Trade," *United States Catholic Miscellany*, December 9, 1843.

79. Quinn, "Three Cheers for the Abolitionist Pope," 87.

80. "Domestic Slavery, considered as a Scriptural Institution, in a correspondence between the Rev. Richard Fuller, of Beaufort, S.C. and the Rev. Francis Wayland, of Providence R.I.," *United States Catholic Miscellany*, December 20, 1845.

81. "The Late Bishop England," *United States Catholic Miscellany*, January 9, 1858.

82. "Church and Abolition," *United States Catholic Miscellany*, June 1, 1850.

83. "Abolitionism," *United States Catholic Miscellany*, December 23, 1854.

84. "A Fugitive Pervert," *United States Catholic Miscellany*, December 31, 1859.

85. "Uncle Tom's Cabin," *United States Catholic Miscellany*, June 11, 1853.

86. "Grace Greenwood," *United States Catholic Miscellany*, February 19, 1853.

87. "Catholics and Slavery," *United States Catholic Miscellany*, October 18, 1856. Corcoran responded to similar attempts to pin social radicalism on Catholics: "Geneva—Calvin," *Miscellany*, March 29, 1851.

88. England, in Messmer, *Works*, 7:343–44.

89. "Southern Quarterly Review," *United States Catholic Miscellany*, October 31, 1851.

90. "Amicable Discussion—Not Controversy," *United States Catholic Miscellany*, October 12, 1850, reprints part of Bachman's controversy over his 1850 book, *The Doctrine of the Unity of the Human Race Examined on the Principles of Science*. The November 9, 1850, edition of the paper ("Protestant Tradition") continued this. Although the editor agreed with Bachman's conclusion, he needled Bachman for his reliance on the doctrine of *sola scriptura*.

91. Sinha, *The Counterrevolution of Slavery*, 125–52; McCardell, *The Idea of a Southern Nation*, 133–40.

92. "The Slave Trade," *United States Catholic Miscellany*, February 7, 1857.

93. "Revival of the African Slave Trade," *United States Catholic Miscellany*, August 1, 1857.

94. *United States Catholic Miscellany*, August 22, 1857.

95. "Glory," *United States Catholic Miscellany*, September 12, 1857.

96. See, Davidson, *The Last Foray*, 106. Davidson studies as a group the 440 slaveholders in South Carolina identified in the 1860 census as owning 100 or more slaves. There was only one Catholic among them, William McKenna. Heisser and White, *Patrick N. Lynch*, 114–25.

97. Ford, "Reconfiguring the Old South," 109.

98. Lynch, "A Few Words on Domestic Slavery in the Confederate States of America," part 1, 70.

99. Ibid., 71.

100. Ibid., 98.

101. Ibid., 87, 95. See Greenberg, "Revolutionary Ideology and the Proslavery Argument," 384, in particular, on the ways in which South Carolinians phrased their defenses of slavery.

102. Ford, *Deliver Us from Evil*, 508.

103. Lynch, "A Few Words on Domestic Slavery," part 1, 93.

104. Lynch, "A Few Words on the Domestic Slavery in the Confederate States of America," part 2, 94, 97, 109, 116.

105. See Noll, *The Civil War as a Theological Crisis*, 51–74, on how the racial characteristic of American slavery overwhelmed sincere Protestant attempts to defend the institution.

106. Lynch, "A Few Words on the Domestic Slavery," part 1, 100.

107. Lynch, "A Few Words on the Domestic Slavery," part 2, 102.

108. Ibid., 102–4. On this question in general, Clarke's *Dwelling Place* illustrates well the issue of separation of married slaves and the destructive effects it had on both white and black societies.

109. Lynch, "A Few Words on the Domestic Slavery," part 2, 105.

110. Ibid., 106–8.

111. Ibid., 110–13.

112. Ibid., 113.

113. This supports the findings of Angela Murphy in *American Slavery, Irish Freedom*, yet in a broader sense. See Noll, *Civil War as a Theological Crisis*, ch. 4, 162.

Conclusion

1. "Our Heading," *Catholic Miscellany* (Charleston, SC), December 29, 1860.

2. "Brownson's Review," *Charleston Catholic Miscellany*, April 6, 1861. Brownson had aggravated a number of Catholic leaders by his comments on the Irish during the 1850s. See McAvoy, "American Cultural Impacts on Catholicism," 49; Moore, *Religious Outsiders and the Making of Americans*, 51–53.

3. "War at Last," *Charleston Catholic Miscellany*, April 13, 1861.

4. See McGreevy, *Catholicism and American Freedom*, 68–90, for a survey of Catholic opinions about the Civil War.

5. Simms, *Sack and Destruction*, 3.

6. Ibid., 5.

7. Ibid., 7.

8. Ibid., 24.

9. Ibid., 14, 15, 35.

10. Ibid., 34.

11. Ibid., 34–35.

12. Ibid., 35.

13. Guilds, *Simms*, 299–300.

14. Simms, *Sack and Destruction*, 35–36.

15. Ibid., 39, 40 (quotation appears on 40).

16. Ibid., 40.

17. England, "Report of Bishop England to the Cardinal Prefect of Propaganda," 320.

18. O'Connell, *Catholicity in the Carolinas and Georgia*, 39.

19. Ibid., 76.

20. Ibid., 46.

21. Ibid., 296.

22. Ibid., 487.

23. Ibid., 628.

24. Ibid., 629.

25. Ibid., 630.

26. Ibid., 268.

27. "Dreadful Conflagration," *Charleston Catholic Miscellany*, December 14, 1861. Note: The date of the paper was misprinted as December 1, 1861.

28. O'Connell, *Catholicity in the Carolinas and Georgia*, 125.

29. Ibid., 212.

30. Ibid., 281.

31. Ibid., 35–36.

32. Ibid., 126. See also Gleeson, "To live and die [for] Dixie," 139–53; Buttimer, "Turning Away from Georgia toward Rome," 17–35. Both of these pieces reach conclusions that differ from mine about the Civil War's legacy for postbellum Catholicism in the southern Atlantic states.

33. O'Connell, *Catholicity in the Carolinas and Georgia*, 35, 629–31.

BIBLIOGRAPHY

Archives and Special Collections

Archives of the Catholic Diocese of Charleston, South Carolina
Georgia Archives, Morrow, Georgia
Irvin Department of Rare Books and Special Collections, Thomas Cooper Library, University of South Carolina
Robert Woodruff Library Special Collections, Emory University
South Carolina State Library, Columbia, South Carolina
South Caroliniana Library, Manuscript Division, Columbia, South Carolina

Newspapers, Nineteenth-Century Journals, and Government Documents

Appendix to the Congressional Globe
Augusta Chronicle (Augusta, GA)
Brownson's Quarterly Review
Charleston Courier (Charleston, SC)
Charleston Mercury (Charleston, SC)
Charleston Observer (Charleston, SC)
Chronicle & Sentinel (Augusta, GA)
Columbus Enquirer (Columbus, GA)
De Bow's Review
Georgia Constitutionalist (Augusta, GA)
The Liberator (Boston, MA)
Milledgeville Federal Union (Milledgeville, GA)
New York Daily Tribune (New York, NY)

Richmond Watchman and Observer (Richmond, VA)
Savannah Daily Georgian (Savannah, GA)
Savannah Daily Republican (Savannah, GA)
Southern Banner (Athens, GA)
Southern Patriot (Charleston, SC)
Southern Quarterly Review
Times (London, England)
Tri-Weekly Chronicle & Sentinel (Augusta, GA)
United States Catholic Miscellany (Charleston, SC)

Books, Articles, Dissertations, and Theses

Abrahamson, James L. *The Men of Secession and Civil War, 1859–1861.* Wilmington, DE: Scholarly Resources, 2000.
Adams, James Luther. "The Voluntary Principle in the Forming of American Religion." In *The Religion of the Republic,* edited by Elwyn A. Smith, 217–46. Philadelphia: Fortress Press, 1971.
Agonito, Joseph. "Ecumenical Stirrings: Catholic-Protestant Relations during the Episcopacy of John Carroll." *Church History* 45, no. 3 (September 1976): 358–73.
Alexander, Erik B. "'The Democracy Must Prepare for Battle': Know-Nothingism in Alabama and Southern Politics, 1851–1859." *Southern Historian* 27 (Spring 2006): 23–37.
Allen, Cuthbert Edward, OSB. "The Slavery Question in Catholic Newspapers, 1850–1865." *US Catholic Historical Society Historical Records and Studies* 26 (1936): 99–169.
Allitt, Patrick. *Catholic Converts: British and American Intellectuals Turn to Rome.* Ithaca, NY: Cornell University Press, 1993.
American Tract Society. "The American Colporteur System" (1836). Reprinted in *The American Tract Society Documents, 1824–1925.* New York: Arno Press, 1972.
Anbinder, Tyler. *Nativism and Slavery: The Northern Know Nothings and the Politics of the 1850s.* New York: Oxford University Press, 1992.
Anderson, Benedict. *Imagined Communities: Reflections on the Origin and Spread of Nationalism.* Rev. ed. New York: Verso, 2006.
Anderton, Douglas L., Richard E. Barrett, and Donald J. Bogue. *The Population of the United States.* 3d ed. New York: Free Press, 1997.
Annals of American History. 18 vols. Chicago: Encyclopedia Britannica, 1968.
Appleby, Joyce. *Inheriting the Revolution.* Cambridge, MA: Belknap Press of Harvard University Press, 2000.

Ashworth, John. "The Jeffersonians: Classical Republicans or Liberal Capitalists?" *Journal of American Studies* 18, no. 3 (1984): 425–35.

Austin, Erik W. *Political Facts of the United States since 1789.* New York: Columbia University Press, 1986.

[Bachman, Catherine]. *John Bachman.* Charleston, SC: Walker, Evans, and Cogswell Co., 1888.

Bachman, John, DD., LLD. *A Defense of Luther and the Reformation against the Charges of John Bellinger, M. D., and Others to Which Are Appended Various Communications of Other Protestant and Roman Catholic Writers Who Engaged in the Controversy.* Charleston, SC: Steam Power Press of Walker and James, 1853.

Banner, James M., Jr. "The Problem of South Carolina." In *The Hofstadter Aegis: A Memorial,* edited by Stanley Elkins and Eric McKitrick, 60–93. New York: Knopf, 1974.

Bartlett, Irving H. *John C. Calhoun: A Biography.* New York: Norton, 1993.

Basil, John D. "South Carolina Catholics before the Roman Discipline, 1670–1820." *Journal of Church and State* 45, no. 4 (Autumn 2003): 787–808.

Bell, Michael Everette. "Regional Identity in the Antebellum South: How German Immigrants Became 'Good' Charlestonians." *South Carolina Historical Magazine* 100, no. 1 (January 1999): 9–28.

Bellows, Barbara. *Benevolence among Slaveholders: Assisting the Poor in Charleston, 1670–1860.* Baton Rouge: Louisiana State University Press, 1993.

Bennett, David H. *The Party of Fear: From Nativist Movements to the New Right in American History.* Chapel Hill: University of North Carolina Press, 1988.

Bergeron, Paul H. "The Nullification Controversy Revisited." *Tennessee Historical Quarterly* 35 (Fall 1976): 263–75.

Berlin, Ira, and Herbert G. Gutman. "Free Men and Slaves: Urban Workingmen in the Antebellum American South." *American Historical Review* 88 (December 1983): 1175–1200.

Bernath, Michael T. *Confederate Minds: The Struggle for Intellectual Independence in the Civil War South.* Chapel Hill: University of North Carolina Press, 2010.

Bianchi, Hanael. *St. George's Day: A Cultural History of England's National Day.* Owing Mills, MD: Caliber and Kempis, 2014.

Billington, Ray Allen. *The Protestant Crusade 1800–1860: A Study of the Origins of American Nativism.* Chicago: Quadrangle Books, 1964. Originally published Macmillan Co., 1938.

Bladek, John David. "'Virginia Is Middle Ground': The Know Nothing Party and the Virginia Gubernatorial Election of 1855." *Virginia Magazine of History and Biography* 106, no. 1 (Winter 1998): 35–70.

Bratt, James D. "The Reorientation of American Protestantism, 1835–1845." *Church History* 67, no. 1 (March 1998): 52–82.

Broussard, James H. "Some Determinants of Know Nothing Electoral Strength in the South, 1856." *Louisiana History* 7, no. 1 (Winter 1966): 5–20.

[Brownson, Orestes]. "Conversations of an Old Man and His Young Friends, No. II." *Brownson's Quarterly Review* 4, no. 2 (April 1850): 228–44.

Butterfield, Herbert. *The Whig Interpretation of History.* New York: Norton, 1965.

Buttimer, Benjamin. "Turning Away from Georgia and Toward Rome: The Diocese of Savannah and the Growth of the Anti-Catholic Movement in Georgia, 1870–1970." *U.S. Catholic Historian* 21, no. 4 (Fall 2003): 17–35.

Byrne, Patricia. "American Ultramontanism." *Theological Studies* 56 (1995): 301–26.

Calhoon, Robert. *Dominion and Liberty: Ideology in the Anglo-American World, 1660–1801.* Arlington Heights, IL: Harlan Davidson, 1994.

Callahan, Helen. "Development of the Roman Catholic Society of Augusta and Richmond County during the Nineteenth Century." *Richmond County History* 1, no. 1 (Winter 1969): 9–14.

Campbell, Sister M. Anne Francis. "Bishop England's Sisterhood, 1829–1929." PhD dissertation, Saint Louis University, 1968.

Cantrell, Gregg. "Southern and Nativist: Kenneth Rayner and the Ideology of 'Americanism.'" *North Carolina Historical Review* 69, no. 2 (April 1992): 131–47.

Capizzi, Joseph E. "For What Shall We Repent? Reflections on the American Bishops, Their Teaching, and Slavery in the United States, 1839–1861." *Theological Studies* 65 (2004): 767–91.

Carey, Anthony Gene. "Too Southern to Be Americans: Proslavery Politics and the Failure of the Know-Nothing Party in Georgia." *Civil War History* 41, no. 1 (1995): 22–40.

Carey, Patrick W. "American Catholic Romanticism, 1830–1888." *Catholic Historical Review* 74, no. 4 (October 1988): 590–606.

———. *An Immigrant Bishop: John England's Adaptation of Irish Catholicism to American Republicanism.* Yonkers, NY: U.S. Catholic Historical Society, 1982.

———. "The Laity's Understanding of the Trustee System, 1785–1855." *Catholic Historical Review* 64, no. 3 (July 1978): 357–76.

———. "Voluntaryism: An Irish Catholic Tradition." *Church History* 48, no. 1 (March 1979): 49–62.

Carpenter, Jesse T. *The South as a Conscious Minority, 1789–1861.* Columbia: University of South Carolina Press, 1990. Originally published New York University Press, 1930.

Carroll, Michael P. *American Catholics and the Protestant Imagination: Rethinking the Academic Study of Religion.* Baltimore, MD: Johns Hopkins University Press, 2007.

Casanova, Jose. "Roman and Catholic and American: The Transformation of Catholicism in the United States." *International Journal of Politics, Culture, and Society* 6, no. 1 (Autumn 1992): 75–111.

Cashin, Edward J. *The Story of Augusta.* Augusta, GA: Richmond County Board of Education, 1980.

————. "Summerville, Retreat of the Old South." *Richmond County History* 5, no. 2 (Summer 1973): 44–59.

Chadwick, Owen. *The Popes and European Revolution.* Oxford: Clarendon Press, 1981.

Chaplin, Joyce E. *An Anxious Pursuit: Agricultural Innovation and Modernity in the Lower South, 1730–1815.* Chapel Hill: University of North Carolina Press, 1993.

Chinnici, Joseph. "American Catholics and Religious Pluralism, 1775–1820." *Journal of Ecumenical Studies* 16 (Fall 1977): 727–46.

Clark, Dennis. "The South's Irish Catholics: A Case of Cultural Confinement." In *Catholics in the Old South: Essays on Church and Culture,* edited by Randall M. Miller and Jon L. Wakelyn, 195–209. Macon, GA: Mercer University Press, 1983.

Clark, Kenneth. *The Gothic Revival: An Essay in the History of Taste.* New York: Scribners, 1950.

Clarke, Erskine. *Dwelling Place: A Plantation Epic.* New Haven, CT: Yale University Press, 2005.

Clarke, Peter. *A Free Church in a Free Society: The Ecclesiology of John England, Bishop of Charleston, 1820–1842.* Hartsville, SC: Center for John England Studies, 1982.

Clarke, Peter, and James Lowell Underwood. "Bishop John England and the Compatibility of the Catholic Church and American Democracy." In *The Dawn of Religious Freedom in South Carolina,* edited by James Lowell Underwood and W. Lewis Burke, 184–210. Columbia: University of South Carolina Press, 2006.

Clarke, Richard Henry. *Lives of the Deceased Bishops of the Catholic Church in the United States.* Vol. 1. New York: Richard H. Clarke, 1888.

Codignola, Luca. "Roman Catholic Conservatism in a New North Atlantic World, 1760–1829." *William and Mary Quarterly,* 3rd ser., 64, no. 4 (October 2007): 717–56.

Colbourn, Trevor. *The Lamp of Experience: Whig History and the Intellectual Origins of the American Revolution.* Indianapolis, IN: Liberty Fund, 1998. Originally published University of North Carolina Press, 1965.

Coleman, Kenneth, ed. *A History of Georgia.* 2nd ed. Athens: University of Georgia Press, 1991.

Commons, John R., Ulrich B. Phillips, Eugene A. Gilmore, Helen L. Sumner, and John B. Andrews, eds. *A Documentary History of American Industrial Society*. Vol. 2. Cleveland, OH: Arthur H. Clark Co., 1910.

Connolly, S.J., ed. *Political Ideas in Eighteenth Century Ireland*. Dublin: Four Courts Press, 2000.

Conser, Walter H., Jr. *Church and Confession: Conservative Theologians in Germany, England, and America, 1815–1866*. Macon, GA: Mercer University Press, 1984.

Conzen, Kathleen Neils. "Mainstreams and Side Channels: The Localization of Immigrant Cultures." *Journal of American Ethnic History* 11, no. 1 (Fall 1991): 5–20.

Conzen, Kathleen Neils, David Gerber, Ewa Morawska, George Pozzetta, and Rudolph J. Vecoli. "The Invention of Ethnicity: A Perspective from the U.S.A." *Journal of American Ethnic History* 12, no. 1 (Fall 1992): 3–41.

Cook, Anna Maria Green. *History of Baldwin County, Georgia*. Spartanburg, SC: Reprint Company, 1978. Originally published Keys-Hearn Printing Co., 1925.

Cooley, Leo P. "Bishop England's Solution to the Negro Problem." MA thesis, St. John's University, 1940.

Cooper, William, Jr. *The South and the Politics of Slavery*. Baton Rouge: Louisiana State University Press, 1978.

Cornelius, Janet Duitsman. *"When I Can Read My Title Clear": Literacy, Slavery, and Religion in the Antebellum South*. Columbia: University of South Carolina Press, 1991.

Corporation of Charleston. *An Account of the Late Intended Insurrection among a Portion of the Blacks of This City*. 3rd ed. Charleston, SC: A. E. Miller, 1822.

Cosgrove, John. "The Hibernian Society of Charleston, South Carolina." *Journal of the American-Irish Historical Society* 25 (1926): 150–58.

Cronin, Mike, and Daryl Adair. *The Wearing of the Green: A History of St. Patrick's Day*. New York: Routledge, 2002.

Curran, Robert Emmett. *Papist Devils: Catholics in British America, 1574–1783*. Washington DC: Catholic University of America Press, 2014.

———. "Rome, the American Church, and Slavery." In *Building the Church in America: Studies in Honor of Monsignor Robert F. Trisco on the Occasion of His Seventieth Birthday*, edited by Joseph C. Linck CO and Raymond J. Kupke, 30–49. Washington, DC: Catholic University of America Press, 1999.

Curti, Merle. "The Impact of the Revolutions of 1848 on American Thought." *Proceedings of the American Philosophical Society* 93, no. 3 (June 1949): 209–15.

Cyclopedia of Georgia. 4 vols. Edited by Allen D. Candler and Clement A. Evans. Spartanburg, SC: Reprint Company, 1972. Originally published State Historical Association, 1906.

D'Agostino, Peter R. *Rome in America: Transnational Catholic Ideology from Risorgimento to Fascism.* Chapel Hill: University of North Carolina Press, 2004.

Dalcho, Frederick. *Practical Considerations Founded on the Scriptures, Relative to the Slave Population of South Carolina.* Charleston, SC: A.E. Miller, 1823.

Dangerfield, George. *The Awakening of American Nationalism, 1815–1828.* New York: Harper & Row, 1965.

———. *The Era of Good Feelings.* New York: Harcourt, Brace and Company, 1952.

Davidson, Chalmers Gaston. *The Last Foray: The South Carolina Planters of 1860, a Sociological Study.* Columbia: University of South Carolina Press, 1971.

Davis, Cyprian, OSB. "Black Catholics in Nineteenth-Century America." *U.S. Catholic Historian* 5, no. 1 (1986): 1–17.

Davis, David Brion. "Some Themes of Counter-Subversion: An Analysis of Anti-Masonic, Anti-Catholic, and Anti-Mormon Literature." *Mississippi Valley Historical Review* 47, no. 2 (September 1960): 205–24.

Davis, John. "Catholic Envy: The Visual Culture of Protestant Desire." In *The Visual Culture of American Religions,* edited by David Morgan and Sally Promey, 105–28. Berkeley: University of California Press, 2001.

Dawson, Christopher. *The Dividing of Christendom.* San Francisco, CA: Ignatius Press, 2009. Originally published Sheed & Ward, 1965.

Decker, Kevin. "Grand and Godly Proportions: Roman Catholic Churches of the Northeast, 1840–1900." PhD dissertation, University at Albany, State University of New York, 2000.

Denney, William H. "South Carolina's Conception of the Union in 1832." *South Carolina Historical Magazine* 78, no. 3 (July 1977): 171–83.

Devanny, John Francis, Jr. "Bishop John England and the Rhetoric of Republicanism." Master's thesis, University of South Carolina, 1995.

Dichtl, John R. *Frontiers of Faith: Bringing Catholicism to the West in the Early Republic.* Lexington: University Press of Kentucky, 2008.

Di Scala, Spencer M. *Italy: From Revolution to Republic, 1700 to the Present.* Boulder, CO: Westview Press, 1995.

Dodd, Donald B., and Wynelle S. Dodd. *Historical Statistics of the South, 1790–1970.* Tuscaloosa: University of Alabama Press, 1973.

Dolan, Jay. "Catholic Attitudes toward Protestants." In *Uncivil Religion: Interreligious Hostility in America,* edited by Robert N. Bellah and Frederick E. Greenspahn, 72–85. New York: Crossroad, 1987.

———. *Catholic Revivalism: The American Experience, 1830–1900.* Notre Dame, IN: University of Notre Dame Press, 1978.

———. *In Search of an American Catholicism.* New York: Oxford University Press, 2002.

Downs, Arthur Channing, Jr. "America's First 'Medieval' Churches." *Historical Magazine of the Protestant Episcopal Church* 45, no. 2 (June 1976): 166–76.

Doyle, David Noel. "The Irish as Urban Pioneers in the United States, 1850–1870." *Journal of American Ethnic History* 10, no. 1–2 (Fall 1990–Winter 1991): 36–59.

Dulles, Avery. *A History of Apologetics*. New York: Corpus Instrumentorum, 1971.

Dunne, Robert. *Antebellum Irish Immigration and Emerging Ideologies of "America": A Protestant Backlash*. Lewiston, NY: Edwin Mellen Press, 2002.

Eaton, Clement. *The Freedom of Thought Struggle in the Old South*. New York: Harper & Row, 1964.

Edgar, Walter. *South Carolina: A History*. Columbia: University of South Carolina Press, 1998.

Egerton, Douglas R. *He Shall Go Out Free: The Lives of Denmark Vesey*. Madison, WI: Madison House, 1999.

Ellis, Richard E. *Aggressive Nationalism: McCulloch v. Maryland and the Foundation of Federal Authority in the Young Republic*. New York: Oxford University Press, 2007.

———. *The Union at Risk: Jacksonian Democracy, States' Rights and the Nullification Crisis*. New York: Oxford University Press, 1987.

Emmons, David M. *Beyond the American Pale: The Irish in the West, 1845–1910*. Norman: University of Oklahoma Press, 2010.

Endres, David J. "Know-Nothings, Nationhood, and the Nuncio: Reassessing the Visit of Archbishop Bedini." *U.S. Catholic Historian* 21, no. 4 (Fall 2003): 1–16.

England, John. *Diurnal of the Right Rev. John England, D.D., First Bishop of Charleston, SC*. Philadelphia: American Catholic Historical Society, 1895.

———. "Letters from the Right Reverend John England, D.D. to the Honorable William Gaston, LL.D." *Records of the American Catholic Historical Society of Philadelphia* 18, no. 4 (December 1907): 367–88.

———. "Letters from the Right Reverend John England, D.D., to the Honorable William Gaston, LL.D., continued." *Records of the American Catholic Historical Association of Philadelphia* 19, no. 1 (March 1908): 98–121.

———. "Letters from the Right Reverend John England, D.D., to the Honorable William Gaston, LL.D., continued." *Records of the American Catholic Historical Association of Philadelphia* 19, no. 2 (June 1908): 140–84.

———. "Report of Bishop England to the Cardinal Prefect of Propaganda." In "Papers Relating to the Church in America: From the Portfolios of the Irish College at Rome, Fourth Series." *Records of the American Catholic Historical Society of Philadelphia* 8, no. 3 (September 1897): 317–29.

Etzioni, Amitai. "Holidays and Rituals: Neglected Seedbeds of Virtue." In *We Are What We Celebrate: Understanding Holidays and Rituals*, edited by Amitai Etzioni and Jared Bloom, 3–40. New York: New York University Press, 2004.

Farmer, James O., Jr. *The Metaphysical Confederacy: James Henley Thornwell and the Synthesis of Southern Values*. Macon, GA: Mercer University Press, 1999. Originally published 1986.

Farrelly, Maura Jane. "American Slavery, American Freedom, American Catholicism." *Early American Studies* 10, no. 1 (Winter 2012): 69–100.

———. *Papist Patriots: The Making of an American Catholic Identity*. New York: Oxford University Press, 2012.

Faust, Drew Gilpin. *The Creation of Confederate Nationalism: Ideology and Identity in the Civil War South*. Baton Rouge: Louisiana State University Press, 1988.

———. *A Sacred Circle: The Dilemma of the Intellectual in the Old South, 1840–1860*. Philadelphia: University of Pennsylvania Press, 1986. Originally published 1977.

Fenton, Elizabeth. *Religious Liberties: Anti-Catholicism and Liberal Democracy in Nineteenth-Century US Literature and Culture*. New York: Oxford University Press, 2011.

Fogarty, Gerald P. "Public Patriotism and Private Politics: The Tradition of American Catholicism." *U.S. Catholic Historian* 4, no. 1 (1984): 1–48.

Foik, Paul. "Pioneer Efforts in Catholic Journalism in the United States (1809–1840)." *Catholic Historical Review* 1, no. 3 (October 1915): 258–70.

Ford, Lacy K., Jr. *Deliver Us from Evil: The Slavery Question in the Old South*. New York: Oxford University Press, 2009.

———. *Origins of Southern Radicalism: The South Carolina Upcountry, 1800–1860*. New York: Oxford University Press, 1988.

———. "A Paternalist's Progress: Insurgency, Orthodoxy, and Reversal in the Old South." *Reviews in American History* 35, no. 1 (March 2007): 46–56.

———. "Reconfiguring the Old South: 'Solving' the Problem of Slavery, 1787–1838." *Journal of American History* 95, no. 1 (June 2008): 95–122.

Formisano, Ronald. *For the People: American Populist Movements from the Revolution to the 1850s*. Chapel Hill: University of North Carolina Press, 2008.

———. "Political Character, Antipartyism and the Second Party System." *American Quarterly* 21, no. 4 (Winter 1969): 683–709.

Foster, David. "Nightmare on Broad Street." *Augusta Magazine* (August–September 1999): 15–20.

Fox-Genovese, Elizabeth, and Eugene D. Genovese. *The Mind of the Master Class: History and Faith in the Southern Slaveholders' Worldview*. New York: Cambridge University Press, 2005.

———. *Slavery in White and Black: Class and Race in the Southern Slaveholders' New World Order*. New York: Cambridge University Press, 2008.

Franchot, Jenny. *Roads to Rome: The Antebellum Protestant Encounter with Catholicism*. Berkeley: University of California Press, 1994.

Frank, Lisa Tendrich. "'Between Death and Dishonor': Defending Confederate Womanhood during Sherman's March." In *Southern Character: Essays in Honor of Bertram Wyatt-Brown*, edited by Lisa Tendrich Frank and Daniel Kilbride, 116–27. Gainesville: University Press of Florida, 2011.

Fraser, Walter J., Jr. *Charleston, Charleston! The History of a Southern City*. Columbia: University of South Carolina Press, 1989.

Frederick, Jeff. "Unintended Consequences: The Rise and Fall of the Know Nothing Party in Alabama." *Alabama Review* 55 (January 2002): 3–33.

Freehling, William W., ed. *The Nullification Era: A Documentary Record*. New York: Harper Torchbooks, 1967.

———. *Prelude to Civil War: The Nullification Controversy in South Carolina, 1816–1836*. New York: Oxford University Press, 1992. Originally published 1965.

Freeman, Joanne. *Affairs of Honor: National Politics in the New Republic*. New Haven, CT: Yale University Press, 2001.

Frese, Joseph R., SJ. "The Catholic Press and Secession, 1860–1861." *Historical Records and Studies* 45 (1957): 79–106.

Furman, Richard. *Exposition of the Views of the Baptists, Relative to the Coloured Population of the United States, in a Communication to the Governor of South-Carolina*. Charleston, SC: A.E. Miller, 1823.

Gagnon, Michael J. *Transition to an Industrial South: Athens, Georgia, 1830–1870*. Baton Rouge: Louisiana State University Press, 2012.

Genovese, Eugene. *The Southern Tradition: The Achievement and Limitations of an American Conservatism*. Cambridge, MA: Harvard University Press, 1994.

———. *The World the Slaveholders Made: Two Essays in Interpretation*. Hanover, NH: Wesleyan University Press, 1988. Originally published 1969.

Giemza, Bryan. *Irish Catholic Writers and the Invention of the American South*. Baton Rouge: Louisiana State University Press, 2013.

Gienapp, William E. "Nativism and the Creation of a Republican Majority in the North before the Civil War." *Journal of American History* 72 (1985): 529–59.

Gilley, Sheridan. "The Roman Catholic Church and the Nineteenth-Century Irish Diaspora." *Journal of Ecclesiastical History* 35, no. 2 (April 1984): 188–207.

Gillikin, Margaret Wilson. "Competing Loyalties: Nationality, Church Governance, and the Development of an American Catholic Identity." *Early American Studies* 11, no. 1 (Winter 2013): 146–60.

Gjerde, Jon. *Catholicism and the Shaping of Nineteenth-Century America*. Edited by S. Deborah Kang. Cambridge: Cambridge University Press, 2012.

Gleason, Philip. "American Catholics and Liberalism, 1789–1960." In *Catholicism and Liberalism: Contributions to American Public Philosophy*, edited by R. Bruce Douglass and David Hollenbach, 45–75. Cambridge: Cambridge University Press, 1994.

——. "American Identity and Americanization." In *Harvard Encyclopedia of American Ethnic Groups*, edited by Stephan Thernstrom, Ann Orlov, and Oscar Handlin, 31–58. Cambridge, MA: Belknap Press of Harvard University Press, 1980.

——. "The New Americanism in Catholic Historiography." *U.S. Catholic Historian* 11, no. 3 (Summer 1993): 1–18.

Gleeson, David T. *The Green and the Gray: The Irish in the Confederate States of America*. Chapel Hill: University of North Carolina Press, 2013.

——. *The Irish in the South, 1815–1877*. Chapel Hill: University of North Carolina Press, 2001.

——. "'To live and die [for] Dixie': Irish Civilians and the Confederate States of America." *Irish Studies Review* 18, no. 2 (May 2010): 139–53.

Gleeson, David T., and Brendan J. Buttimer. "We Are Irish Everywhere: Irish Immigrant Networks in Charleston, South Carolina, and Savannah, Georgia." In *Irish Migration, Networks and Ethnic Identities since 1750*, edited by Donald M. MacRaild and Enda Delany, 39–61. New York: Routledge, 2015.

Goodrich, Carter. *Government Promotion of American Canals and Railroads, 1800–1890*. New York: Columbia University Press, 1960.

Greenberg, Kenneth S. "Representation and the Isolation of South Carolina, 1776–1860." *Journal of American History* 64, no. 3 (December 1977): 723–43.

——. "Revolutionary Ideology and the Proslavery Argument: The Abolition of Slavery in Antebellum South Carolina." *Journal of Southern History* 42, no. 3 (August 1976): 365–84.

Griffin, Susan M. *Anti-Catholicism and Nineteenth-Century Fiction*. Cambridge: Cambridge University Press, 2004.

Grinde, Donald A., Jr. "Building the South Carolina Railroad." *South Carolina Historical Magazine* 77, no. 2 (April 1976): 84–96.

Guarneri, Carl J. *The Utopian Alternative: Fourierism in Nineteenth-Century America*. Ithaca, NY: Cornell University Press, 1991.

Guilday, Peter. *A History of the Councils of Baltimore, 1791–1884*. New York: Arno Press and the New York Times, 1969.

——. *The Life and Times of John England, First Bishop of Charleston*. 2 vols. New York: America Press, 1927.

——. *The National Pastorals of the American Hierarchy, 1792–1919*. Washington, DC: National Catholic Welfare Council, 1923.

Guilds, John Caldwell. *Simms: A Literary Life*. Fayetteville: University of Arkansas Press, 1992.

Guinn, Ashley Paige. "Among Kith and Kin: The Irish in Antebellum Charleston, South Carolina." Master's thesis, University of South Carolina, 2007.

Gutzman, Kevin R.C. *Virginia's American Revolution: From Dominion to Republic, 1776–1840*. Lanham, MD: Lexington Books, 2007.

Haddox, Thomas F. *Fears and Fascinations: Representing Catholicism in the American South*. New York: Fordham University Press, 2005.

Hanley, Mark Y. *Beyond a Christian Commonwealth: The Protestant Quarrel with the American Republic, 1830–1860*. Chapel Hill: University of North Carolina Press, 1994.

Hatch, Nathan O. *The Democratization of American Christianity*. New Haven, CT: Yale University Press, 1989.

Havens, Mary. "The Liturgical Traditions II: Lutherans." In *Religion in South Carolina*, edited by Charles H. Lippy, 59–66. Columbia: University of South Carolina Press, 1993.

Haynes, Sam W. *Unfinished Revolution: The Early American Republic in a British World*. Charlottesville: University of Virginia Press, 2010.

Heath, Milton Sydney. *Constructive Liberalism: The Role of the State in Economic Development in Georgia to 1860*. Cambridge, MA: Harvard University Press, 1954.

Heidler, David S. *Pulling the Temple Down: The Fire-Eaters and the Destruction of the Union*. Mechanicsburg, PA: Stackpole Books, 1994.

Heisser, David C.R. "Bishop Lynch's People: Slaveholding by a South Carolina Prelate." *South Carolina Historical Magazine* 102, no. 3 (July 2001): 238–62.

Heisser, David C.R., and Stephen J. White Sr. *Patrick N. Lynch, 1817–1882: Third Catholic Bishop of Charleston*. Columbia: University of South Carolina Press, 2015.

Hennesey, James. *American Catholics: A History of the Roman Catholic Community in the United States*. New York: Oxford University Press, 1981.

———. "Roman Catholicism: The Maryland Tradition." *Thought* 51, no. 202 (September 1976): 282–95.

Heyrman, Christine Leigh. *Southern Cross: The Beginnings of the Bible Belt*. Chapel Hill: University of North Carolina Press, 1997.

Higham, John. "Integrating America: The Problem of Assimilation in the Nineteenth Century." *Journal of American Ethnic History* 1, no. 1 (Fall 1981): 7–25.

Hill, Harvey. "American Catholicism? John England and 'The Republic in Danger.'" *Catholic Historical Review* 89, no. 2 (April 2003): 240–57.

Holifield, E. Brooks. *The Gentlemen Theologians: American Theology in Southern Culture, 1795–1860*. Durham, NC: Duke University Press, 1978.

———. "Theology as Entertainment: Oral Debate in American Religion." *Church History* 67, no. 3 (September 1998): 499–520.

———. *Theology in America: Christian Thought from the Age of the Puritans to the Civil War*. New Haven, CT: Yale University Press, 2003.

Holland, Edwin. *A Refutation of the Calumnies Circulated against the Southern and Western States Respecting the Institution and Existence of Slavery among Them. To which is added, A Minute and Particular Account of the Actual State and Condition of their Negro Population. Together with Historical Notices of all the Insurrections that have taken place since the Settlement of the Country*. Charleston, SC: A.E. Miller, 1822.

Holt, Michael F. "The Politics of Impatience: The Origins of Know Nothingism." *Journal of American History* 60 (1973): 309–31.

———. *The Rise and Fall of the American Whig Party: Jacksonian Politics and the Onset of the Civil War*. New York: Oxford University Press, 1999.

Horry, Albert. *An Address Delivered in Charleston before the Agricultural Society of South Carolina at the Anniversary Meeting, on Tuesday, the 19th August 1828*. Charleston, SC: A.E. Miller, 1828.

Howard, Charles Wallace. *A Sermon Delivered at the Re-Opening and Dedication of the French Protestant Church of Charleston, S.C. on Sunday, the 11th Day of May, 1845*. Charleston, SC: Burges & James, Printers, 1845.

Howe, Daniel Walker. *What Hath God Wrought: The Transformation of America, 1815–1848*. New York: Oxford University Press, 2007.

Huff, A.V., Jr. "The Eagle and the Vulture: Changing Attitudes toward Nationalism in Fourth of July Orations Delivered in Charleston, 1778–1860." *South Atlantic Quarterly* 73, no. 1 (Winter 1974): 10–22.

Humphreys, Margaret. *Yellow Fever and the South*. New Brunswick, NJ: Rutgers University Press, 1992.

Hunter, James Davison. "To Change the World" (2002). http://71513.netministry .com/images/TO_CHANGE_THE_WORLD_HUNTER.pdf.

The Irish Volunteers Memorial Meeting and Military Hall Festival, October–November 1877, Together with a Brief Sketch of the Company. Charleston, SC: News and Courier Book and Job Presses, 1878.

Irons, Charles F. *The Origins of Proslavery Christianity: White and Black Evangelicals in Colonial and Antebellum Virginia*. Chapel Hill: University of North Carolina Press, 2008.

Jackson, Alvin. *Ireland 1798–1998: Politics and War*. Oxford: Blackwell, 1999.

Jameson, J. Franklin., ed. "Correspondence of John C. Calhoun." *Annual Report of the American Historical Association for the Year 1899*. Vol. 2. Washington, DC: Government Printing Office, 1900.

Jefferson, Thomas. *Thomas Jefferson: Writings*. New York: Literary Classics of the United States, 1984.

Jenkins, Philip. *The Lost History of Christianity*. New York: Harper One, 2008.

Jervey, Theodore D. *Robert Y. Hayne and His Times*. New York: Da Capo Press, 1970. Originally published Macmillan Co., 1909.

John, Richard R. "Recasting the Information Infrastructure for the Industrial Age." In *A Nation Transformed by Information*, edited by Alfred D. Chandler Jr. and James W. Cortada, 55–105. New York: Oxford University Press, 2000.

————. *Spreading the News: The American Postal System from Franklin to Morse.* Cambridge, MA: Harvard University Press, 1995.

Jones, Charles C., Jr., and Salem Dutcher. *Memorial History of Augusta, Georgia.* Spartanburg, SC: Reprint Company, 1980.

Joyce, Dee Dee. "White, Worker, Irish, and Confederate: Irish Workers' Constructed Identity in Late Antebellum Charleston, South Carolina." PhD dissertation, State University of New York at Binghamton, 2002.

Kane, Paula. "The Supernatural and Slavery: Catholics, Power, and Oppression." In *The Problem of Evil: Slavery, Freedom, and the Ambiguities of American Reform*, edited by Steven Mintz and John Stauffer, 199–209. Amherst: University of Massachusetts Press, 2007.

Kastor, Peter J. *The Nation's Crucible: The Louisiana Purchase and the Creation of America.* New Haven, CT: Yale University Press, 2004.

Kearns, Daniel F. "Bishop John England and the Possibilities of Catholic Republicanism." *South Carolina Historical Magazine* 102, no. 1 (January 2001): 47–67.

Kehoe, Lawrence, ed. *Complete Works of the Most Rev. John Hughes, D.D.* 2 vols. New York: Catholic Publication House, 1864.

Kelly, Joseph. "Charleston's Bishop John England and American Slavery." *New Hibernia Review* 5, no. 4 (Winter 2001): 48–56.

Kelly, Mary C. "A 'sentinel(s) of our liberties': Archbishop John Hughes and Irish-American Intellectual Negotiation in the Civil War Era." *Irish Studies Review* 18, no. 2 (May 2010): 155–72.

Kenny, Kevin. *The American Irish: A History.* New York: Longman, 2000.

————. "Race, Violence, and Anti-Irish Sentiment in the Nineteenth Century." In *Making the Irish American: History and Heritage of the Irish in the United States*, edited by J.J. Lee and Marion R. Casey, 364–78. New York: New York University Press, 2006.

Kenrick, Francis. "The Works of the Right Rev. John England First Bishop of Charleston, collected and arranged under the immediate Advice and Direction of his immediate successor, the Right Rev. Ignatius Aloysius Reynolds." *Brownson's Quarterly Review* 4, no. 2 (April 1850): 137–59.

Kervick, Francis William Wynn. "Patrick Charles Keely, Architect: A Record of His Life and Work." South Bend, IN: Privately printed, 1953.

Kilde, Jeanne Halgren. *When Church Became Theater: The Transformation of Evangelical Architecture and Worship in Nineteenth-Century America.* New York: Oxford University Press, 2002.

Klebaner, Benjamin Joseph. "Public Poor Relief in Charleston, 1800–1860." *South Carolina Historical Magazine* 55, no. 4 (October 1954): 210–20.

Knobel, Dale T. *"America for the Americans": The Nativist Movement in the United States*. New York: Twayne Publishers, 1996.

———. *Paddy and the Republic: Ethnicity and Nationality in Antebellum America*. Middletown, CT: Wesleyan University Press, 1986.

Komlos, John H. *Louis Kossuth in America, 1851–1852*. Buffalo, NY: East European Institute, 1973.

Krebsbach, Suzanne. "Black Catholics in Antebellum Charleston." *South Carolina Historical Magazine* 108, no. 2 (April 2007): 143–59.

Kurtz, William. *Excommunicated from the Union: How the Civil War Created a Separate Catholic America*. New York: Fordham University Press, 2016.

Larson, John Lauritz. "'Bind the Republic Together': The National Union and a Struggle for a System of Internal Improvements." *Journal of American History* 74, no. 2 (September 1987): 363–87.

———. *Internal Improvement: National Public Works and the Promise of Popular Government in the Early United States*. Chapel Hill: University of North Carolina Press, 2001.

Laurie, Bruce. *Beyond Garrison: Antislavery and Social Reform*. Cambridge: Cambridge University Press, 2005.

Lence, Ross, ed. *Union and Liberty: The Political Philosophy of John C. Calhoun*. Indianapolis, IN: Liberty Fund, 1992.

Levin, Kevin. "So It Was a Holy Cause after All." *Civil War Memory* (blog). September 10, 2009. http://cwmemory.com/2009/09/10/so-it-was-a-holy-cause -after-all/.

———. "Update on Jefferson Davis's Crown of Thorns." *Civil War Memory* (blog). September 27, 2009. http://cwmemory.com/2009/09/27/update-on-jefferson -daviss-crown-of-thorns/.

Levine, Bruce. "Conservatism, Nativism, and Slavery: Thomas R. Whitney and the Origins of the Know-Nothing Party." *Journal of American History* 88, no. 2 (September 2001): 459–60.

Litwicki, Ellen M. "'Our Hearts Burn with Ardent Love for Two Countries': Ethnicity and Assimilation." In *We Are What We Celebrate: Understanding Holidays and Rituals*, edited by Amitai Etzioni and Jared Bloom, 213–45. New York: New York University Press, 2004.

Lofton, Edward Dennis. "Rev. Doctor James A. Corcoran and the *United States Catholic Miscellany* Concerning the Question of Slavery and the Confederacy." *Records of the American Catholic Historical Society of Philadelphia* 93 (1982): 86–97.

Loveland, Anne C. *Southern Evangelicals and the Social Order, 1800–1860*. Baton Rouge: Louisiana State University Press, 1980.

Lowman, Mary Marcian. "James Andrew Corcoran: Editor, Theologian, Scholar (1820–1889)." *Records of the American Catholic Historical Society of Philadelphia* 69 (1958): 67–97.

Lynch, Patrick. "A Few Words on Domestic Slavery in the Confederate States of America." Part 1. Edited by David C. R. Heisser. *Avery Review* 2, no. 1 (Spring 1999): 64–103.

———. "A Few Words on the Domestic Slavery in the Confederate States of America." Part 2. Edited by David C. R. Heisser. *Avery Review* 3, no. 1 (Spring 2000): 93–123.

Madden, Richard C. *Catholics in South Carolina: A Record.* Lanham, MD: University Press of America, 1985.

Maier, Pauline. "The Road Not Taken: Nullification, John C. Calhoun, and the Revolutionary Tradition in South Carolina." *South Carolina Historical Magazine* 82, no. 1 (January 1981): 1–19.

Maizlish, Stephen E. "The Meaning of Nativism and the Crisis of the Union: The Know-Nothing Movement in the Antebellum North." In *Essays on American Antebellum Politics, 1840–1860,* edited by Stephen E. Maizlish and John J. Kushma, 166–98. College Station: Texas A&M University Press, 1982.

Marchio, James. "Nativism in the Old South: Know-Nothingism in Antebellum South Carolina." *Southern Historian* 8 (1987): 39–53.

Marraro, Howard R. *American Opinion on the Unification of Italy, 1846–1861.* New York: Columbia University Press, 1932.

———. "Lincoln's Offer of a Command to Garibaldi: Further Light on a Disputed Point of History." *Journal of the Illinois State Historical Society* 36, no. 3 (September 1943): 237–70.

Marrs, Aaron W. *Railroads in the Old South: Pursuing Progress in a Slave Society.* Baltimore, MD: Johns Hopkins University Press, 2009.

Mathews, Donald. *Religion in the Old South.* Chicago: University of Chicago Press, 1977.

McAleer, Philip. "Keely, 'The Irish Pugin of America.'" *Irish Arts Review* 4, no. 3 (Autumn 1987): 16–24.

McAvoy, Thomas. "American Cultural Impacts on Catholicism." In *The Religion of the Republic,* edited by Elwyn A. Smith, 45–75. Philadelphia: Fortress Press, 1971.

———. "Americanism and Frontier Catholicism." *Review of Politics* 5 (July 1943): 275–301.

———. "The Formation of a Catholic Minority in the United States 1820–1860." *Review of Politics* 10, no. 1 (January 1948): 13–34.

McCardell, John. *The Idea of a Southern Nation: Southern Nationalists and Southern Nationalism, 1830–1860.* New York: Norton, 1979.

McDannell, Colleen. *The Christian Home in Victorian America, 1840–1900.* Bloomington: Indiana University Press, 1986.

McDonald, Forrest. *Novus Ordo Seclorum: The Intellectual Origins of the Constitution.* Lawrence: University Press of Kansas, 1985.

McGreevy, John. "Catholicism and Abolition: A Historical (and Theological) Problem." In *Figures in the Carpet: Finding the Human Person in the American Past*, edited by Wilfred M. McClay, 406–27. Grand Rapids, MI: Eerdmans, 2007.

———. *Catholicism and American Freedom: A History*. New York: Norton, 2003.

McNally, Michael J. "A Peculiar Institution: A History of Catholic Parish Life in the Southeast (1850–1980)." In *The American Catholic Parish: A History from 1850 to the Present*, vol. 1, edited by Jay P. Dolan, 121–234. New York: Paulist Press, 1987.

McNeil, Lou F. *Recovering American Catholic Inculturation: John England's Jacksonian Populism and Romanticist Adaptation*. Lanham, MD: Rowman & Littlefield, 2008.

Meagher, Timothy J. *Inventing Irish America: Generation, Class, and Ethnic Identity in a New England City, 1880–1928*. South Bend, IN: University of Notre Dame Press, 2001.

Meehan, Andrew B. "Canonical Visitation." In *The Catholic Encyclopedia*, 15:479–80. 15 vols. New York: Robert Appleton Co., 1912.

Melish, Joanne Pope. *Disowning Slavery: Gradual Emancipation and "Race" in New England, 1780–1860*. Ithaca, NY: Cornell University Press, 1998.

Messmer, Sebastian G., ed. *Works of the Right Reverend John England*. 7 vols. Cleveland, OH: Arthur H. Clark Company, 1908.

The Metropolitan Catholic Almanac and Laity's Directory for 1844. Baltimore, MD: Fielding Lucas Jr., 1844.

The Metropolitan Catholic Almanac and Laity's Directory, for the Year of Our Lord 1851. Baltimore, MD: Fielding Lucas Jr., 1850.

Miller, David W. "Irish Catholicism and the Great Famine." *Journal of Social History* 9, no. 1 (Autumn 1975): 81–98.

Miller, Kerby A. *Emigrants and Exiles: Ireland and the Irish Exodus to North America*. New York: Oxford University Press, 1985.

Miller, Randall M. "Catholics in a Protestant World: The Old South Example." In *Varieties of the Southern Religious Experience*, edited by Samuel S. Hill, 115–34. Baton Rouge: Louisiana State University Press, 1988.

———. "A Church in Cultural Captivity: Some Speculations on Catholic Identity in the Old South." In *Catholics in the Old South: Essays on Church and Culture*, edited by Randall M. Miller and Jon L. Wakelyn, 11–52. Macon, GA: Mercer University Press, 1983.

———. "The Enemy Within: Some Effects of Foreign Immigrants on Antebellum Southern Cities." *Southern Studies* 24, no. 1 (Spring 1985): 30–53.

———. "A Failed Mission: The Catholic Church and Black Catholics in the Old South." In *Catholics in the Old South: Essays on Church and Culture*, edited by Randall M. Miller and Jon L. Wakelyn, 147–70. Macon, GA: Mercer University Press, 1983.

———. "Introduction." In *Catholics in the Old South: Essays on Church and Culture*, edited by Randall M. Miller and Jon L. Wakelyn, 3–10. Macon, GA: Mercer University Press, 1983.

———. "Roman Catholicism in South Carolina." In *Religion in South Carolina*, edited by Charles H. Lippy, 82–102. Columbia: University of South Carolina Press, 1993.

Mitchell, Arthur. *The History of the Hibernian Society of Charleston, South Carolina, 1799–1981*. Charleston, SC: n.p., 1981.

———. *South Carolina Irish*. Charleston, SC: History Press, 2011.

Mize, Sandra Yocum. "Defending Roman Loyalties and Republican Values: The 1848 Italian Revolution in American Catholic Apologetics." *Church History* 60, no. 4 (December 1991): 480–92.

Moltke-Hansen, David. "Protecting Interests, Maintaining Rights, Emulating Ancestors: U.S. Constitution Bicentennial Reflections on 'the Problem of South Carolina,' 1787–1860." *South Carolina Historical Magazine* 89, no. 3 (July 1988): 160–82.

———. "Southern Literary Horizons in Young America: Imaginative Development of a Regional Geography." *Studies in the Literary Imagination* 42, no. 1 (Spring 2009): 1–31.

Moore, R. Laurence. "Religion, Secularization, and the Shaping of the Culture Industry in Antebellum America." *American Quarterly* 41, no. 2 (June 1989): 216–42.

———. *Religious Outsiders and the Making of Americans*. New York: Oxford University Press, 1986.

Moriarty, Thomas F. "The Irish American Response to Catholic Emancipation." *Catholic Historical Review* 66, no. 3 (July 1980): 353–73.

Morrison, Michael A. "American Reaction to European Revolutions, 1848–1852: Sectionalism, Memory, and the Revolutionary Heritage." *Civil War History* 49, no. 2 (June 2003): 111–32.

Morse, Samuel F.B. *Foreign Conspiracy against the Liberties of the United States*. 5th ed. New York: H.A. Chapin & Co., 1841.

———. *Imminent Dangers to the Free Institutions of the United States through Foreign Immigration and the Present State of the Naturalization Laws*. New York: E.B. Clayton, 1835.

Moss, Kenneth. "St. Patrick's Day Celebrations and the Formation of Irish-American Identity, 1845–1875." *Journal of Social History* 29, no. 1 (Autumn 1995): 125–48.

Murphy, Angela. *American Slavery, Irish Freedom: Abolition, Immigrant Citizenship, and the Transatlantic Movement for Irish Repeal*. Baton Rouge: Louisiana State University Press, 2010.

Noll, Mark A. *The Civil War as a Theological Crisis.* Chapel Hill: University of North Carolina Press, 2006.

Nord, David Paul. "The Evangelical Origins of Mass Media in America, 1815–1835." *Journalism Monographs* 88 (May 1984): 1–30.

———. "Religious Reading and Readers in Antebellum America." *Journal of the Early Republic* 15, no. 2 (Summer 1995): 241–72.

Oberman, Heiko A. *Luther: Man between God and the Devil.* Translated by Eileen Walliser-Schwarzbart. New York: Image Books, 1992.

O'Brien, David J. *Public Catholicism.* 2nd ed. New York: Orbis Books, 1996.

O'Brien, Michael. *Conjectures of Order: Intellectual Life in the American South, 1810–1860.* 2 vols. Chapel Hill: University of North Carolina Press, 2004.

O'Brien, Michael J. "The Irish in Charleston, South Carolina." *Journal of the American Irish Historical Society* 25 (1926): 134–46.

Ochenkowski, J.P. "The Origins of Nullification in South Carolina." *South Carolina Historical Magazine* 83, no. 2 (April 1982): 121–53.

O'Connell, Jeremiah Joseph. *Catholicity in the Carolinas and Georgia: Leaves of Its History.* New York: D. & J. Sadlier & Co., 1879.

O'Connor, Mary Doline. *The Life and Letters of M. P. O'Connor.* New York: Dempsey & Carroll, 1893.

Olwell, Robert. *Masters, Slaves, and Subjects: The Culture of Power in the South Carolina Low Country, 1740–1790.* Ithaca, NY: Cornell University Press, 1998.

Overdyke, W. Darrell. *The Know Nothing Party in the South.* Gloucester, MA: Peter Smith, 1968. Originally published Louisiana State University Press, 1950.

Pagliarini, Marie Anne. "The Pure American Woman and the Wicked Catholic Priest: An Analysis of Anti-Catholic Literature in Antebellum America." *Religion and American Culture* 9, no. 1 (Winter 1999): 97–128.

Panzer, Joel S. *The Popes and Slavery.* New York: Alba House, 1996.

"Papers Relating to the Church in America: From the Portfolios of the Irish College at Rome, Third Series." *Records of the American Catholic Historical Society of Philadelphia* 8, no. 2 (June 1897): 195–240.

"Papers Relating to the Church in America: From the Portfolios of the Irish College at Rome, Fourth Series." *Records of the American Catholic Historical Society of Philadelphia* 8, no. 3 (September 1897): 294–329.

Parsons, Lynn Hunt. *The Birth of Modern Politics: Andrew Jackson, John Quincy Adams, and the Election of 1828.* New York: Oxford University Press, 2009.

Pasley, Jeffrey L. *"The Tyranny of Printers": Newspaper Politics in the Early American Republic.* Charlottesville: University of Virginia Press, 2001.

Pasquier, Michael. *Fathers on the Frontier: French Missionaries and the Roman Catholic Priesthood in the United States, 1789–1870.* New York: Oxford University Press, 2010.

———. "'Though Their Skin Remains Brown, I Hope Their Souls Will Soon Be White': Slavery, French Missionaries, and the Roman Catholic Priesthood in the American South, 1789–1865." *Church History* 77, no. 2 (June 2008): 337–70.

Pasulka, Diana Walsh. "The Eagle and the Dove: Constructing Catholic Identity through Word and Image in Nineteenth-Century United States." *Material Religion* 4, no. 3 (November 2008): 306–25.

Pease, Jane H., and William H. Pease. "The Economics and Politics of Charleston's Nullification Crisis." *Journal of Southern History* 47, no. 3 (August 1981): 335–62.

———. *The Web of Progress: Private Values and Public Styles in Boston and Charleston, 1828–1843.* Athens: University of Georgia Press, 1991.

Pettegree, Andrew. *Brand Luther: 1517, Printing, and the Making of the Reformation.* New York: Penguin Books, 2015.

Phillips, Ulrich Bonnell. *A History of Transportation in the Eastern Cotton Belt to 1860.* New York: Octagon Books, 1968. Originally published Columbia University Press, 1908.

Pierce, John R., and Jim Writer. *Yellow Jack: How Yellow Fever Ravaged America and Walter Reed Discovered Its Deadly Secrets.* New York: John Wiley & Sons, 2005.

Pinheiro, John C. *Missionaries of Republicanism: A Religious History of the Mexican-American War.* New York: Oxford University Press, 2014.

Pocock, J.G.A. *The Machiavellian Moment: Florentine Political Thought and the Atlantic Republican Tradition.* Princeton, NJ: Princeton University Press, 1975.

"Political Philosophy of South Carolina." *Southern Quarterly Review* 7, no. 13 (January 1853): 120–40.

Poston, Jonathan H. *The Buildings of Charleston: A Guide to the City's Architecture.* Columbia: University of South Carolina Press, 1997.

Potter, David M. "The Historian's Use of Nationalism and Vice Versa." *American Historical Review* 67, no. 4 (July 1962): 924–50.

Powers, Bernard. *Black Charlestonians: A Social History, 1822–1885.* Fayetteville: University of Arkansas Press, 1994.

Pugin, A.W.N. *The Present State of Ecclesiastical Architecture in England.* London: Charles Dolman, 1843.

———. *The True Principles of Pointed or Christian Architecture.* London: John Weale, 1841.

Quigley, Paul. *Shifting Grounds: Nationalism and the American South, 1848–1865.* New York: Oxford University Press, 2012.

———. "'That History Is Truly the Life of Nations': History and Southern Nationalism in Antebellum South Carolina." *South Carolina Historical Magazine* 106, no. 1 (January 2005): 7–33.

Quinn, John F. "'Three Cheers for the Abolitionist Pope!': American Reaction to Gregory XVI's Condemnation of the Slave Trade, 1840–1860." *Catholic Historical Review* 90, no. 1 (January 2004): 67–93.

Rable, George. *The Confederate Republic: A Revolution against Politics.* Chapel Hill: University of North Carolina Press, 1994.

Rahe, Paul A. *Republics Ancient and Modern: Classical Republicanism and the American Revolution.* Chapel Hill: University of North Carolina Press, 1992.

Ratner, Lorman A., and Dwight L. Teeter Jr. *Fanatics and Fire Eaters: Newspapers and the Coming of the Civil War.* Urbana: University of Illinois Press, 2004.

Ravenel, Beatrice St. Julien. *Architects of Charleston.* Columbia: University of South Carolina Press, 1992. Originally published 1945.

Remini, Robert. "Martin Van Buren and the Tariff of Abominations." *American Historical Review* 63, no. 4 (July 1958): 903–17.

Reynolds, Ignatius, ed. *The Works of the Right Reverend John England.* 5 vols. Baltimore, MD: John Murphy & Co., 1849.

Reynolds, James A. *The Catholic Emancipation Crisis in Ireland, 1823–1829.* Westport, CT: Greenwood Press, 1970.

Reynolds, Larry J. *European Revolutions and the American Literary Renaissance.* New Haven, CT: Yale University Press, 1988.

———. *Righteous Violence: Revolution, Slavery, and the American Renaissance.* Athens: University of Georgia Press, 2011.

Riach, Douglas C. "Daniel O'Connell and American Anti-Slavery." *Irish Historical Studies* 20, no. 77 (March 1976): 3–25.

Rice, Madeleine Hooke. *American Catholic Opinion in the Slavery Controversy.* Gloucester, MA: Peter Smith, 1964.

Ridley, Jasper. *Garibaldi.* New York: Viking Press, 1974.

Risjord, Norman K. *The Old Republicans: Southern Conservatism in the Age of Jefferson.* New York: Columbia University Press, 1965.

Robertson, David. *Denmark Vesey.* New York: Vintage Books, 1999.

Rodgers, Daniel T. "Republicanism: The Career of a Concept." *Journal of American History* 79, no. 1 (June 1992): 11–38.

Ross, Cecil S.H. "Pulpit and Stump: The Clergy and the Know Nothings in Mississippi." *Journal of Mississippi History* 48 (1986): 271–82.

Rothbard, Murray. *The Panic of 1819: Reactions and Policies.* New York: Columbia University Press, 1962.

Rousey, Dennis C. "Aliens in the WASP Nest: Ethnocultural Diversity in the Antebellum Urban South." *Journal of American History* 79, no. 1 (June 1992): 152–64.

———. "Friends and Foes of Slavery: Foreigners and Northerners in the Old South." *Journal of Social History* 35, no. 2 (Winter 2001): 373–96.

Salley, F.M. *History of Irish Volunteers Company from 1798 to 1836.* WPA Project, College of Charleston, 1935. http://lcdl.library.cofc.edu/lcdl/catalog/lcdl: 20205.

Sams, Steven Michael. "The Cauldron of Enmities: The Friends of Ireland and the Conflict between Liberalism and Democracy in the Early Nineteenth Century Atlantic World." Master's thesis, Georgia State University, 2006.

Saunders, R. Frank, and George Rogers, "Bishop John England of Charleston: Catholic Spokesman and Southern Intellectual, 1820–1842." *Journal of the Early Republic* 13 (Fall 1993): 301–22.

Schmucker, Samuel Simon. *The Papal Hierarchy Viewed in the Light of Prophecy and History: Being a Discourse Delivered in the English Lutheran Church. Gettysburg, Feb. 2, 1845.* 2nd ed. Gettysburg, PA: H.C. Neinstedt, 1845.

Schultz, Harold. *Nationalism and Sectionalism in South Carolina, 1852–1860.* New York: Da Capo Press, 1969. Originally published Duke University Press, 1950.

Schultz, Nancy Lusignan. *Fire and Roses: The Burning of the Charlestown Convent, 1834.* New York: Free Press, 2000.

Seabrook, Whitemarsh. *A Concise View of the Critical Situation, and Future Prospects of the Slave-holding States, in relation to their Coloured Population.* 2nd ed. Charleston, SC: A.E. Miller, 1825.

———. *An Essay on the Management of Slaves, and Especially, on their Religious Instruction; Read before the Agricultural Society of St. John's Colleton.* Charleston, SC: A.E. Miller, 1834.

Sell, Edward S. *The Geography of Georgia.* 3rd ed. Oklahoma City, OK: Harlow Publishing Co., 1961.

The Seventh Census of the United States: 1850. Edited by J.B.D. DeBow. Washington, DC: Robert Armstrong, 1853.

Severens, Kenneth. *Charleston: Antebellum Architecture and Civic Destiny.* Knoxville: University of Tennessee Press, 1988.

Sharpe, James. *Remember, Remember: A Cultural History of Guy Fawkes Day.* Cambridge, MA: Harvard University Press, 2005.

Shaw, Russell. *American Church: The Remarkable Rise, Meteoric Fall, and Uncertain Future of Catholicism in America.* San Francisco, CA: Ignatius Press, 2013.

Sheidley, Harlow. "The Webster-Hayne Debate: Recasting New England's Sectionalism." *New England Quarterly* 67, no. 1 (March 1994): 5–29.

Shivers, Forrest. *The Land Between: A History of Hancock County, Georgia to 1940.* Spartanburg, SC: Reprint Company, 1990.

Shugerman, Jed Handelsman. "The Louisiana Purchase and South Carolina's Reopening of the Slave Trade in 1803." *Journal of the Early Republic* 22, no. 2 (Summer 2002): 263–90.

Silver, Christopher. "A New Look at Old South Urbanization: The Irish Worker in Charleston, South Carolina, 1840–1860." *South Atlantic Urban Studies* 3 (1979): 141–72.

Simms, Kristina. *Macon: Georgia's Central City.* Chatsworth, CA: Windsor Publications, 1989.

Simms, William Gilmore. "Charleston, the Palmetto City." *Harper's New Monthly Magazine* 15, no. 85 (June 1857).

———. "Kossuth and Intervention." *Southern Quarterly Review* 6, no. 11 (July 1852): 221–34.

———. *Sack and Destruction of the City of Columbia, S.C. to which is added A List of the Property Destroyed.* Columbia, SC: Power Press of Daily Phoenix, 1865.

———. *Views and Reviews in American Literature History and Fiction.* 1st ser. Edited by C. Hugh Holman. Cambridge, MA: Belknap Press of Harvard University Press, 1962.

———. *The Wigwam and the Cabin.* Rev. ed. New York: Redfield, 1859.

Sinha, Manisha. *The Counterrevolution of Slavery: Politics and Ideology in Antebellum South Carolina.* Chapel Hill: University of North Carolina Press, 2000.

Skeen, C. Edward. "Calhoun, Crawford, and the Politics of Retrenchment." *South Carolina Historical Magazine* 73, no. 3 (July 1972): 141–55.

Smith, Denis Mack. *Italy: A Modern History.* Ann Arbor: University of Michigan Press, 1969.

Smith, Elwyn A. "The Fundamental Church-State Tradition of the Catholic Church in the United States." *Church History,* 38, no. 4 (December 1969): 486–505.

Smith, Harold T. "The Know-Nothings in Arkansas." *Arkansas Historical Quarterly* 34, no. 4 (Winter 1975): 291–303.

Smith, Mark M. "Remembering Mary, Shaping Revolt: Reconsidering the Stono Rebellion." *Journal of Southern History* 67, no. 3 (August 2001): 513–34.

Smith IV, Miles. "From Savannah to Vienna: William Henry Stiles, the Revolutions of 1848, and Southern Conceptions of Order." *American Nineteenth Century History* 14, no. 1 (2013): 27–51.

Smith, Ryan K. *Gothic Arches, Latin Crosses: Anti-Catholicism and American Church Designs in the Nineteenth Century.* Chapel Hill: University of North Carolina Press, 2006.

Smith, Timothy L. "Religion and Ethnicity in America." *American Historical Review* 83, no. 5 (December 1978): 1155–85.

Snay, Mitchell. *Gospel of Disunion: Religion and Separatism in the Antebellum South.* Chapel Hill: University of North Carolina Press, 1997. Originally published Cambridge University Press, 1993.

South Carolina Synod of the Lutheran Church in America. *A History of the Lutheran Church in South Carolina.* Columbia, SC: R.L. Bryan, 1971.

"A Southern Teaching Order: The Sisters of Mercy of Charleston, SC, A.D. 1829–1904, by a Member of the Order." *Records of the American Catholic Historical Society of Philadelphia* 15, no. 3 (September 1904): 249–65.

Spalding, Thomas W. "The Catholic Frontiers." *U.S. Catholic Historian* 12, no. 4 (Fall 1994): 1–15.

————. "The Maryland Tradition." *U.S. Catholic Historian* 8, no. 4 (Fall 1989): 51–58.

Spencer, Donald S. *Louis Kossuth and Young America: A Study of Sectionalism and Foreign Policy, 1848–1852*. Columbia: University of Missouri Press, 1977.

Stanton, Phoebe B. *The Gothic Revival and American Church Architecture*. Baltimore, MD: Johns Hopkins University Press, 1968.

Stearns, Peter N. *1848: The Revolutionary Tide in Europe*. New York: Norton, 1974.

Steinfels, Peter. "The Failed Encounter: The Catholic Church and Liberalism in the Nineteenth Century." In *Catholicism and Liberalism: Contributions to American Public Philosophy*, edited by R. Bruce Douglass and David Hollenbach, 19–44. Cambridge: Cambridge University Press, 1994.

Stephens, Lester D. "The Literary and Philosophical Society of South Carolina: A Forum for Intellectual Progress in Antebellum Charleston." *South Carolina Historical Magazine* 104, no. 3 (July 2003): 154–75.

————. *Science, Race, and Religion in the American South: John Bachman and the Charleston Circle of Naturalists, 1815–1895*. Chapel Hill: University of North Carolina Press, 2000.

Stern, Andrew H.M. *Southern Crucifix, Southern Cross: Catholic-Protestant Relations in the Old South*. Tuscaloosa: University of Alabama Press, 2012.

————. "Southern Harmony: Catholic-Protestant Relations in the Antebellum South." *Religion and American Culture* 17, no. 2 (2007): 165–90.

Stock, Leo Francis. "Catholic Participation in the Diplomacy of the Southern Confederacy." *Catholic Historical Review* 16, no. 1 (April 1930): 1–18.

Stokes, Christopher. "Catholics in Beulahland: The Church's Encounter with Anti-Catholicism, Nativism, and Anti-Abolitionism in the Carolinas and Georgia, 1820–1845." PhD dissertation, Rice University, 2001.

Strum, Harvey. "South Carolina and Irish Famine Relief, 1846–1847." *South Carolina Historical Magazine* 103, no. 2 (April 2002): 130–52.

Sydnor, Charles. *The Development of Southern Sectionalism, 1819–1848*. Baton Rouge: Louisiana State University Press, 1948.

Tate, Adam. "Catholics and Southern Honor: Rev. Patrick Lynch's Paper War with Rev. James Henley Thornwell." *Catholic Historical Review* 99, no. 3 (July 2013): 455–79.

————. "Confronting Abolitionism: Bishop John England and a Catholic Response to Slavery." *Journal of the Historical Society* 9 no. 3 (September 2009): 373–404.

———. "A Historiography of States' Rights: John Taylor of Caroline's *New Views of the Constitution*," *Southern Studies* 18, no. 1 (Spring–Summer 2011): 10–28.

———. "The Power of Historical Narrative: Bishop John England, American Catholicism, and the National Jubilee of 1826." In *Catholicism and Historical Narrative*, edited by Kevin Schmiesing, 151–72. Lanham, MD: Rowman & Littlefield, 2014.

———. "South Carolina Catholics and the Know Nothing Challenge: The Charleston Elections of 1855." *Catholic Social Science Review* 18 (2013): 105–18.

Tentler, Leslie Woodcock. "'How I Would Save them All': Priests on the Michigan Frontier." *U.S. Catholic Historian* 12, no. 4 (Fall 1994): 17–35.

Thigpen, Thomas Paul. "Aristocracy of the Heart: Catholic Lay Leadership in Savannah, 1820–1870." PhD dissertation, Emory University, 1995.

Thompson, John J., Jr. *The Church, the South and the Future*. Westminster, MD: Christian Classics, 1988.

Tise, Larry. *Proslavery: A History of the Defense of Slavery in America, 1701–1840*. Athens: University of Georgia Press, 1987.

Tocqueville, Alexis de. *Democracy in America*. Translated by Gerald E. Bevan. New York: Penguin Books, 2003.

Tyrrell, Ian R. "Drink and Temperance in the Antebellum South: An Overview and Interpretation." *Journal of Southern History* 48, no. 4 (November 1982): 485–510.

Von Frank, Albert. "John Brown, James Redpath, and the Idea of Revolution." *Civil War History* 52, no. 2 (June 2006): 142–60.

Waddell, Gene. *Charleston Architecture, 1670–1860*. Vol. 1. Charleston, SC: Wyrick & Co., 2003.

———. "Introduction: John Bachman's Works and Life." In *John Bachman: Selected Writings on Science, Race, and Religion*, edited by Gene Waddell, 1–21. Athens: University of Georgia Press, 2011.

Wallace, W. Jason. *Catholics, Slaveholders, and the Dilemma of American Evangelicalism, 1835–1860*. South Bend, IN: University of Notre Dame Press, 2010.

Walters, Ronald G. *American Reformers, 1815–1860*. Rev. ed. New York: Hill and Wang, 1997.

Walther, Eric H. *The Fire-Eaters*. Baton Rouge: Louisiana State University Press, 1992.

Ward, James A. "A New Look at Antebellum Southern Railroad Development." *Journal of Southern History* 39, no. 3 (August 1973): 409–20.

Weir, Robert M. "The South Carolinian as Extremist." *South Atlantic Quarterly* 74 (December 1975): 86–103.

Whelan, Kevin. *The Tree of Liberty: Radicalism, Catholicism, and the Construction of Irish Identity, 1760–1830*. South Bend, IN: University of Notre Dame Press, 1996.

Wikramanayake, Marina. *A World in Shadow: The Free Black in Antebellum South Carolina*. Columbia: University of South Carolina Press, 1973.

Wilkins, Joe. "Window on Freedom: South Carolina's Response to British West Indian Slave Emancipation, 1833–1834." *South Carolina Historical Magazine* 85, no. 2 (April 1984): 135–44.

Williams, Donald M. *Shamrocks and Pluff Mud: A Glimpse of the Irish in the Southern City of Charleston, South Carolina*. n.p.: Privately published, 2005.

Willingham, Robert M., Jr. *The History of Wilkes Country, Georgia*. Washington, GA: Wilkes Publishing Co., 2002.

Wilson, David A. *United Irishmen, United States: Immigrant Radicals in the Early Republic*. Ithaca, NY: Cornell University Press, 1998.

Wolffe, John. "Anti-Catholicism and Evangelical Identity in Britain and the United States, 1830–1860." In *Evangelicalism: Comparative Studies of Popular Protestantism in North America, the British Isles, and Beyond, 1700–1990*, edited by Mark A. Noll, David W. Bebbington, and George A. Rawlyk, 179–97. New York: Oxford University Press, 1994.

Wood, Gordon. "Conspiracy and the Paranoid Style: Causality and Deceit in the Eighteenth Century." *William and Mary Quarterly* 39, no. 3 (July 1982): 401–41.

———. *The Creation of the American Republic, 1776–1787*. Chapel Hill: University of North Carolina Press, 1969.

Wood, W. K. "The Georgia Railroad and Banking Company." *Georgia Historical Quarterly* 57, no. 4 (Winter 1973): 544–61.

Woods, James M. *A History of the Catholic Church in the American South, 1513–1900*. Gainesville: University Press of Florida, 2011.

Wright, Willard E., ed. "Some Wartime Letters of Bishop Lynch." *Catholic Historical Review* 43, no. 1 (April 1957): 20–37.

"Writings of Bishop England," *De Bow's Review of the Southern and Western States*, n.s., 11, no. 4 (July 1851): 96–97.

Wyatt-Brown, Bertram. *Southern Honor: Ethics and Behavior in the Old South*. New York: Oxford University Press, 1982.

Wyly-Jones, Susan. "The 1835 Anti-Abolition Meetings in the South: A New Look at the Controversy over the Abolition Postal Campaign." *Civil War History* 47, no. 4 (2001): 289–309.

Young, Jeffrey Robert. *Domesticating Slavery: The Master Class in Georgia and South Carolina, 1670–1837*. Chapel Hill: University of North Carolina Press, 1999.

———, ed. *Proslavery and Sectional Thought in the Early South, 1740–1829*. Columbia: University of South Carolina Press, 2006.

Zanca, Kenneth J. *American Catholics and Slavery, 1789–1866: An Anthology of Primary Documents*. Lanham, MD: University Press of America, 1994.

Zboray, Ronald J. *A Fictive People: Antebellum Economic Development and the American Reading Public*. New York: Oxford University Press, 1993.

INDEX

A D A M   T A T E

is a professor of history and chair of the Department of

Humanities at Clayton State University.

www.ingramcontent.com/pod-product-compliance
Lightning Source LLC
Chambersburg PA
CBHW021150160426
42812CB00078B/493